A M A T E U R P H O T O G R A P H Y 1

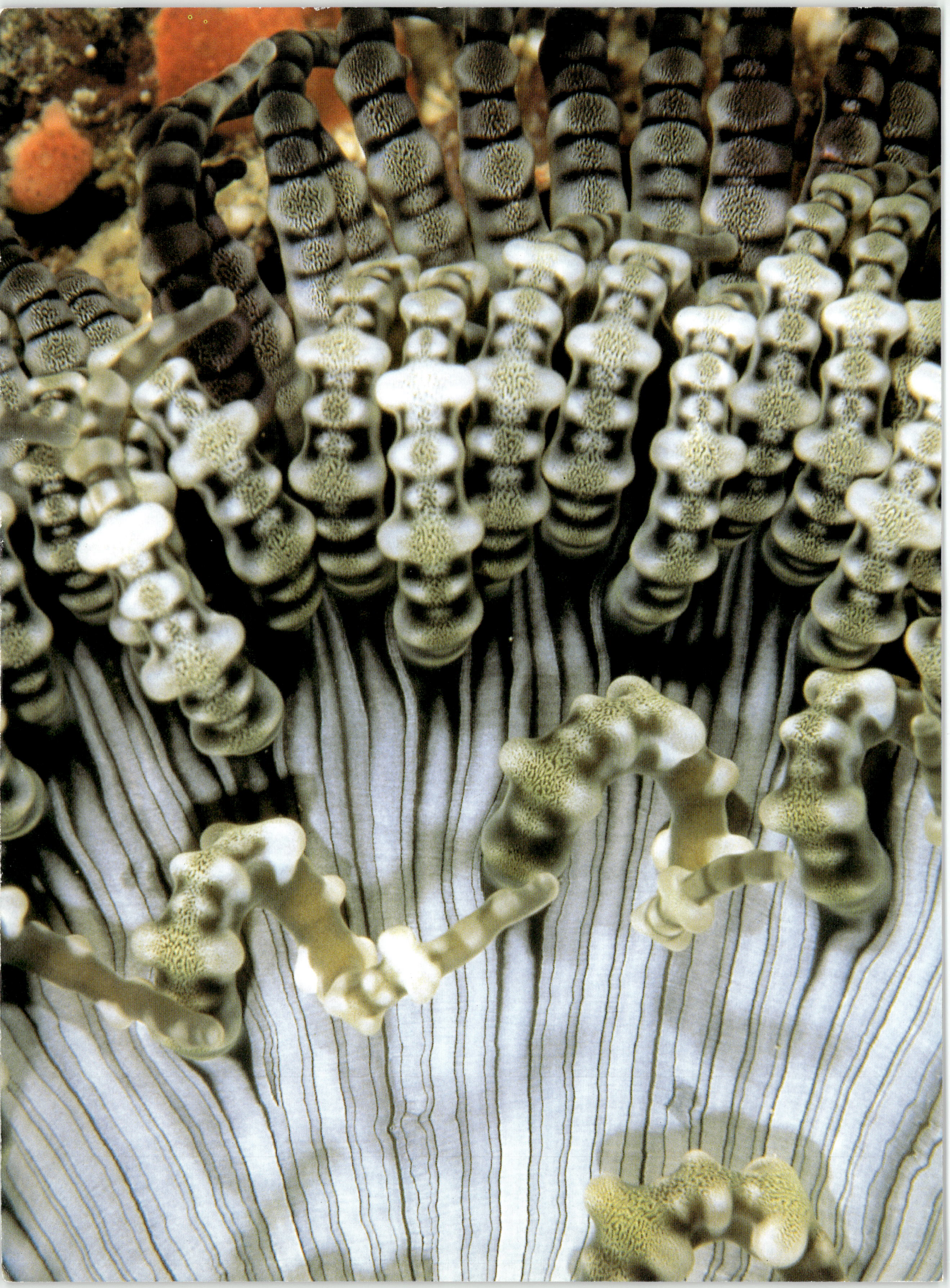

GRAPHIS AMATEUR PHOTOGRAPHY 1

THE INTERNATIONAL ANNUAL OF AMATEUR PHOTOGRAPHY

DAS INTERNATIONALE JAHRBUCH ÜBER AMATEUR-PHOTOGRAPHIE

LE RÉPERTOIRE INTERNATIONAL DE LA PHOTOGRAPHIE AMATEUR

EDITED BY • HERAUSGEGEBEN VON • EDITE PAR:

B. MARTIN PEDERSEN

PUBLISHER AND CREATIVE DIRECTOR: B. MARTIN PEDERSEN

BOOK PUBLISHER: ROB DRASIN

EDITORS: CLARE HAYDEN, HEINKE JENSSEN

ASSOCIATE EDITORS: PEGGY CHAPMAN, DANIEL IMAL

ART DIRECTOR: JOHN JEHEBER

DESIGNER: JENNIFER RUF

GRAPHIS INC.

(OPPOSITE) PHOTO BY CONSTANTINO PETRINOS

(COVER) PHOTO BY PAUL KOZAL

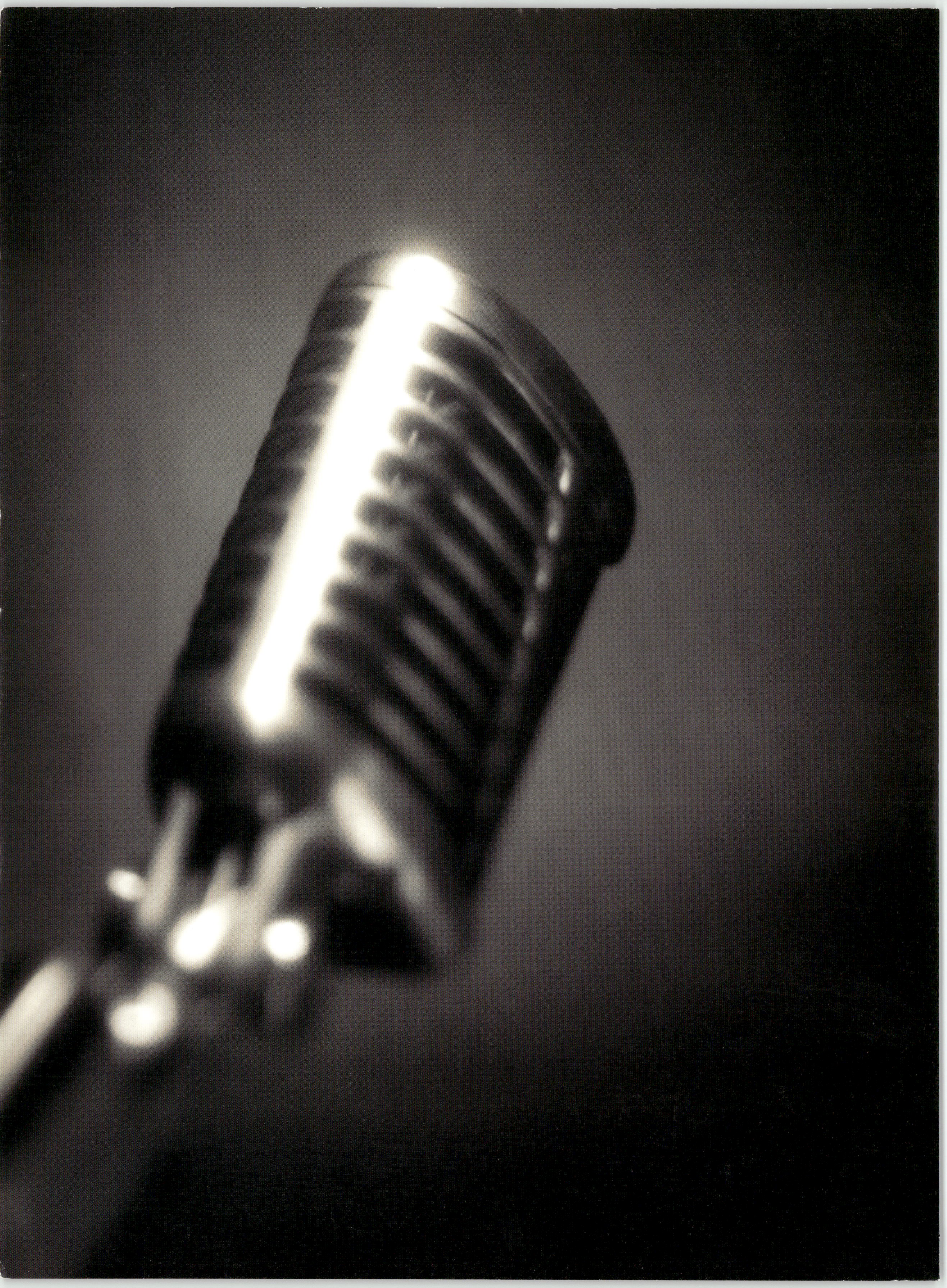

CONTENTS

INHALT

SOMMAIRE

REMARKS

WE EXTEND OUR HEARTFELT THANKS TO CONTRIBUTORS THROUGHOUT THE WORLD WHO HAVE MADE IT POSSIBLE TO PUBLISH A WIDE AND INTERNATIONAL SPECTRUM OF THE BEST WORK IN THIS FIELD.

ENTRY INSTRUCTIONS FOR NEXT YEAR'S ANNUAL MAY BE REQUESTED AT:
GRAPHIS INC.
141 LEXINGTON AVENUE
NEW YORK, NY 10016-8193

ANMERKUNGEN

UNSER DANK GILT DEN EINSENDERN AUS ALLER WELT, DIE ES UNS DURCH IHRE BEITRÄGE ERMÖGLICHT HABEN, EIN BREITES, INTERNATIONALES SPEKTRUM DER BESTEN ARBEITEN ZU VERÖFFENTLICHEN.

TEILNAHMEBEDINGUNGEN FÜR DAS NÄCHSTE JAHRBUCH SIND ERHÄLTLICH BEIM:
GRAPHIS INC.
141 LEXINGTON AVENUE
NEW YORK, NY 10016-8193

REMERCIEMENTS

NOUS REMERCIONS LES PARTICIPANTS DU MONDE ENTIER QUI ONT RENDU POSSIBLE LA PUBLICATION DE CET OUVRAGE OFFRANT UN PANORAMA COMPLET DES MEILLEURS TRAVAUX RÉALISÉS DANS CE DOMAINE.

LES MODALITÉS D'INSCRIPTION PEUVENT ÊTRE OBTENUES AUPRÈS DE:
GRAPHIS INC.
141 LEXINGTON AVENUE
NEW YORK, NY 10016-8193

ISBN: 1-888001-34-8

PRINTED IN HONG KONG BY DAI NIPPON.

(Opposite) Photo by K.C. Armstrong • (Following spread) Photo by Stuart Brown

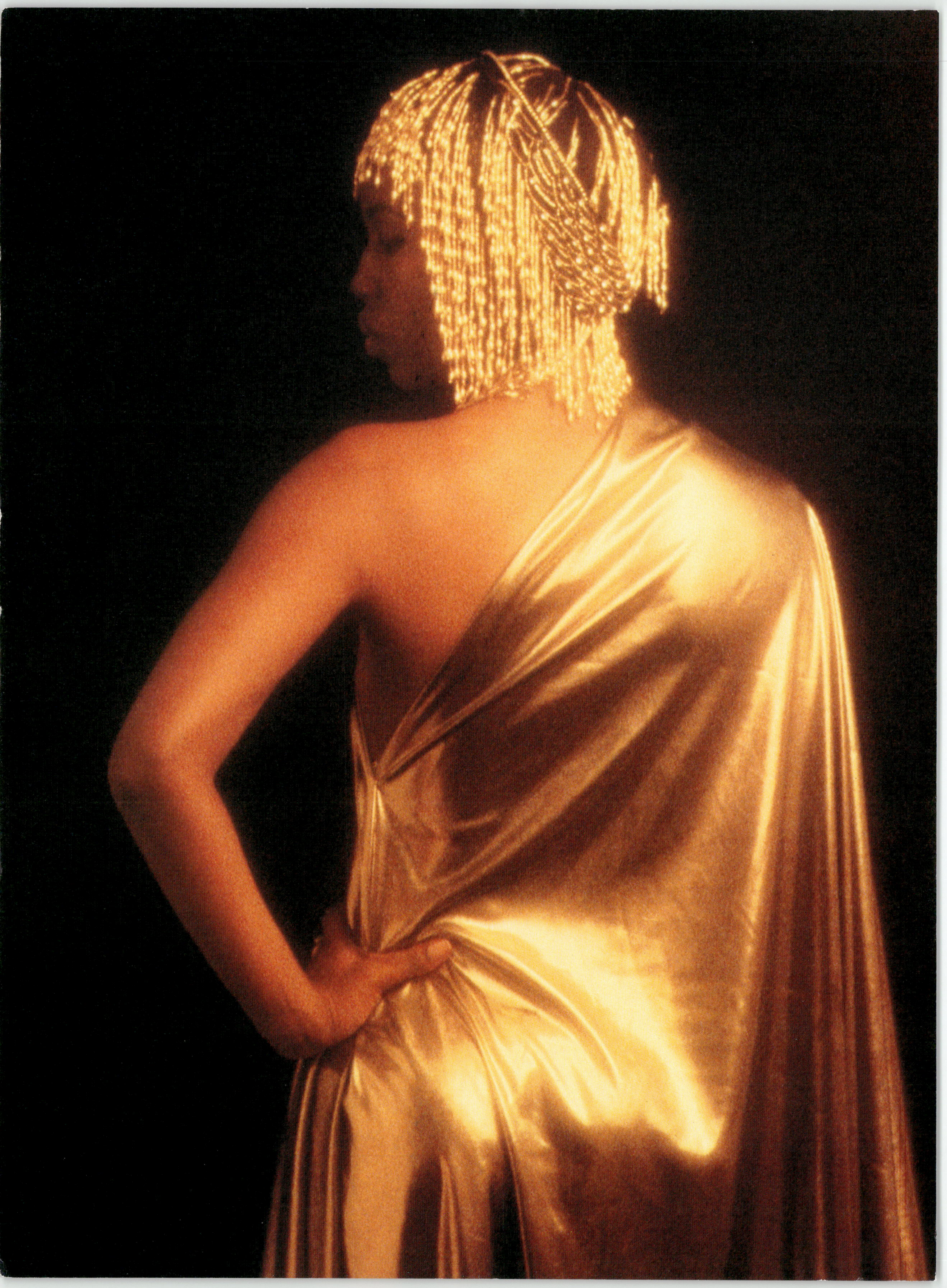

INTRODUCTION

EINLEITUNG

INTRODUCTION

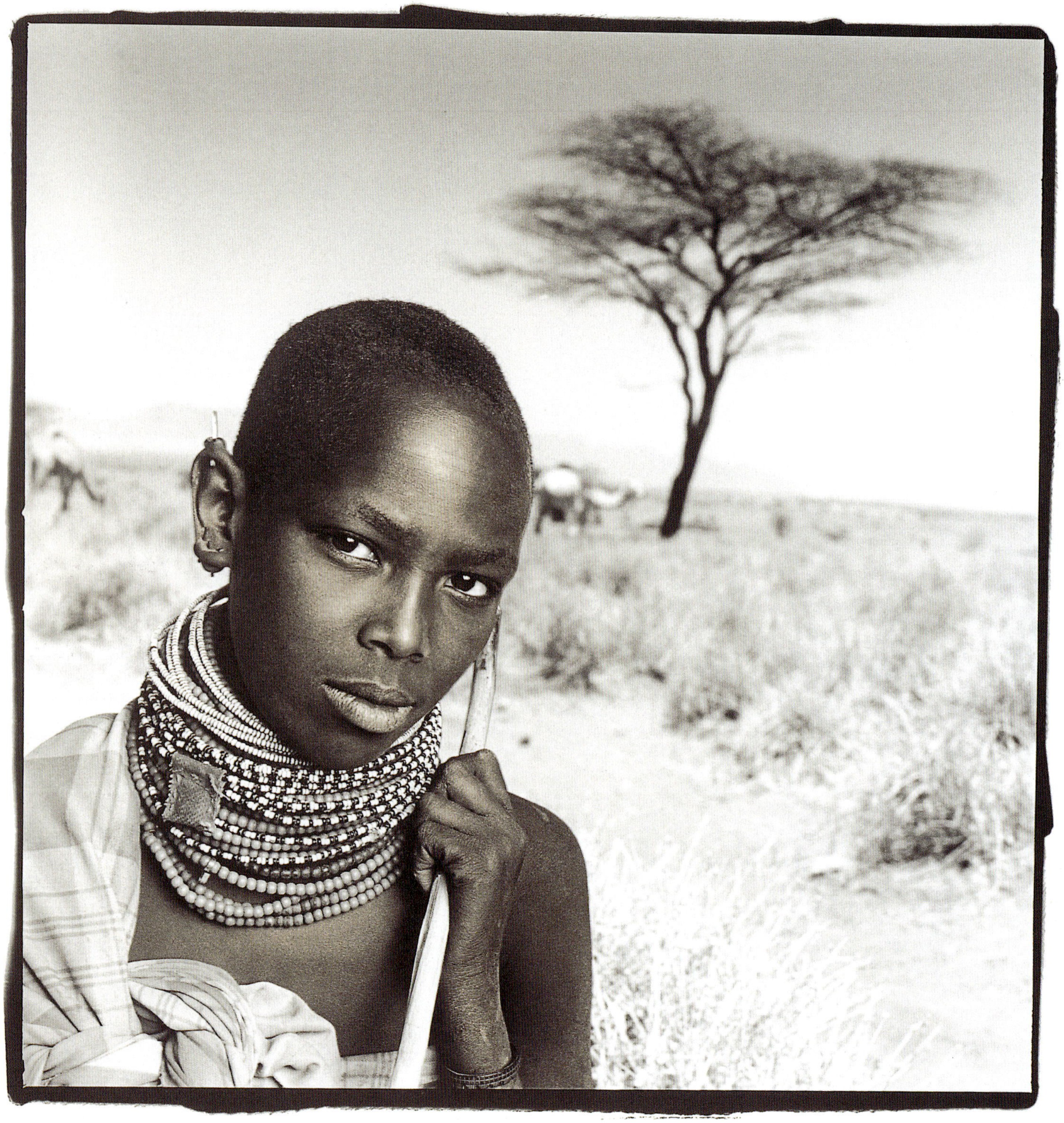

Baragoi, Kenya

Lothuru 12

Phil Borges

It was in the late sixties that I first became infatuated with photography. I was a second-year dental student living in San Francisco's Haight Ashbury district. So much was happening—summer of love, Filmore Auditorium, free concerts in Golden Gate Park. I used some of my student loan money and bought a Minolta SRT101. The parks and recreation department had a wonderfully underutilized darkroom that I began to inhabit four to five nights per week. For the next three years it was hard keeping my mind on teeth. • I managed to graduate in 1969. Broke and heavily in student loan debt, I put photography aside and immersed myself in a thriving orthodontic practice in the San Francisco Bay area. For eighteen years I straightened teeth and used my free time to travel to remote areas around the world. It was a great profession, working with kids, setting my own schedule, and having more money than I needed. Perfect! The only problem was a nagging feeling that began to grow as the years went by that something was

Phil Borges is a Seattle-based photographer who divides his time between editorial and commercial assignments and documentary projects which focus on different cultures and subcultures.

I realize how fortunate I have been to be able to follow a path that was sometimes illuminated no more than one step

missing. I didn't fully understand my dissatisfaction. • It wasn't until 1986 that I broke out the old Minolta and loaded it with Tri-X to record my son's birth. The old infatuation started to grab me again. A month later I enrolled in a beginning black-and-white photography class at a local community college and fell in love with the darkroom. Eighteen months later I had sold my practice, moved my family to Seattle and declared myself a photographer. I didn't have a license to practice dentistry in the state of Washington—a real bridge burning. It was such an insecure time. Had I killed the golden goose? Was I going to spend the rest of my life in poverty? • Having no clients and no jobs and a lot of time, I started trying to find myself in the infinite world of choices called 'photography.' Early on I found I was drawn to black-and-white and that I very seldom took a photo without a person in it. I started tearing photos that grabbed me from magazines and pinning them on the wall. A definite pattern started to emerge. I began experimenting in the darkroom and shooting different types of film. A friend introduced me to 70mm black-and-white infrared film. I learned a masking technique in a weekend photo workshop and used it to selectively tone my prints. Before long I realized that my work had its own unique look. • A teacher in one of my classes in community college had drilled into us the importance of building a body of work instead of taking single photos. The idea is to start with something you are attracted to and begin to explore it photographically and keep exploring until you have a strong collection of photos that hold together in some way. Looking back I realized I have built my photographic career on his advice. I have used the images from my personal projects to attract commercial assignments. So everything I do in photography is originally generated from work that I am attracted to. • My personal projects focus on different cultures and sub-cultures. I find photography gives me an excuse to enter the world of various groups of people that are very different from me and the people I'm normally around. I love it. I've had the opportunity to explore the lives of bicycle messengers in San Francisco, a Seattle street gang, Native Americans at powwows, Huichol Indians in Mexico, Tibetans in exile and in their homeland, and most recently the Samburu and Turkana tribes in East Africa. • Originally it was the commercial work—advertising, corporate and editorial assignments—that financially allowed me to pursue my projects. However, in the last year these personal projects have begun to be the major source of my support (mainly through fine art print sales and stock). • I realize how fortunate I have been to be able to follow a path that sometimes was illuminated no more than one step at a time. It has been so different than the first half of my life—getting on the conveyor belt of school, being shot out with a degree and having a relatively predictable set of choices on how to proceed. Photography has required me to act on my hunches, go through a lot of trial and error and be willing to embrace the unknown. It hasn't always been comfortable, but, I no longer have that nagging feeling that something is missing.

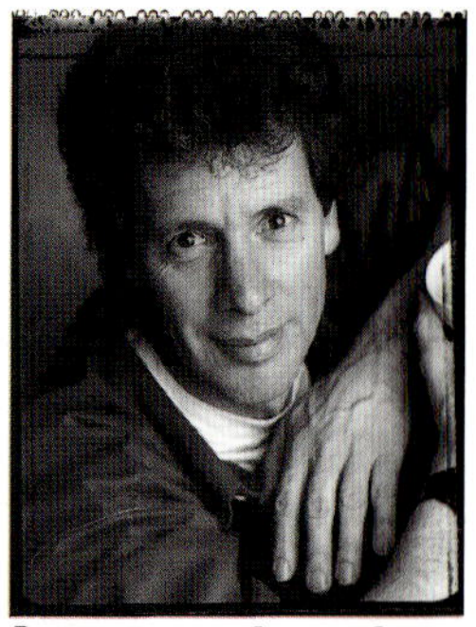

PORTRAIT BY JULEE GEIER

In den späten sechziger Jahren habe ich mich zum ersten Mal in die Photographie verliebt. Ich studierte Zahnmedizin im dritten Semester und lebte im Haight-Ashbury-Distrikt von San Francisco. Es passierte so viel - Sommer, Liebe, das Filmore West (die berühmteste Rock-Adresse der Welt), eintrittsfreie Konzerte im Golden Gate Park. Mit einem Teil meines Stipendiums kaufte ich eine Minolta SRT101. Es gab eine wunderbare, kaum benutzte Dunkelkammer, die vom Park- und Freizeit-Departement der Stadt zur Verfügung gestellt wurde, und ich begann hier vier bis fünf Nächte pro Woche zu verbringen. In den nächsten drei Jahren fiel es mir schwer, meine Gedanken auf Zähne zu konzentrieren. • Trotzdem schaffte ich 1969 das Examen. Angesichts der Schulden, die ich durch das Studium hatte, vergass ich die Photographie und begann, in einer gutgehenden Praxis für Kieferorthopädie im San Francisco Bay-Distrikt zu arbeiten. 18 Jahre lang richtete ich Zähne und nutzte meine Freizeit, um in die entlegensten Winkel der Erde zu reisen. Es war ein grossartiger Beruf, ich arbeitete mit Kindern, konnte meine Zeit selbst einteilen und verdiente mehr Geld, als ich brauchte. Perfekt! Das einzige Problem war das nagende Gefühl, das sich im Laufe der Jahre einstellte und mir sagte, dass mir etwas entging. Ich begriff meine Unzufriedenheit nicht ganz. • Erst 1986 grub ich die alte Minolta wieder aus, um die Geburt meines Sohnes zu photographieren. Und es packte mich wieder. Einen Monat später schrieb ich mich in einen Anfänger-Kursus für Schwarzweiss-Photographie in einem benachbarten College ein, und ich verliebte mich in die Dunkelkammer. Achtzehn Monate später verkaufte ich meine Praxis, zog mit meiner Familie nach Seattle und nannte mich Photograph. Ich hatte keine Bewilligung, im Staate Washington als Zahnarzt zu praktizieren – damit hatte ich sämtliche Brücken hinter mir abgebrochen. Es war eine völlig unsichere Sache. Hatte ich die goldene Gans geschlachtet? Würde ich für den Rest meines Lebens arm sein? Ich hatte weder Kunden noch Aufträge, aber jede Menge Zeit, und ich begann, mich in der Welt der Photographie, die so unendlich viele Möglichkeiten bietet, zu orientieren. Am Anfang fühlte ich mich zur Schwarzweiss-Photographie hingezogen, und nur ganz selten machte ich eine Aufnahme ohne Person im Bild. Ich schnitt Photos, die mich berührten, aus Zeitschriften aus und heftete sie an die Wand. Es ergab sich schnell ein ganz bestimmtes Muster. Ich experimentierte in der Dunkelkammer und probierte verschiedene Filme aus. Ein Freund zeigte mir den Schwarzweiss-Infrarot-Film. In einem Wochenend-Photo-Workshop eignete ich mir eine Maskiertechnik an, die ich dann beim selektiven Kolorieren meiner Abzüge anwendete. Bald stellte ich fest, dass meine Arbeiten etwas Besonderes hatten. • Ein Lehrer am College hatte immer wieder betont, wie wichtig es sei, ein zusammenhängendes Werk zu schaffen, statt einzelne Photos zu

PHIL BORGES DER ALS PHOTOGRAPH IN SEATTLE LEBT, TEILT SEINE ZEIT ZWISCHEN AUFTRAGSPHOTOGRAPHIE FÜR WERBE- UND REDAKTIONELLE ZWECKE UND FREIEN DOKUMENTARISCHEN PROJEKTEN ÜBER VERSCHIEDENE KULTUREN UND SUBKULTUREN.

at a time ... It hasn't always been comfortable, but I no longer have that nagging feeling that something is missing.

machen. Die Idee war, dass man mit etwas beginnen sollte, das einen ansprach, um es dann photographisch zu erkunden und zwar kontinuierlich, bis man zu einer starken Sammlung von Photos gelangen würde, die einen Zusammenhang haben. Rückblickend stelle ich fest, dass sein Rat meine Photo-Karriere bestimmt hat. Ich benutzte Bilder meiner freien Projekte, um Kunden zu gewinnen. Alle meine photographischen Arbeiten sind also aus etwas erwachsen, was mich fasziniert. • Bei meinen persönlichen Projekten befasse ich mich vor allem mit verschiedenen Kulturen und Subkulturen. Photographie gibt mir einen Vorwand, mich in die Welt ganz unterschiedlicher Gruppen von Menschen zu begeben, die ganz anders leben als ich und die Leute, mit denen ich normalerweise verkehre. Mir gefällt das sehr. Ich hatte Gelegenheit, das Leben von Velo-Kurieren in San Francisco kennenzulerenen, sowie das einer Strassenbande in Seattle, von Ureinwohnern Amerikas in Pow Wows, der Huichol-Indianer in Mexiko, von Tibetern im Exil und in ihrer Heimat und das der Samburu- und Turkana-Stämme in Ostafrika. • Am Anfang finanzierte ich meine persönlichen Projekte durch kommerzielle Aufträge für Werbung, Firmen und Redaktionen. Im letzten Jahr jedoch haben diese Projekte (vor allem durch den Verkauf von Abzügen und Archivphotos) meinen Unterhalt finanziert. • Während ich diesen Text niederschreibe, wird mir bewusst, wieviel Glück ich hatte auf meinem Weg, auf dem manchmal nur gerade der nächste Schritt abzusehen war. Es war so anders als in der ersten Hälfte meines Lebens - erst Schule, dann Studium, alles war ziemlich vorgezeichnet. Die Photographie hat mich gezwungen, nach meinem Gefühl zu handeln, viel auszuprobieren, Irrtümer zu riskieren und mich auf unbekanntes Terrain zu wagen. Es war nicht immer angenehm, aber ich habe nicht mehr das Gefühl, dass mir etwas entgangen ist.

Je suis tombé amoureux de la photographie vers la fin des années soixante. J'étais étudiant en deuxième année de chirurgie dentaire et j'habitais le quartier Haight Ashbury de San Francisco. Tant de choses s'y passaient – un été d'amour, l'amphithéâtre Filmore, des concerts gratuits au Golden Gate Park. J'ai utilisé une partie de ma bourse d'étudiant pour m'acheter un appareil-photo Minolta SRT101. J'ai commencé à passer quatre ou cinq nuits par semaine dans l'atelier de photographie qui appartenait au département de gestion du parc. Heureusement, cet atelier était presque toujours libre. Pendant les trois années suivantes, il m'était difficile de me concentrer sur les problèmes dentaires. • Fauché et très endetté en 1969, j'ai néanmoins obtenu mon diplôme. J'ai mis la photographie de côté pour me consacrer à mon cabinet d'orthodontiste, qui m'a rendu prospère dans la région de San Francisco. Pendant 18 ans, j'ai arrangé des dents et profité de mon temps libre pour voyager dans les régions lointaines. C'était une excellente profession, dans laquelle j'aimais travailler avec des enfants, fixer moi-même mes horaires, et gagner plus d'argent que je n'en avais besoin. Parfait! Le seul problème était qu'il me manquait quelque chose. Je ne comprenais pas entièrement mon mécontentement. • Ce n'est qu'en 1986 que j'ai repris le vieil appareil Minolta et l'ai chargé d'une pellicule Tri-x afin de photographier la naissance de mon fils. J'ai retrouvé mon ancien amour. Un mois plus tard, je me suis inscrit à l'université de ma région dans un cours pour débutants en photographie noir et blanc. Je suis tombé amoureux de l'atelier. Dix-huit mois plus tard, j'avais vendu mon cabinet d'orthodontiste, déménagé avec ma famille à Seattle, et m'étais profilé comme photographe. Je n'avais pas de permis d'orthodontiste dans l'Etat de Washington – je brûlais toutes les étapes. Je n'étais sur de rien. Avais-je tué la poule aux œufs d'or? Allais-je vivre le reste de ma vie dans la pauvreté? • Sans clients, sans emploi et avec beaucoup de temps libre, j'ai tenté de trouver ma voie dans le monde infini de la photographie. Très tôt, j'ai découvert que le noir et blanc me fascinait, et qu'il était très rare que je prenne une photographie sans qu'une personne y figure. J'ai commencé à déchirer dans des revues des photographies qui m'attiraient, et à les coller sur le mur. Un modèle en est né. J'ai commencé à faire des expériences dans mon atelier et à me servir de différentes pellicules. Un ami m'a montré une pellicule noir et blanc infrarouge. J'ai appris grâce à un cours de week-end une technique permettant de masquer une partie d'une photographie; je m'en suis servi ponctuellement afin de donner une tonicité à mes épreuves. Après peu de temps, je me suis rendu compte que mon travail avait ses propres aspects qui le rendaient unique. • Un professeur qui enseignait dans un de mes cours à l'université nous avait bien fait entrer dans la tête l'importance de créer un tout au lieu de prendre des photographies individuelles. L'idée était de commencer avec quelque chose qui vous attirait, de pouvoir en faire l'exploration d'un point de vue photographique, et de continuer à l'examiner jusqu'au moment où vous aviez construit une collection de photographies liées les unes aux autres par un aspect particulier. Lorsque j'y pense, je me rends compte que j'ai construit ma carrière de photographe selon ce conseil. Je me suis servi des images de mes projets personnels pour trouver des travaux commerciaux. Ceci veut dire que tout ce que je fais en photogrpahie naît d'un travail qui m'attire. • Mes projets personnels se concentrent sur des cultures différentes et des sous-cultures. Je trouve que la photographie me permet d'entrer dans un monde de divers groupes de personnes qui sont très différentes de moi et de ceux qui m'entourent. J'adore cela. J'ai profité de mes projets pour aller découvrir la vie des coursiers à vélo de San Francisco, un gang à Seattle, des Indiens d'Amérique dans leurs assemblées, des Indiens de la tribu des Huichol au Mexique, des Tibétains en exil et au Tibet, et plus récemment les tribus des Samburu et Turkana en Afrique de l'Est. • Au début, mes travaux commerciaux – la publicité et des travaux pour les entreprises et les publications – ont financé mes projets personnels. Mais depuis cette année, mes propres projets sont devenus la source principale de mes revenus (grâce aux ventes de mes gravures des beaux-arts.) • En écrivant ceci, je me rends compte de ma chance de pouvoir suivre un chemin qui ne s'est parfois révélé que petit par petit. C'est tout à fait différent de la première moitié de ma vie. En suivant la voie universitaire, je m'y suis retrouvé avec un diplôme en poche et un ensemble de choix sans surprise. Grâce à la photographie, j'ai appris à suivre mon intuition, à procéder uniquement par tâtonnements, et à embrasser l'inconnu. Ceci n'a pas toujours été réconfortant, mais je n'ai plus ce sentiment d'insatisfaction.

Phil Borges, un laureat en photographie, vit a Seattle, ou il partage son temps entre ses missions commerciales/redactionelles et ses projets de documentaire, qui se concentrent sur des cultures partout dans le monde.

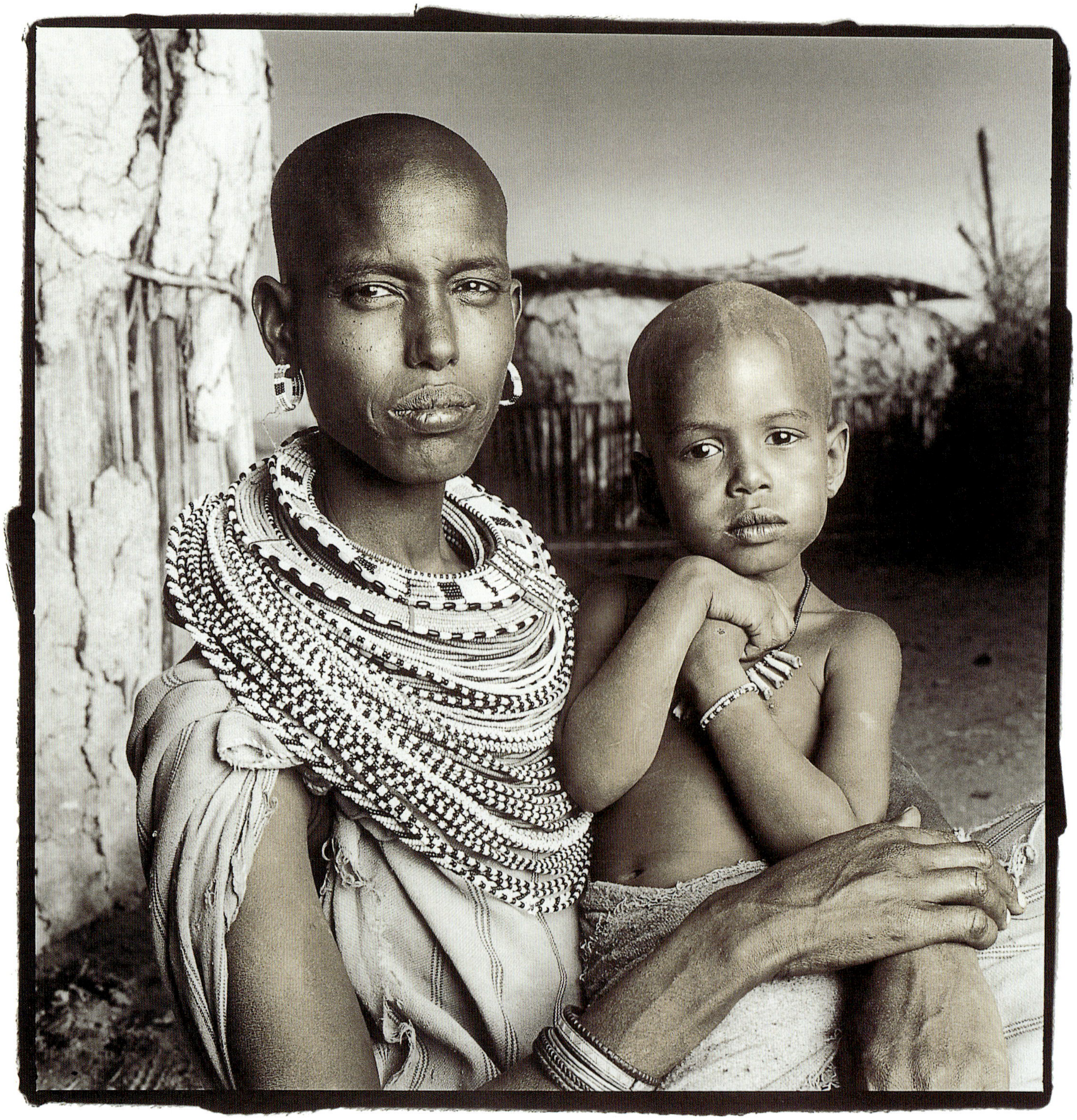

Lesirikan, Kenya

Oriena 34
Seneyia 18 mos.

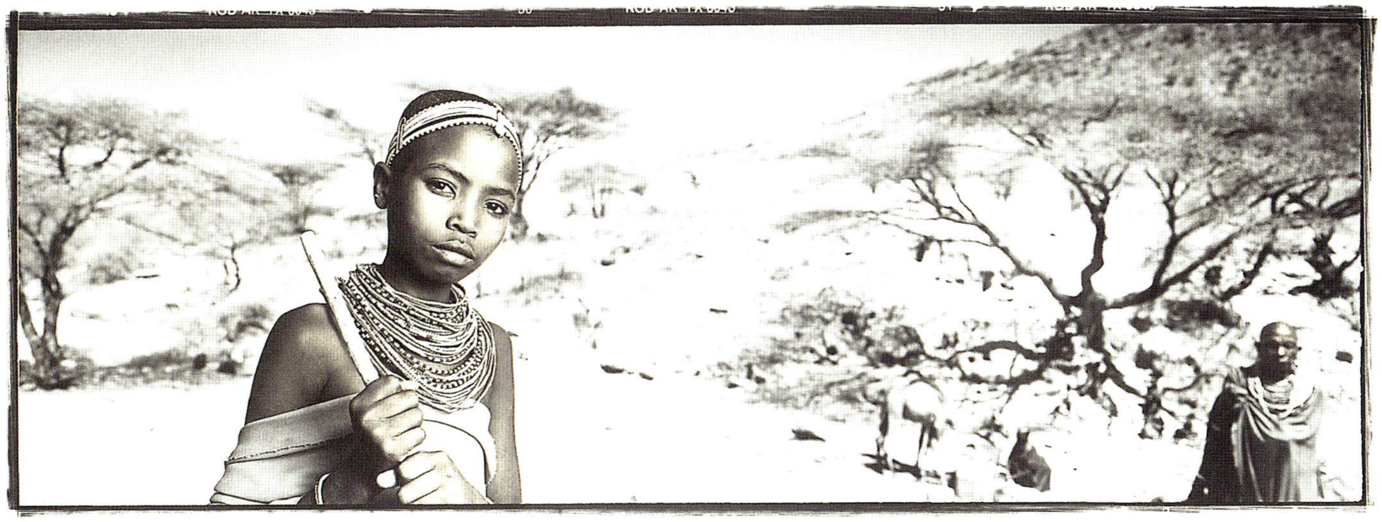

Ndoto Range, Kenya

Lekarate 9

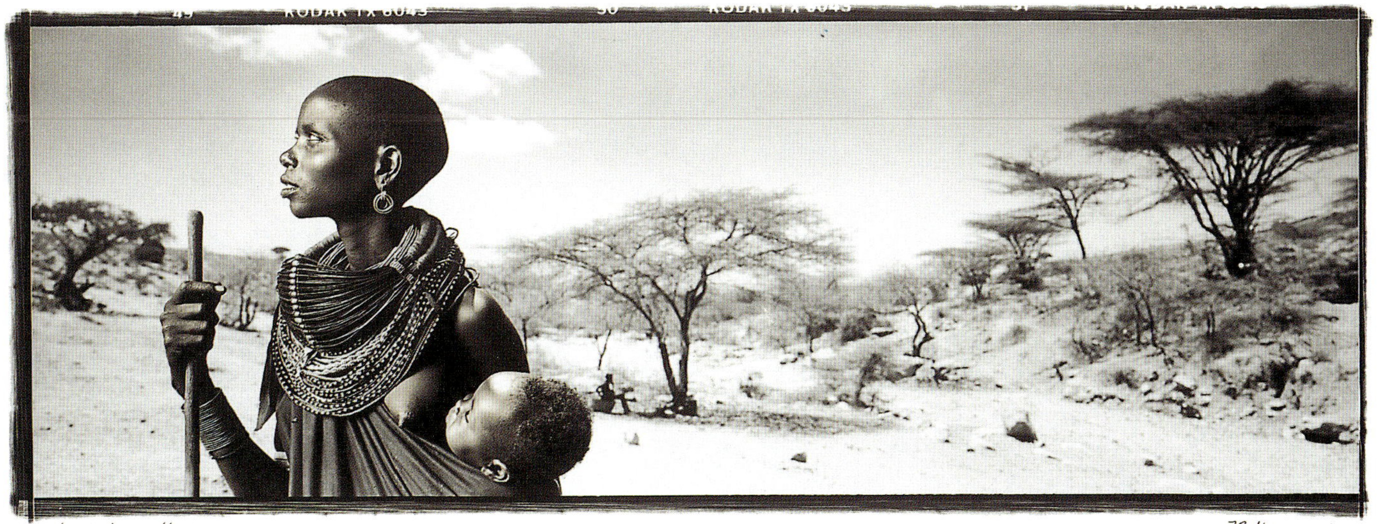

Lesirikan, Kenya

Nolina 24
Seneyia 5mos.

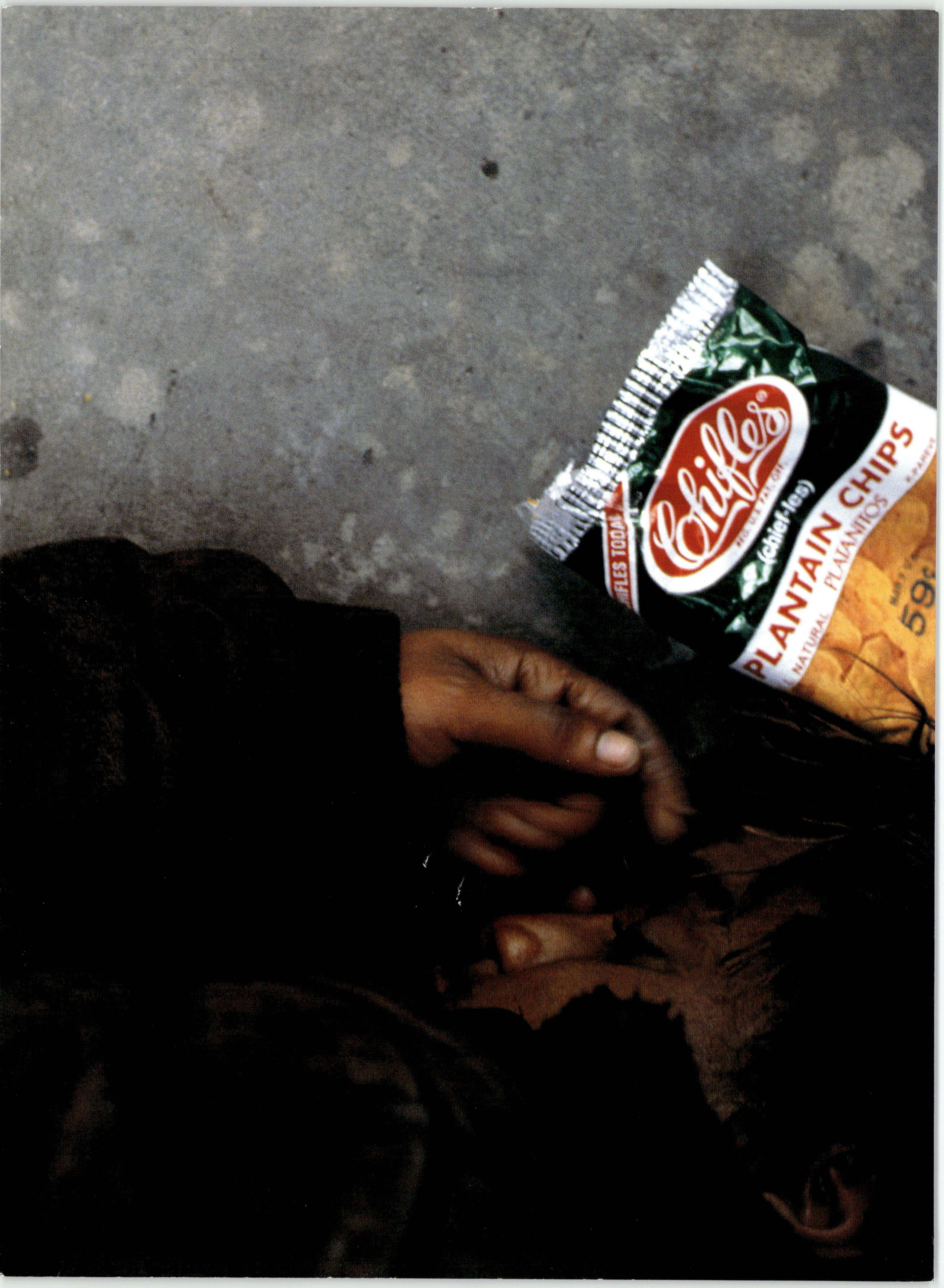
Chifles
(chief-lees)
PLANTAIN CHIPS
PLATANITOS

JOURNALISM

JOURNALISMUS

JOURNALISME

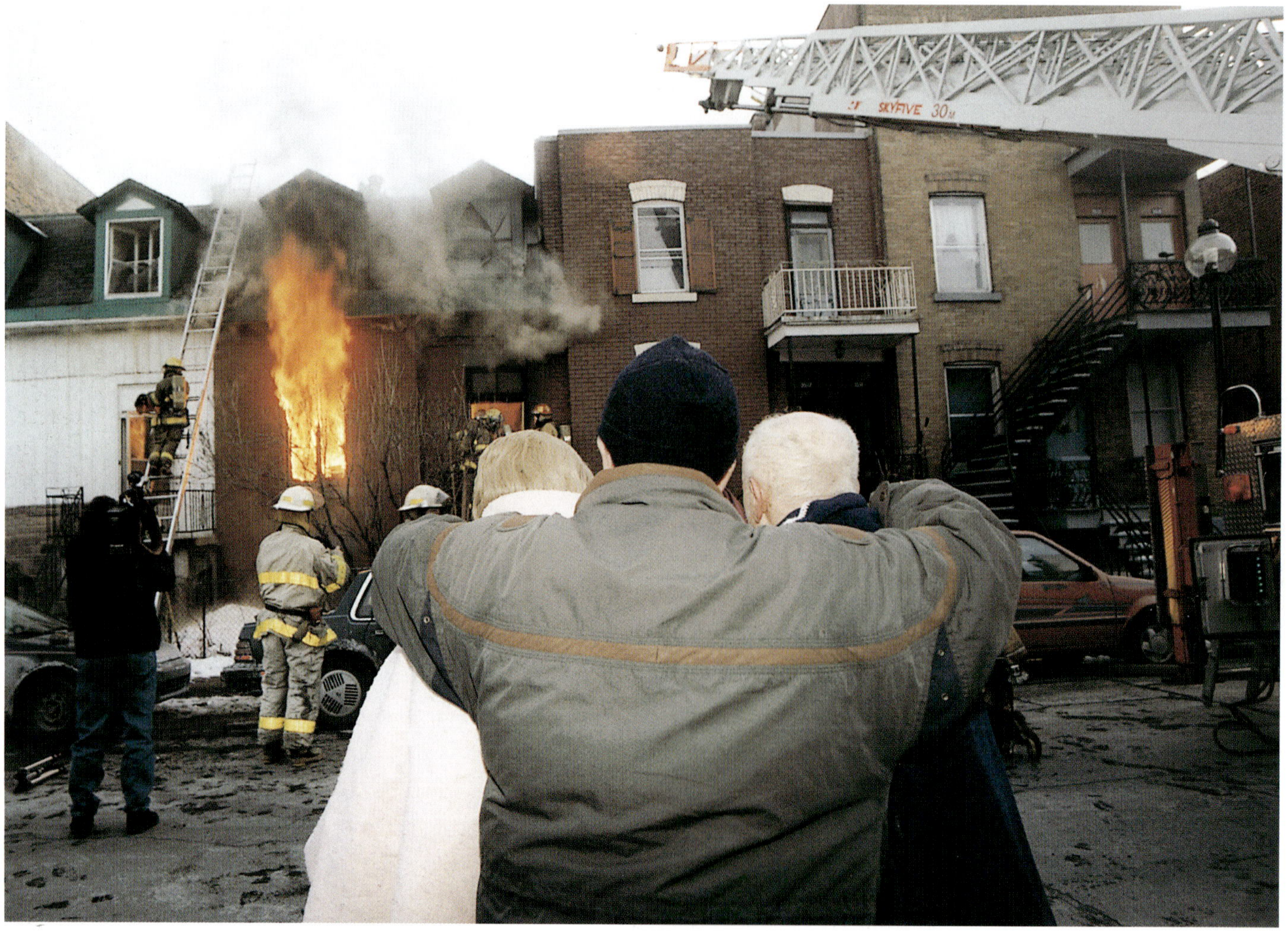

(PREVIOUS SPREAD) *Kosuke Yuki* ■ (THIS PAGE) *Patrick Sanfacon*

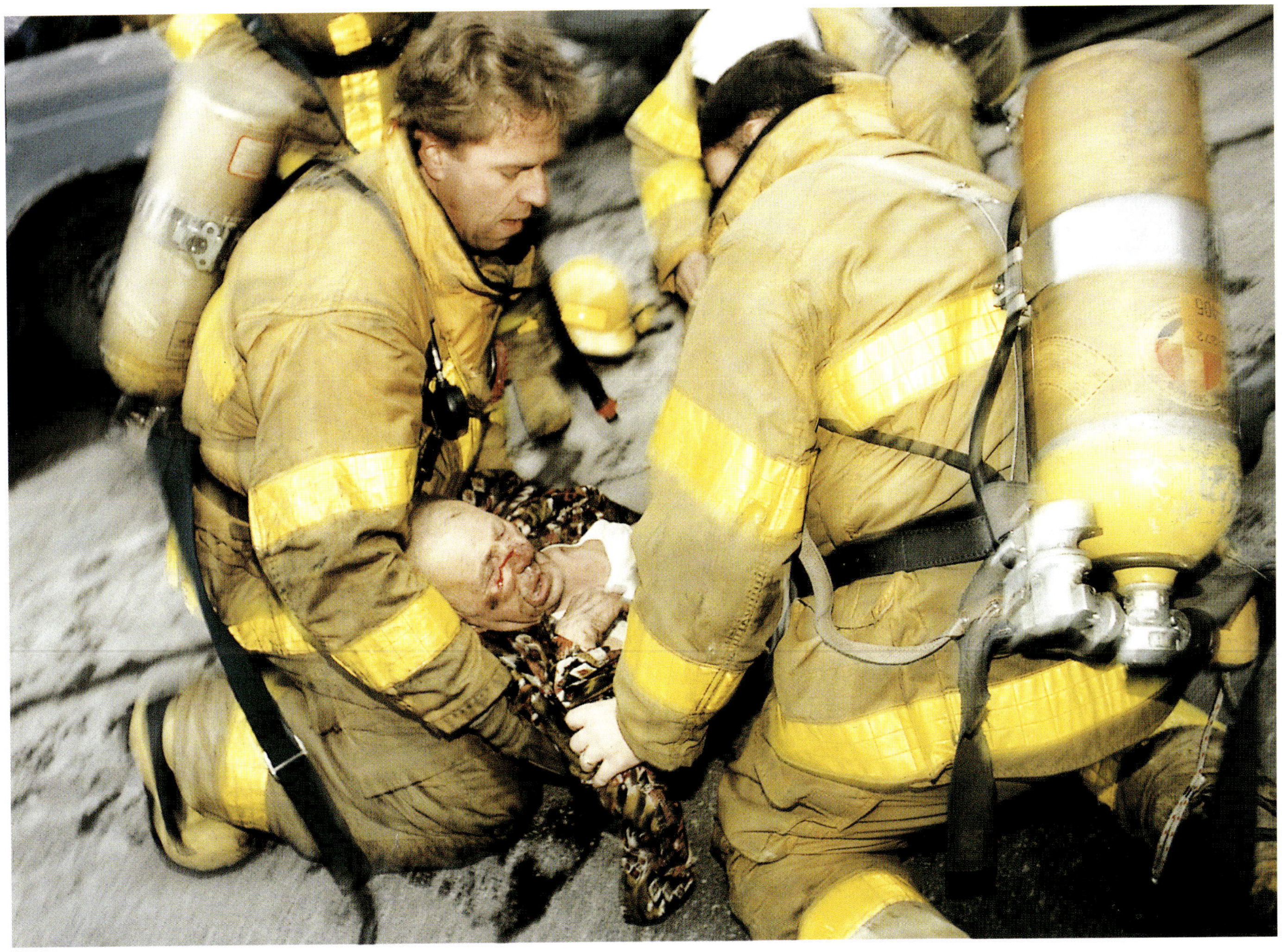

Patrick Sanfacon

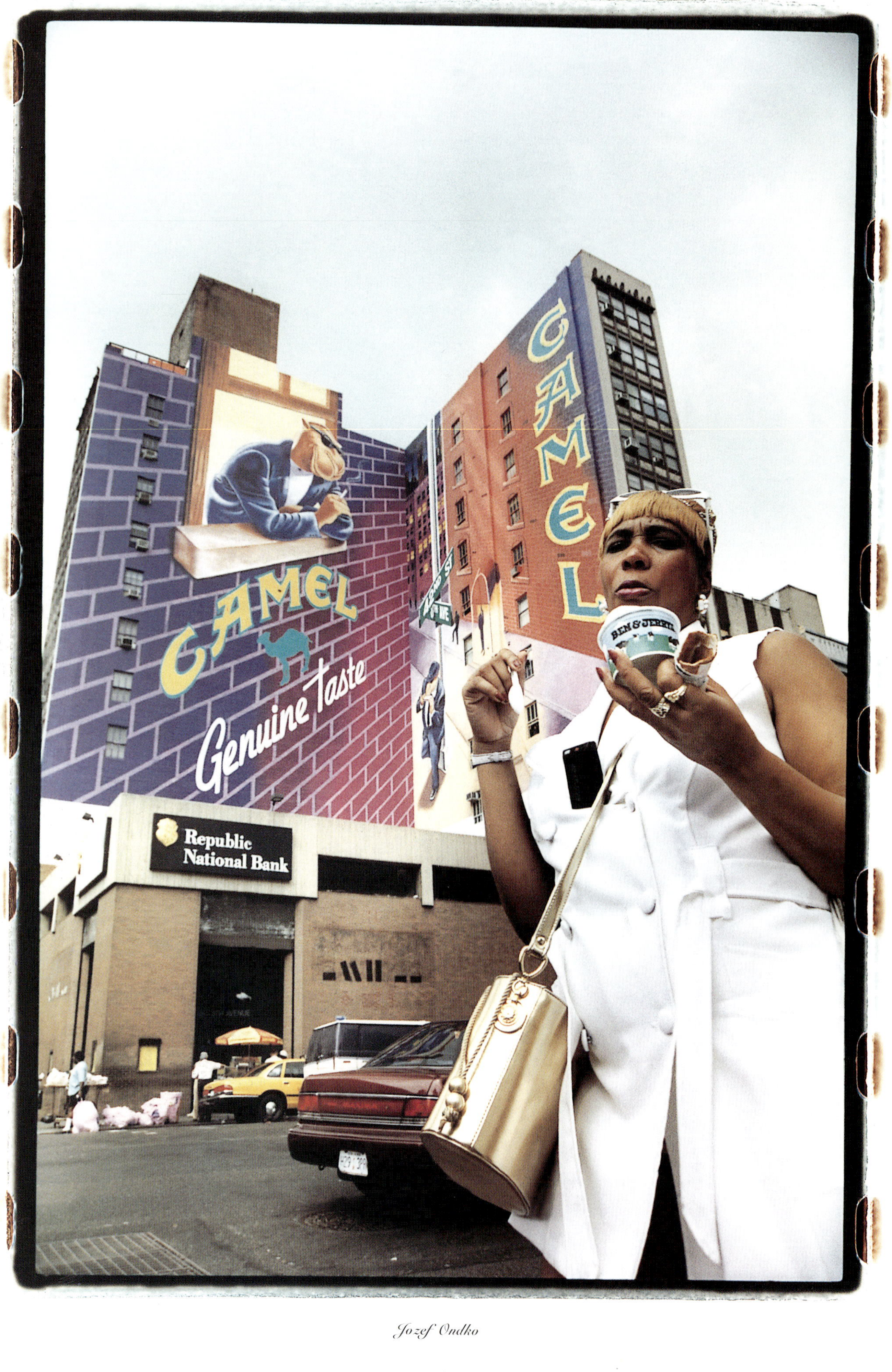
CAMEL
Genuine taste
CAMEL
Republic
National Bank
BEN & JERRY'S

Jozef Ondko

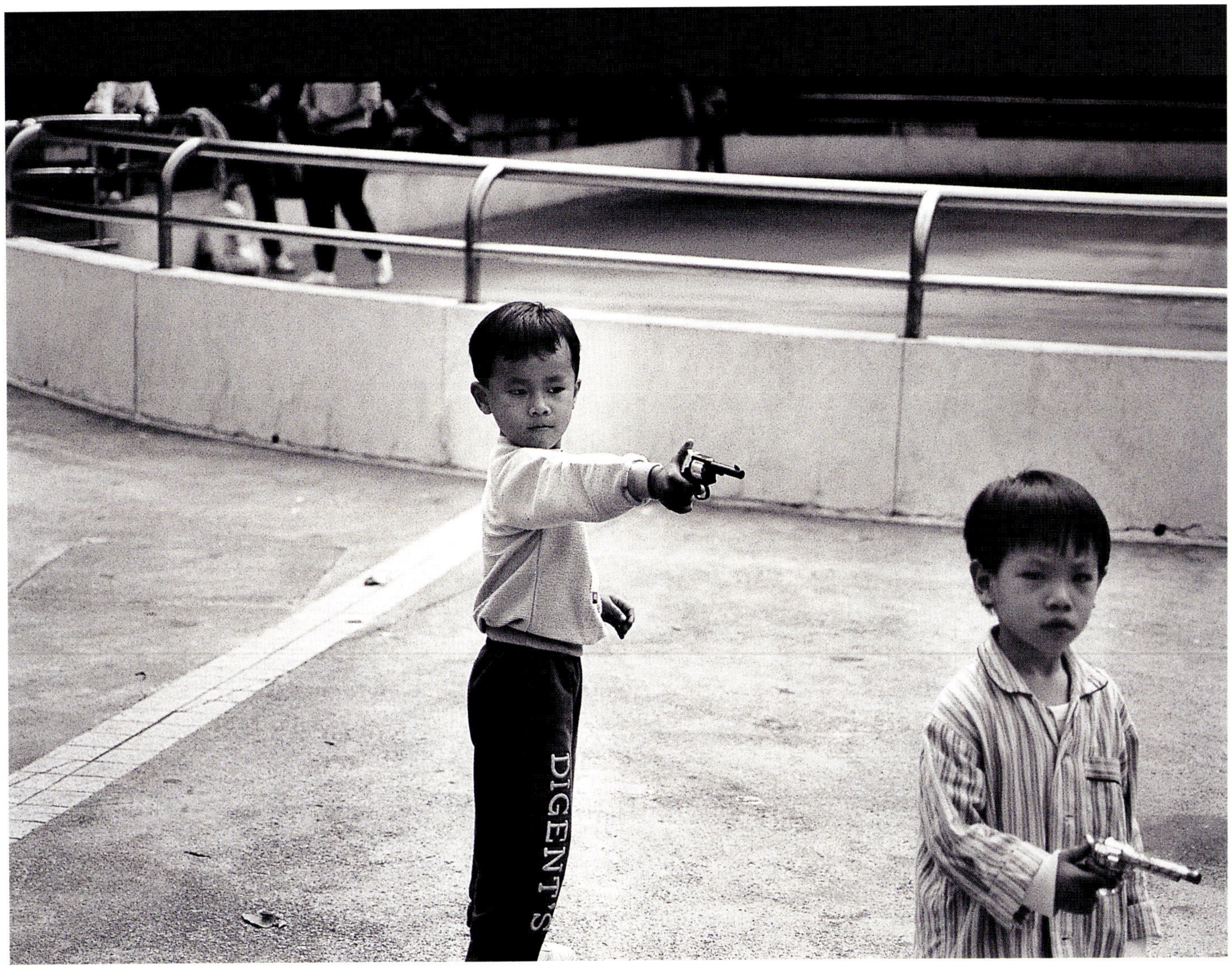

Lorne Resnick

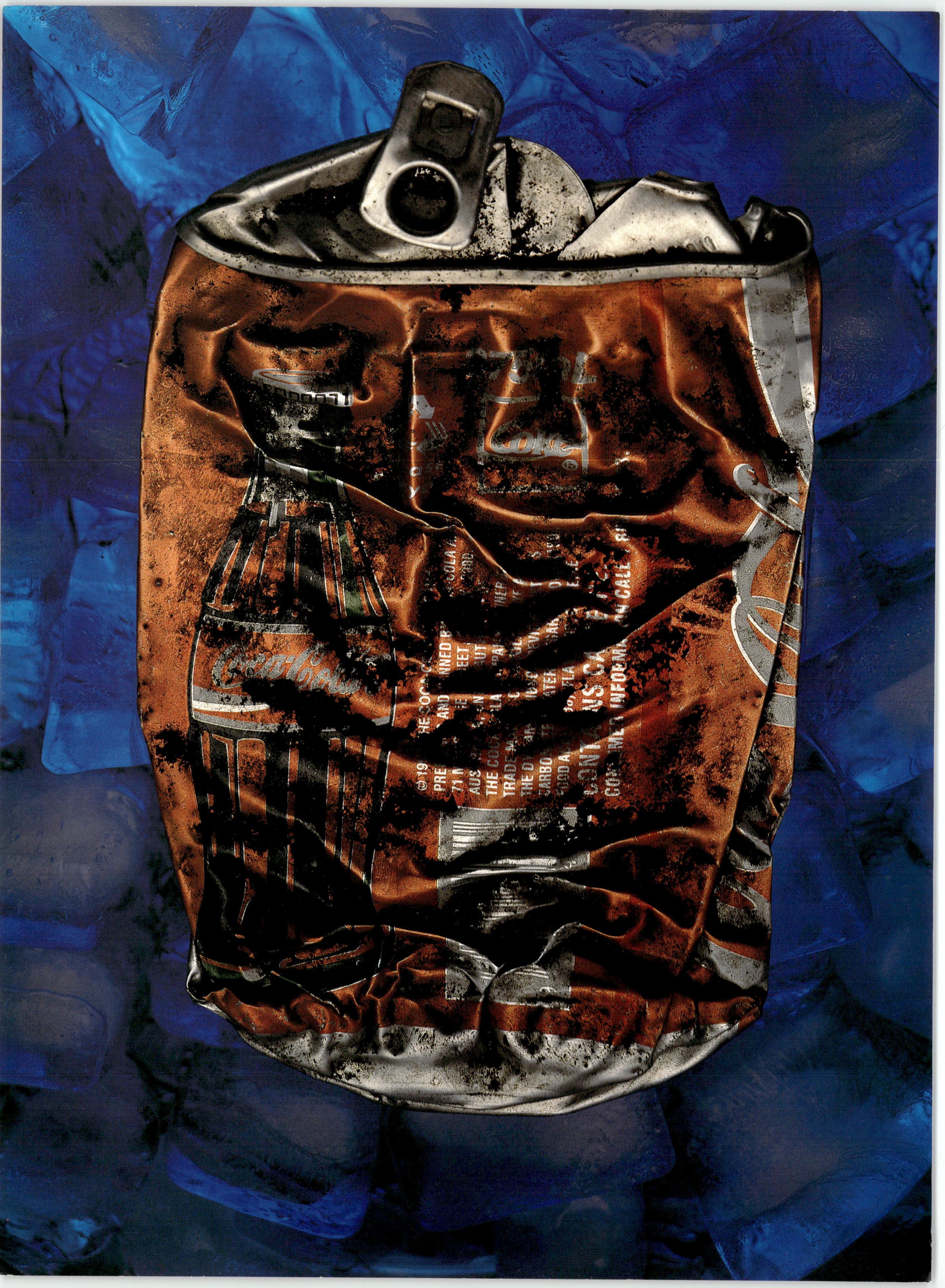

STILL LIFE

STILLEBEN

NATURE MORTE

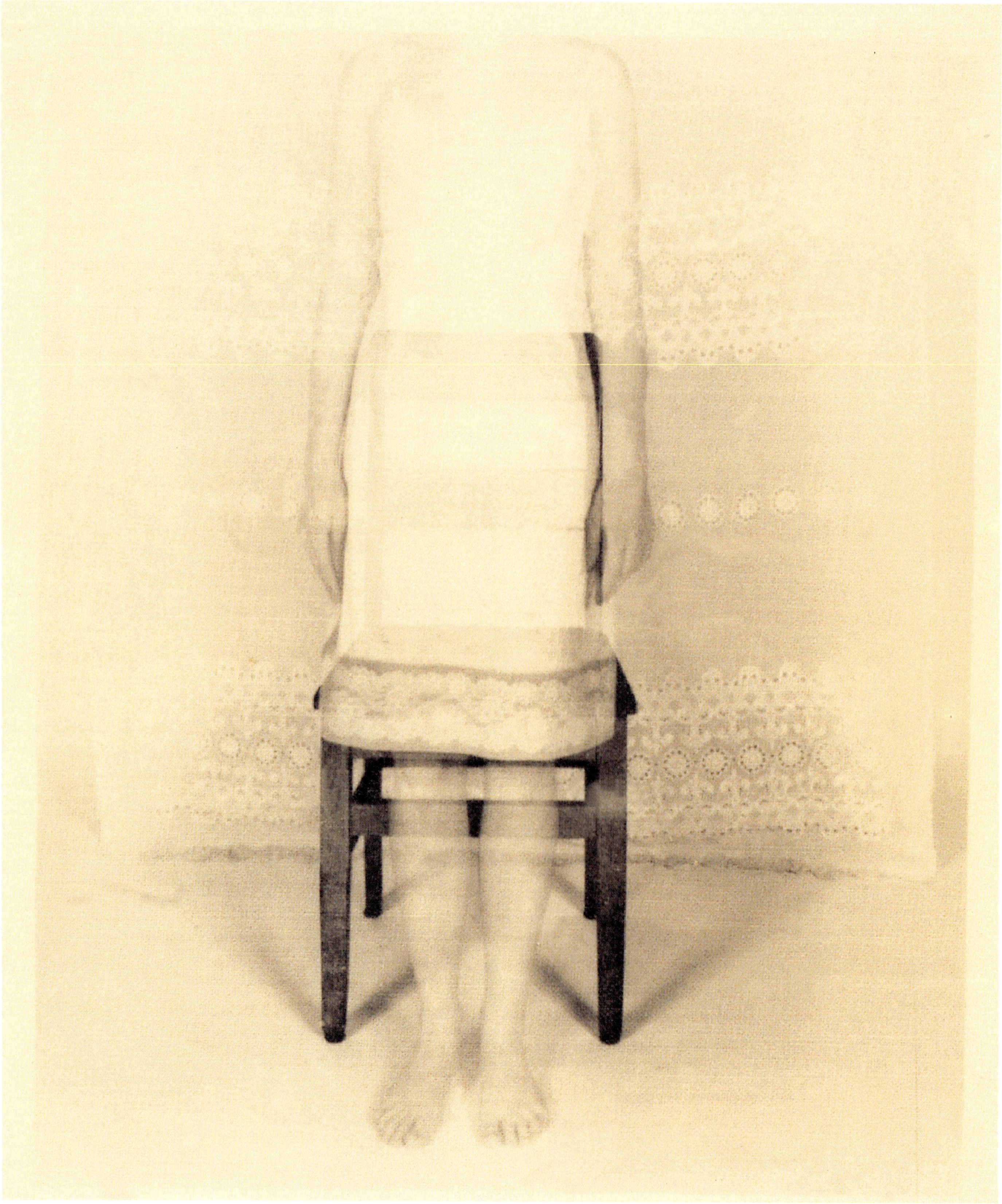

(PREVIOUS SPREAD) *Michael Davies* ■ (THIS PAGE) *Andrea Pickens*

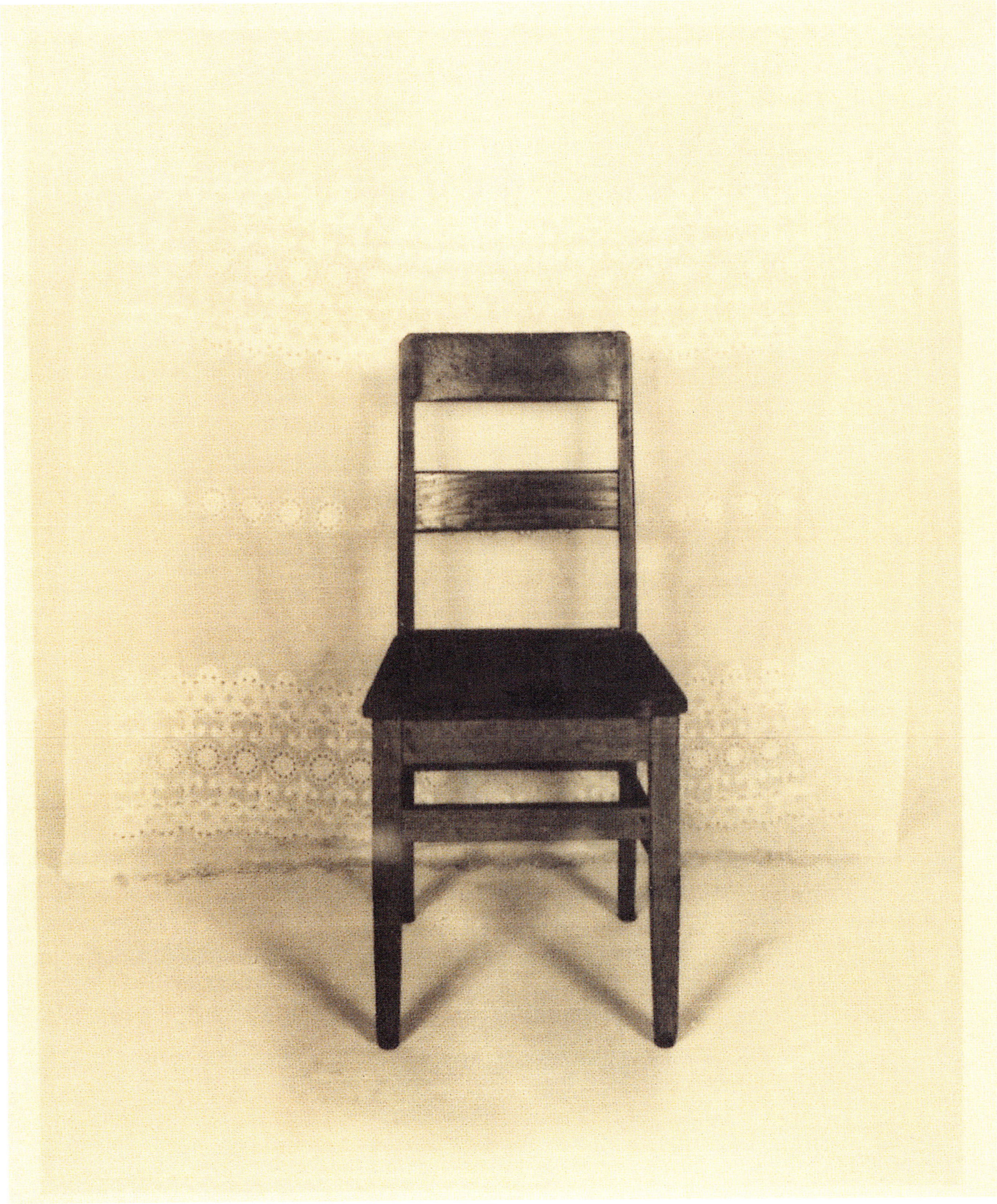

Andrea Pickens

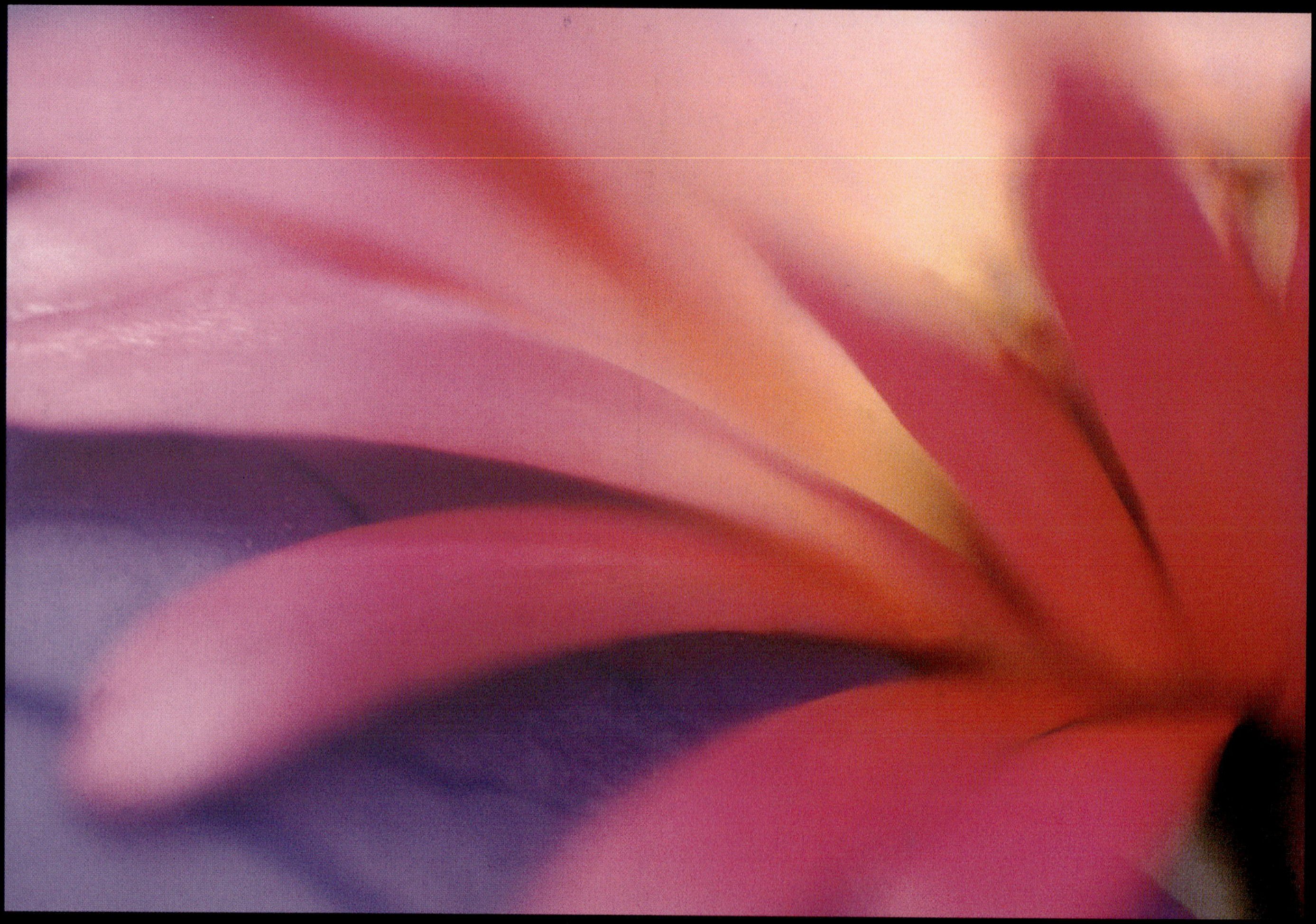

James Colony

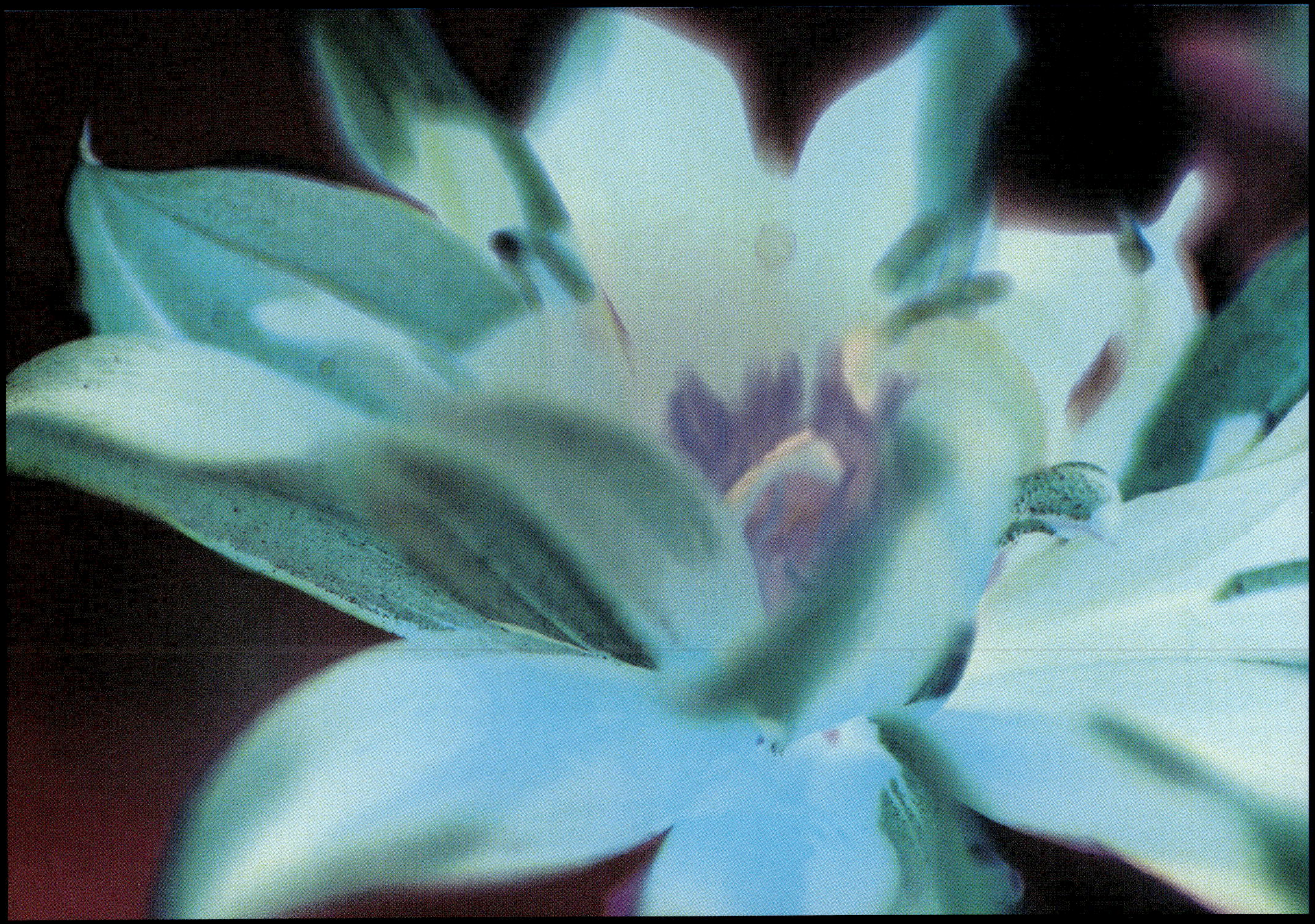

James Colony

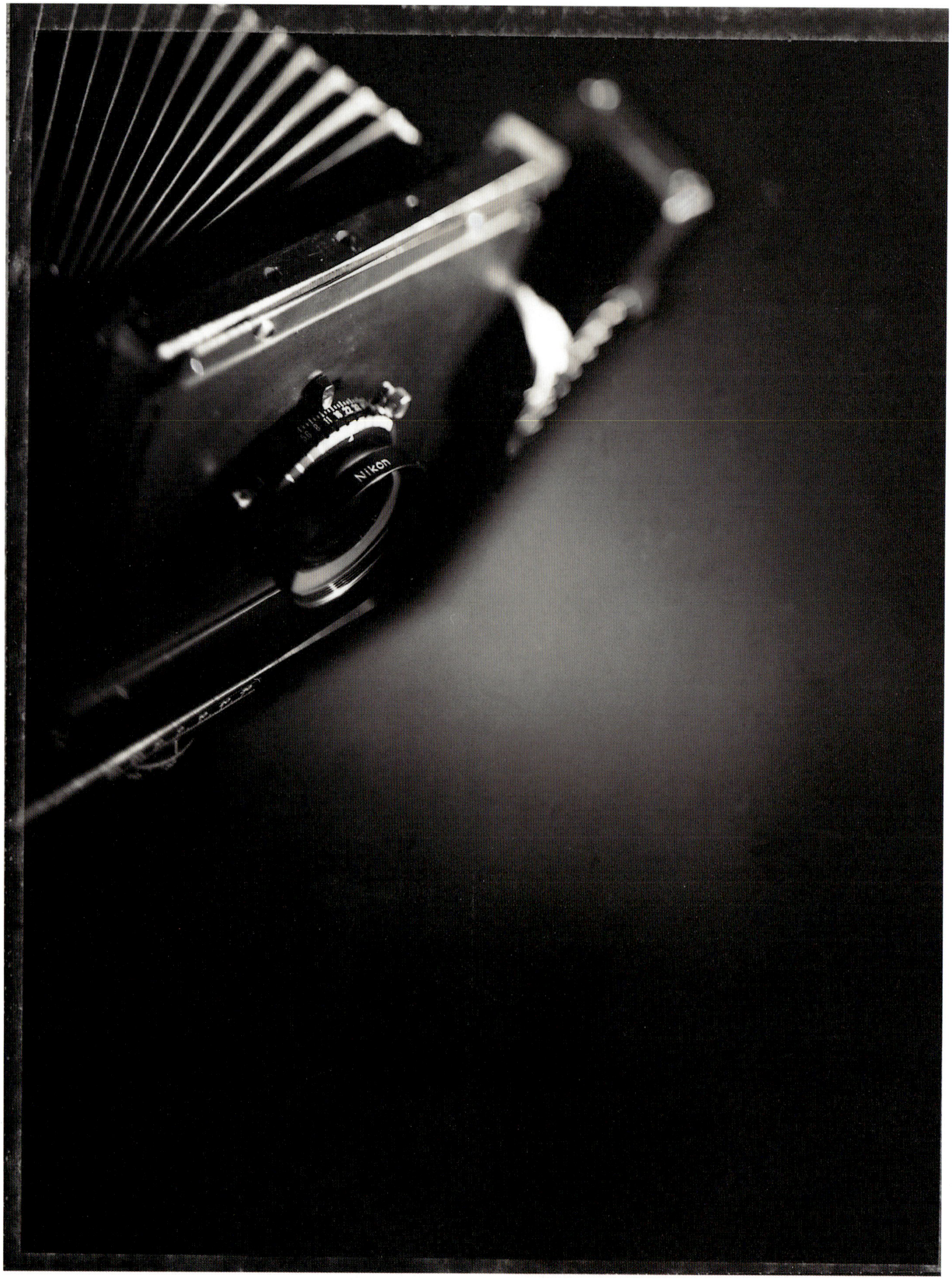

K.C. Armstrong

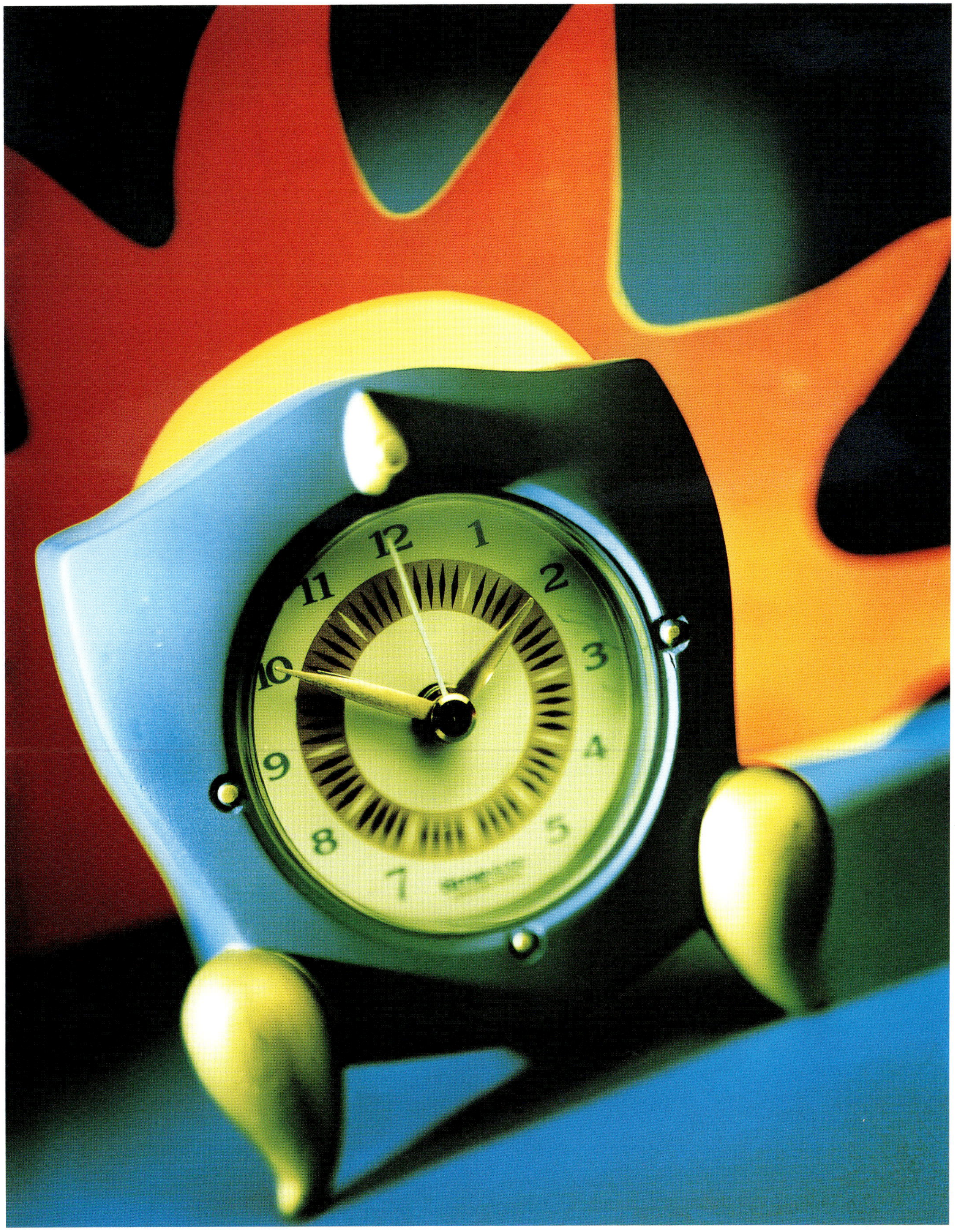

K.C. Armstrong

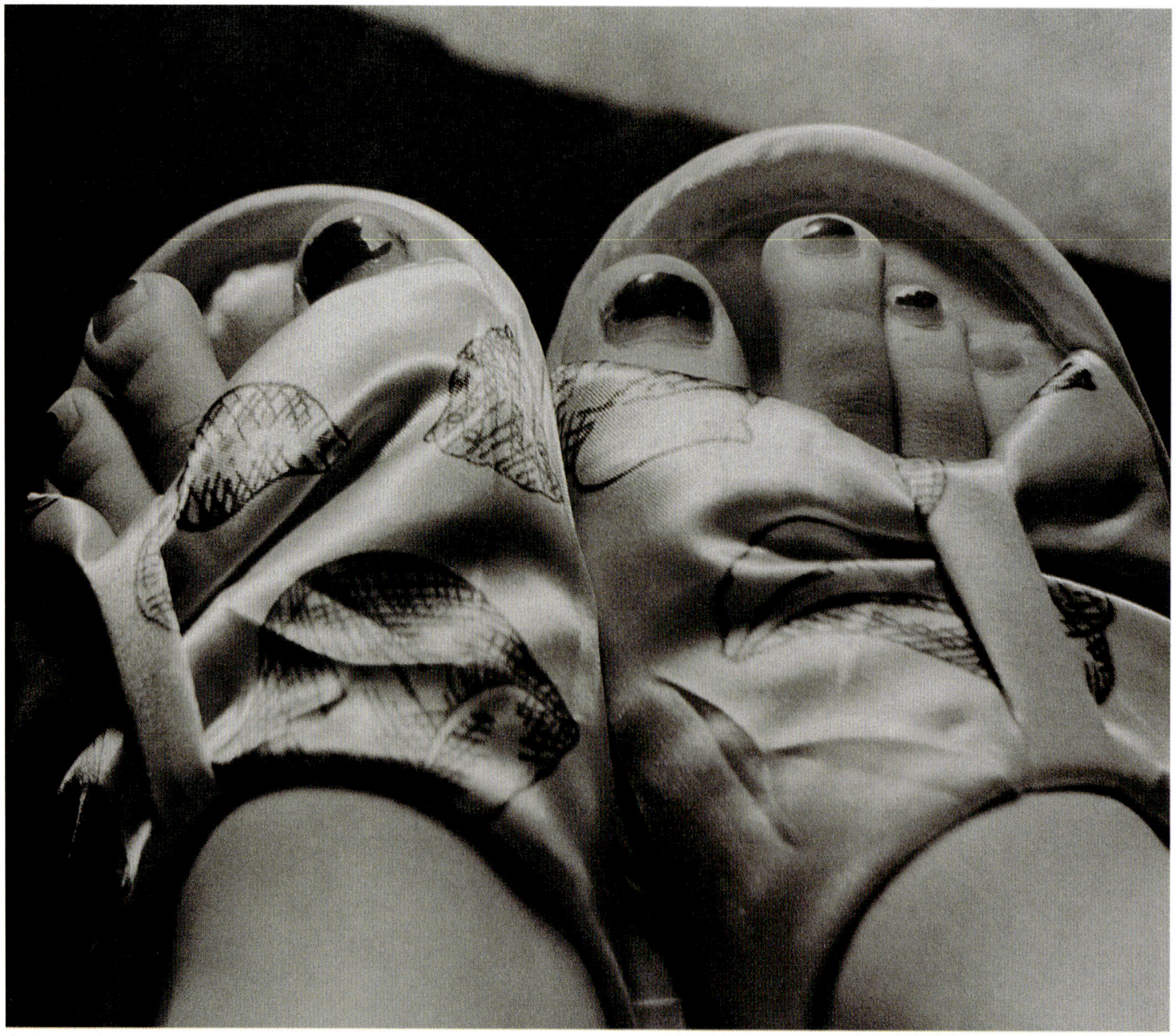

Beth Vagley

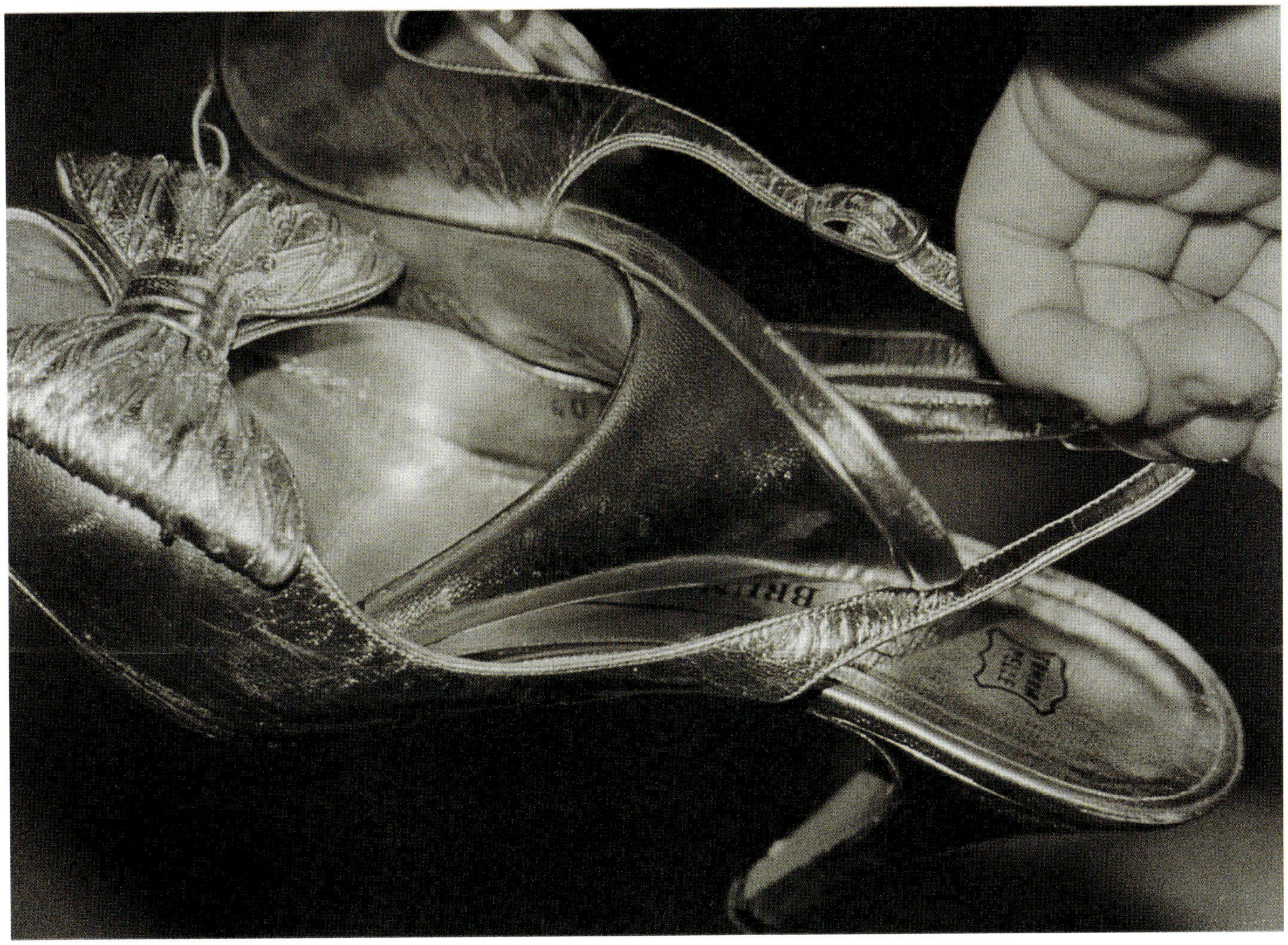

Beth Vagley

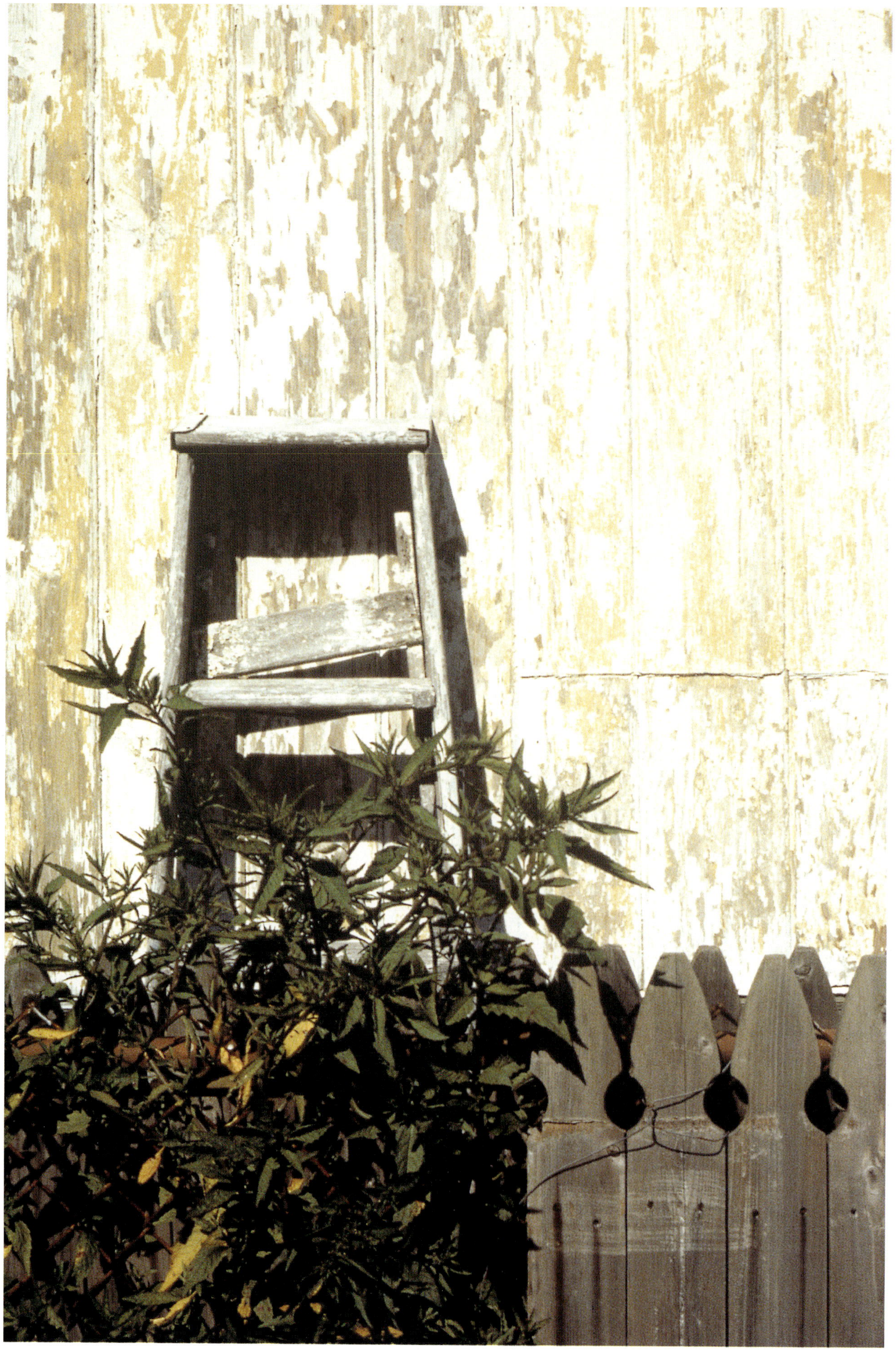

Marcelino Pagan

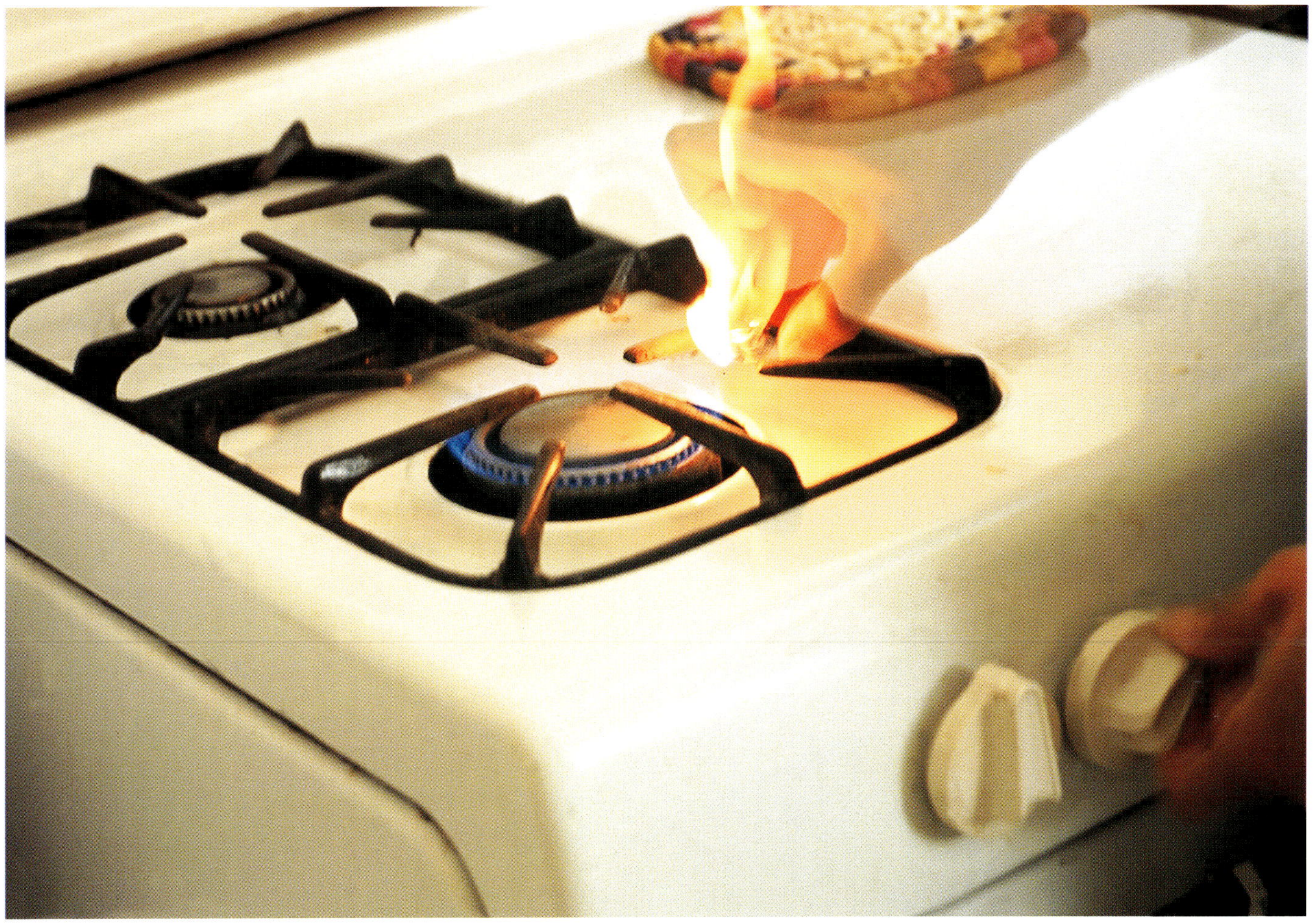

Noel Kurzen

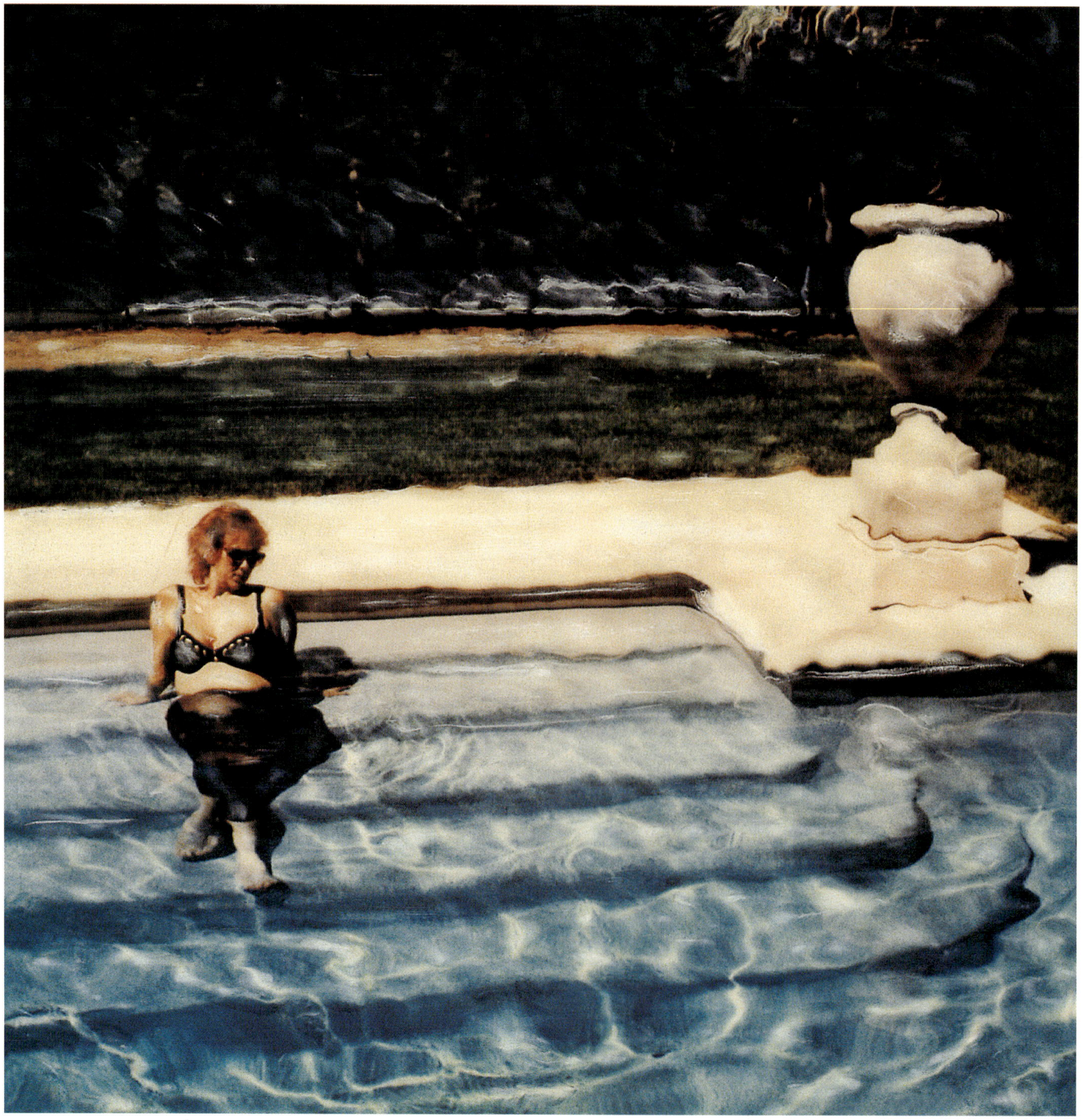

Paul Cutright

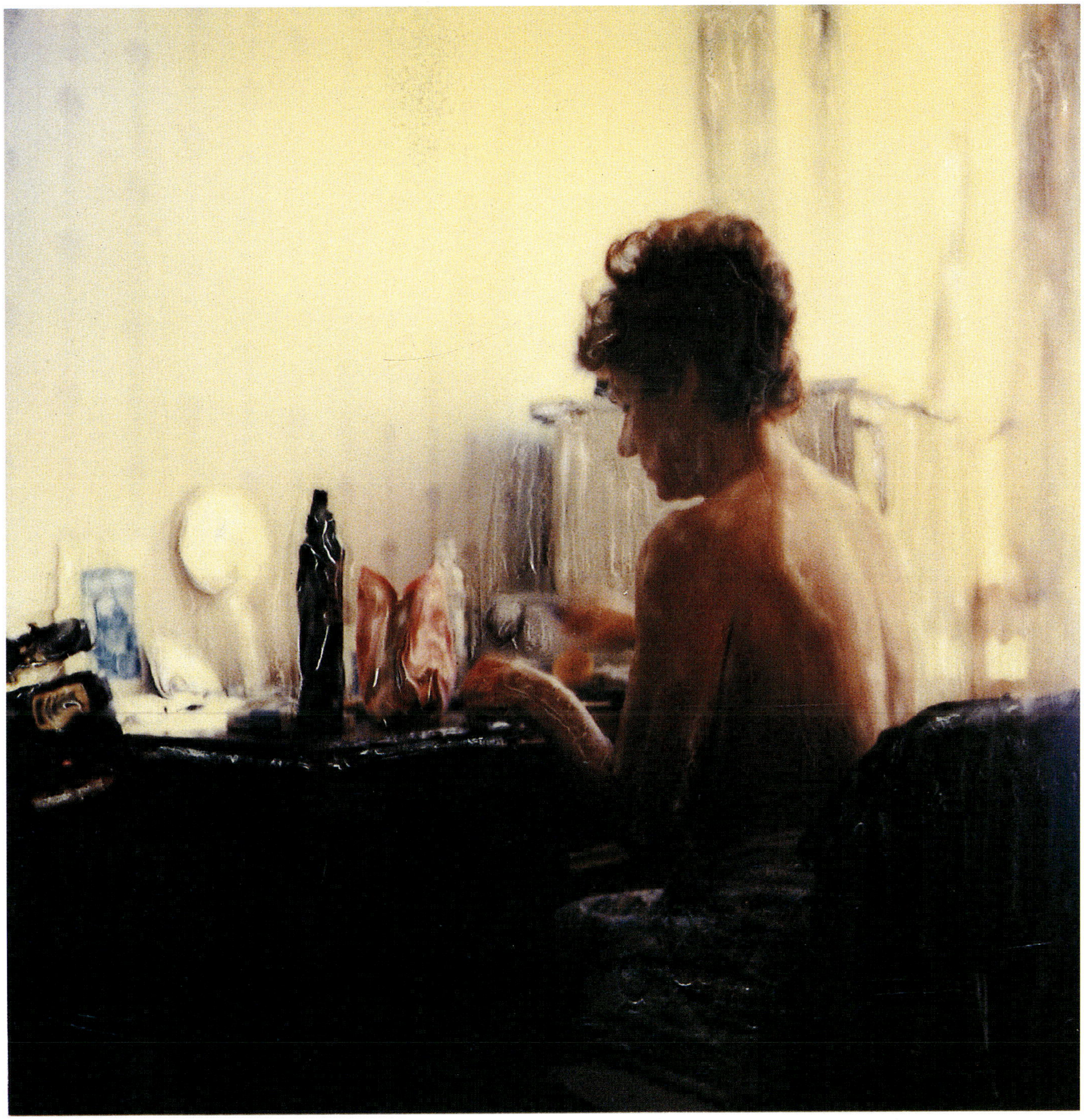

Paul Cutright

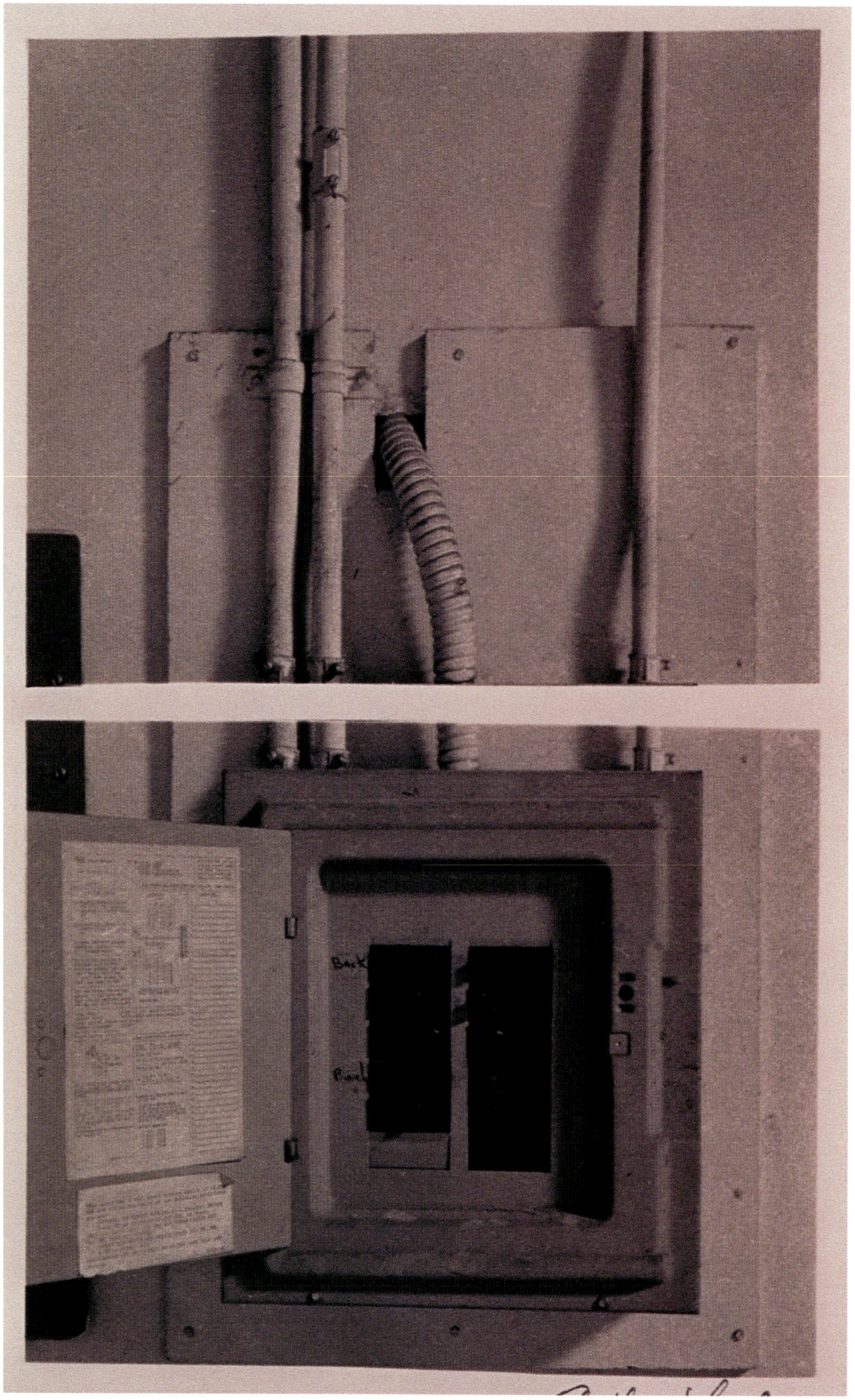

Anthony Lawson

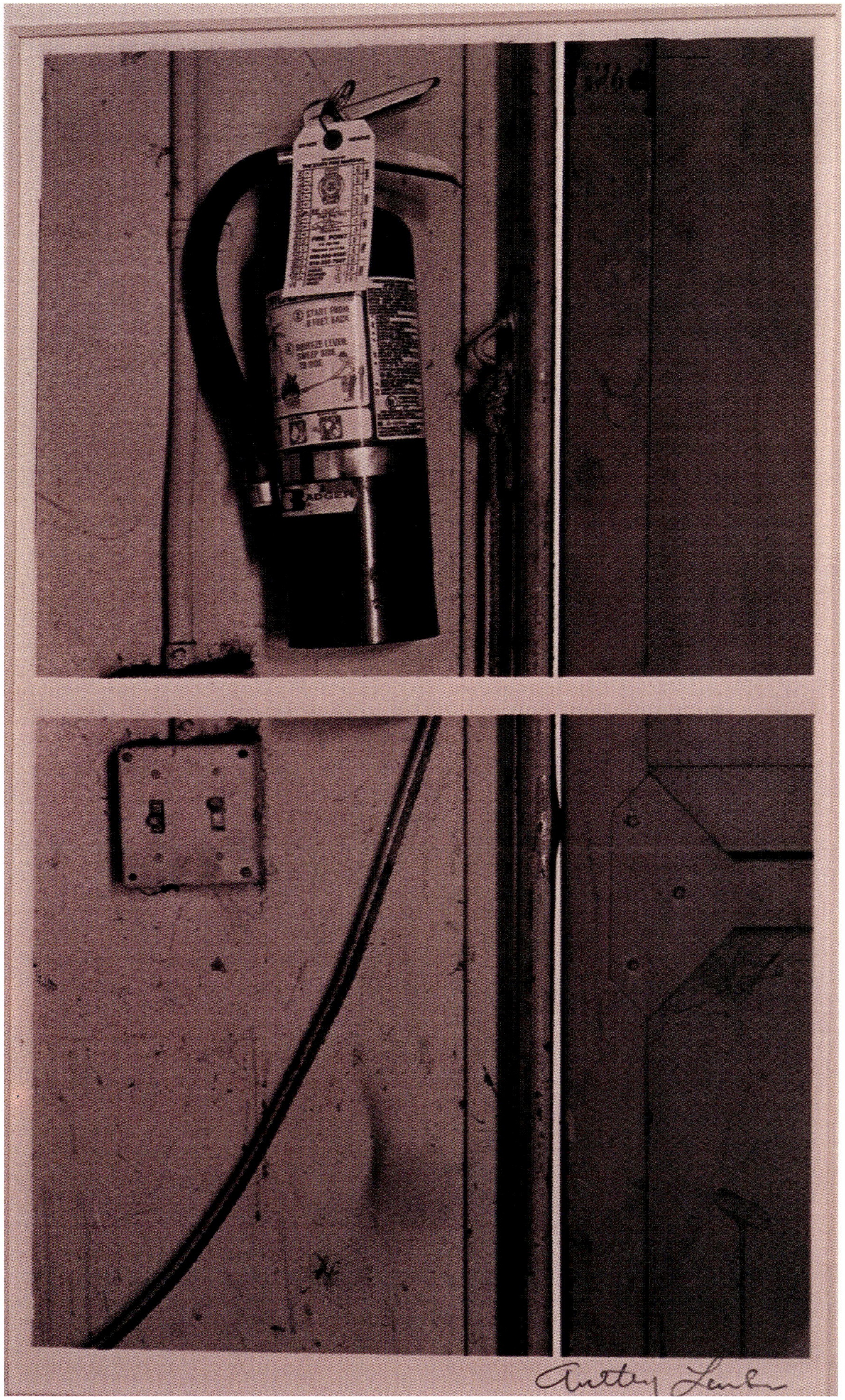

Anthony Lawson

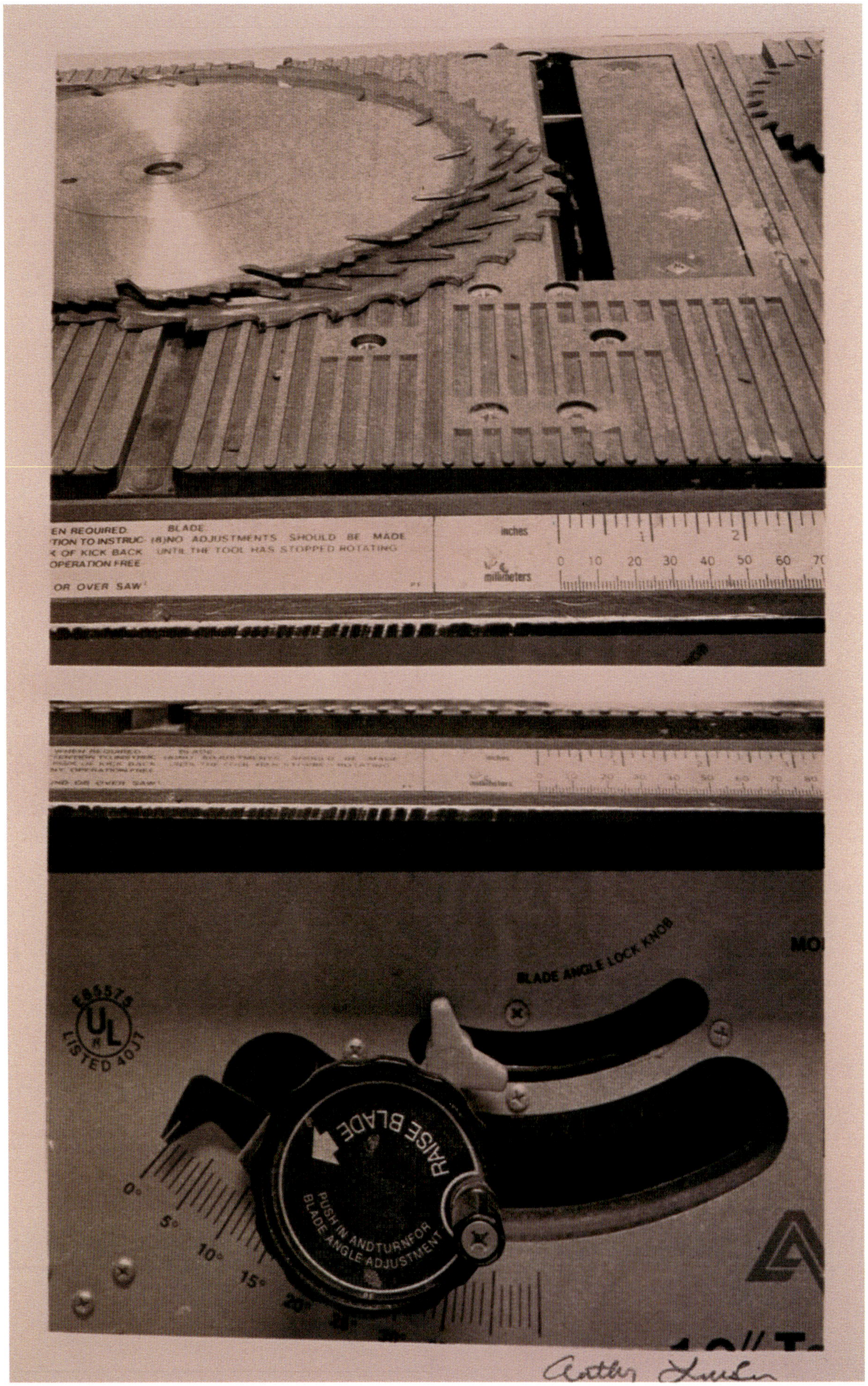

Anthony Lawson

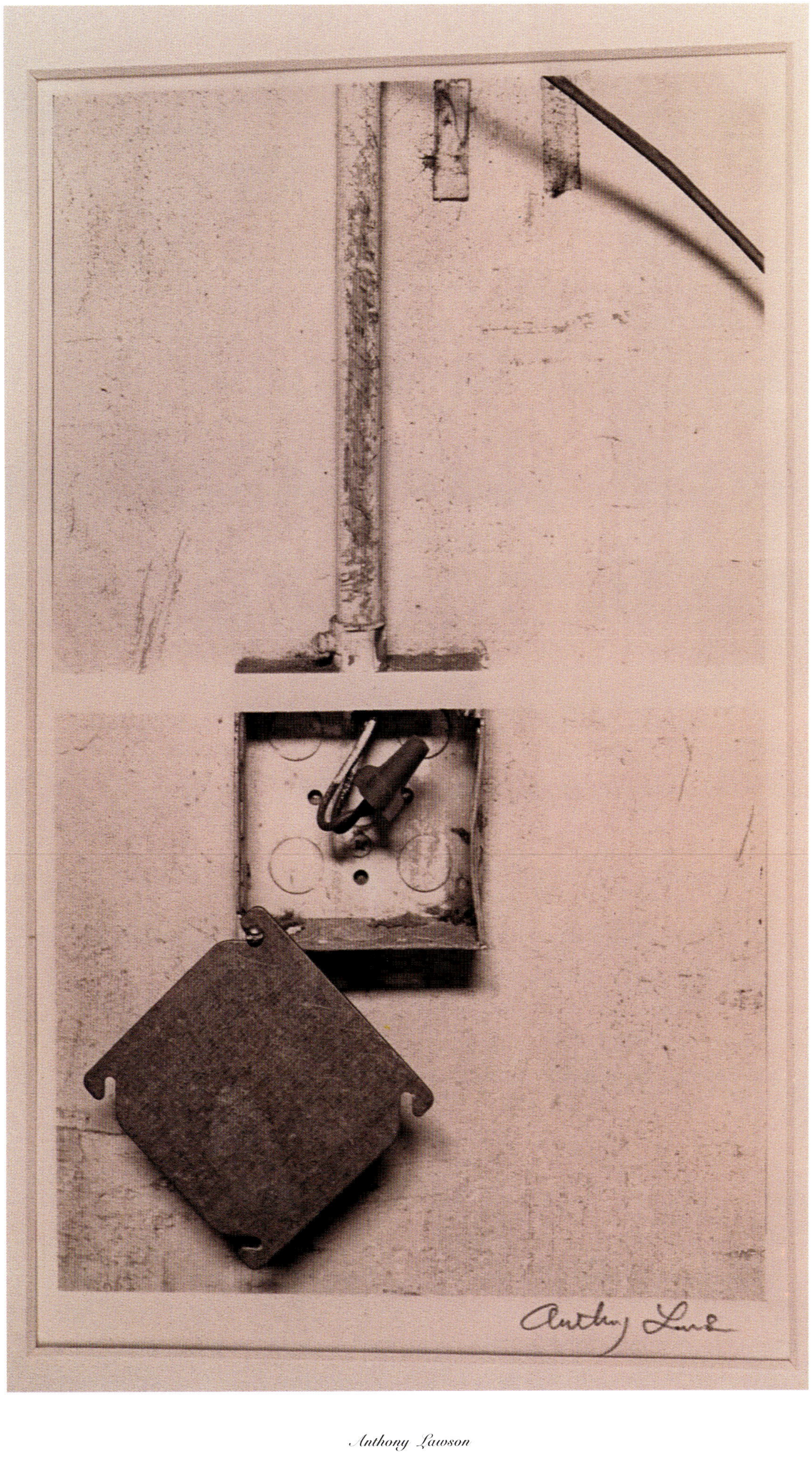

Anthony Lawson

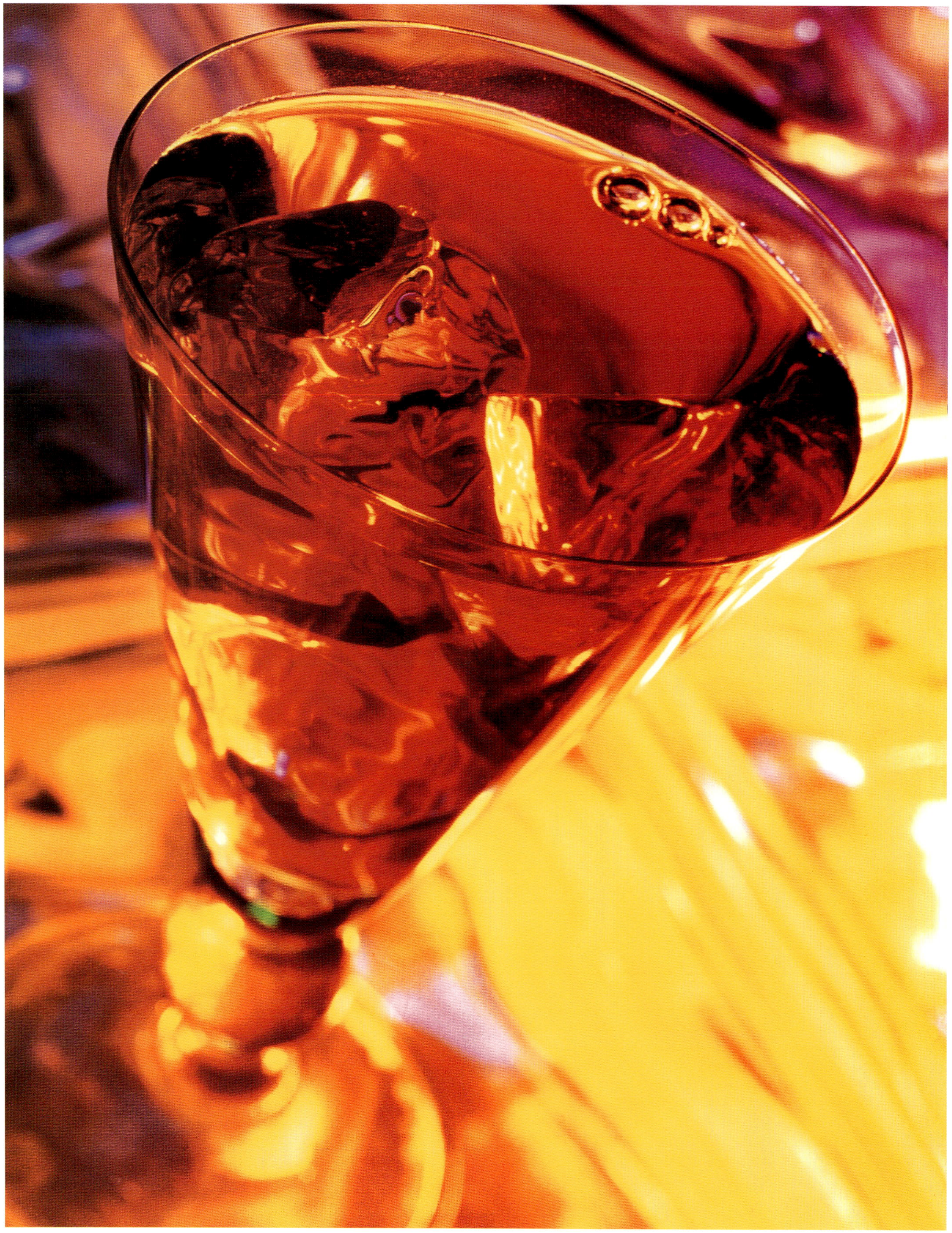

Karina Karla Serna

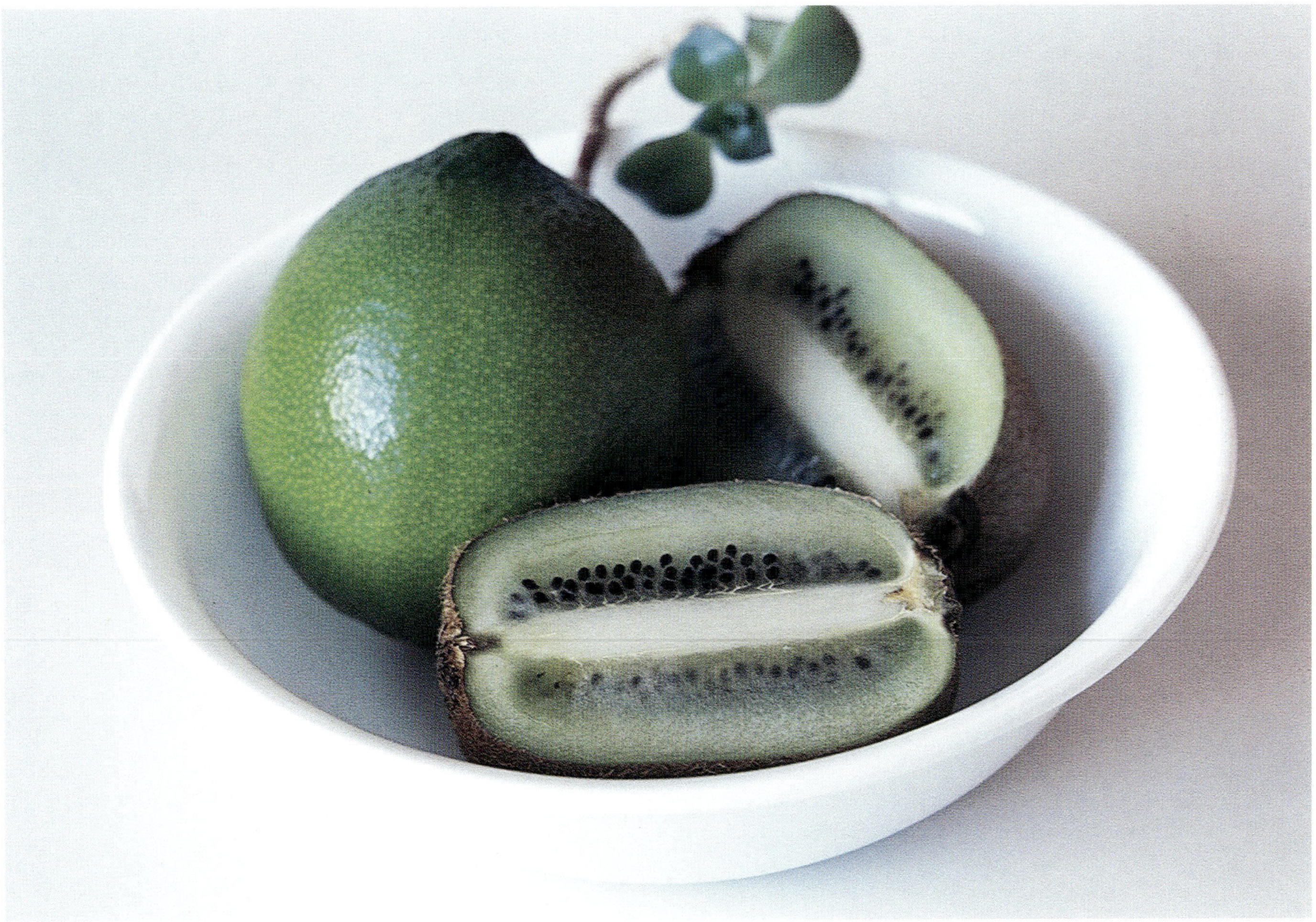

Peter Worth

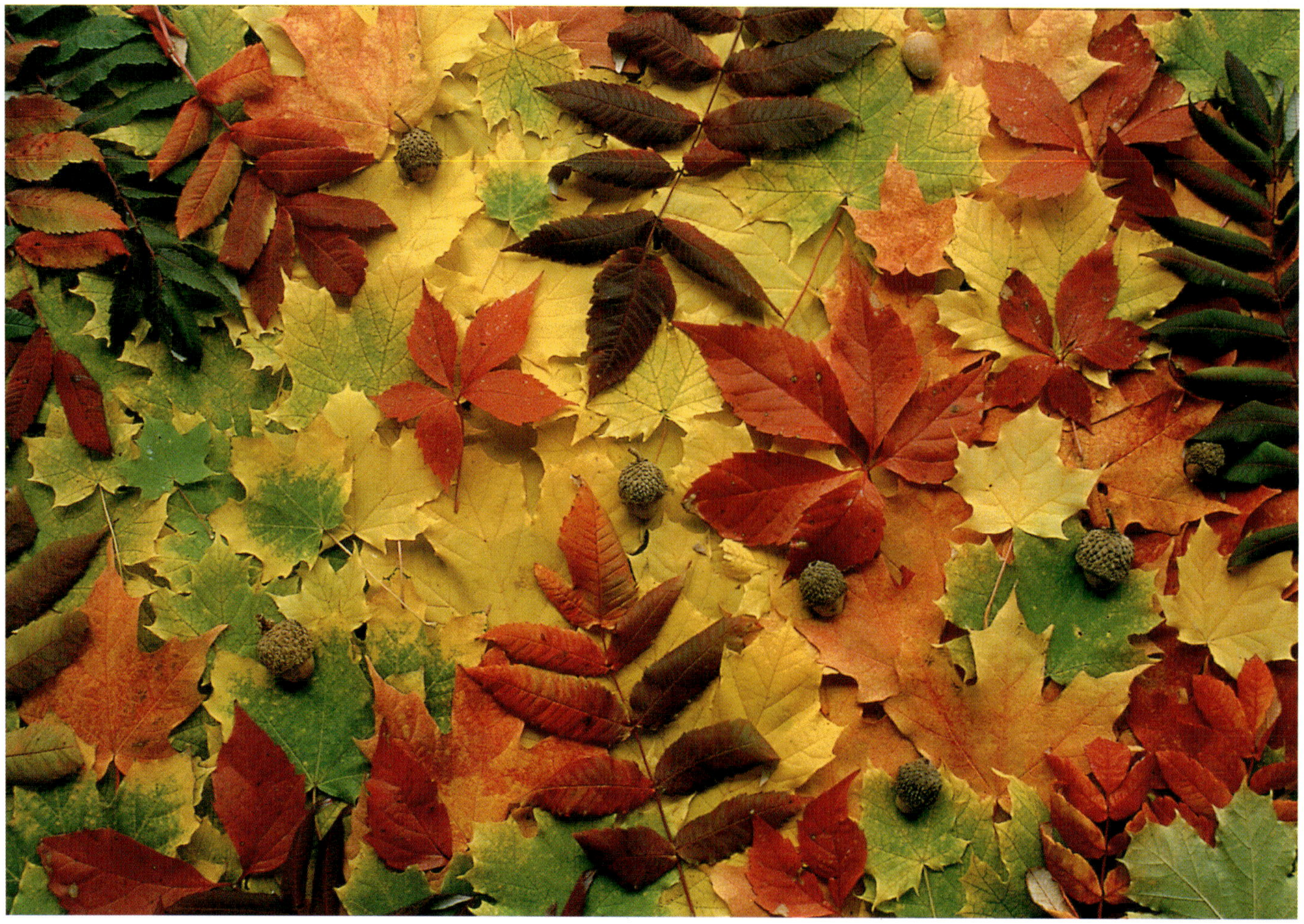

George Day

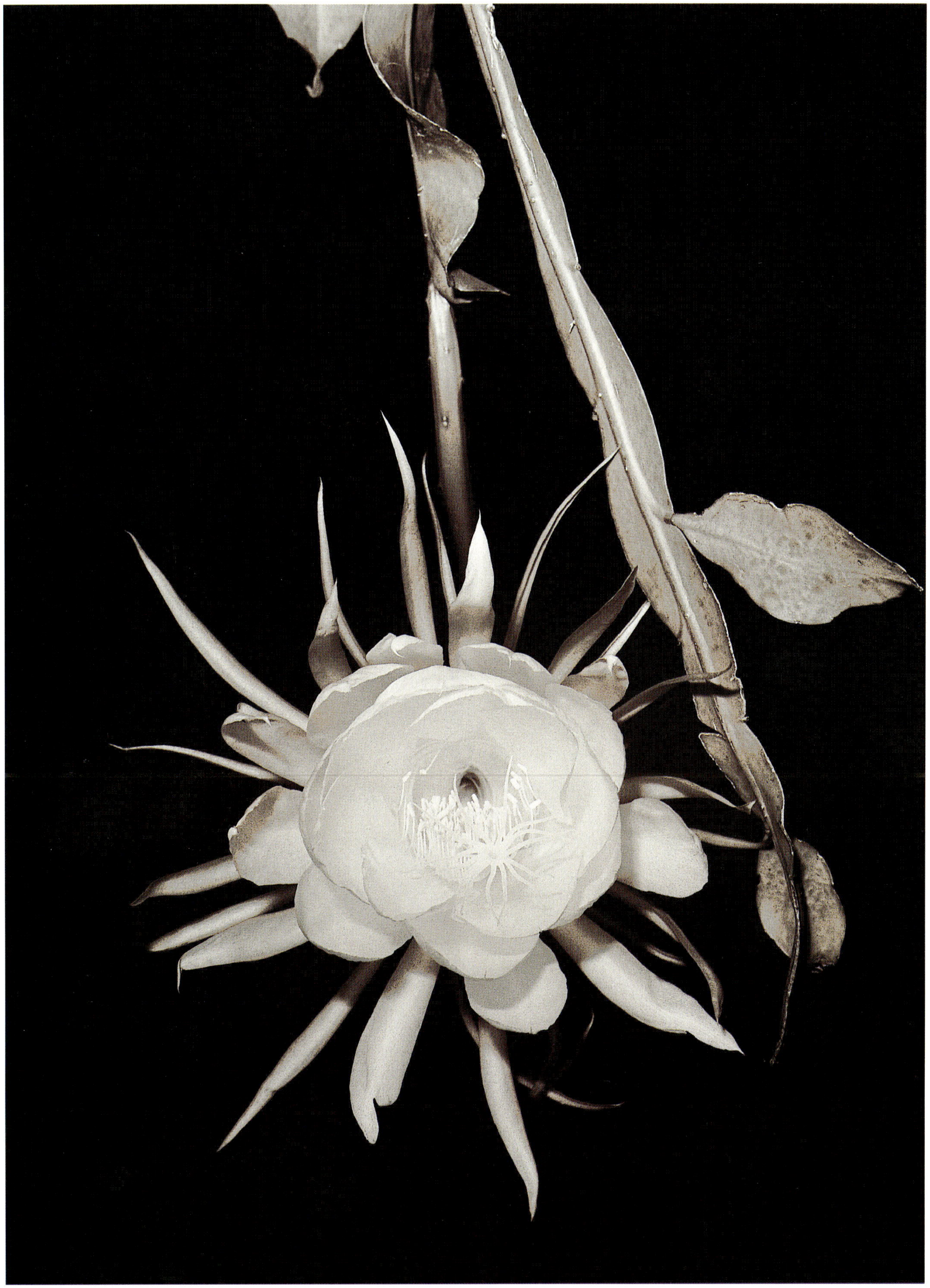

Roger Pfingston

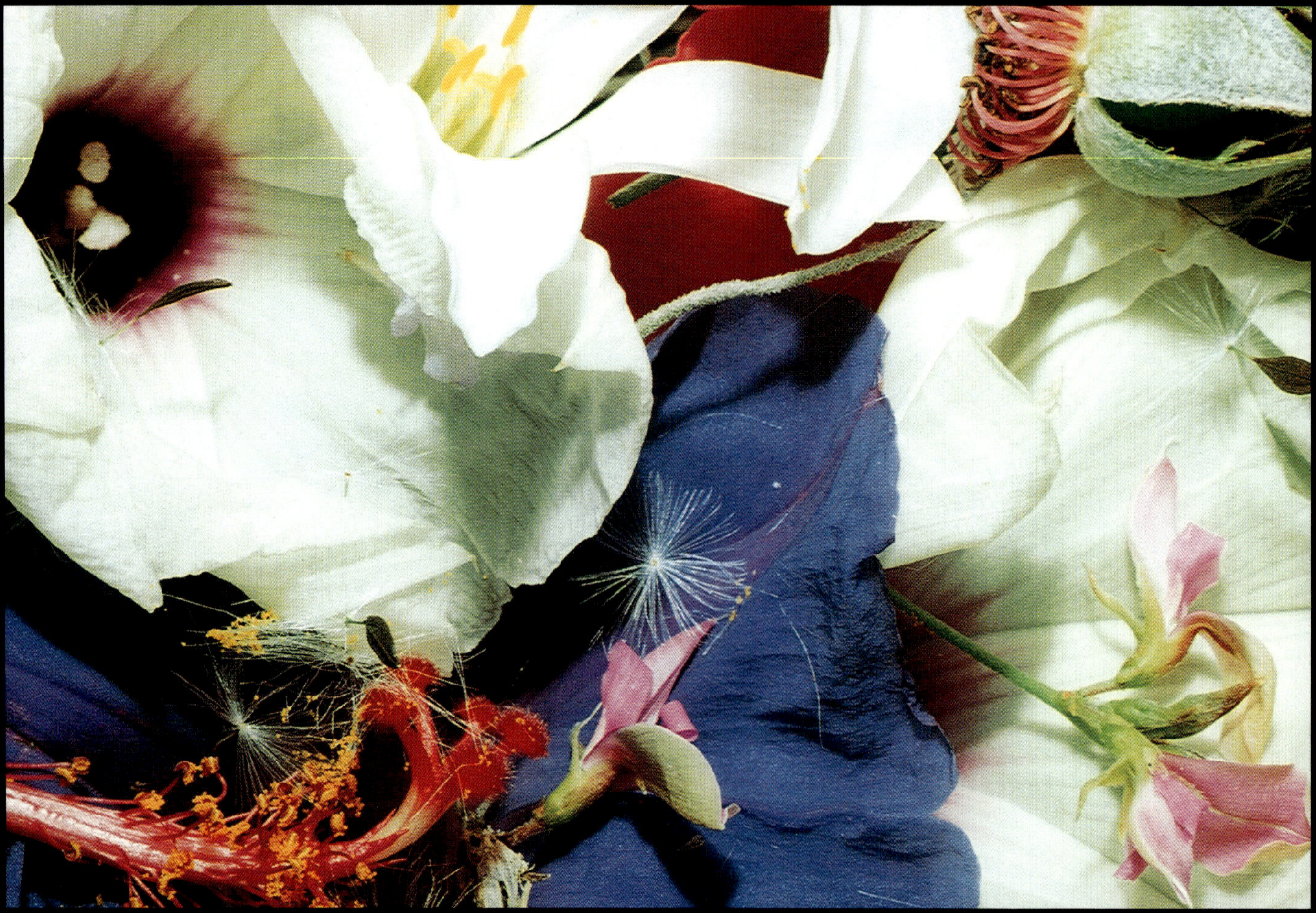

H.C. Turk

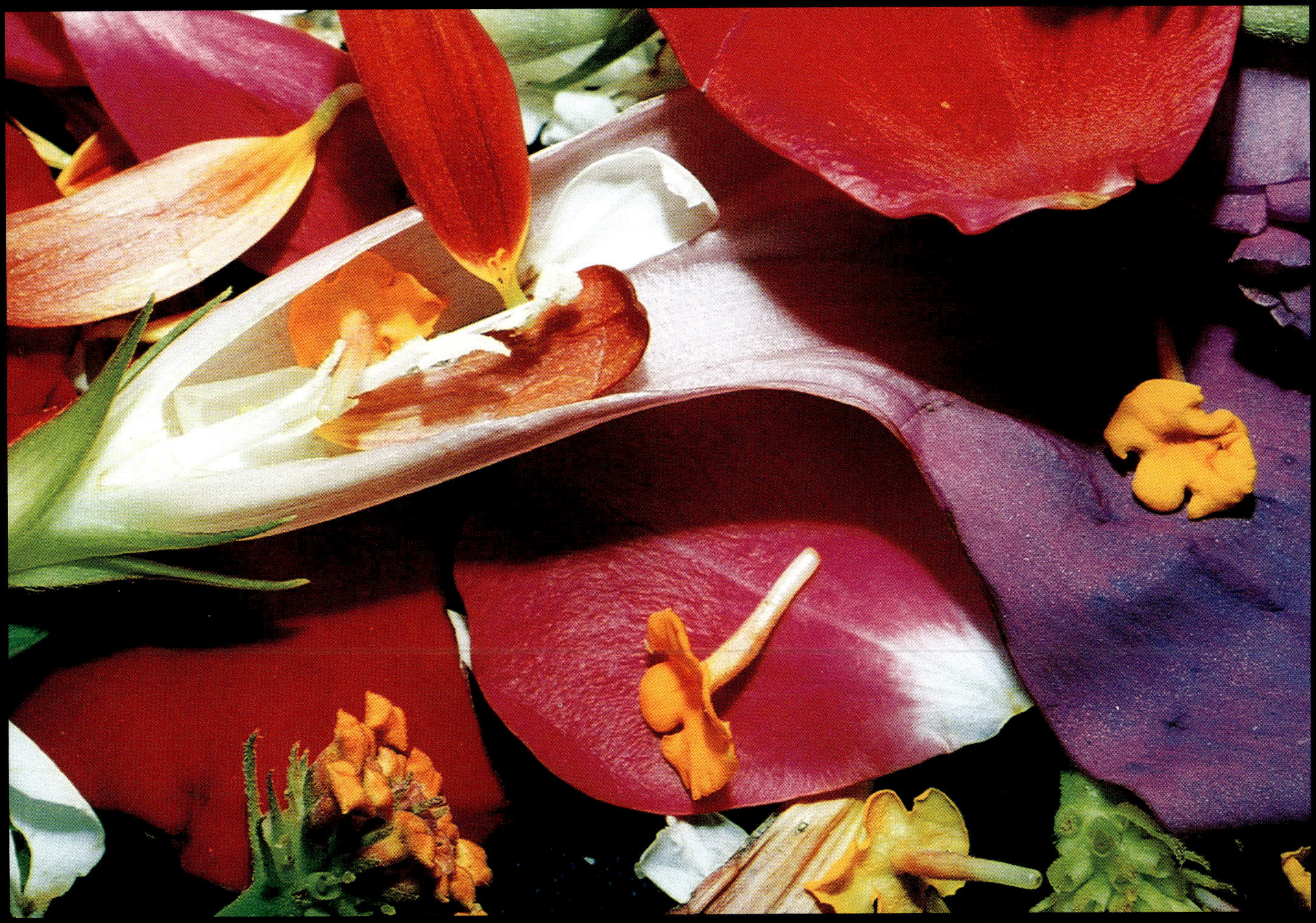

H.C. Turk

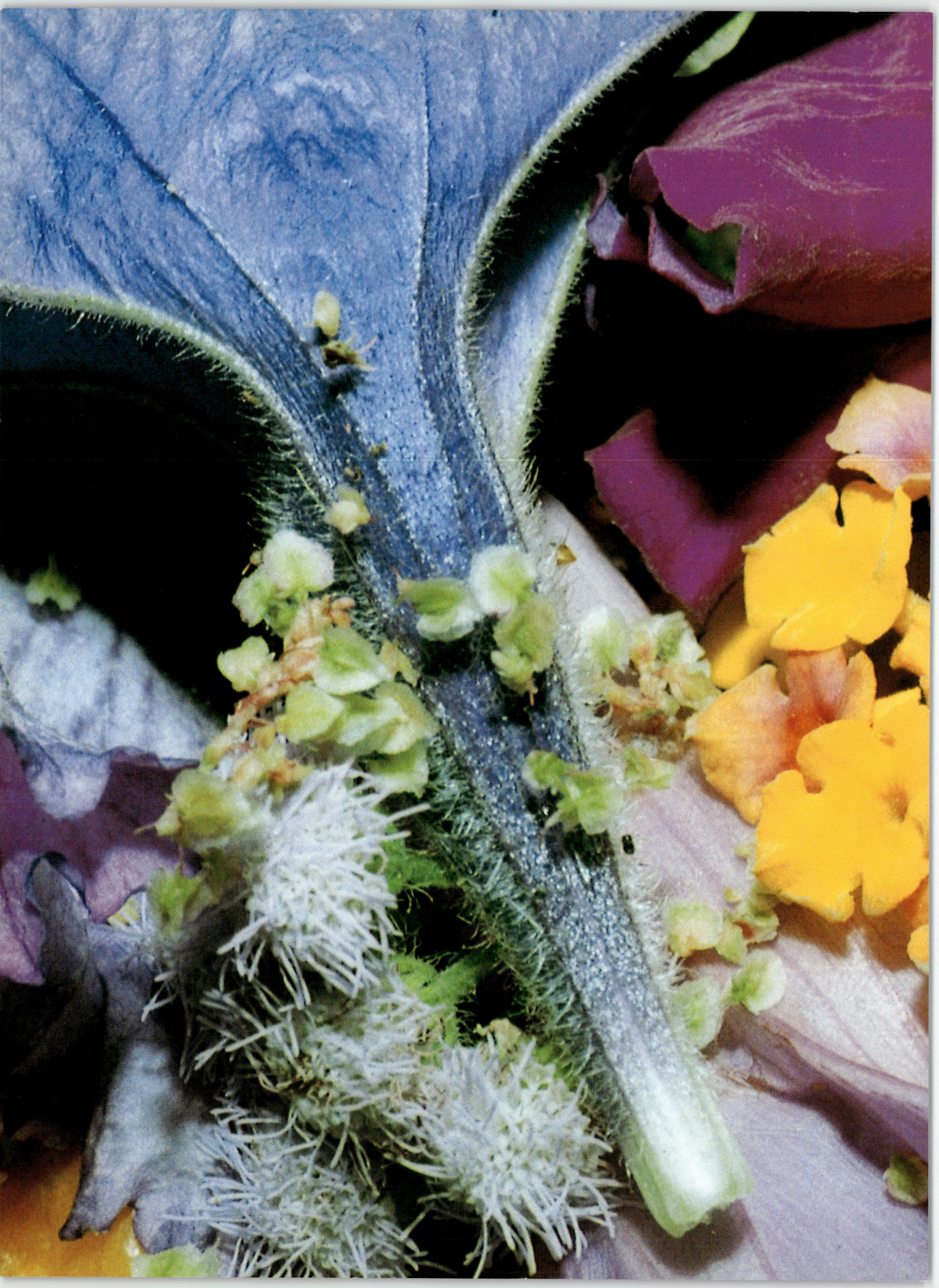

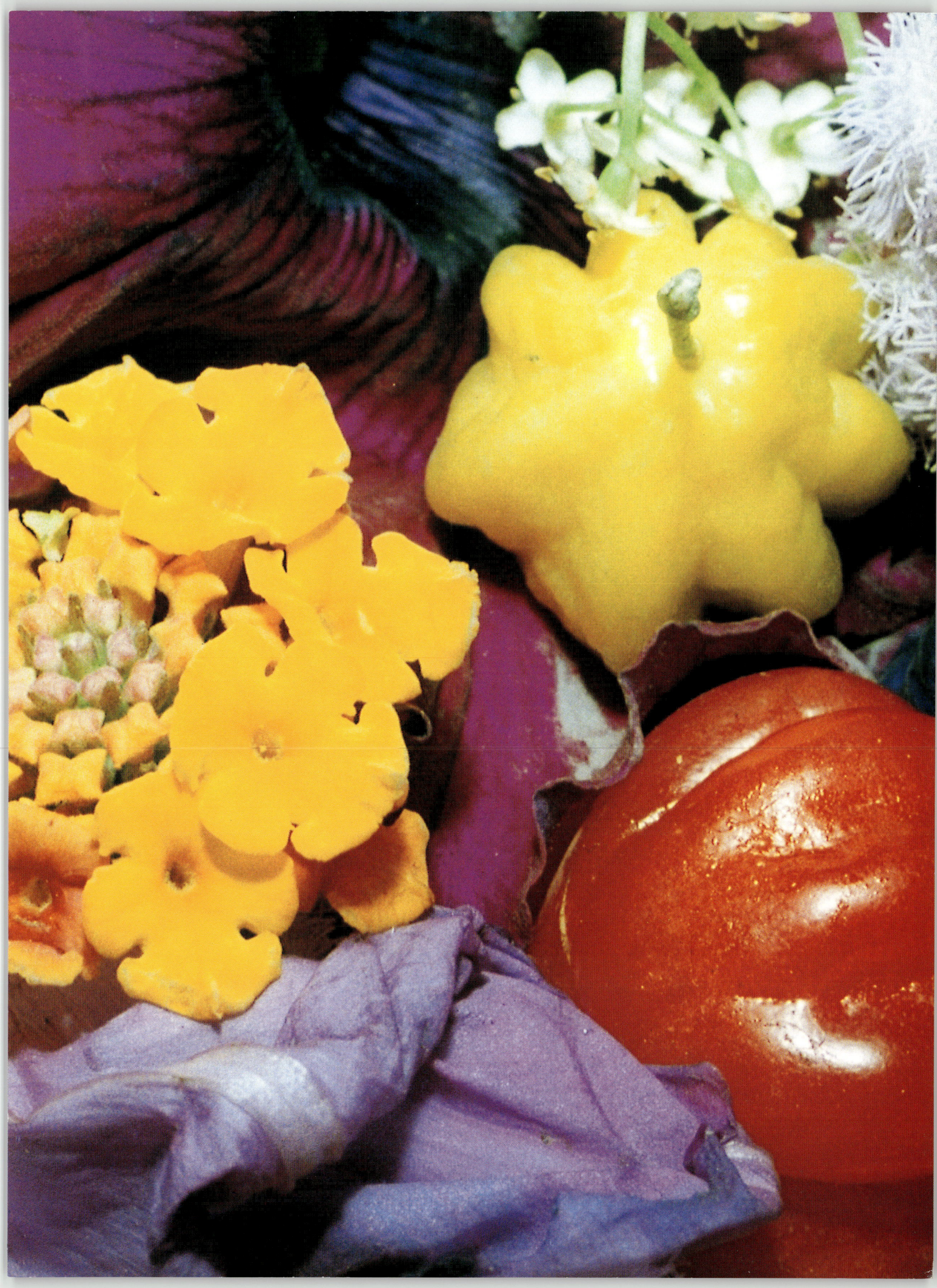

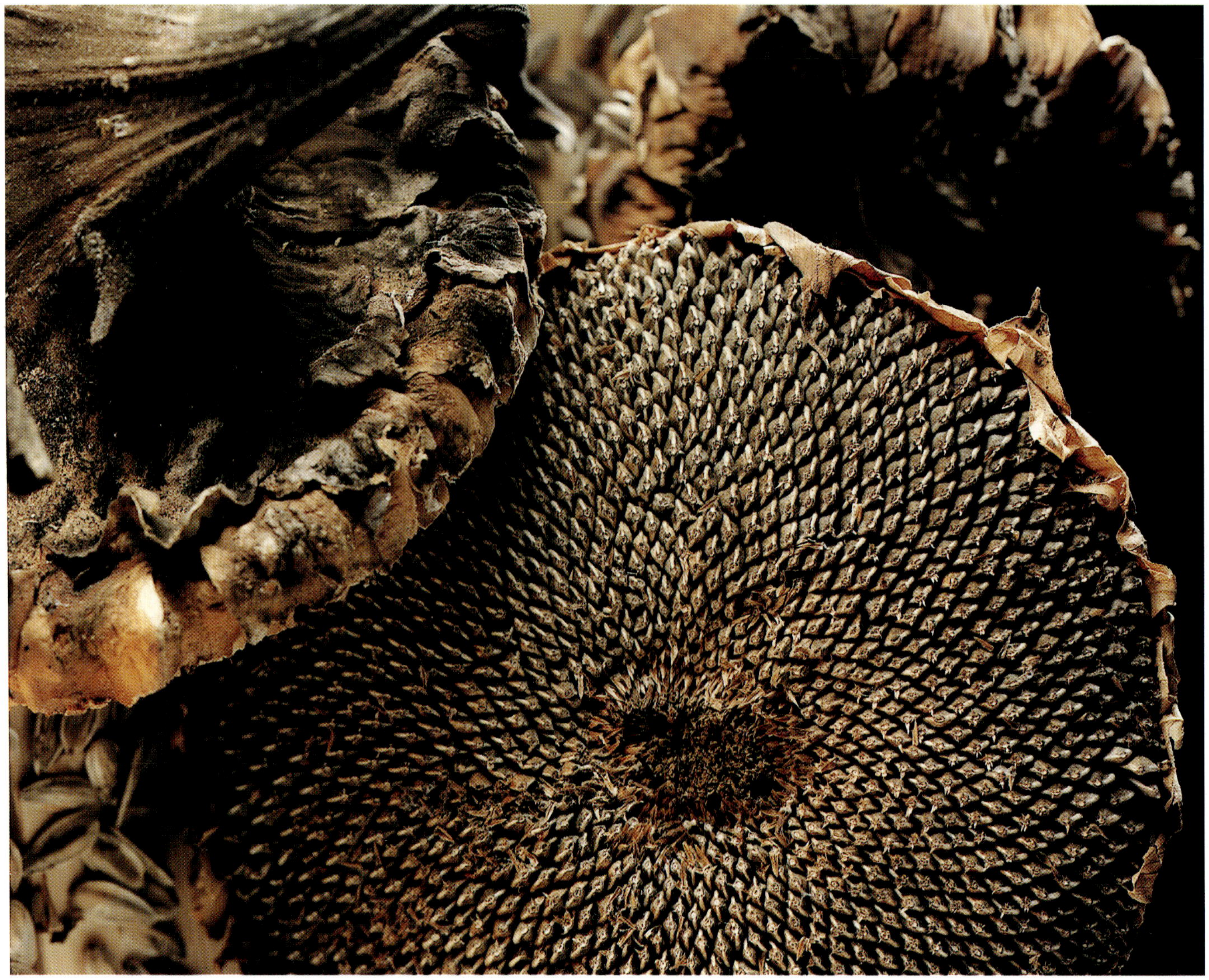

(PREVIOUS SPREAD) *H.C. Turk* ■ (THIS PAGE) *Assaf Haber*

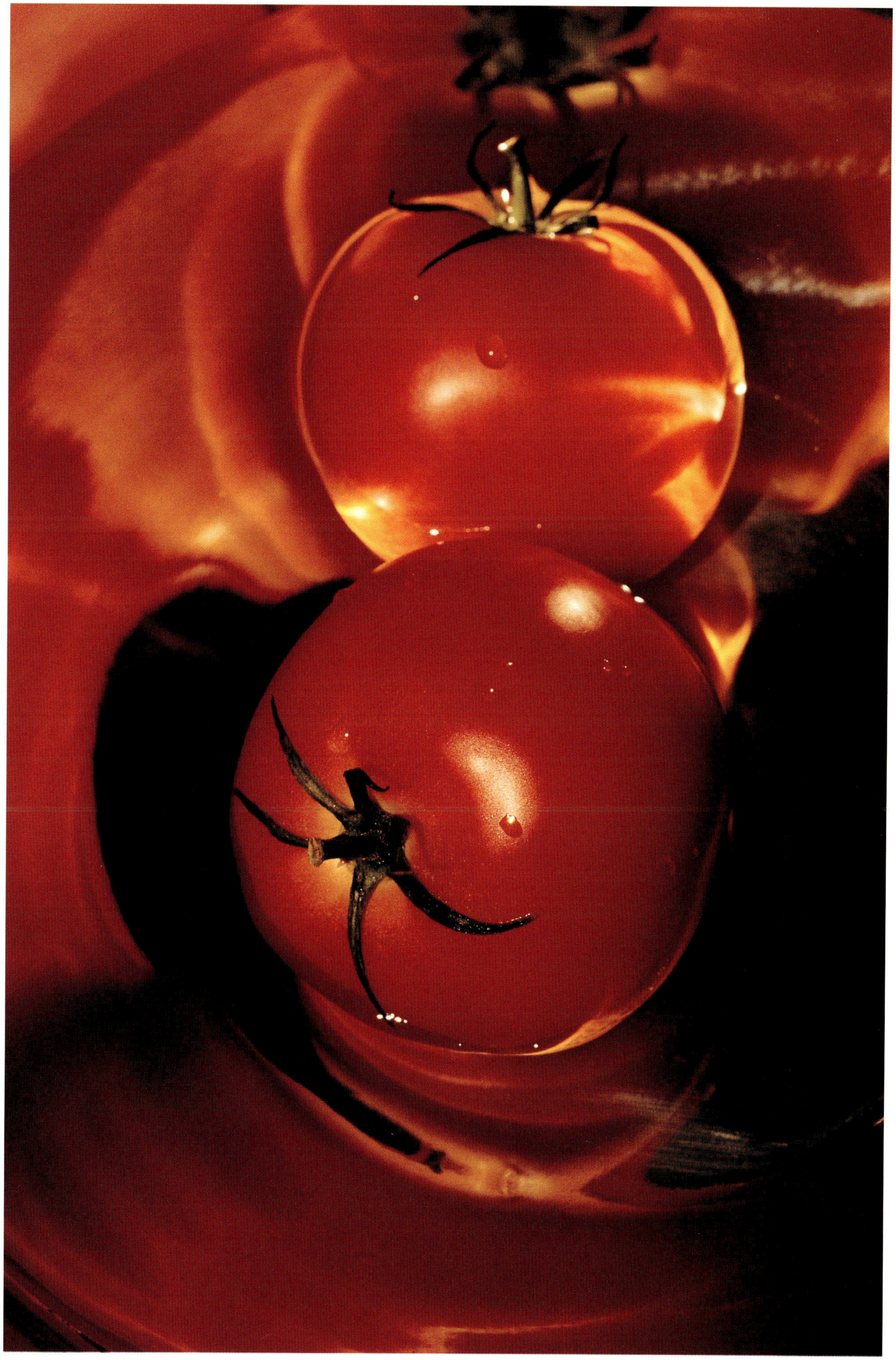

Helena Fierlinger

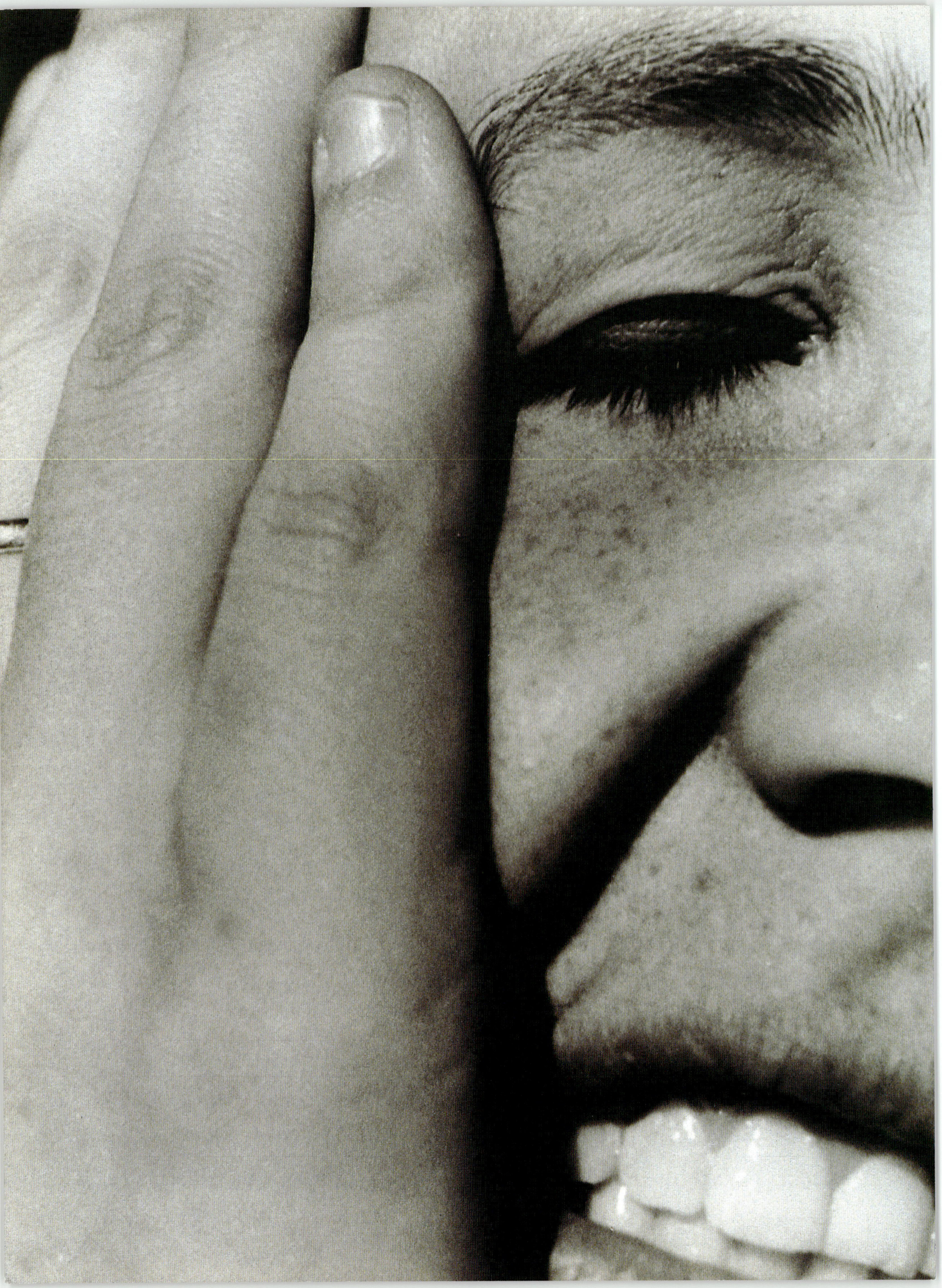

PEOPLE

MENSCHEN

PERSONNES

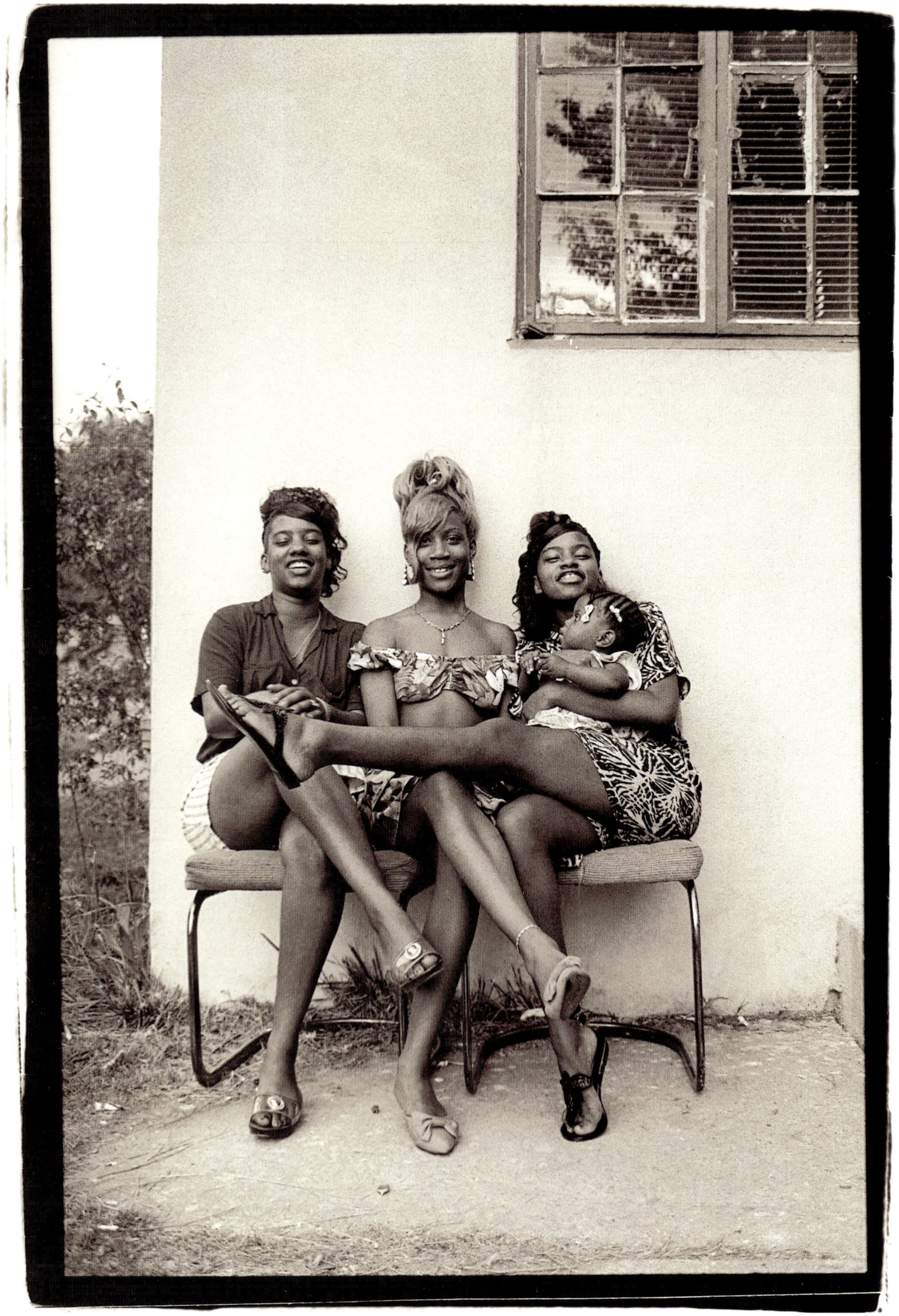

(PREVIOUS SPREAD) *Beth Vagley* ■ (THIS PAGE) *Michael R. Reese*

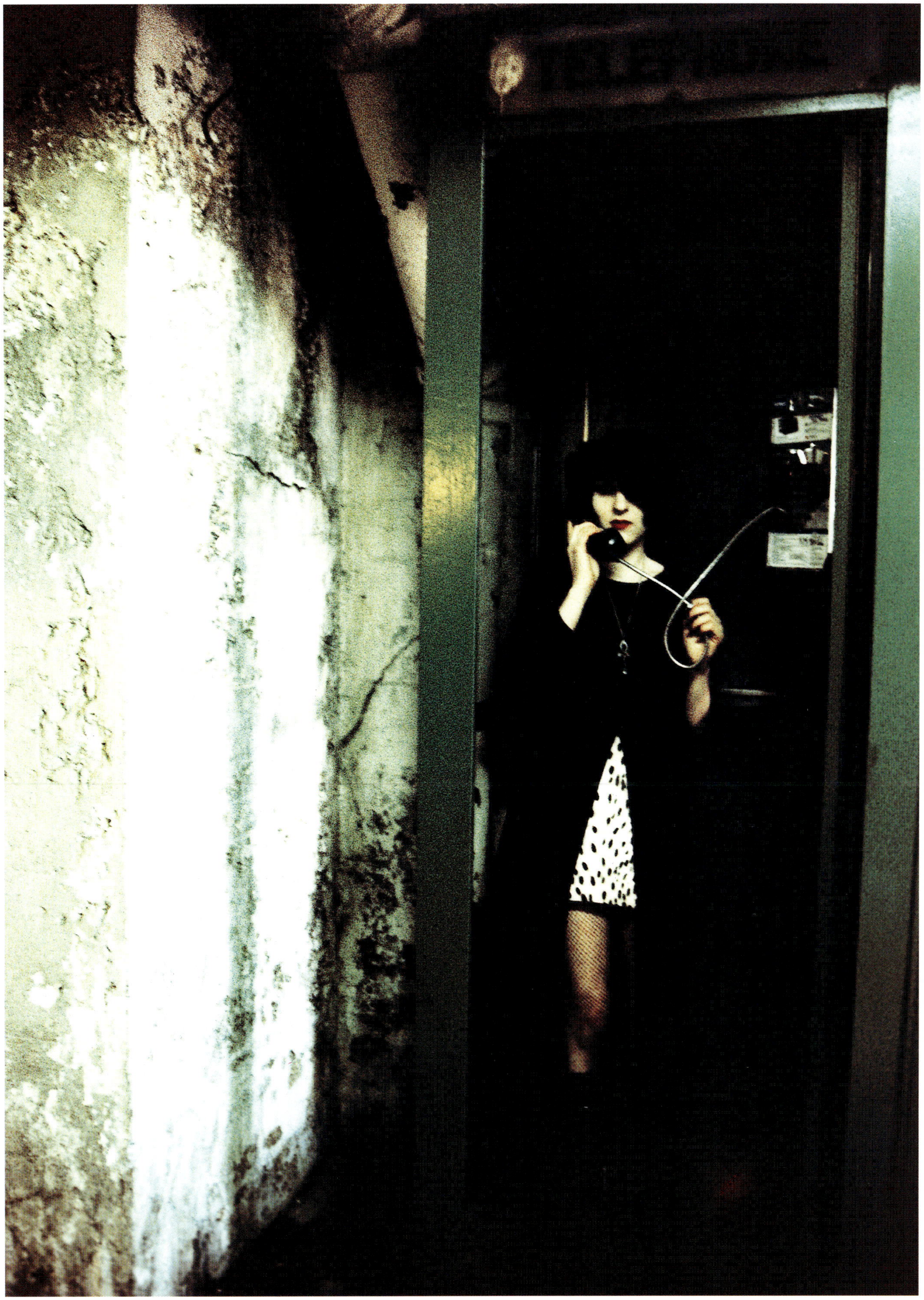

Miwa Nishio

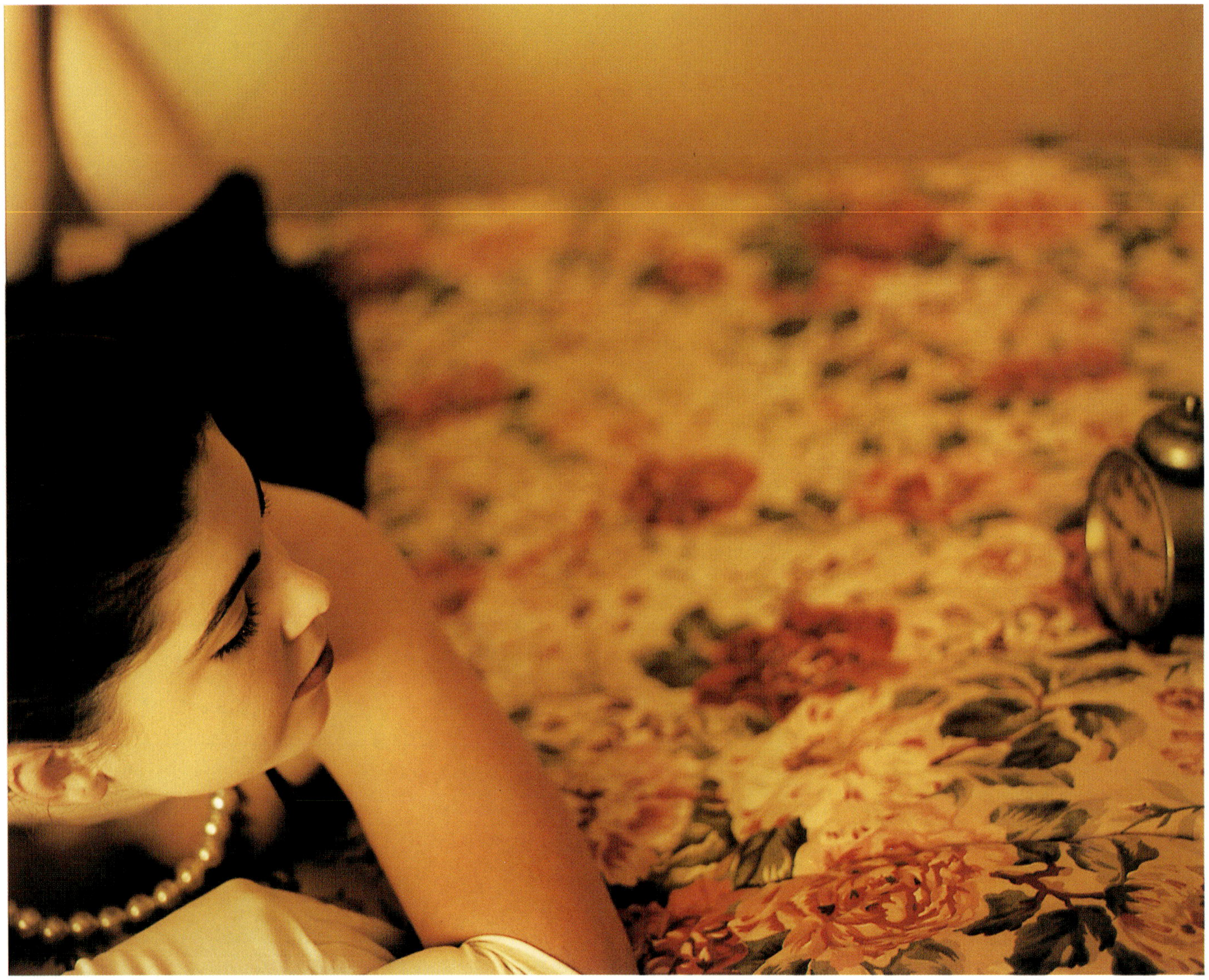

Nathan Teutle

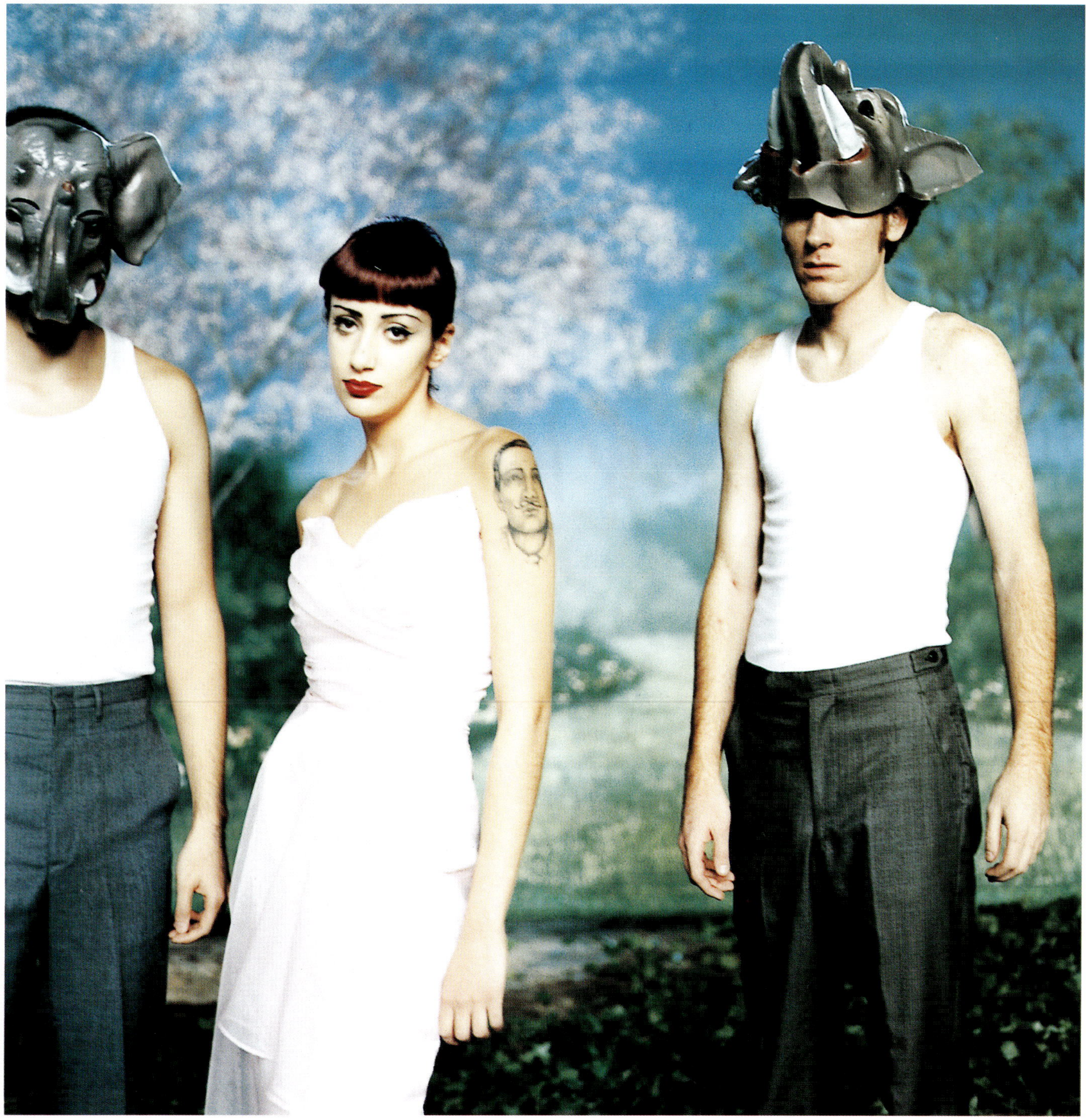

Norma Zuniga

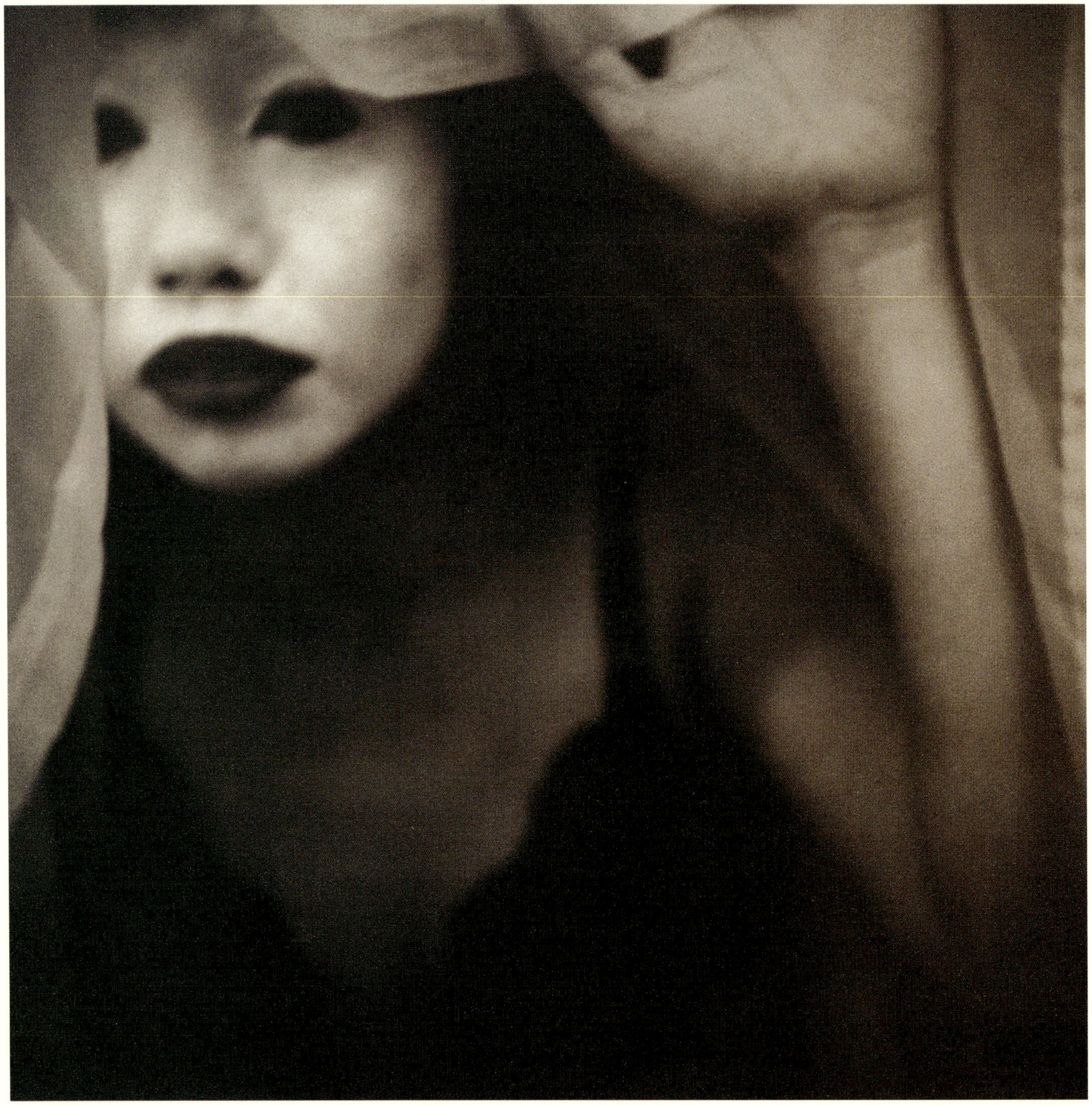

Charles Brackman

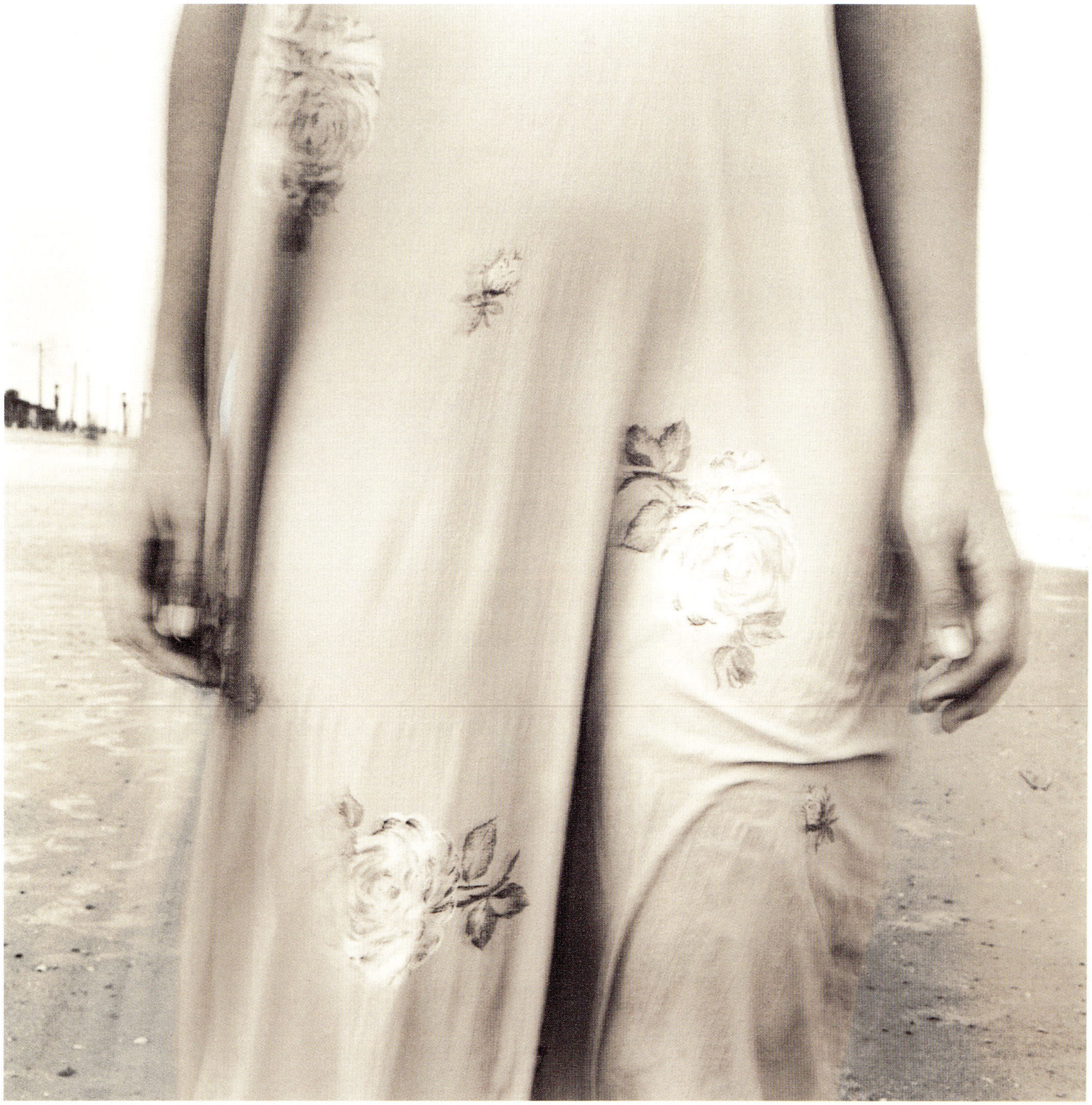

Charles Brackman

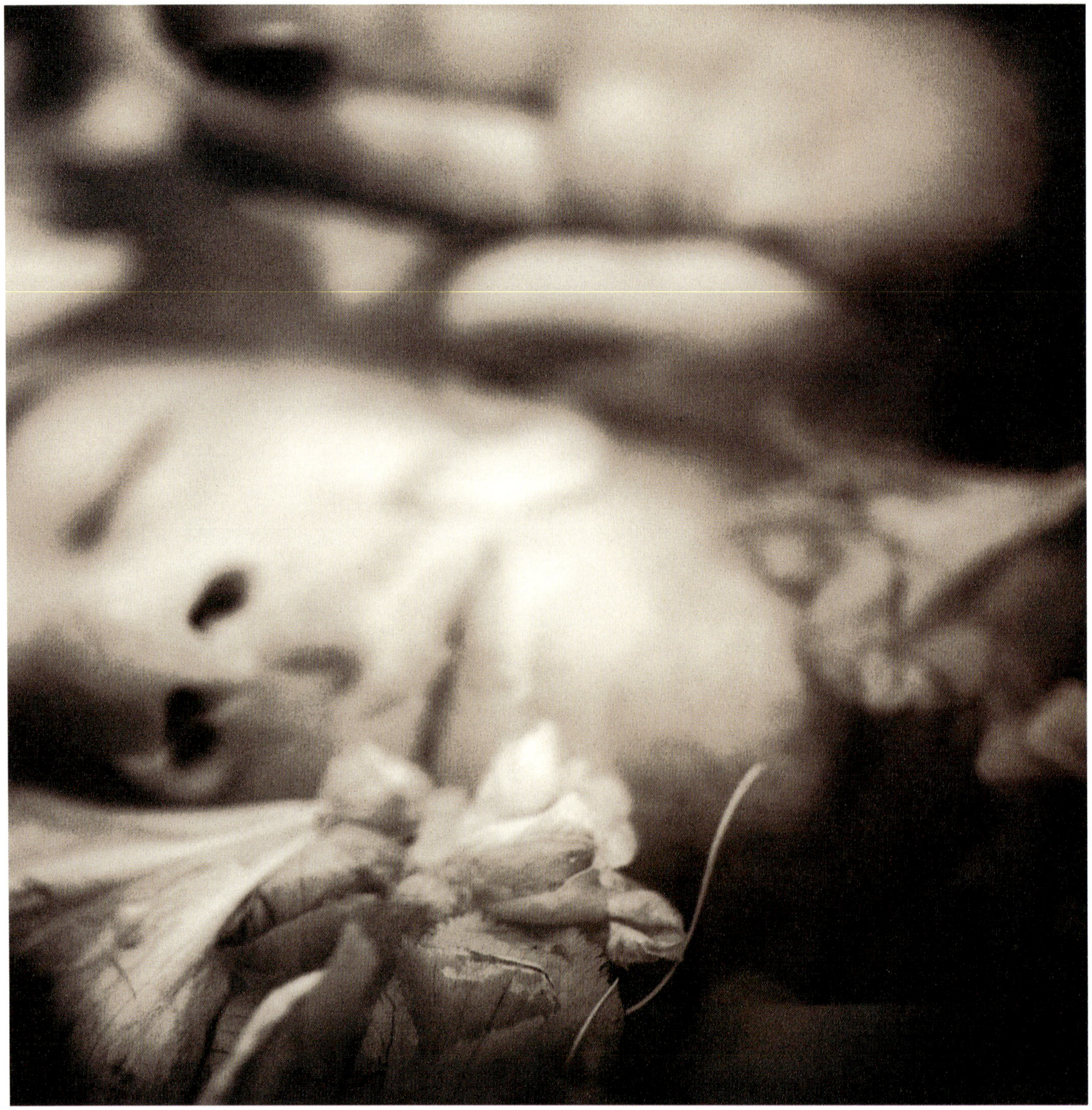

Charles Brackman

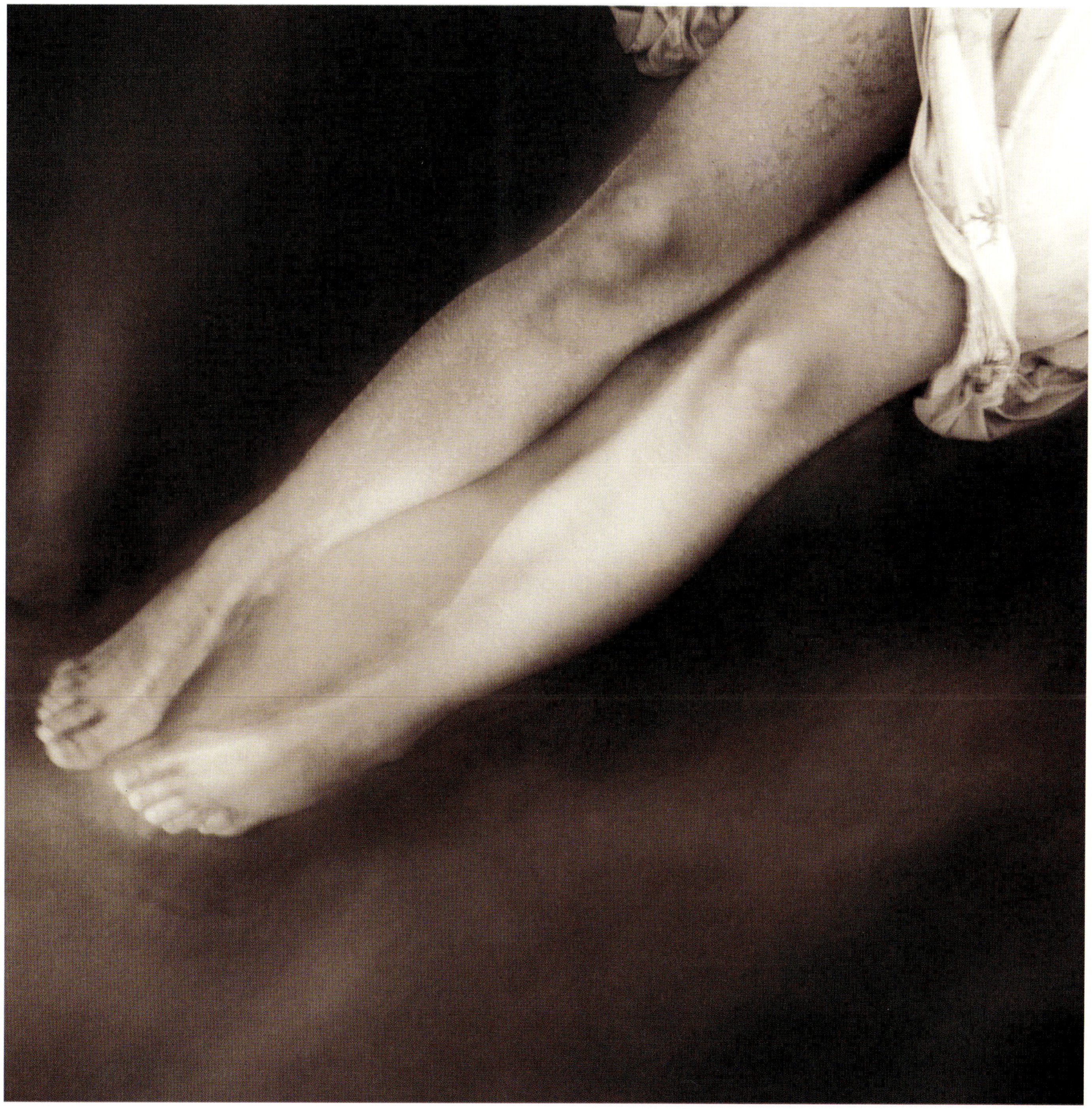

Charles Brackman

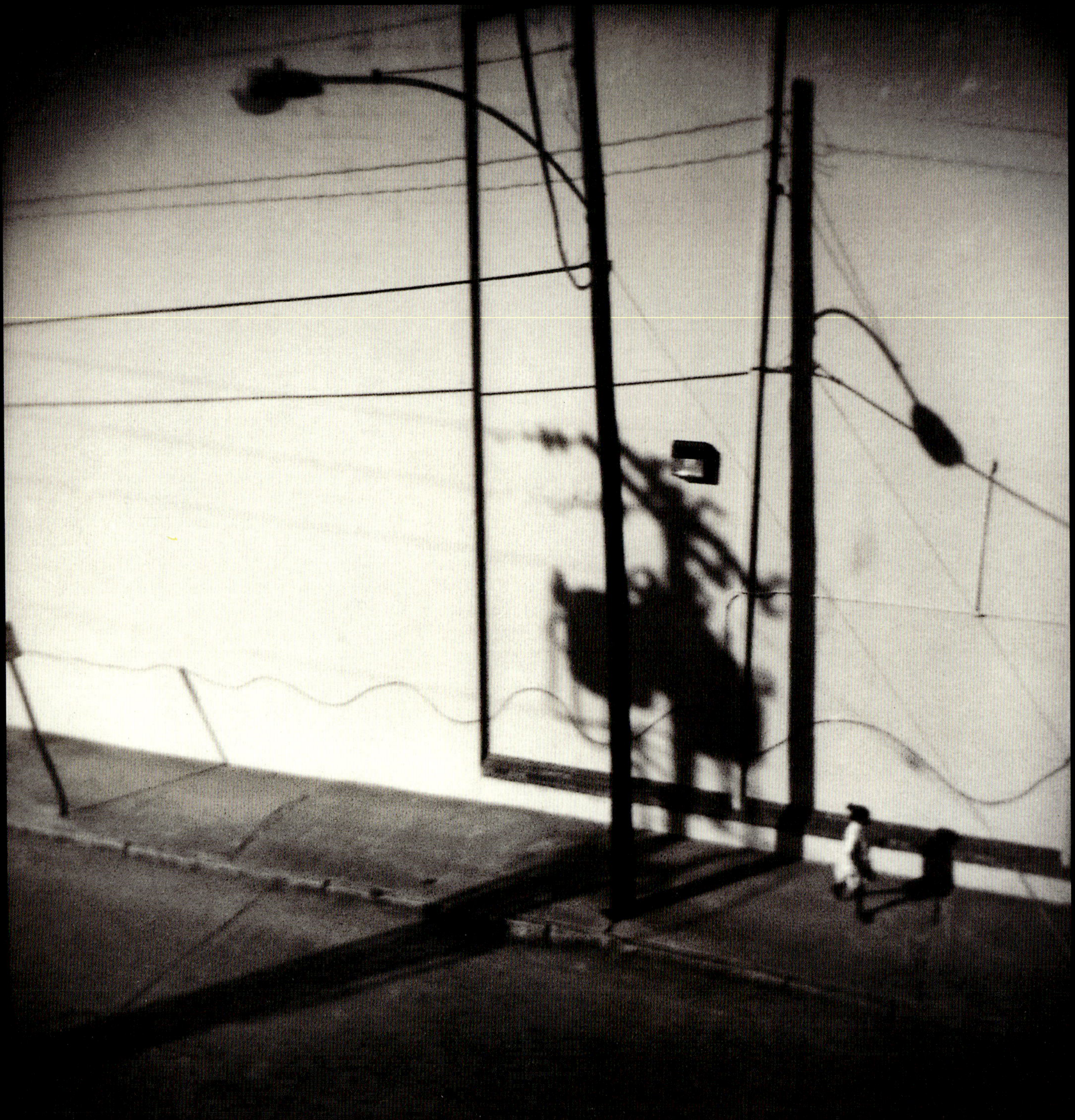

Charles Brackman

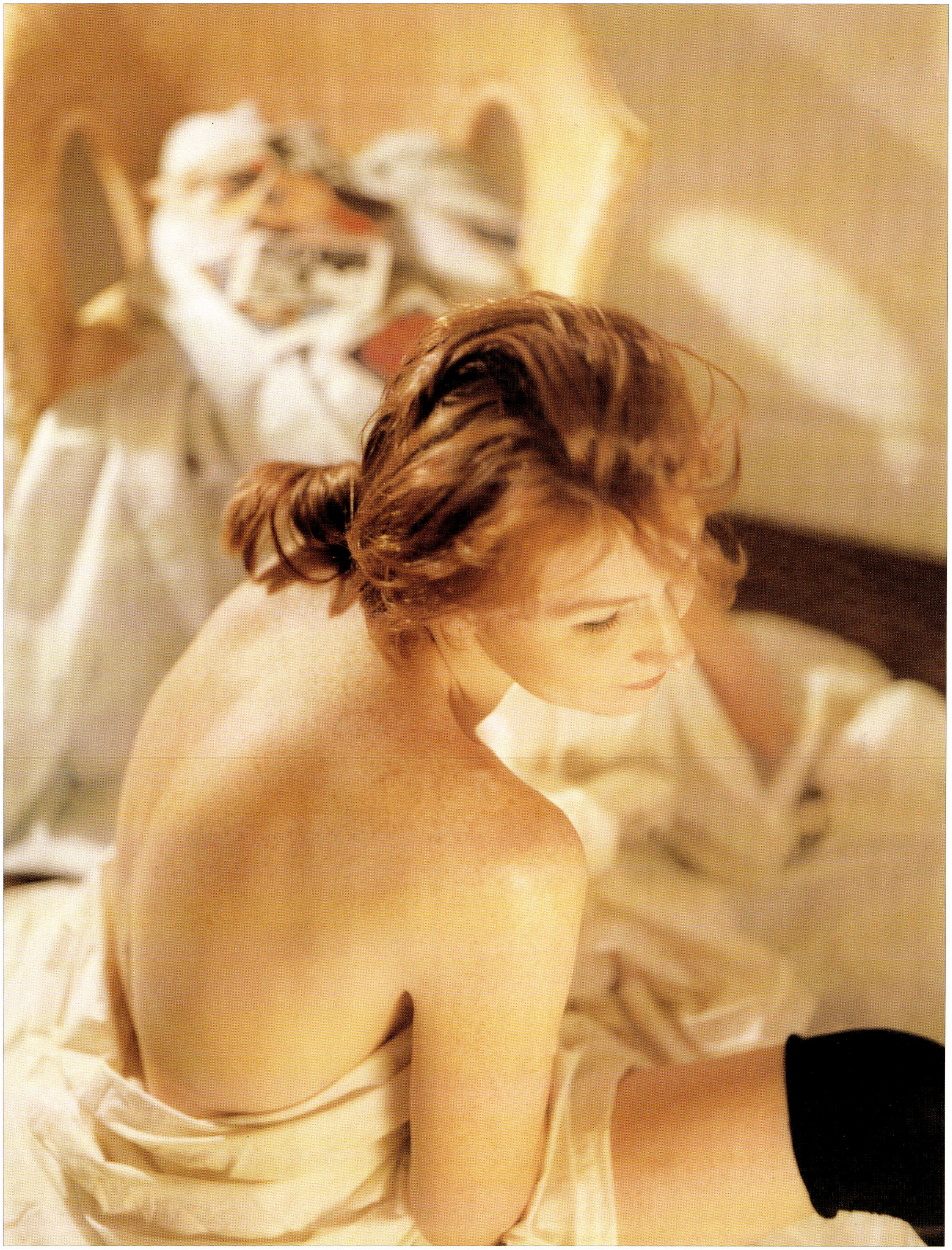

Melvin N. Moten Jr.

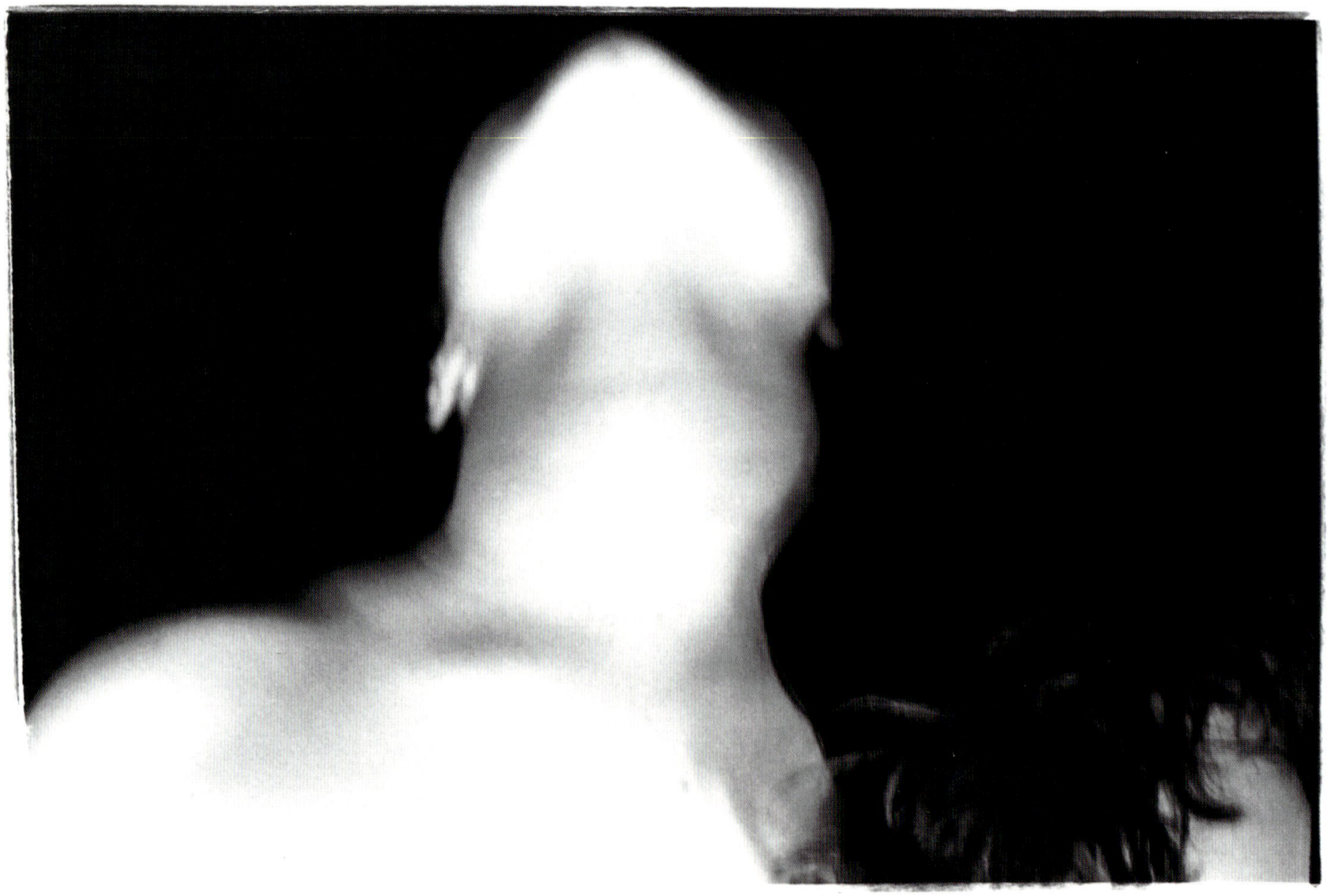

Catherine Satterwhite

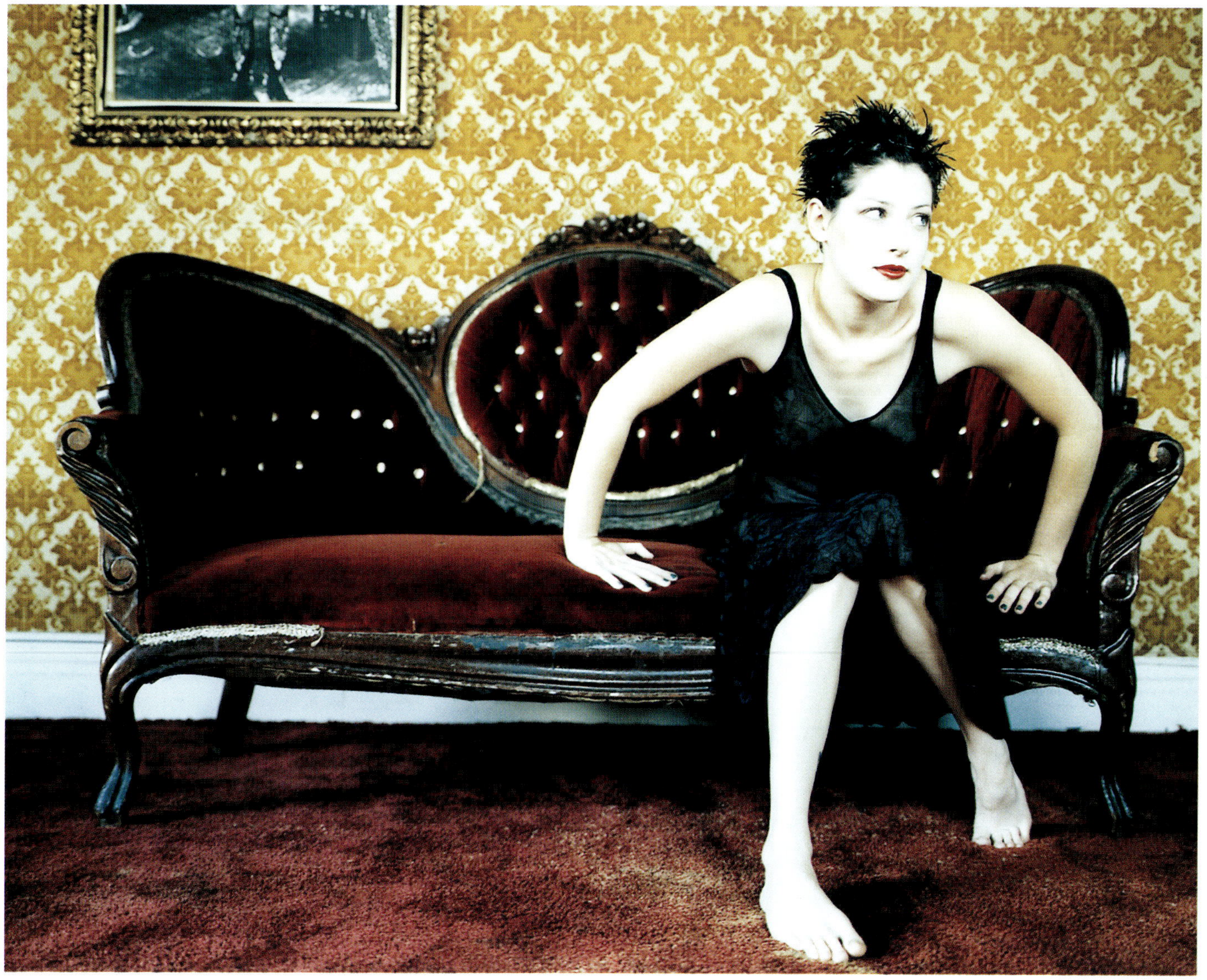

Norma Zuniga

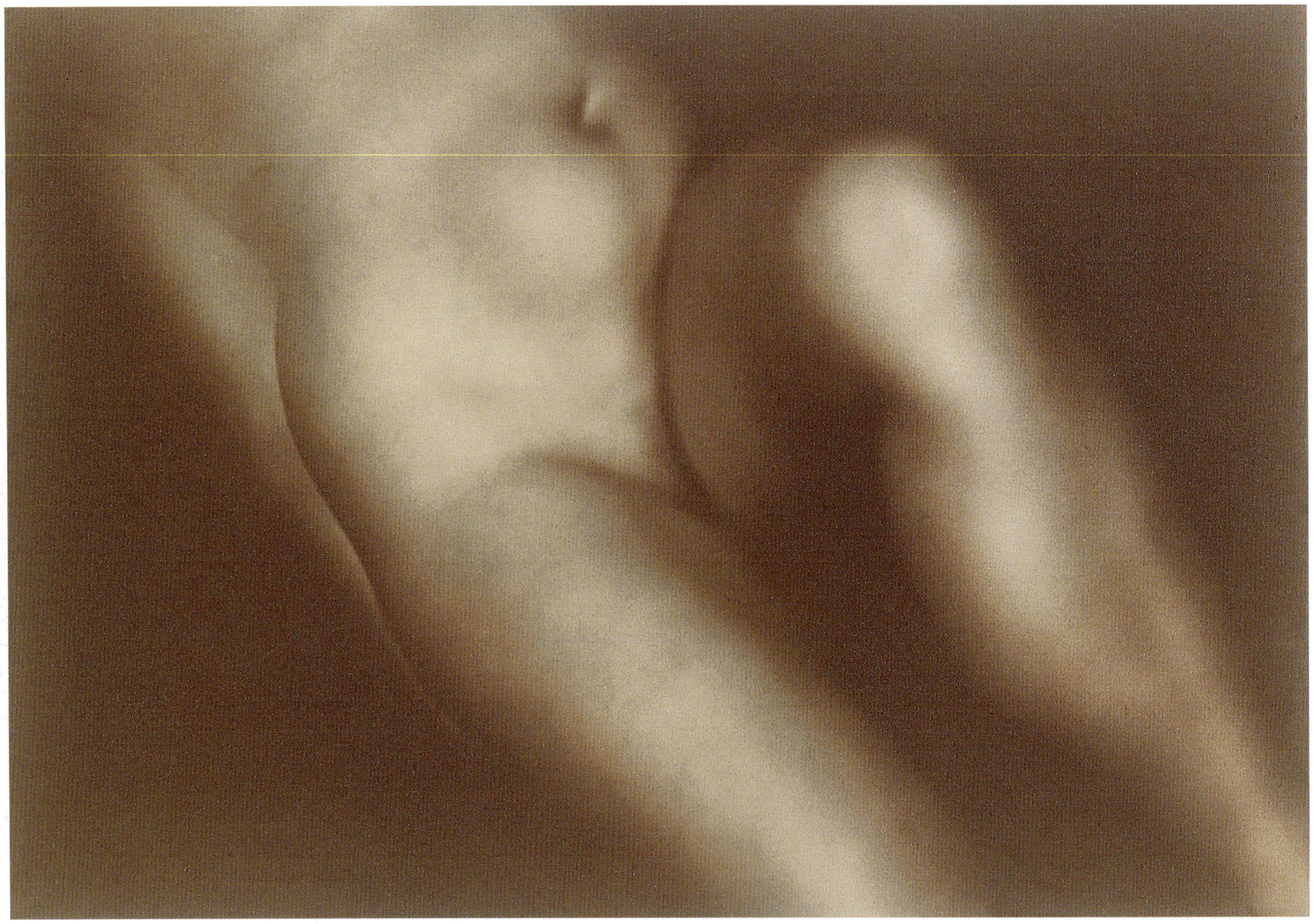

Martin Cooper

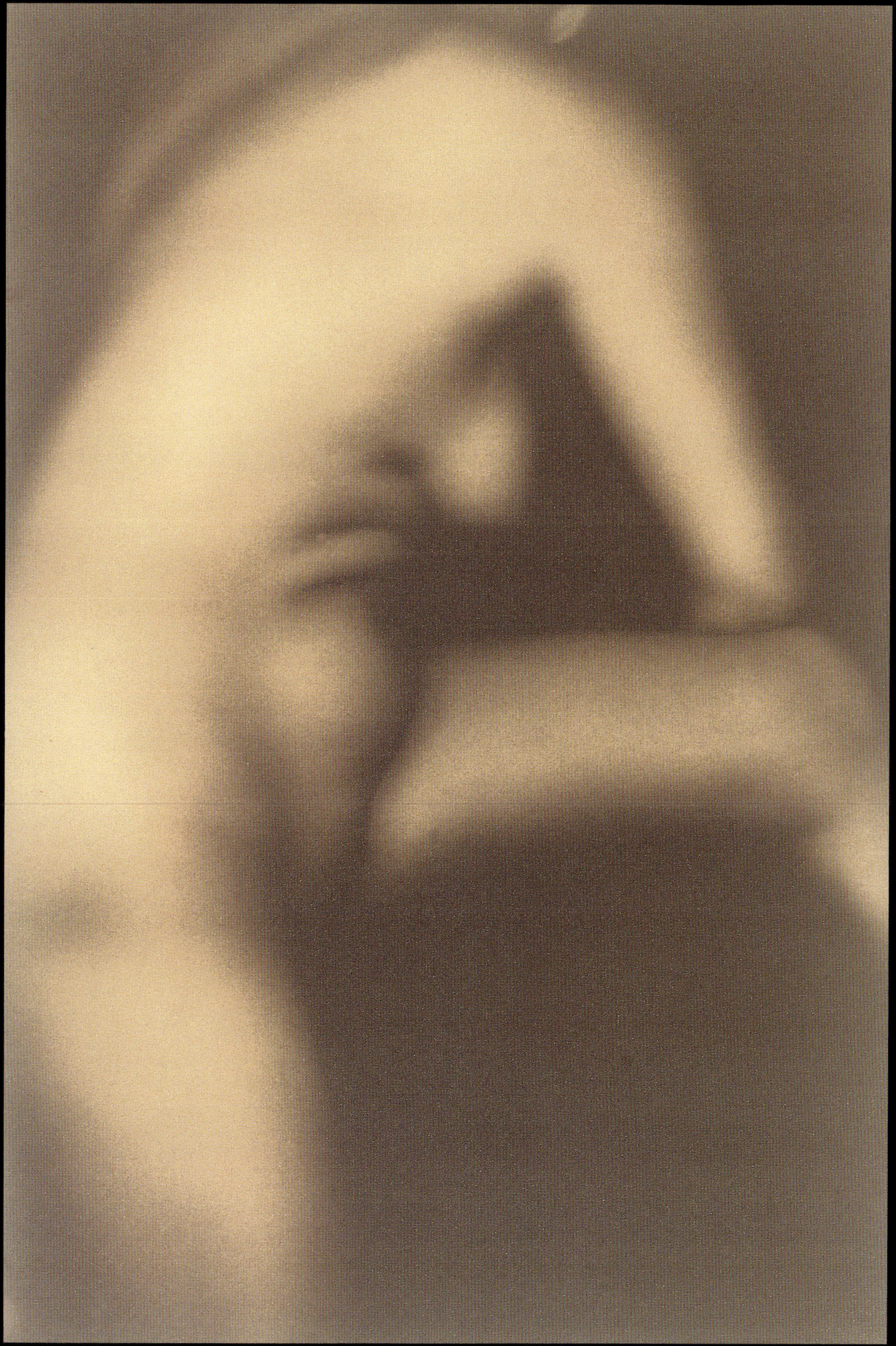

Martin Cooper

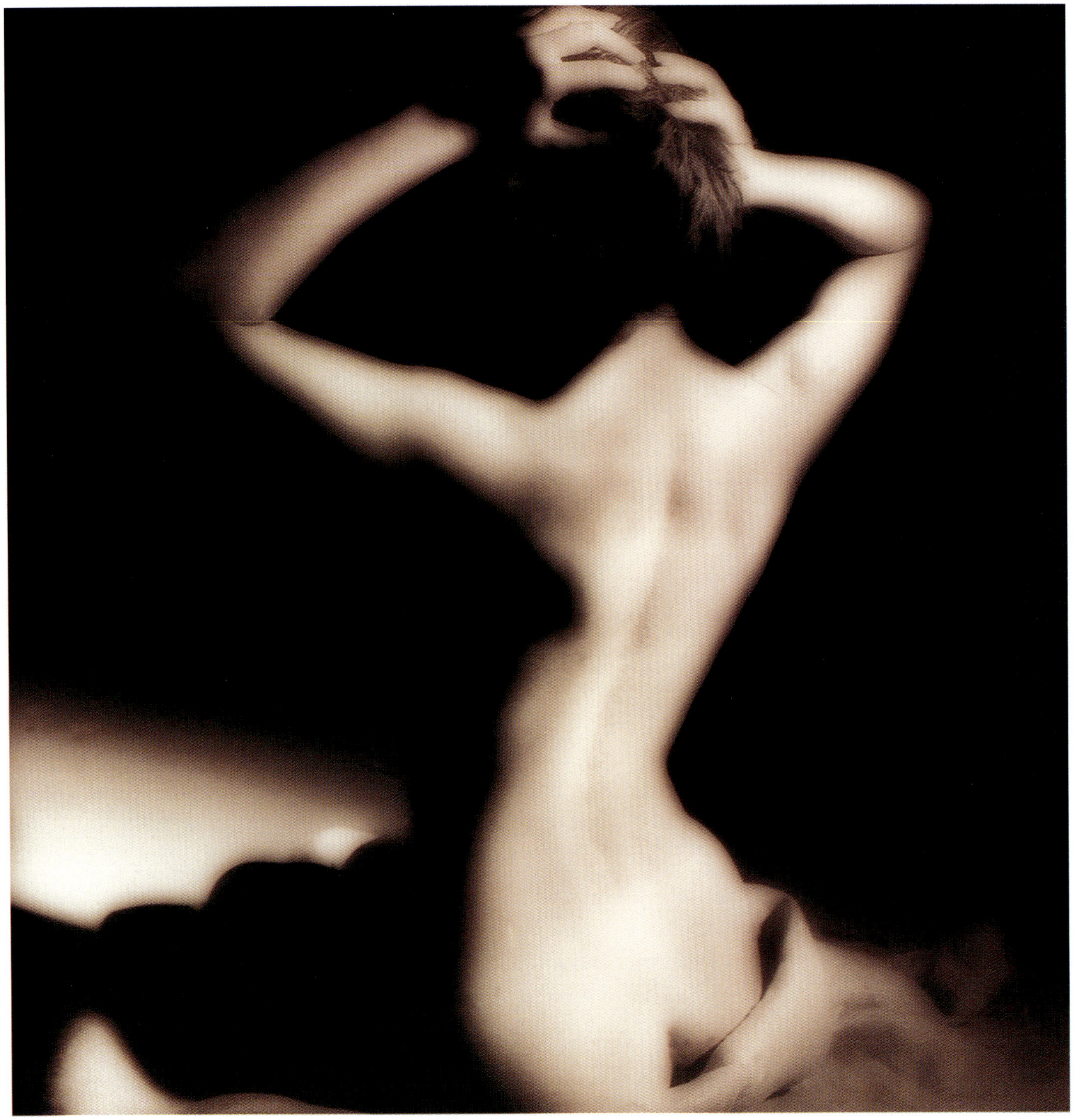

Michael Wylot

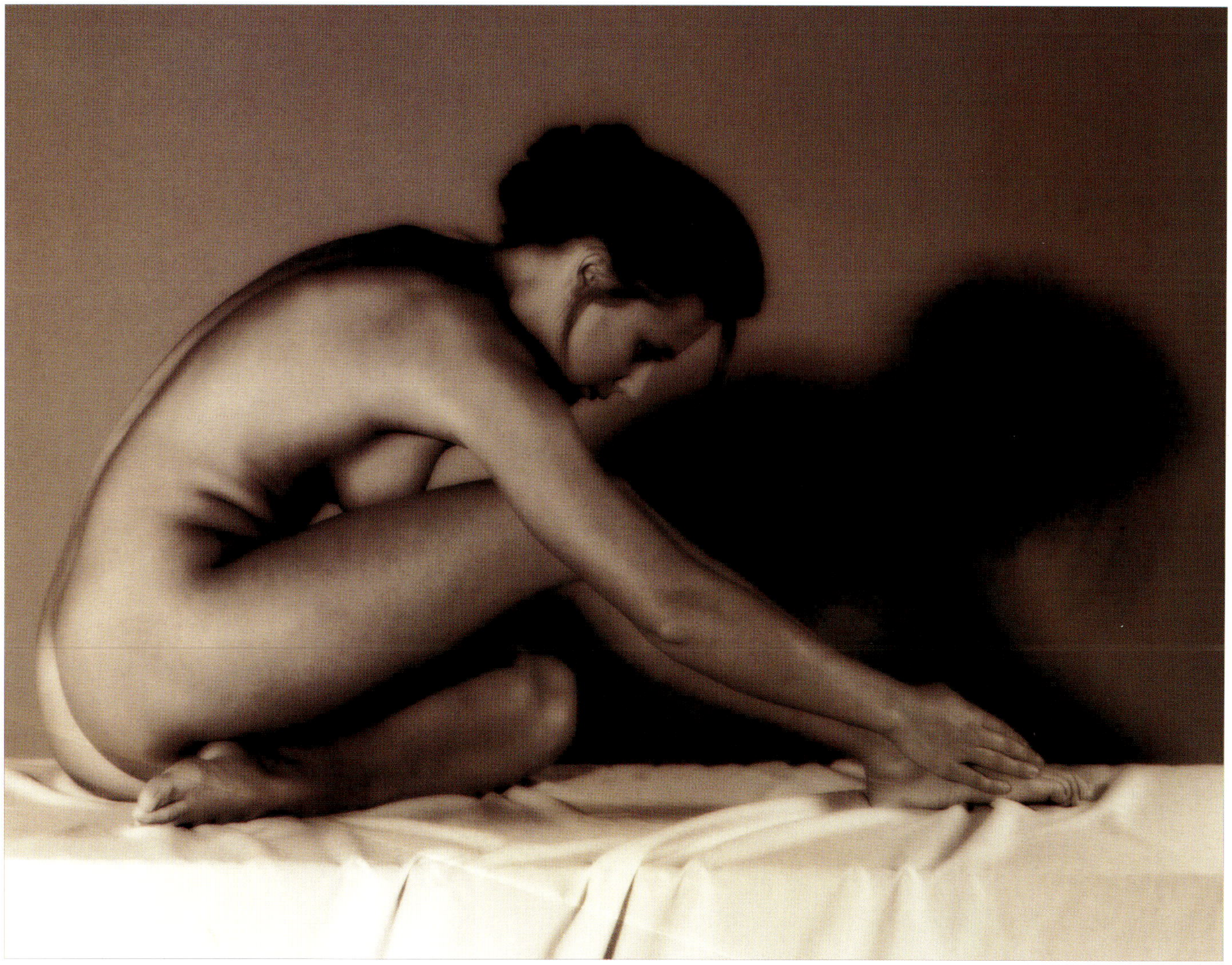

Kevin E. McWilliams

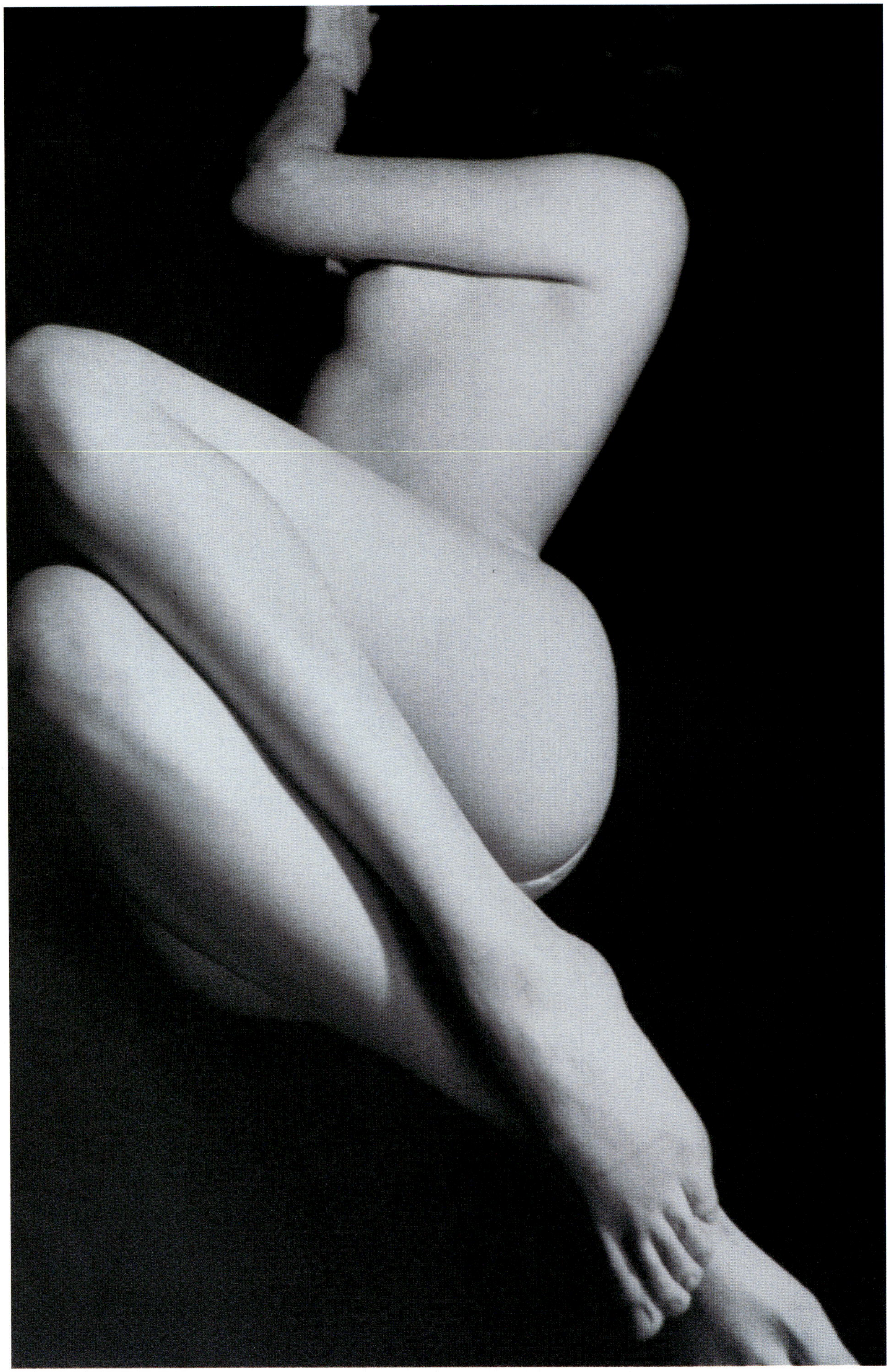

Laura Savidge

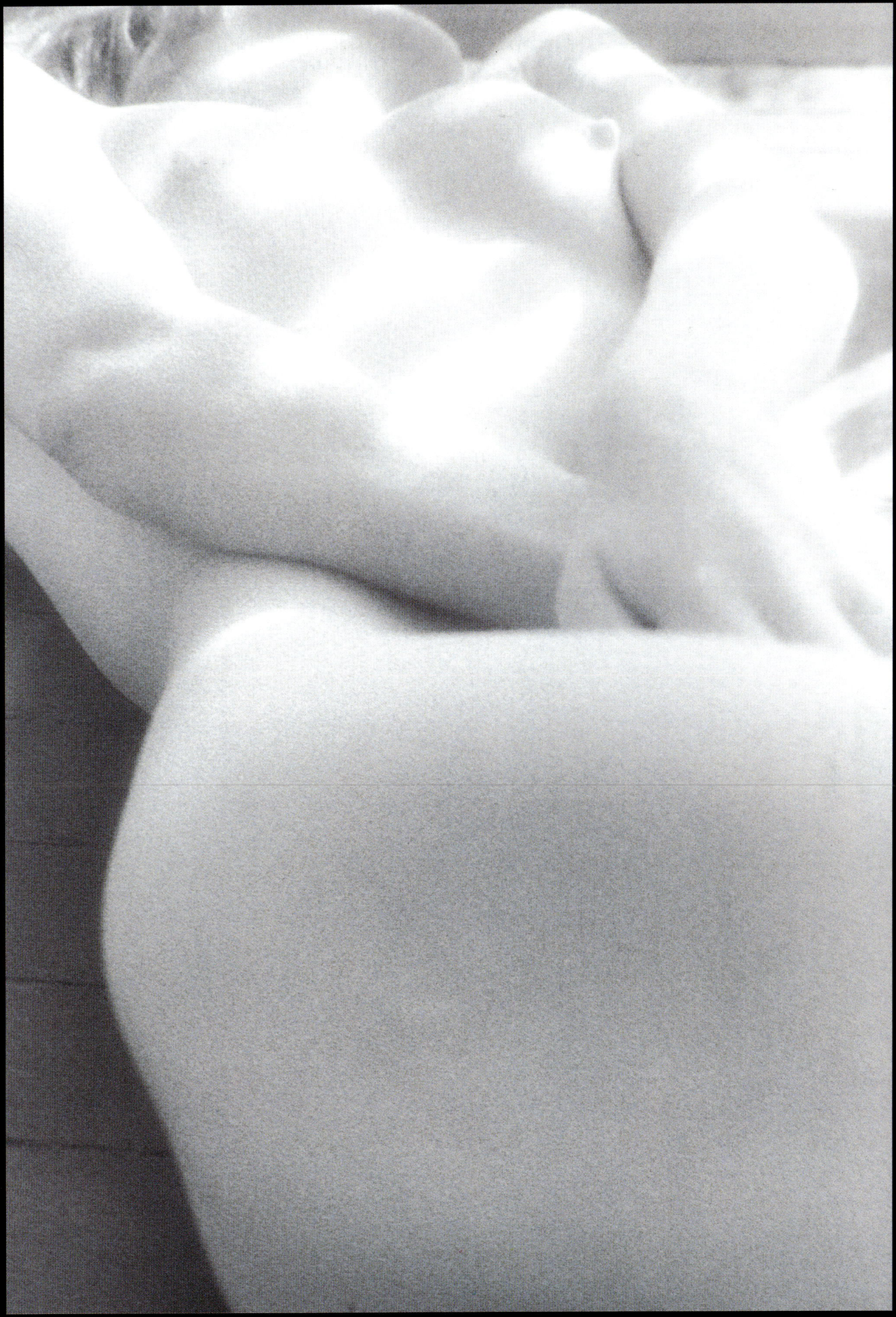

Laura Savidge

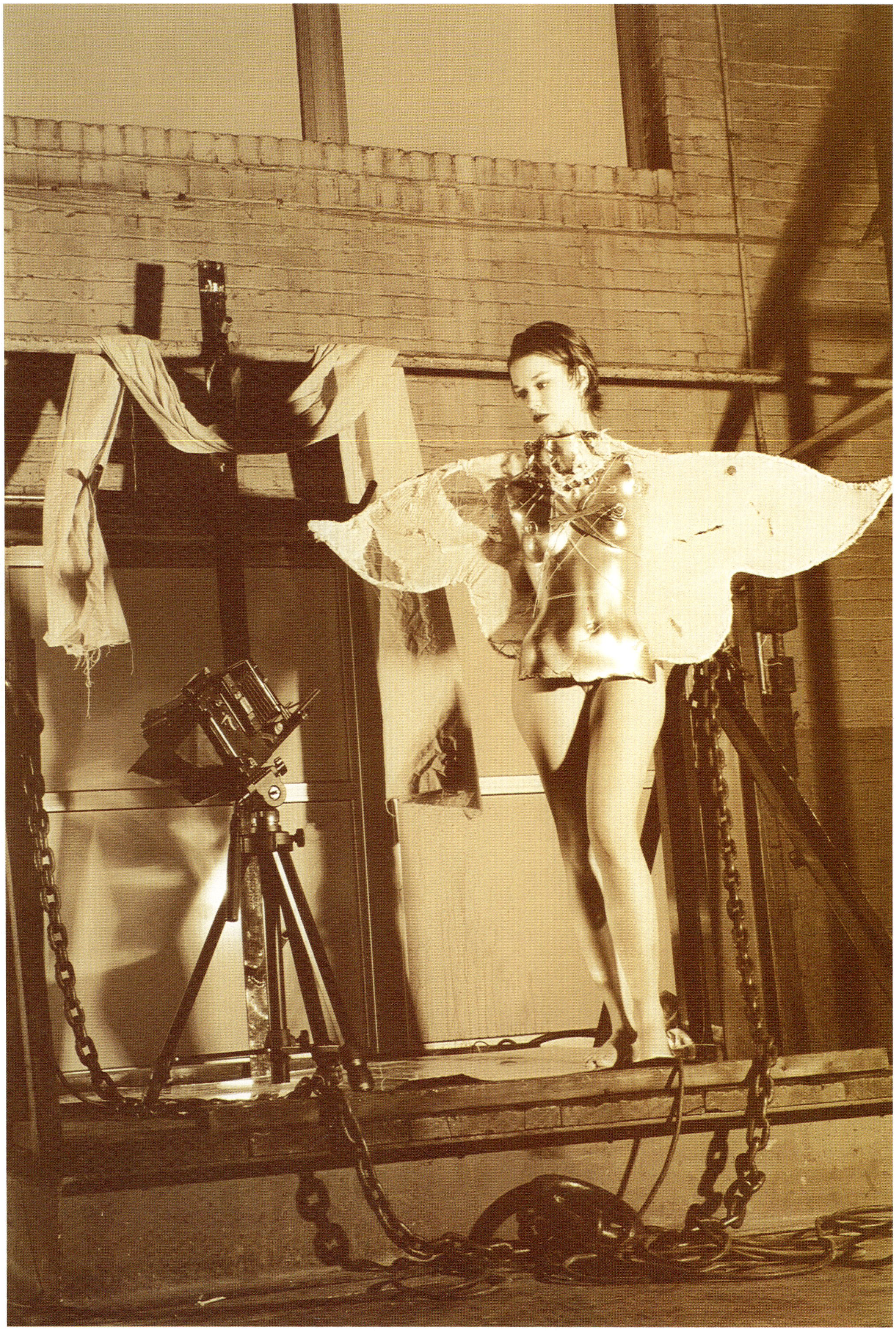

Christopher Lovenguth

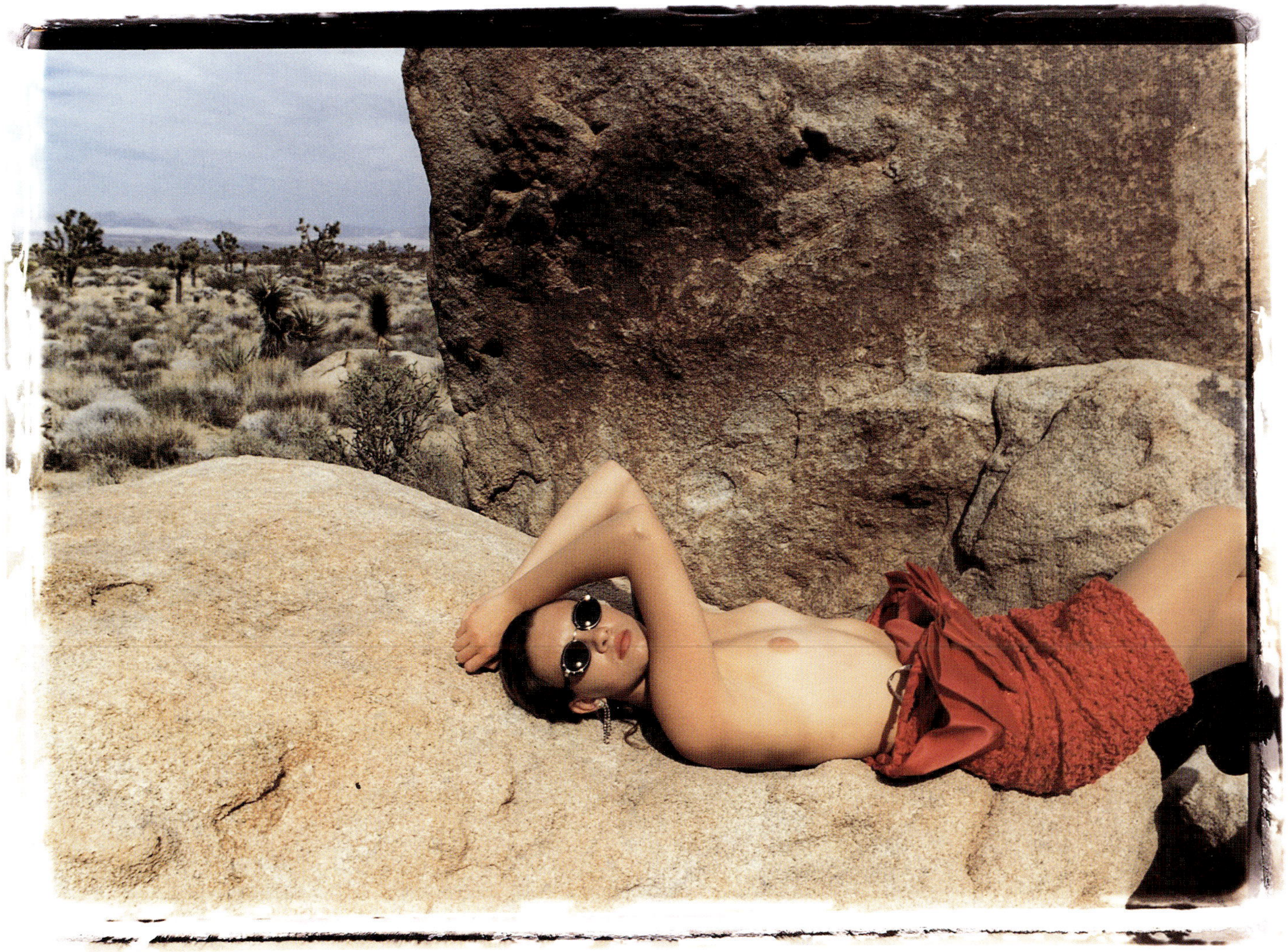

R. Michael Walker

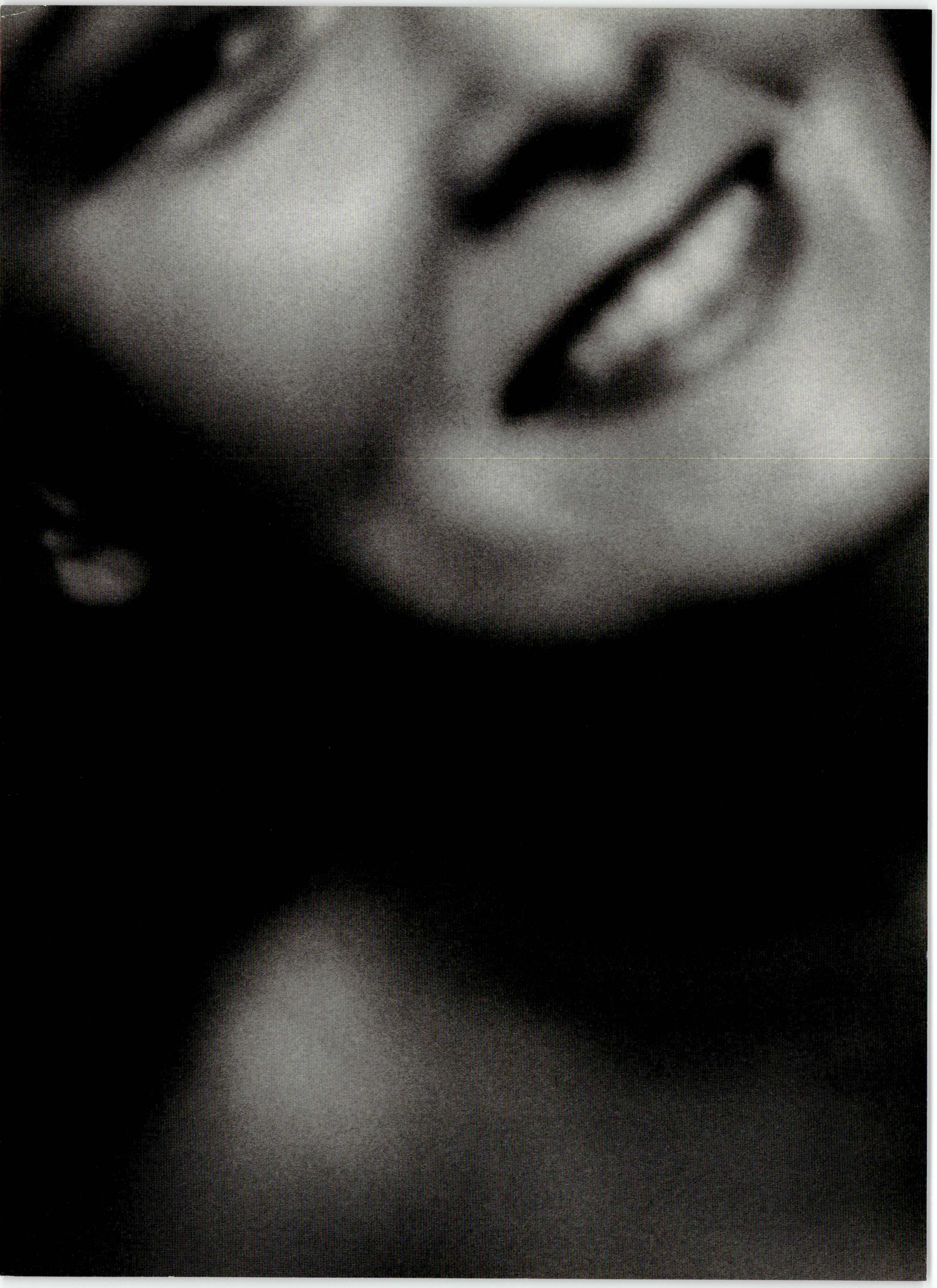

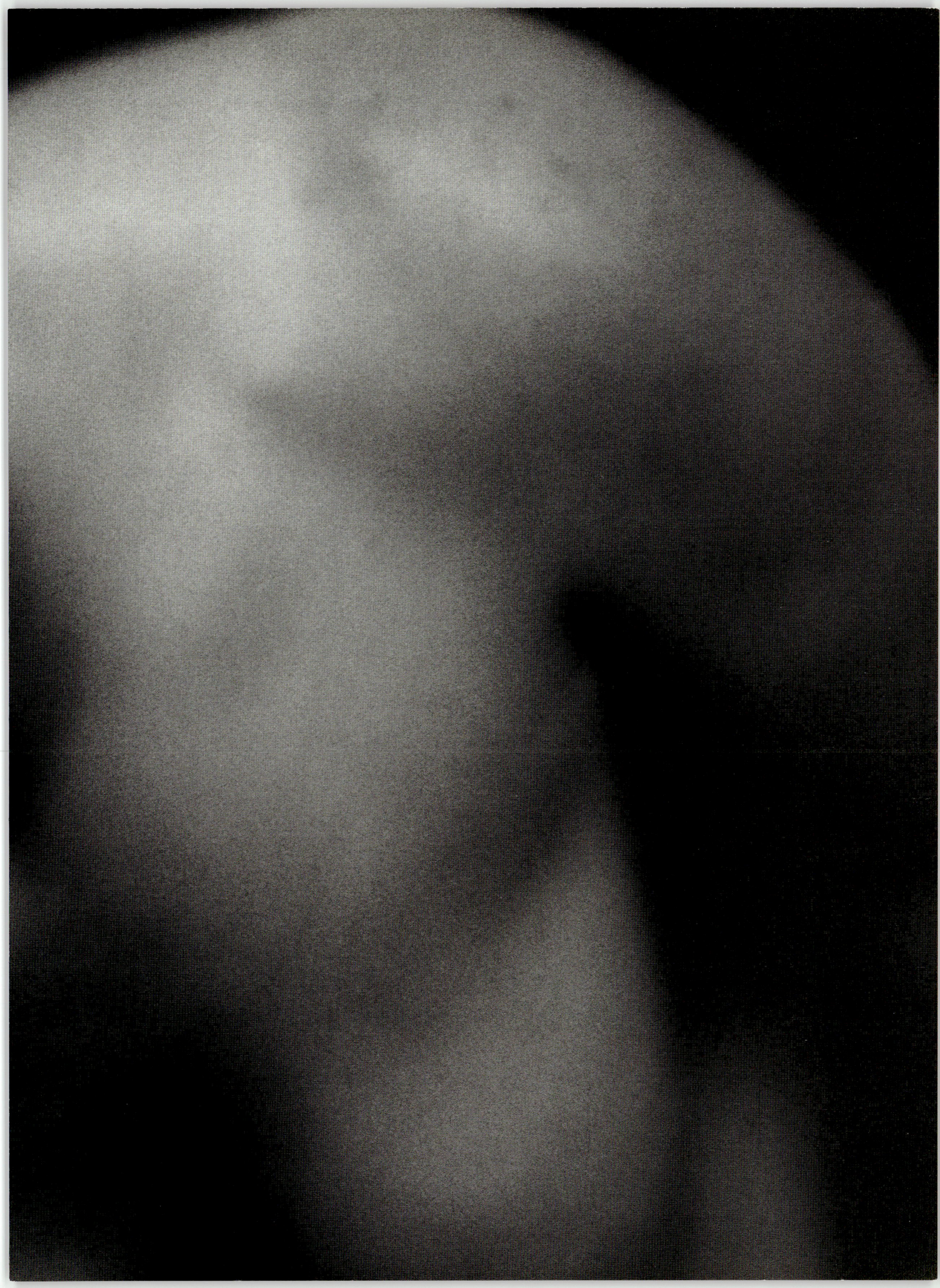

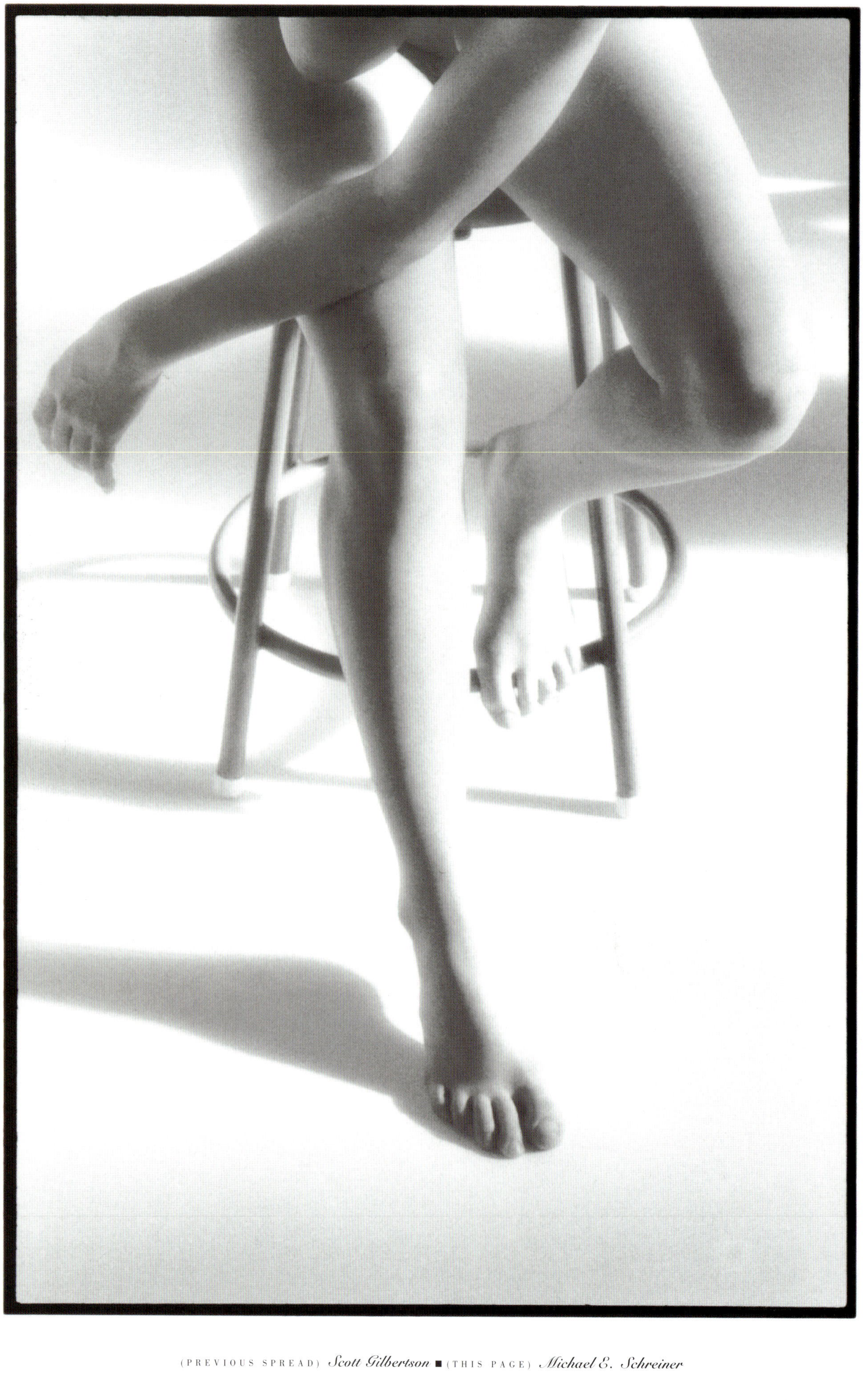

(PREVIOUS SPREAD) *Scott Gilbertson* ■ (THIS PAGE) *Michael E. Schreiner*

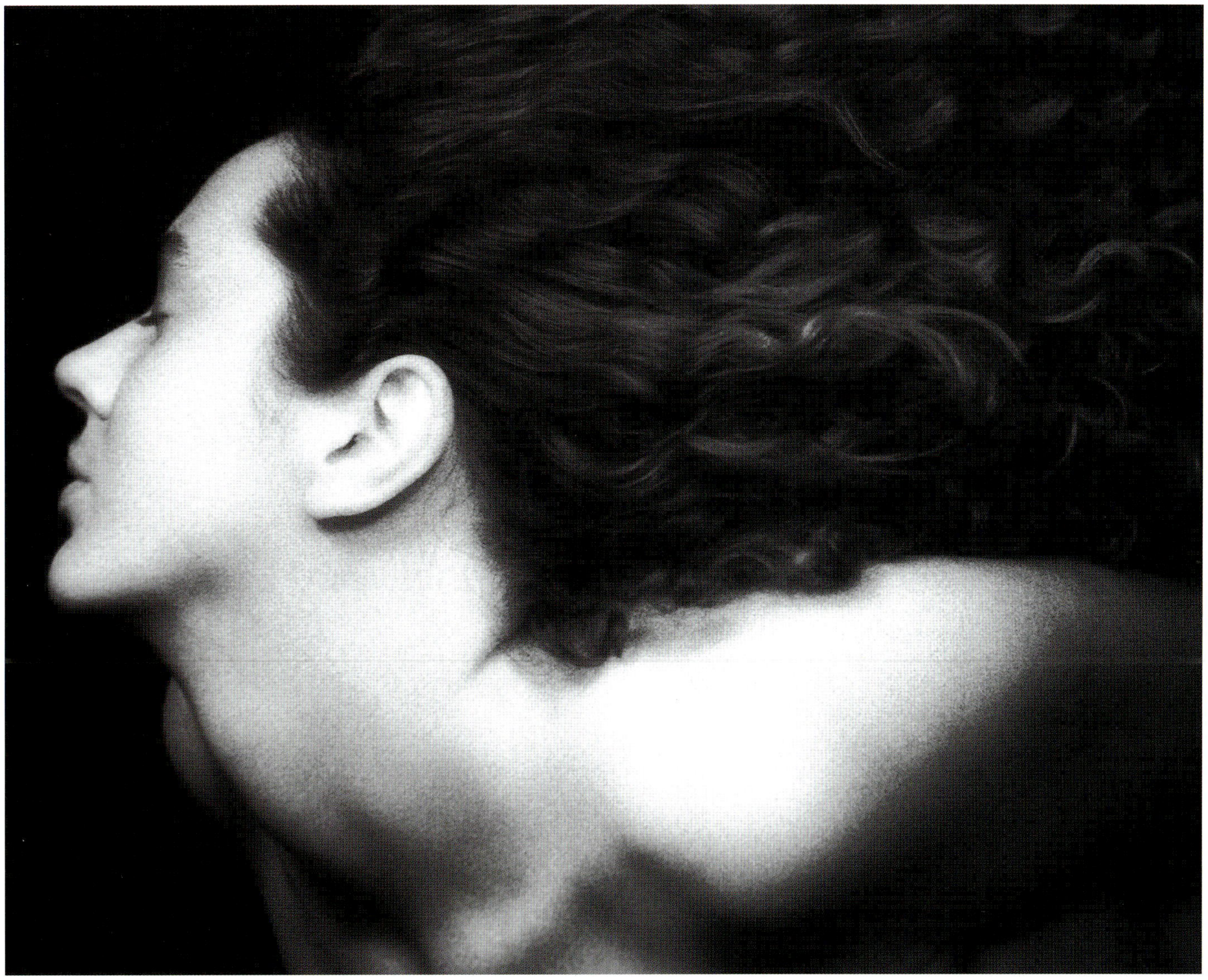

Joe Rice

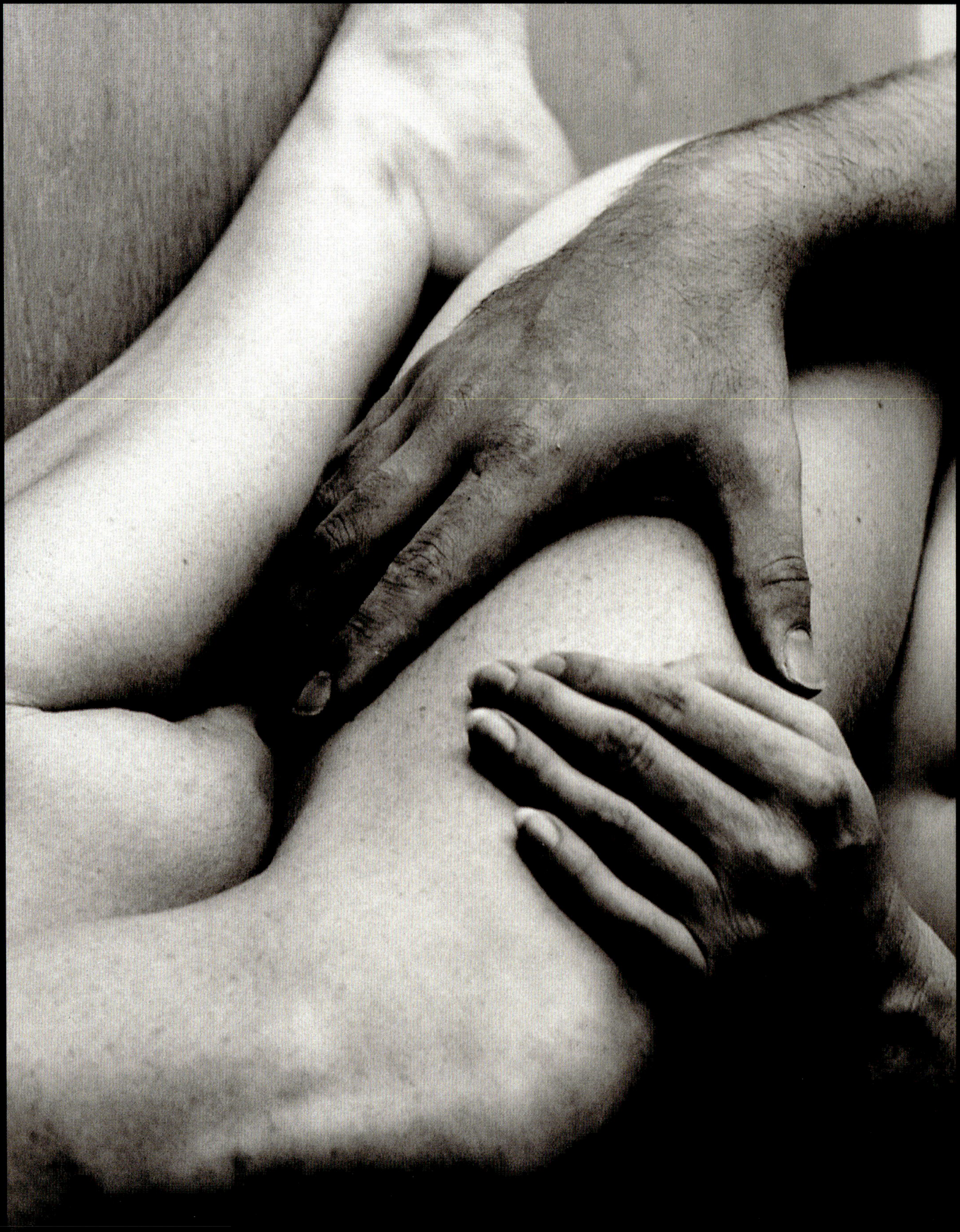

Scott Gilbertson

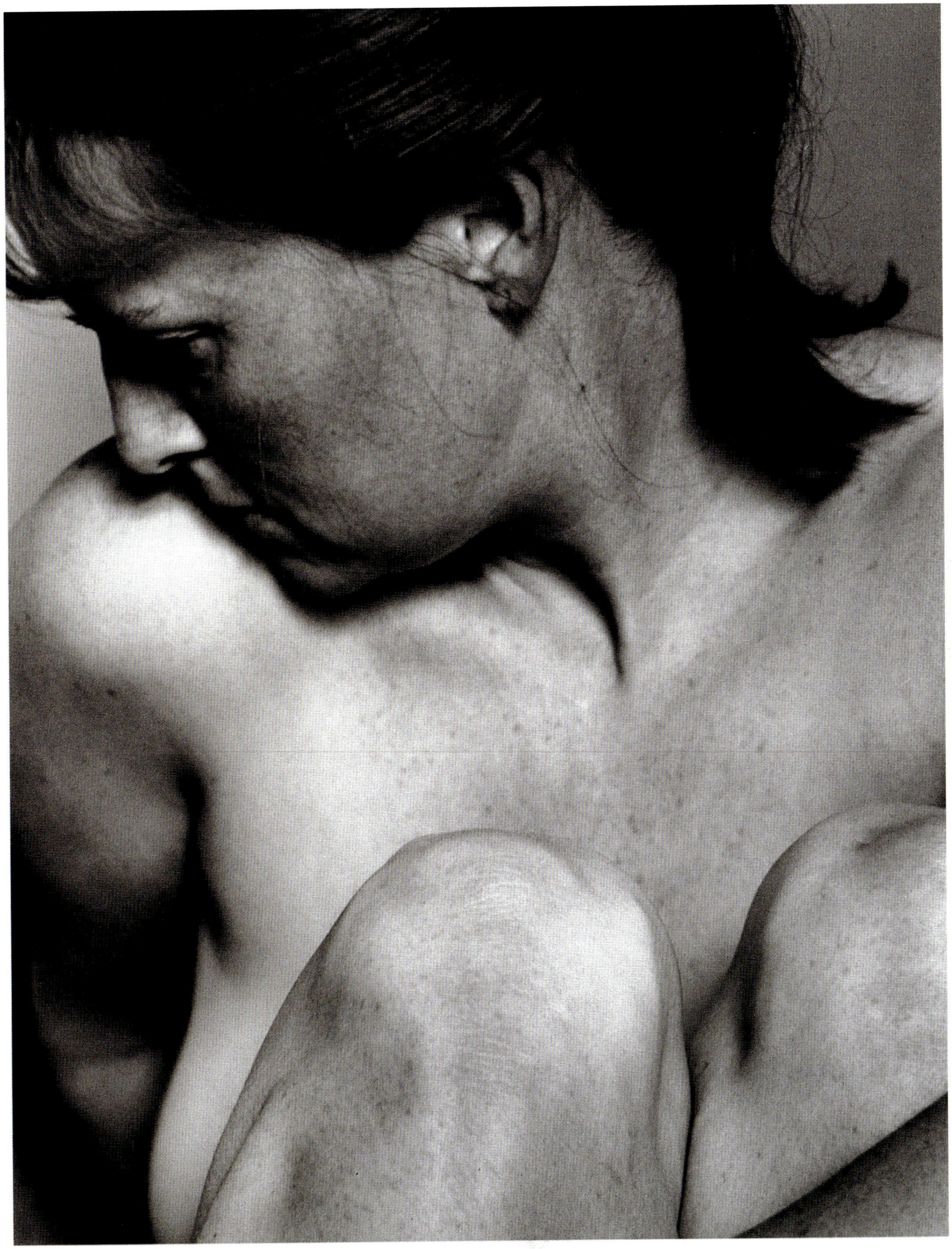

Scott Gilbertson

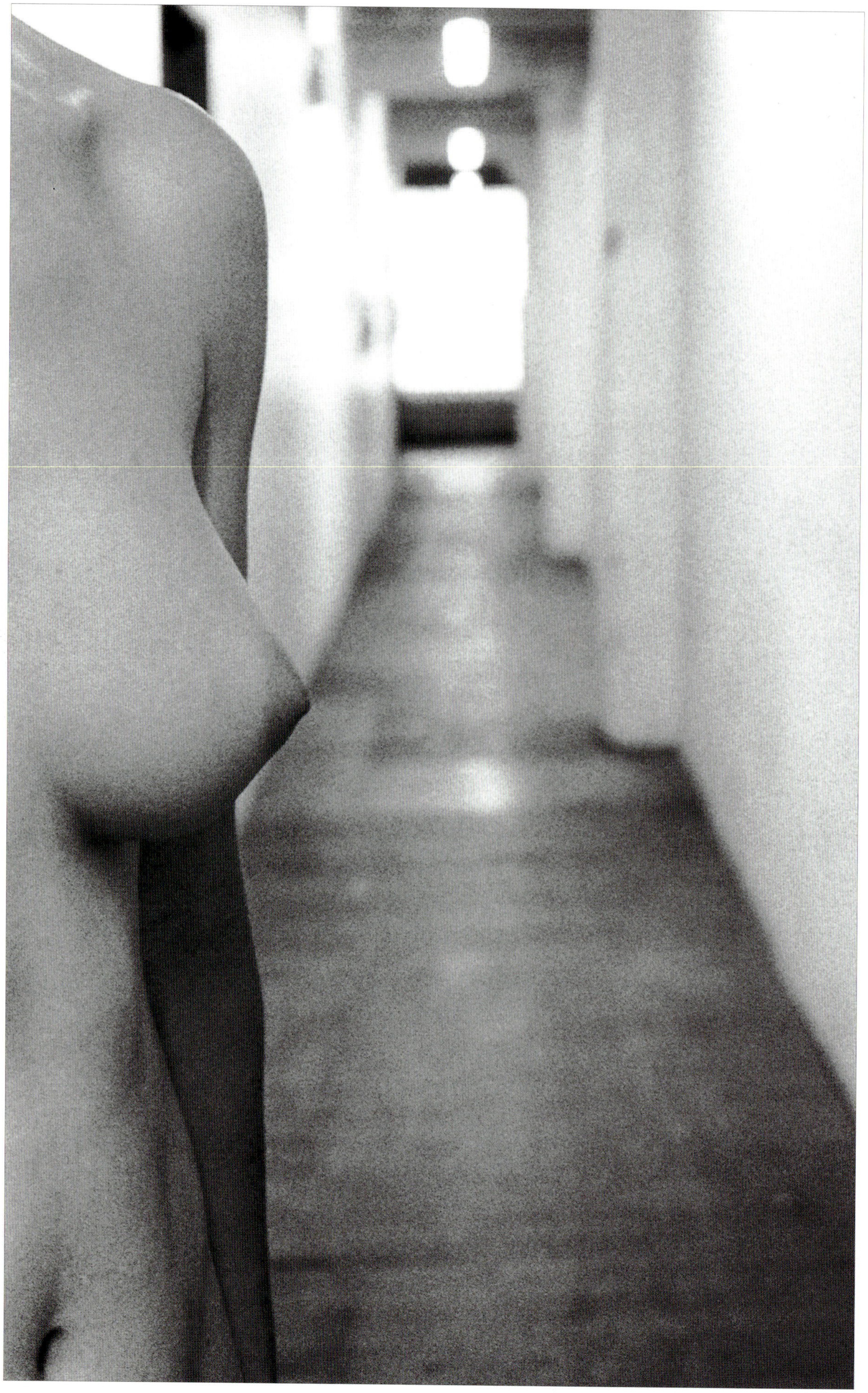

Bob Todrick

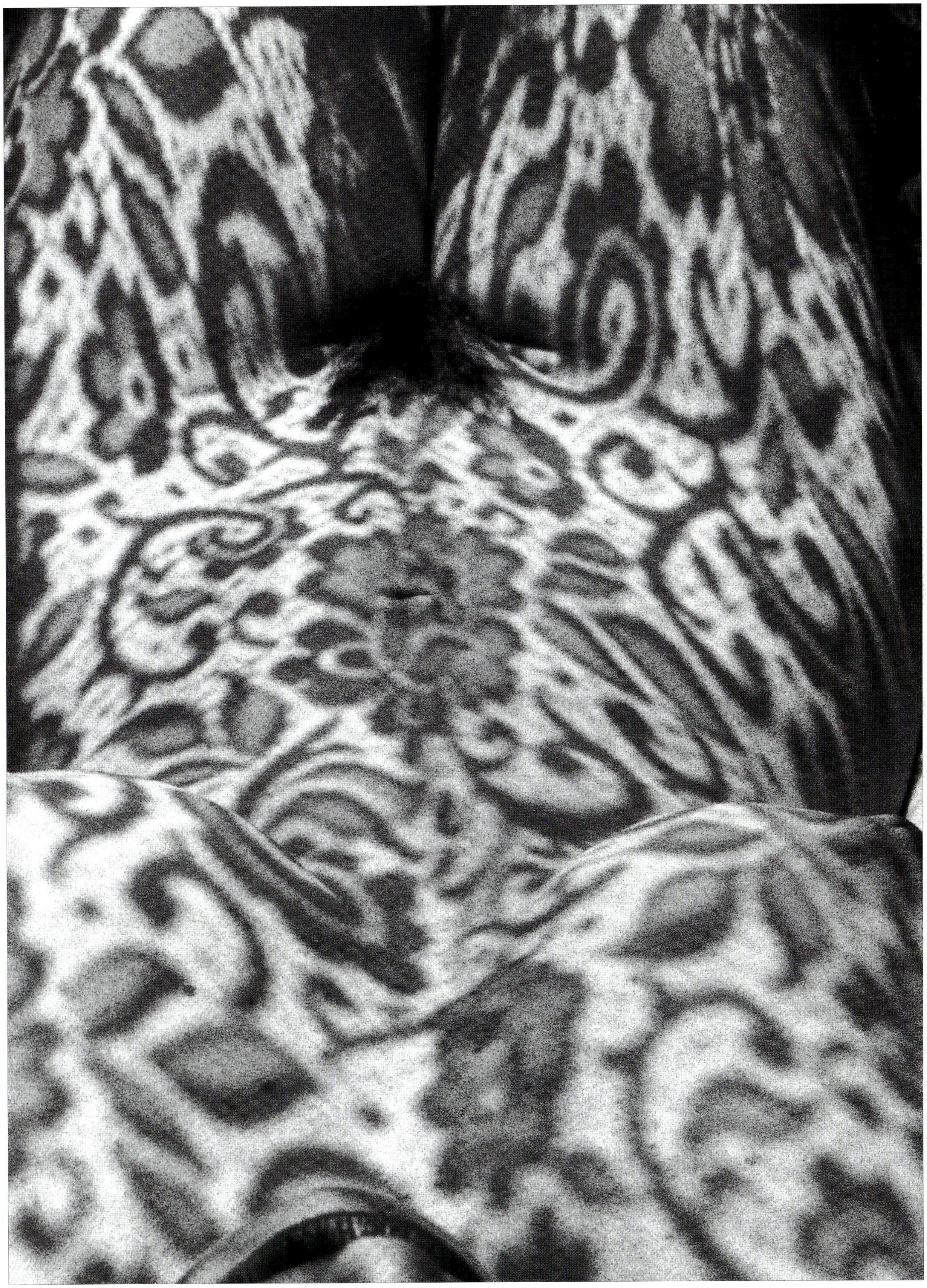

Jorge Marquardt

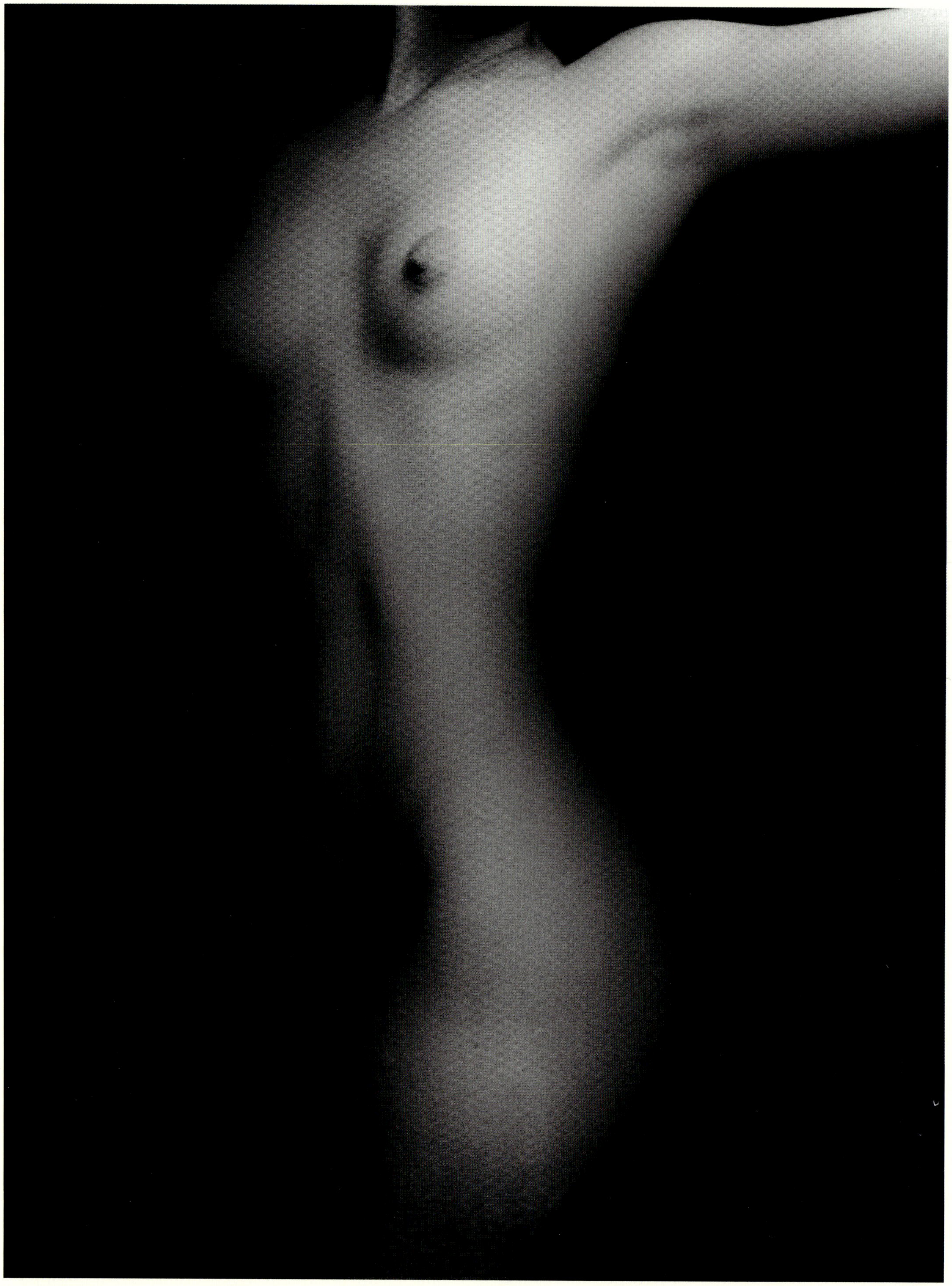

David Lundberg

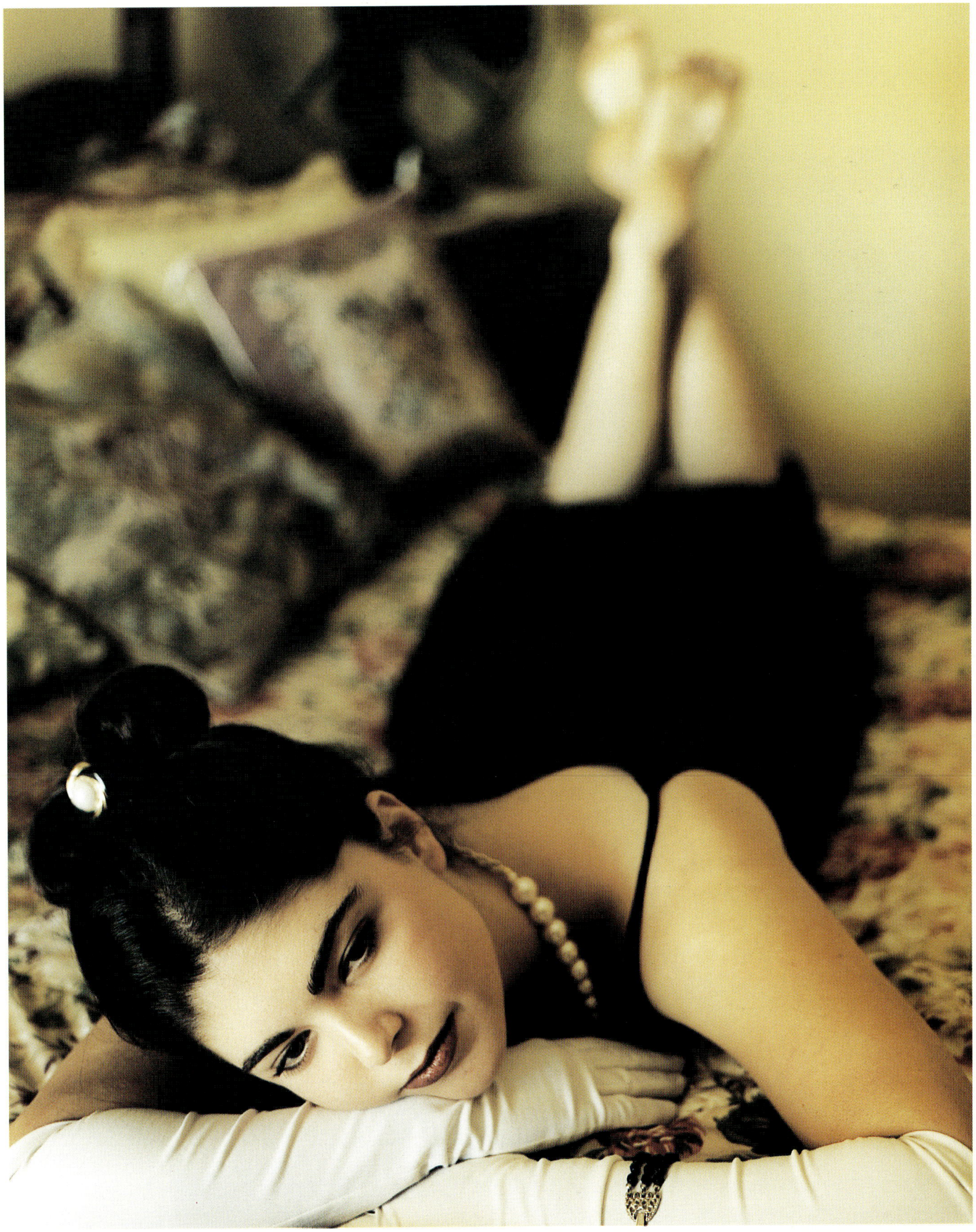

Nathan Teutle

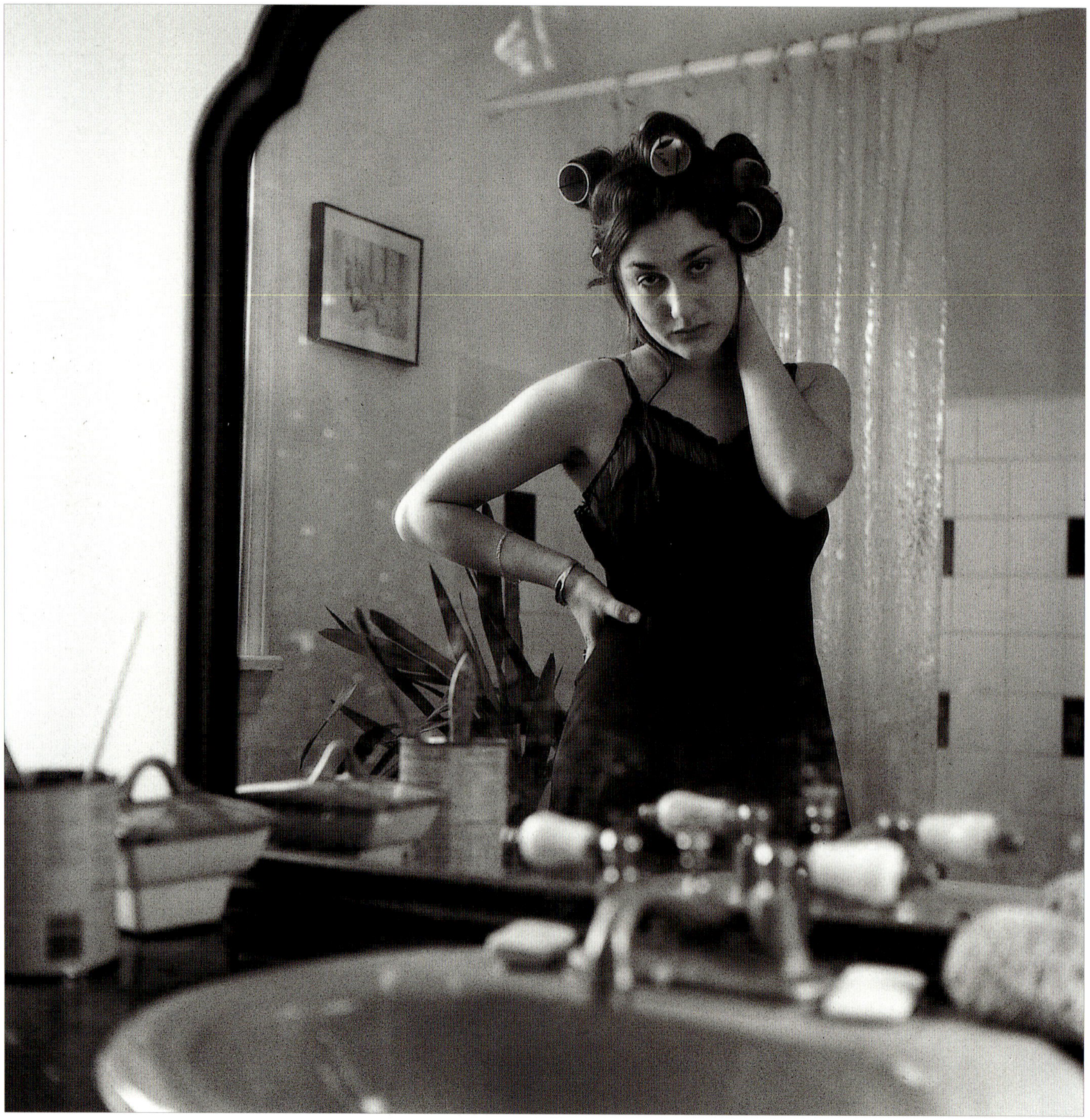

Wendy M. Newman

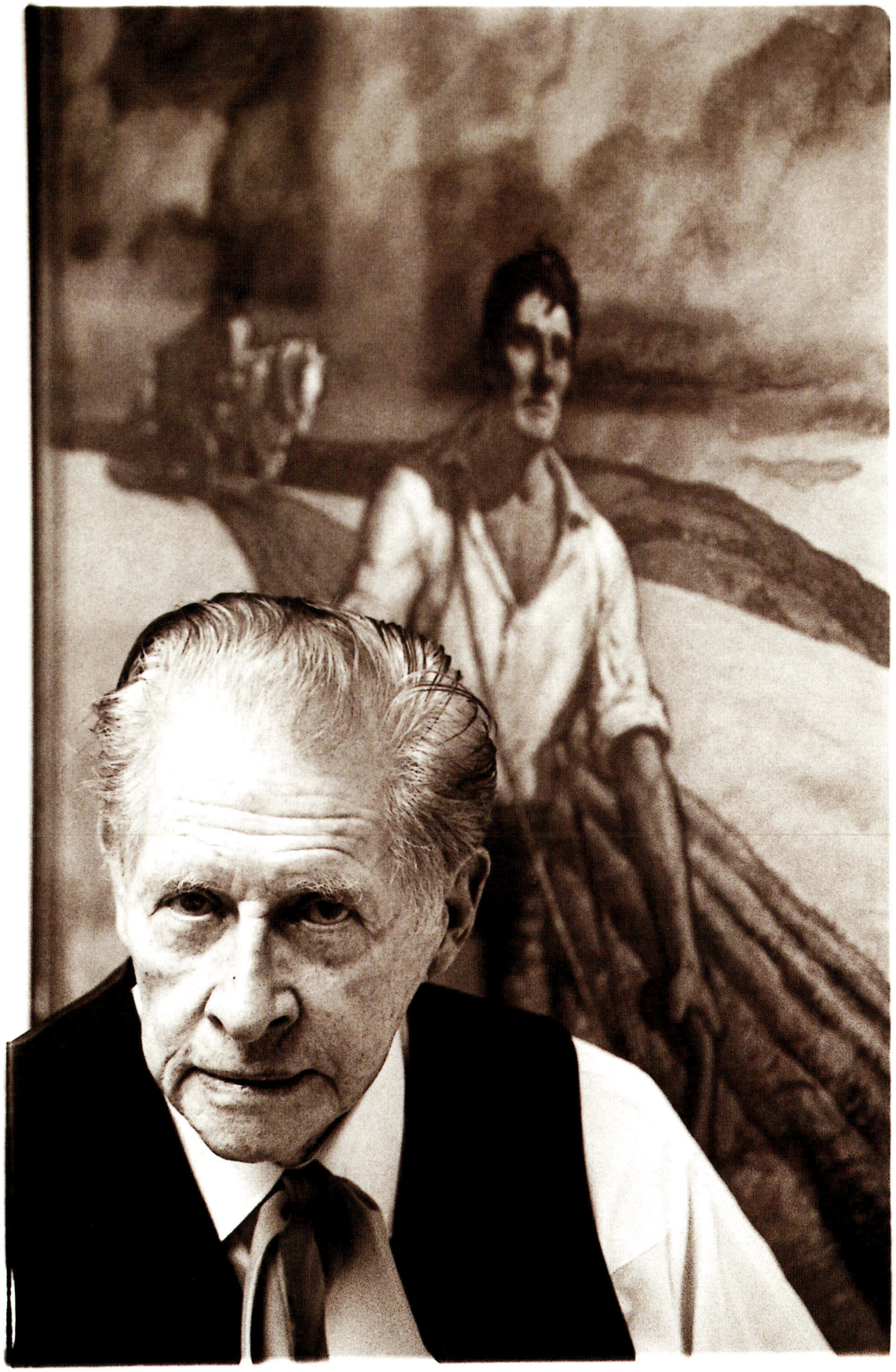

Paul Kozal

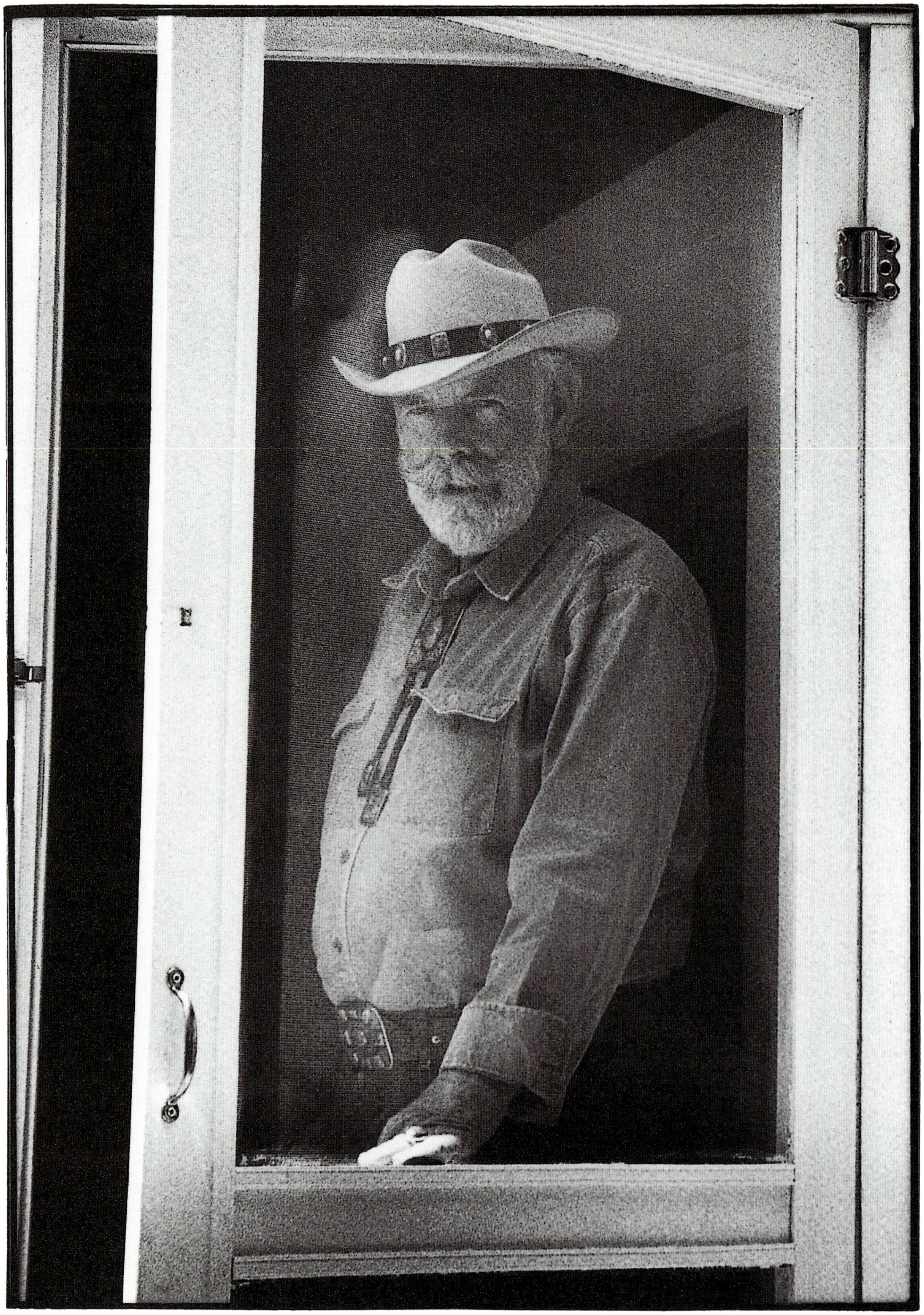

Paul Kozal

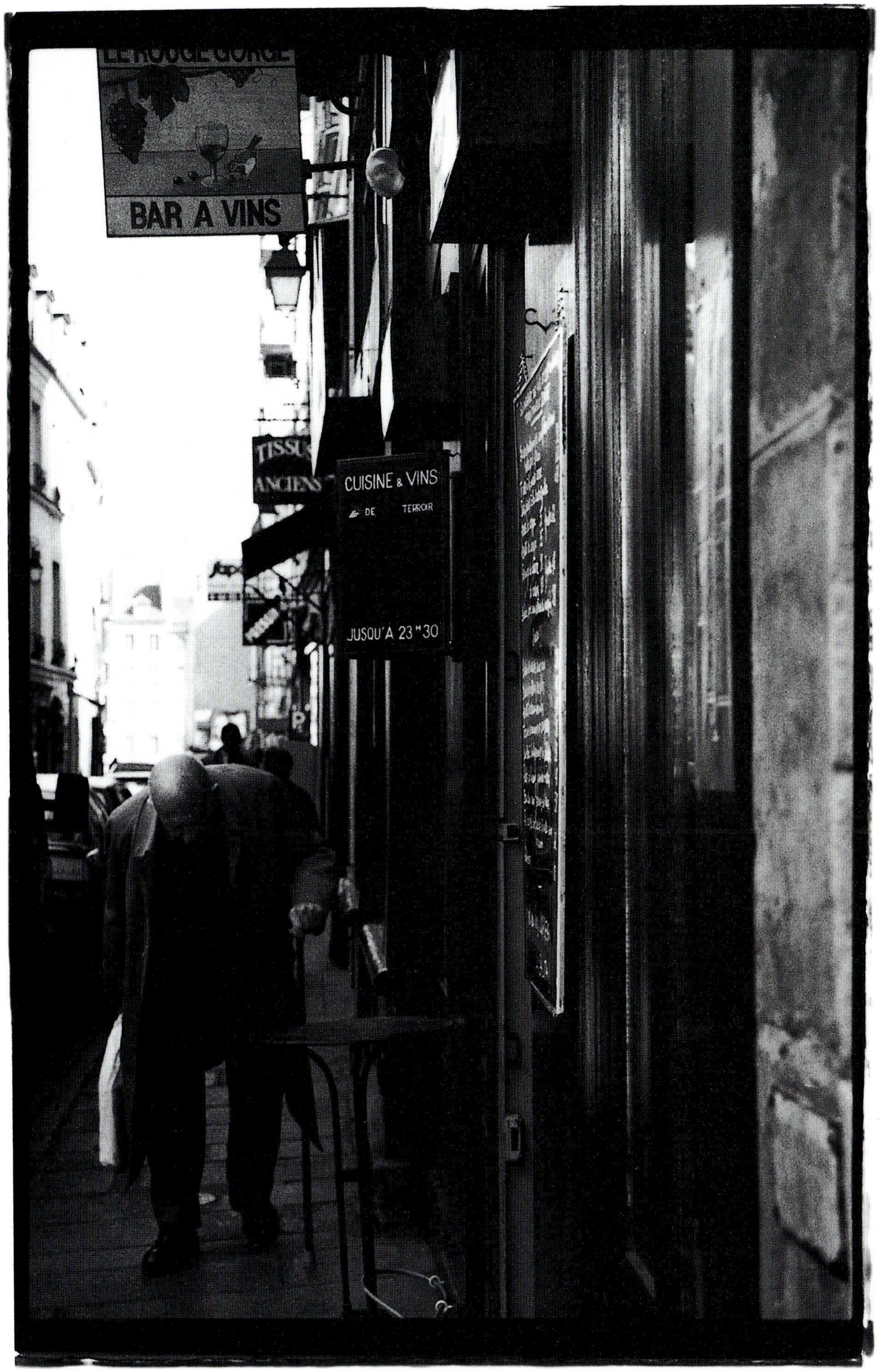

Edie Pereira

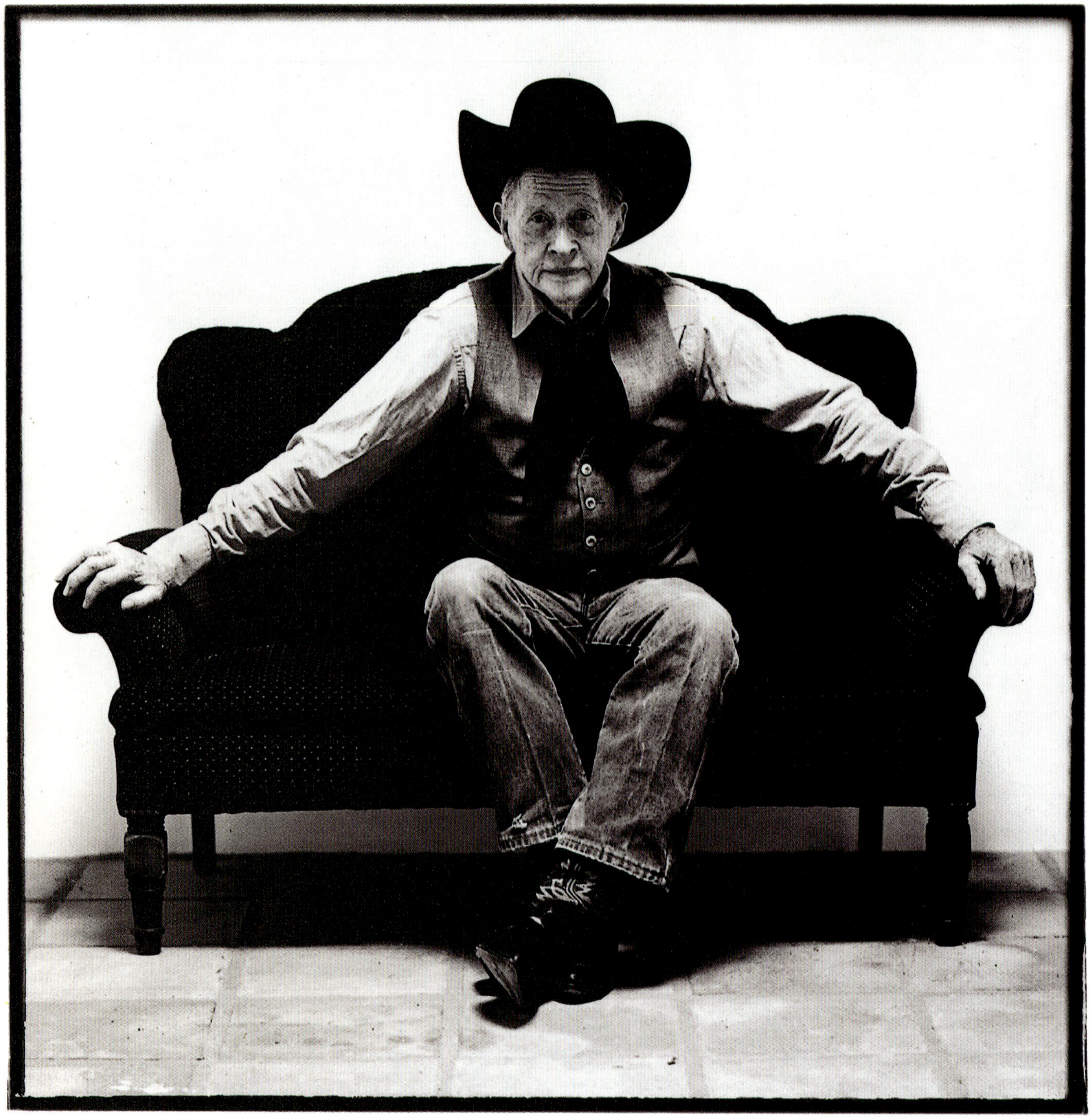

Paul Kozal

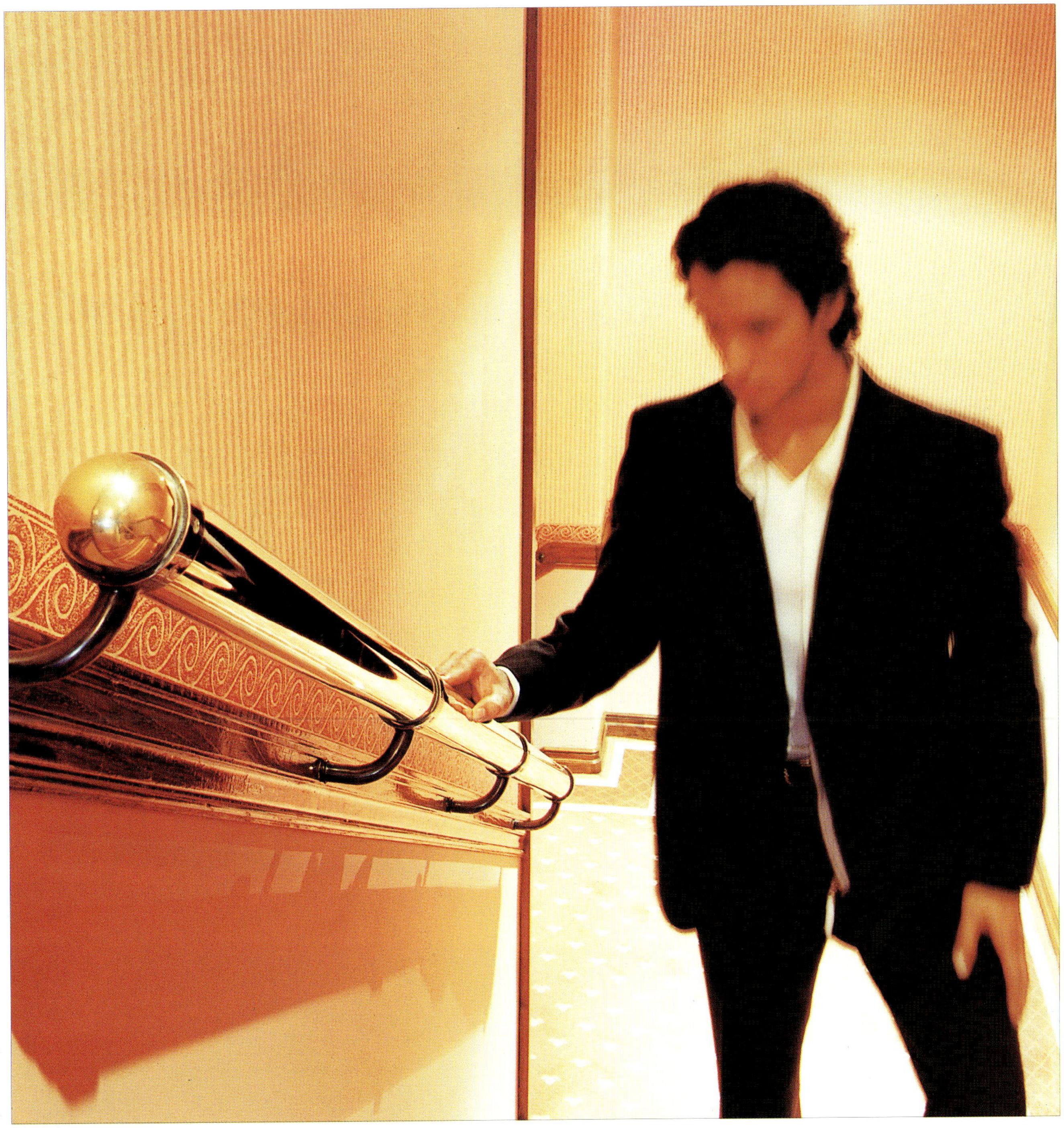

Sérgio Leitaõ

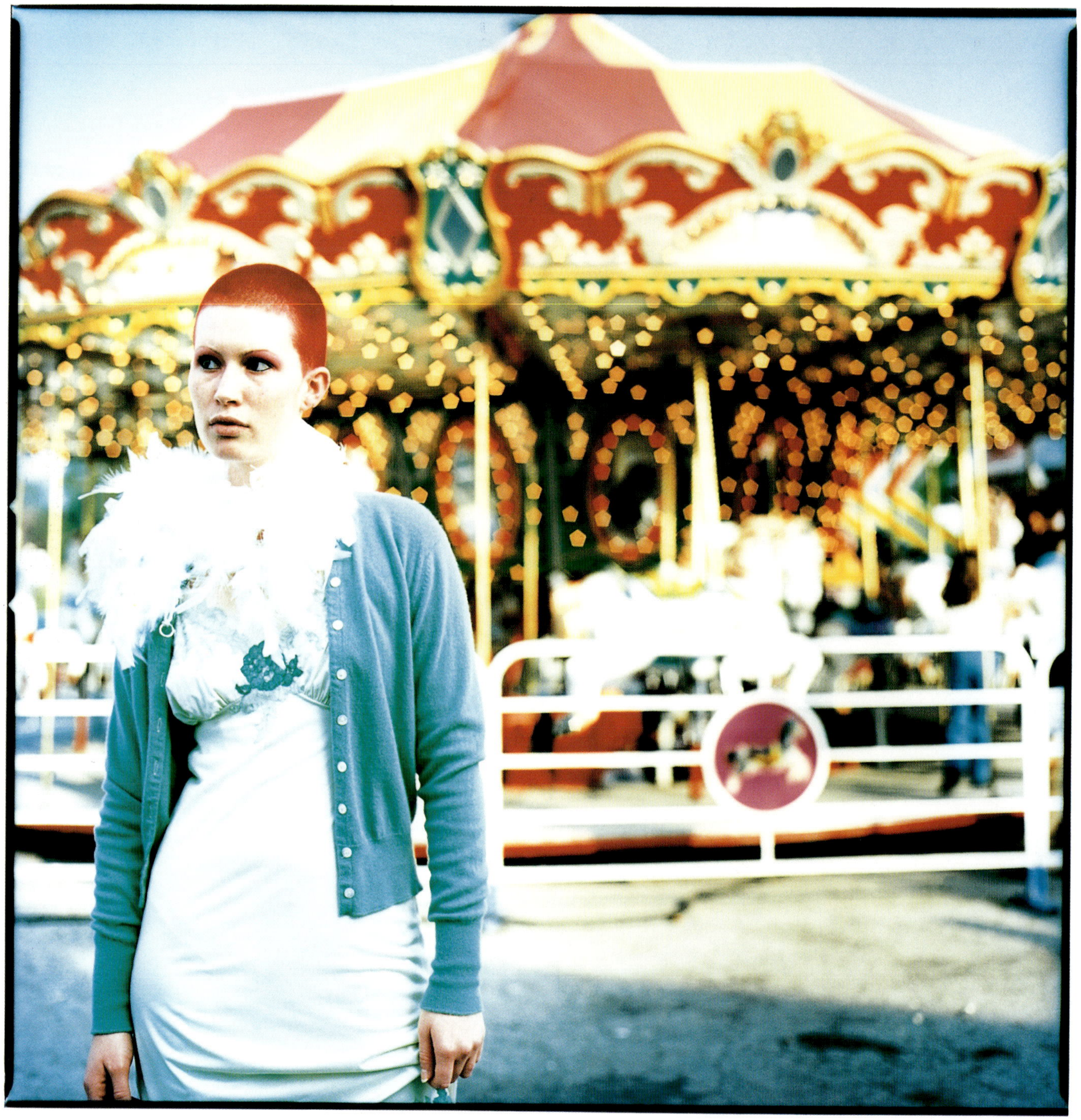

Norma Zuniga

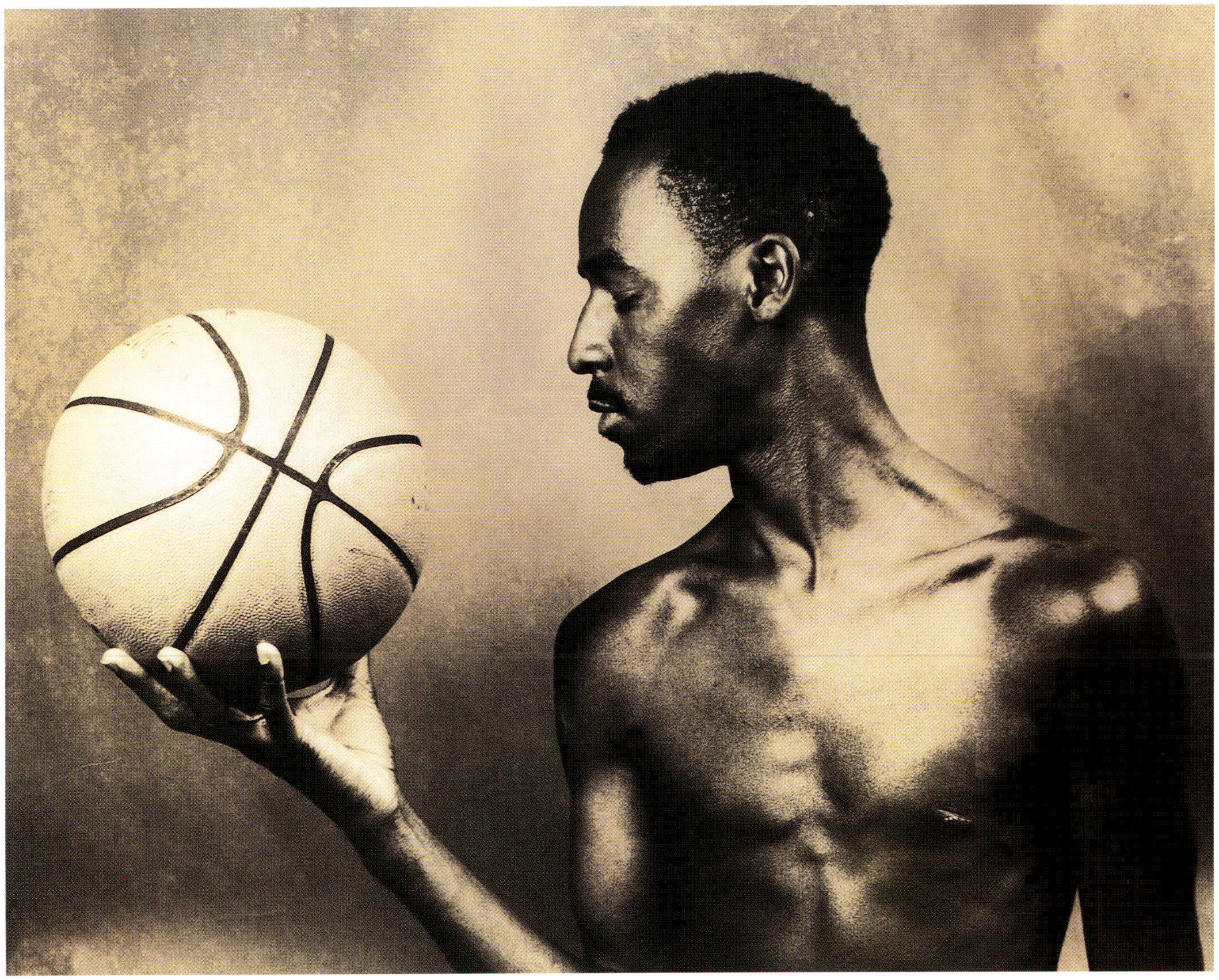

Michael R. Reese

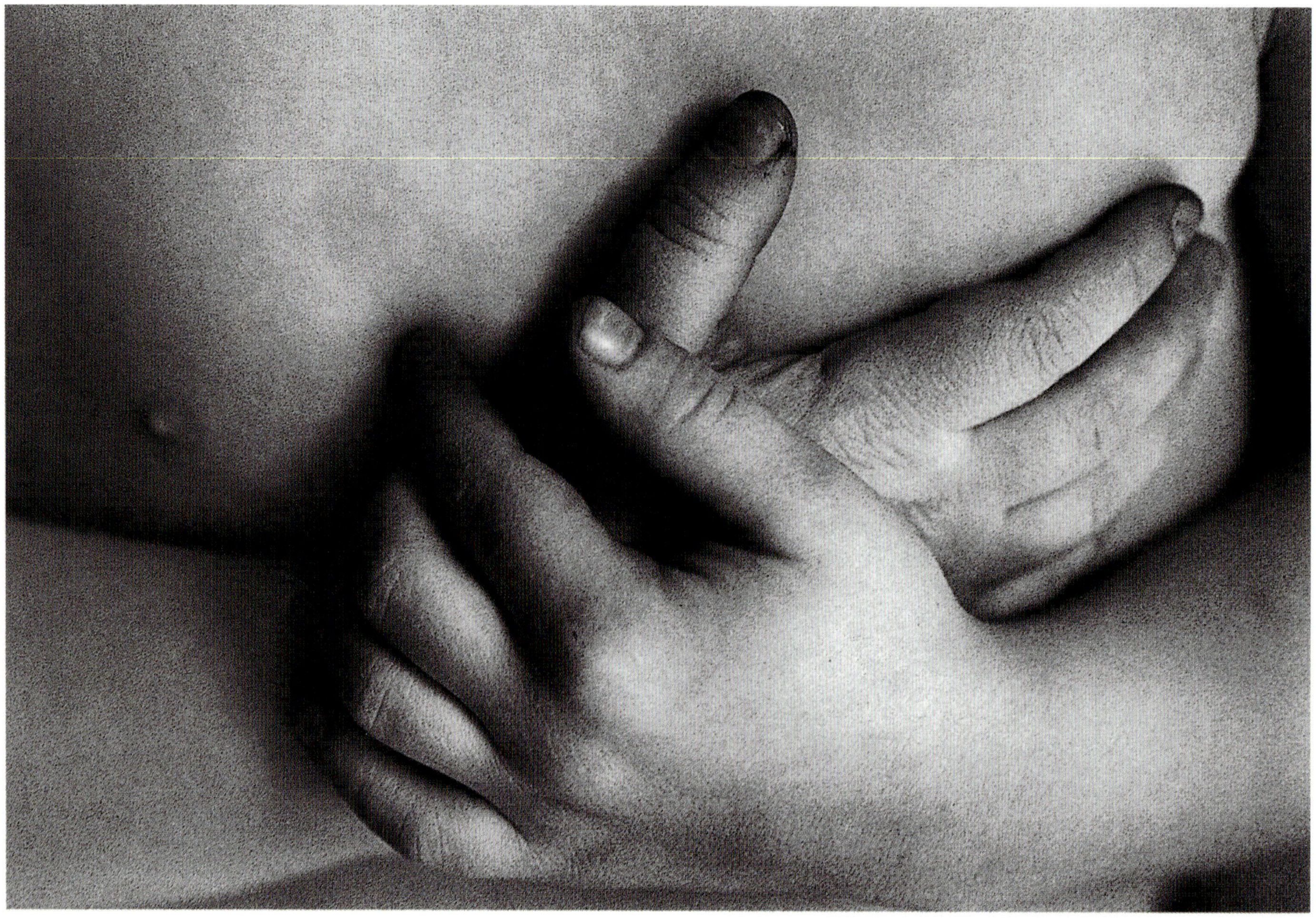

Malinda Kilmer

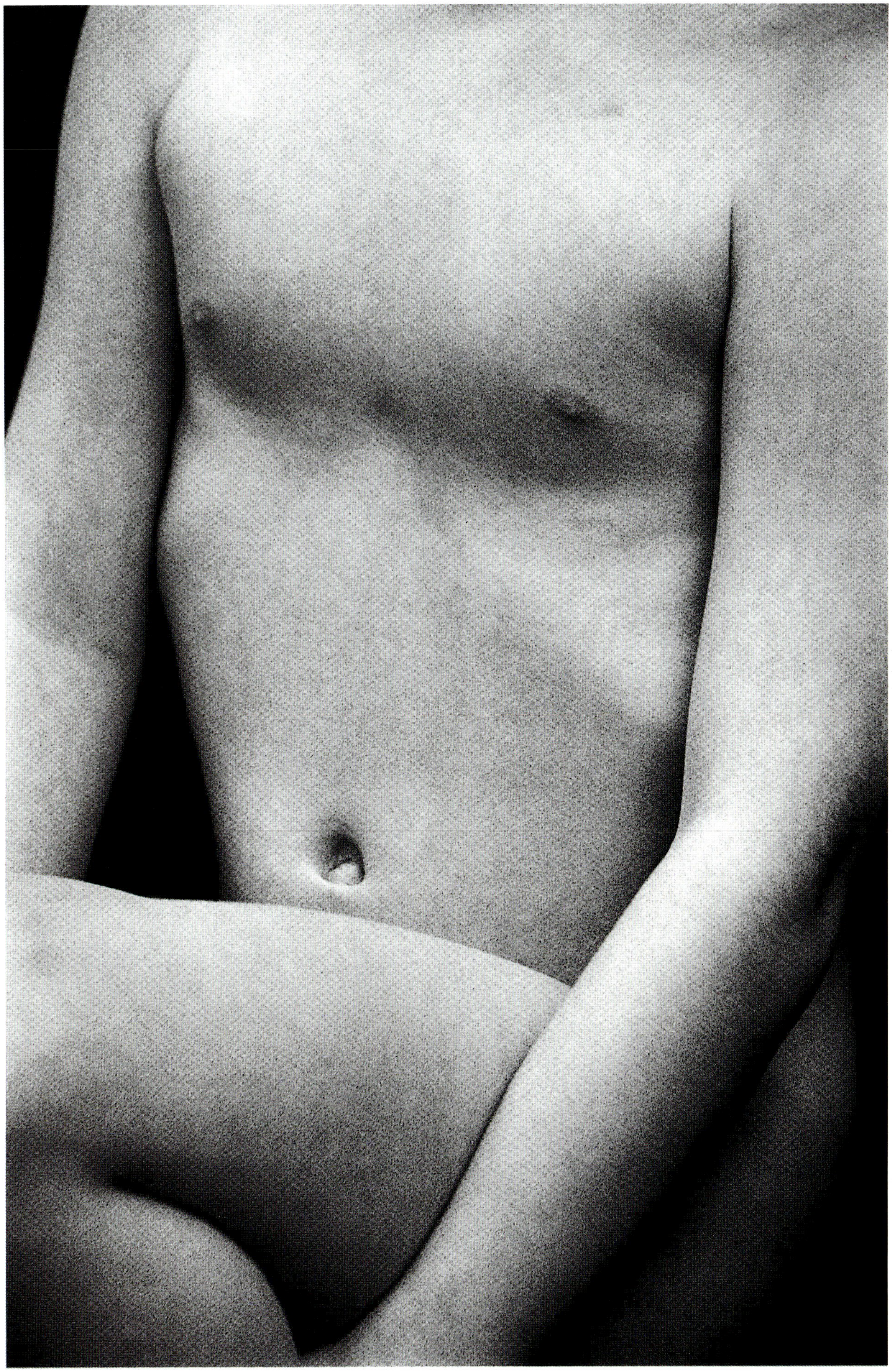

Malinda Kilmer

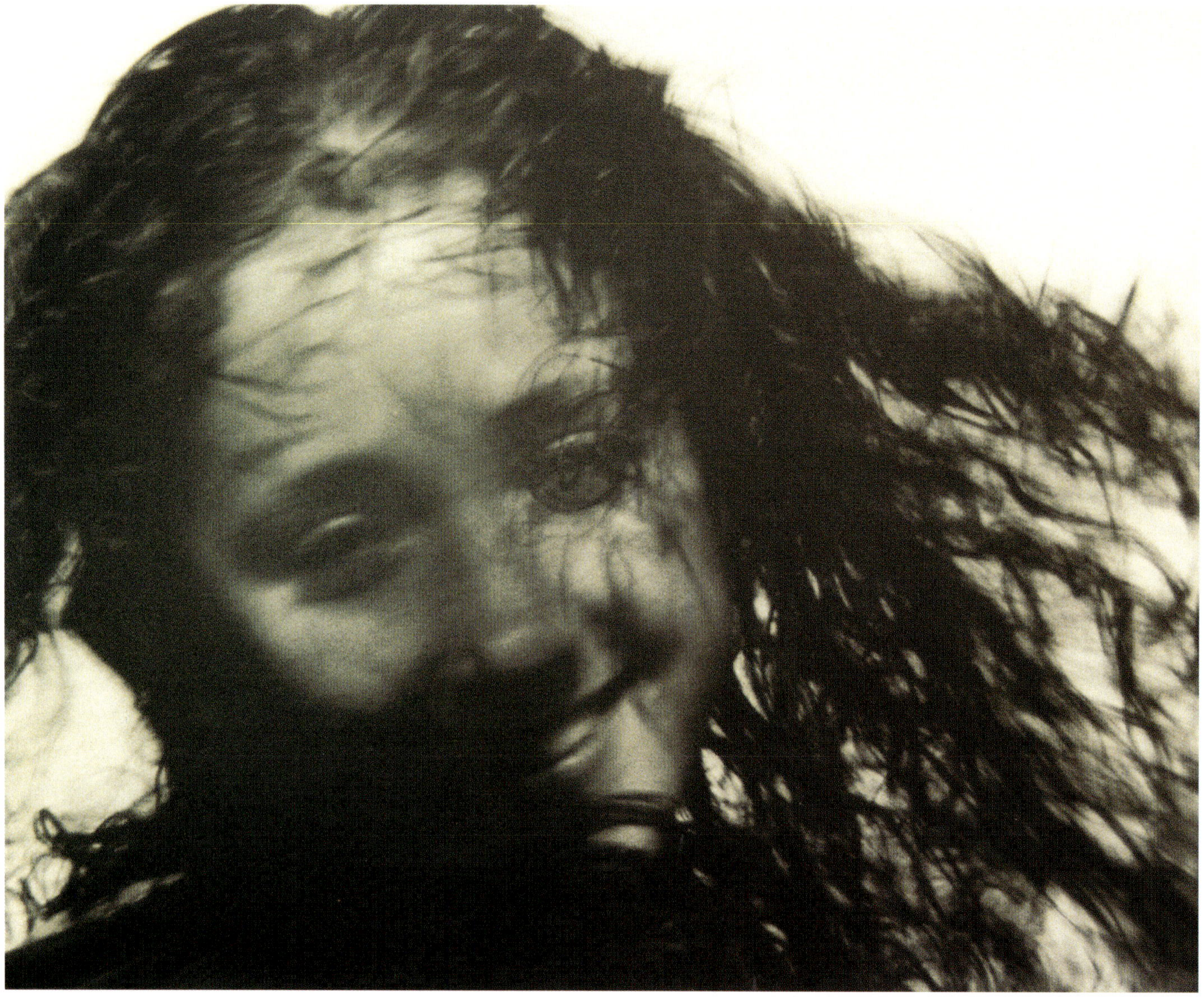

Gordon Eckler

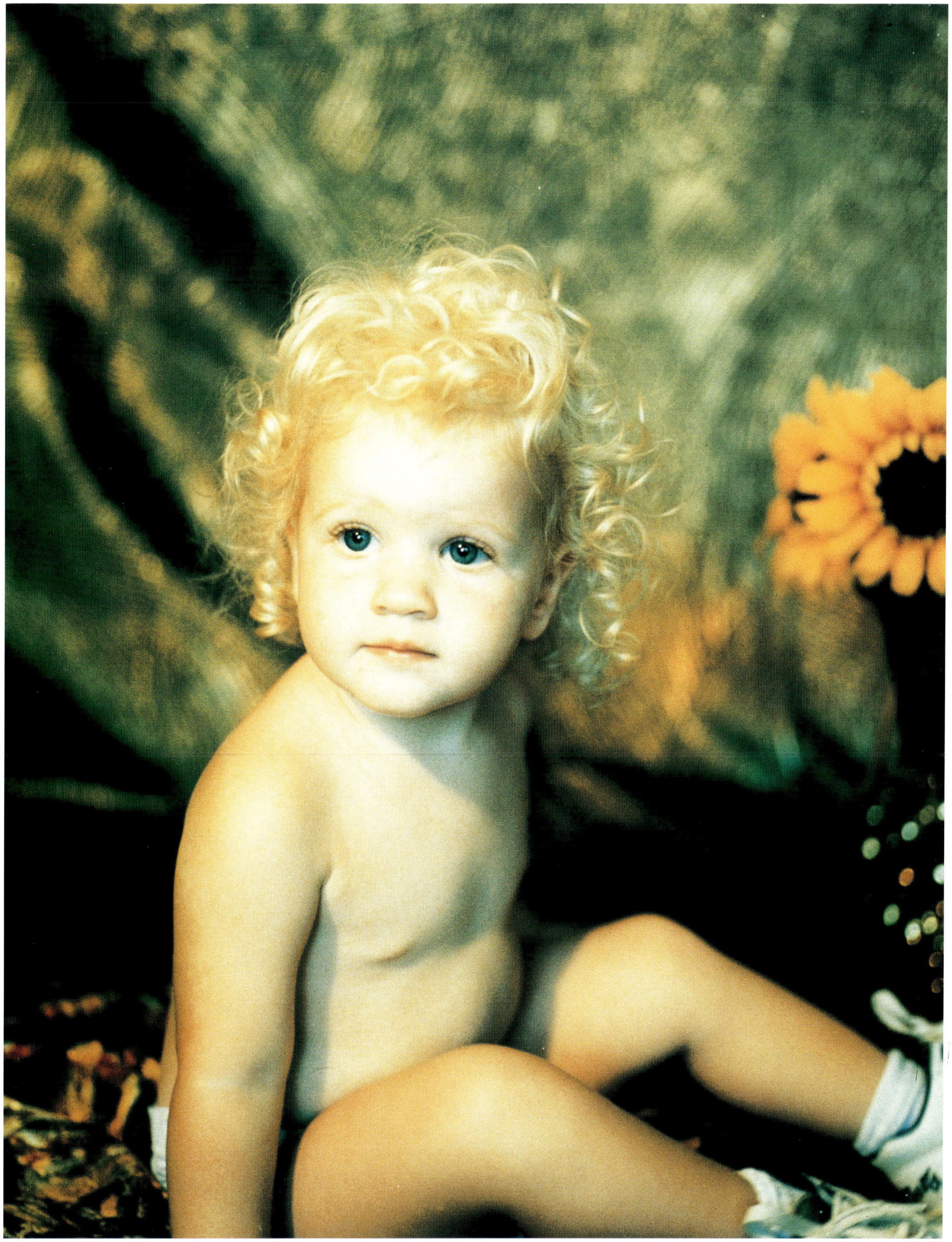

Darriel Caston

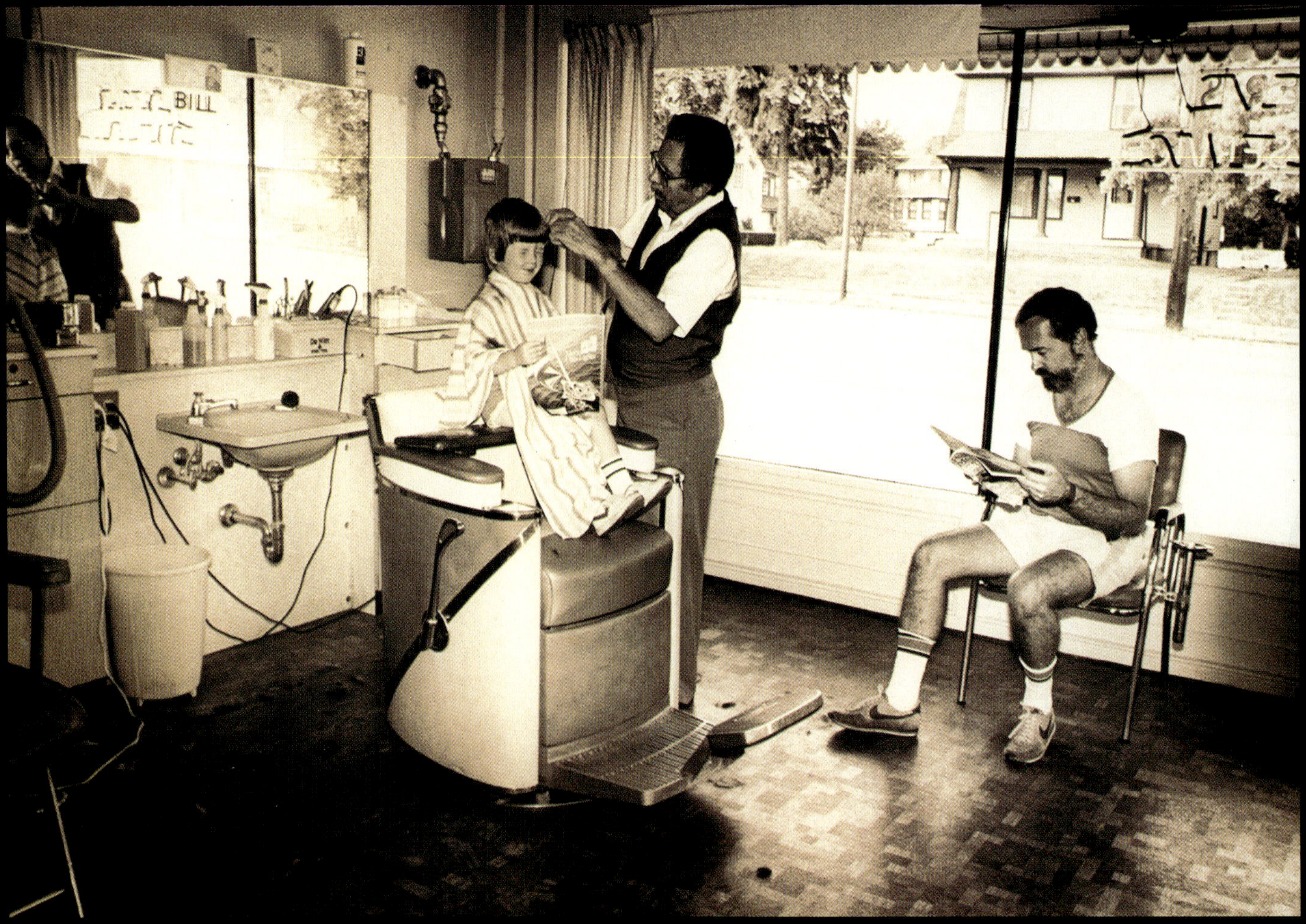

Robert Parkey III

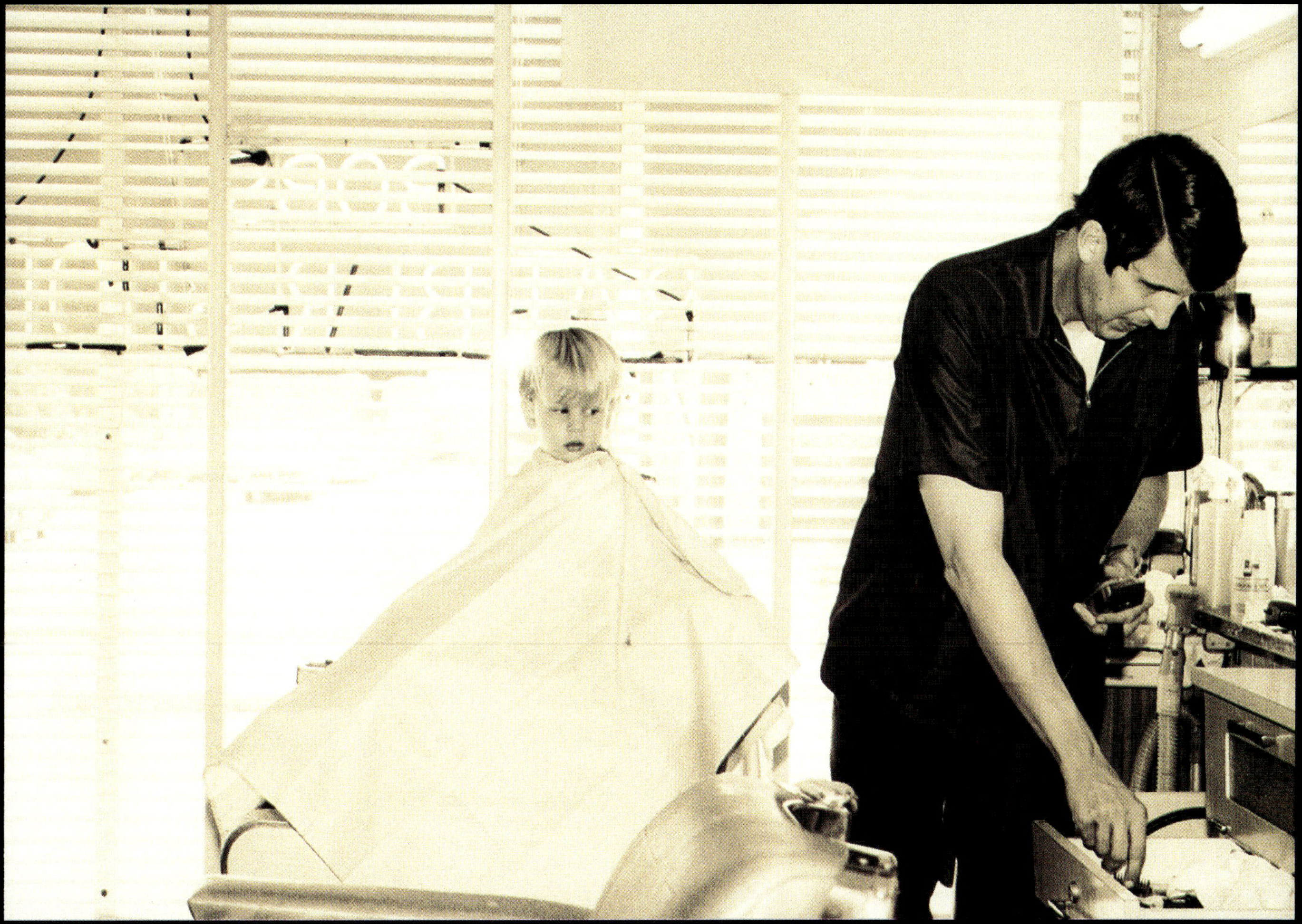

Robert Parkey III

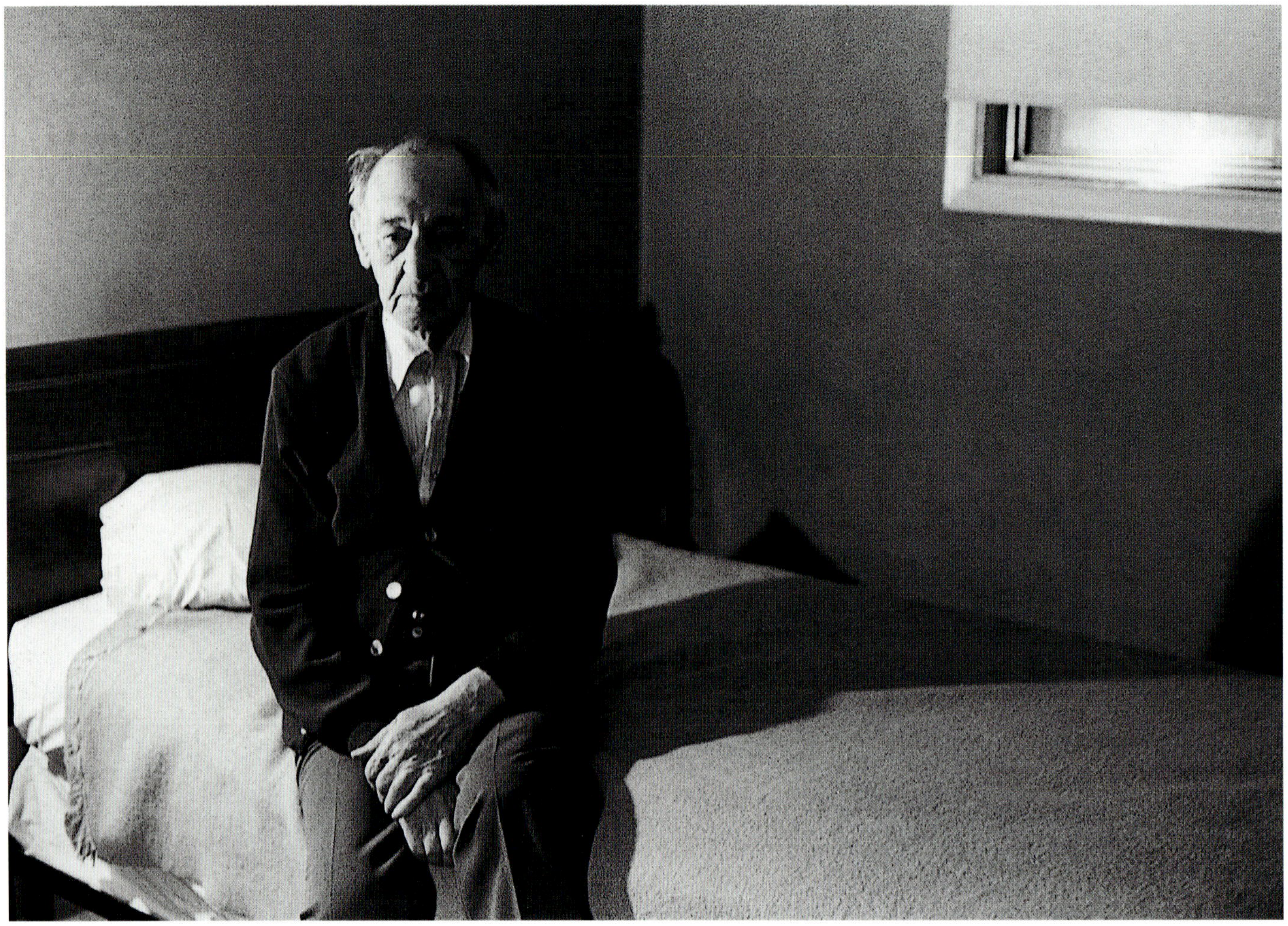

Sara-Jo Matthys

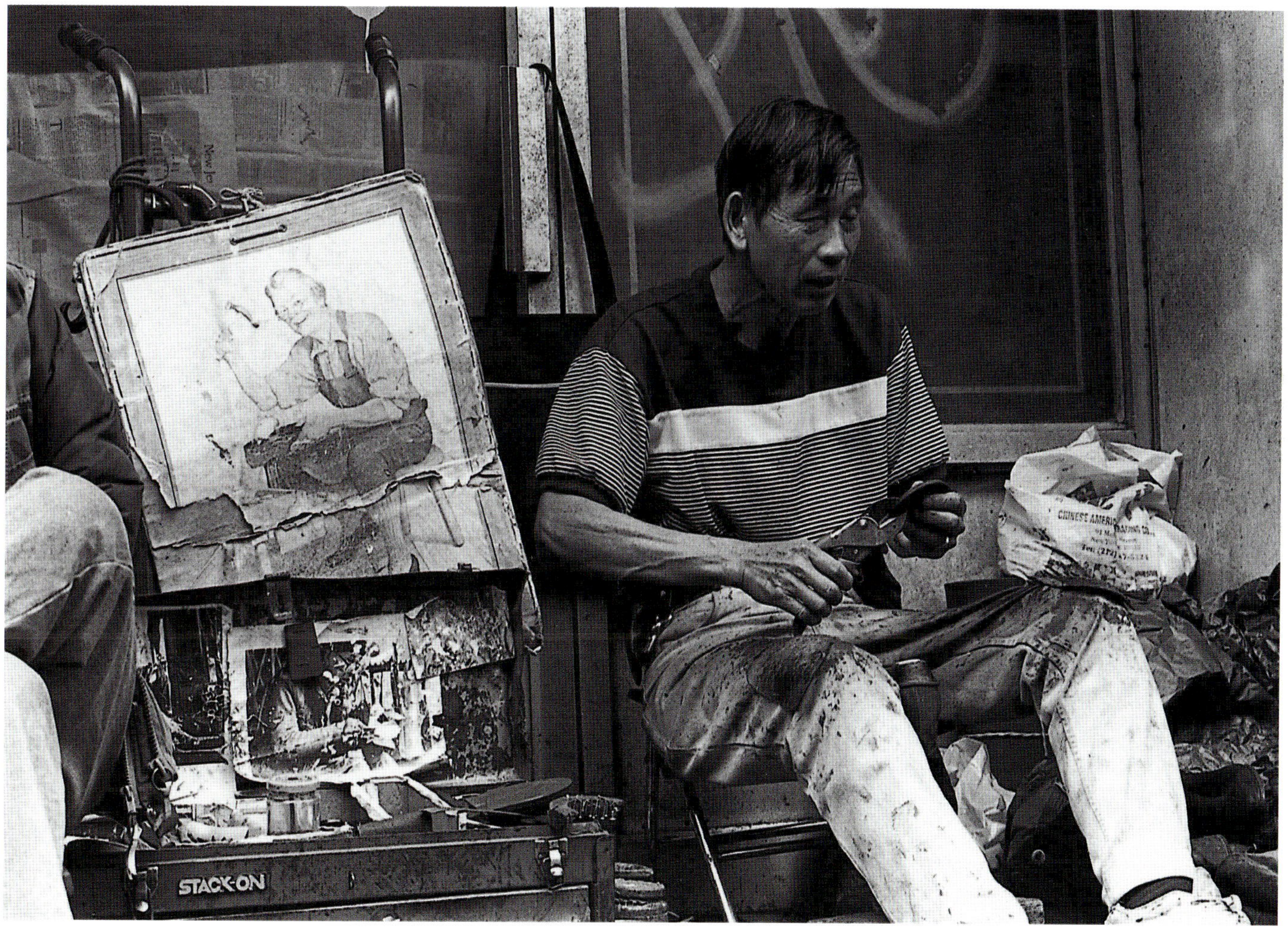

Liza L. Betof

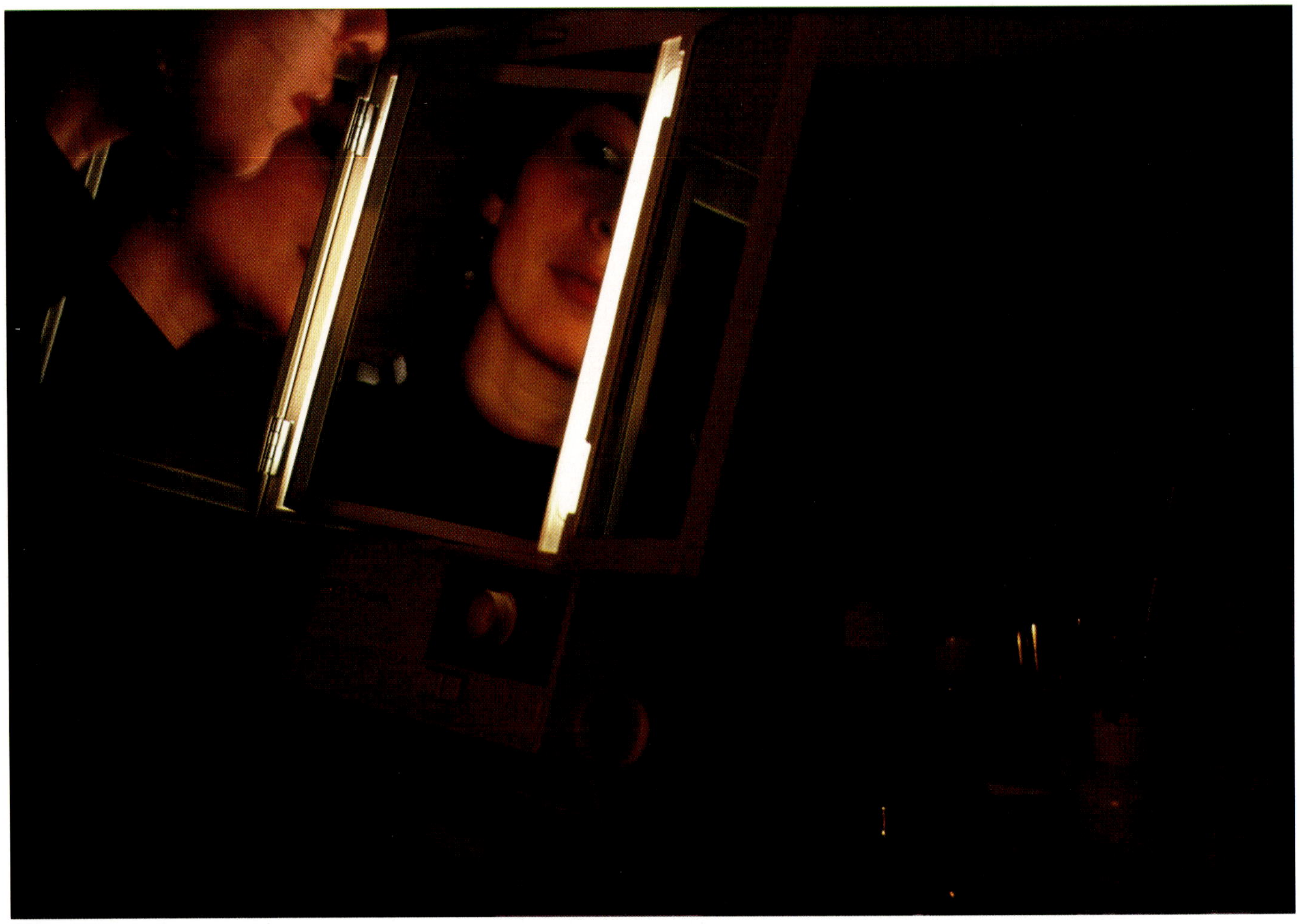

Jo Ann Lore

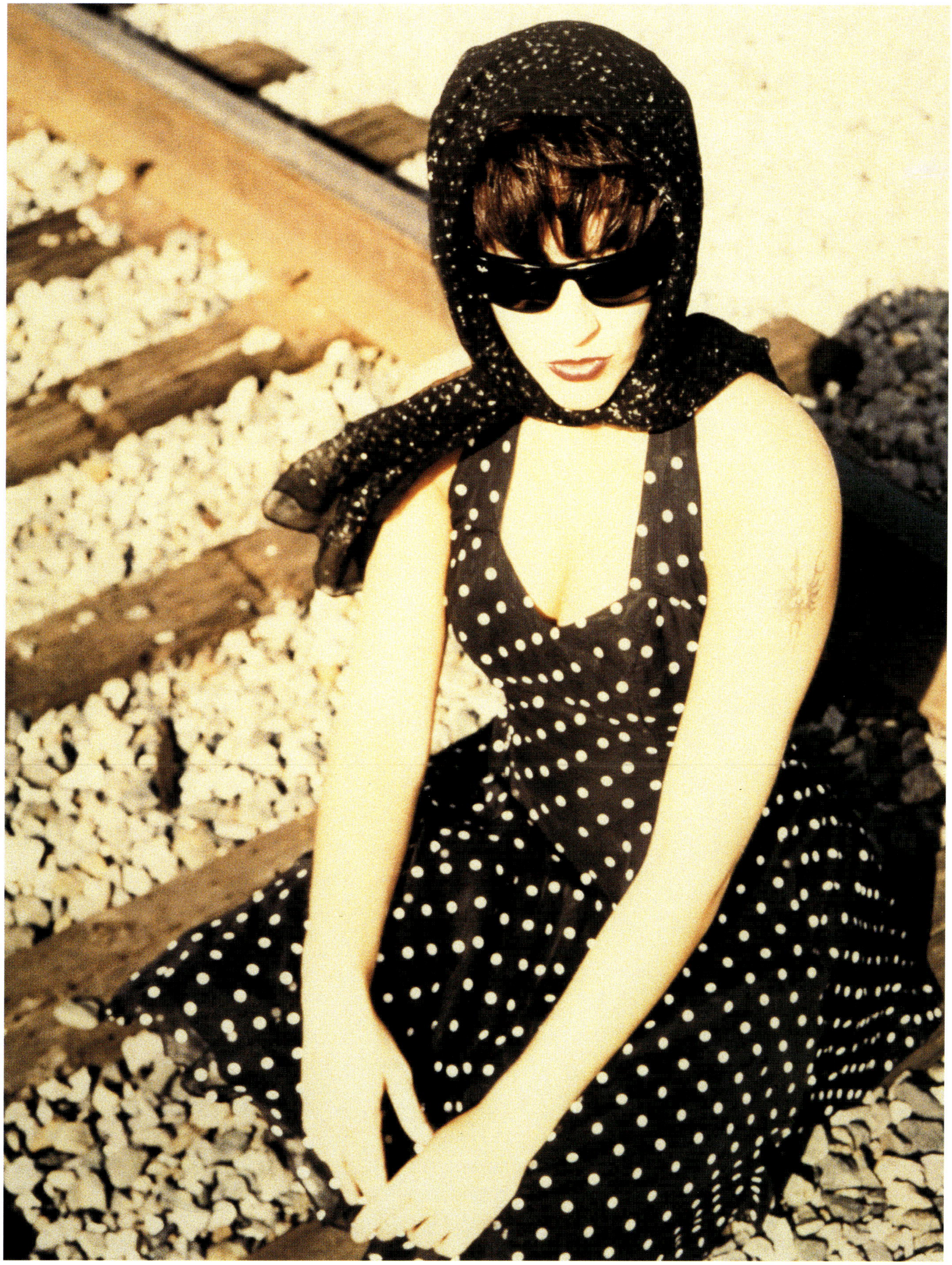

Michael S. Dobson

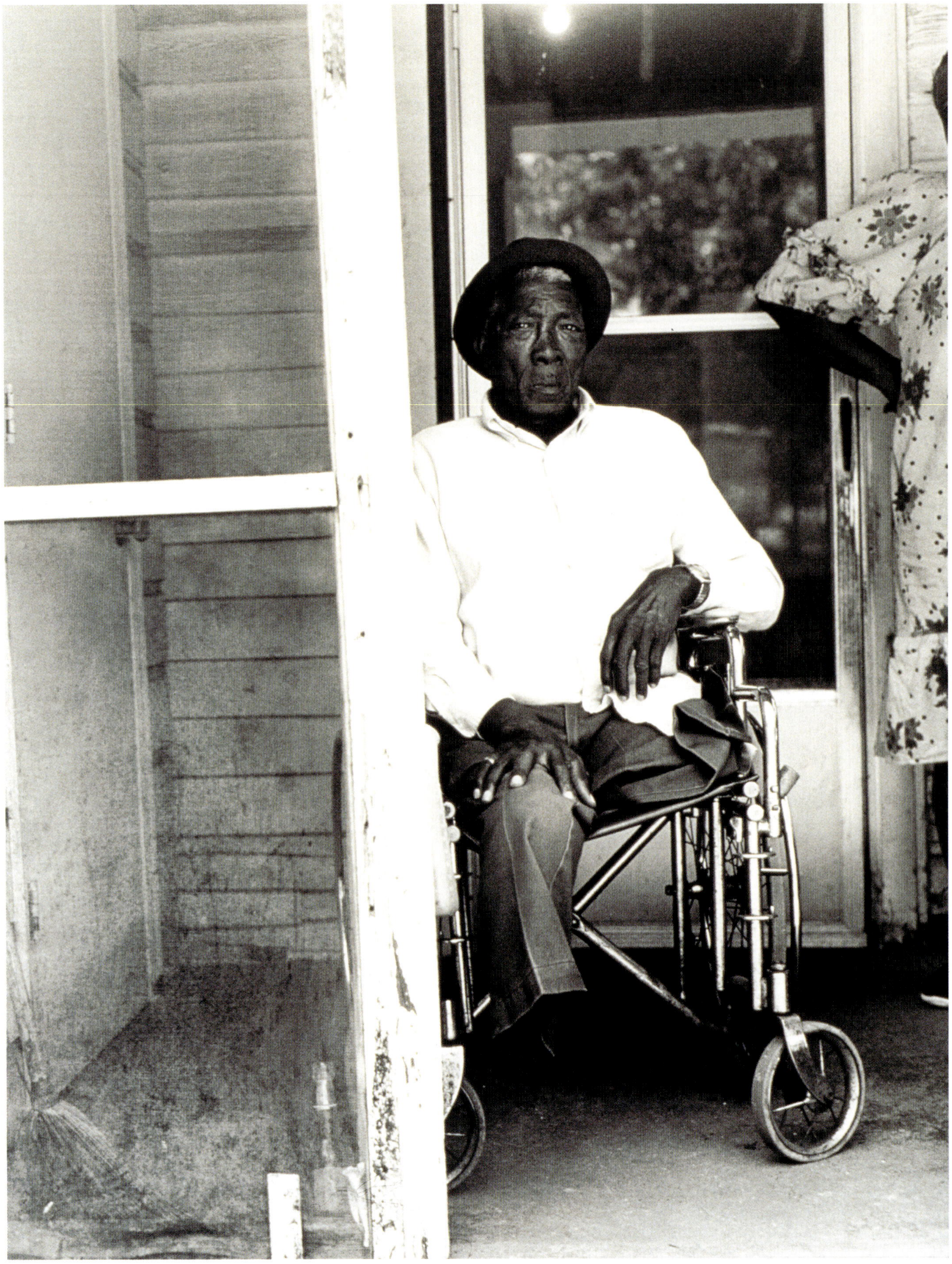

Perry Dilbeck

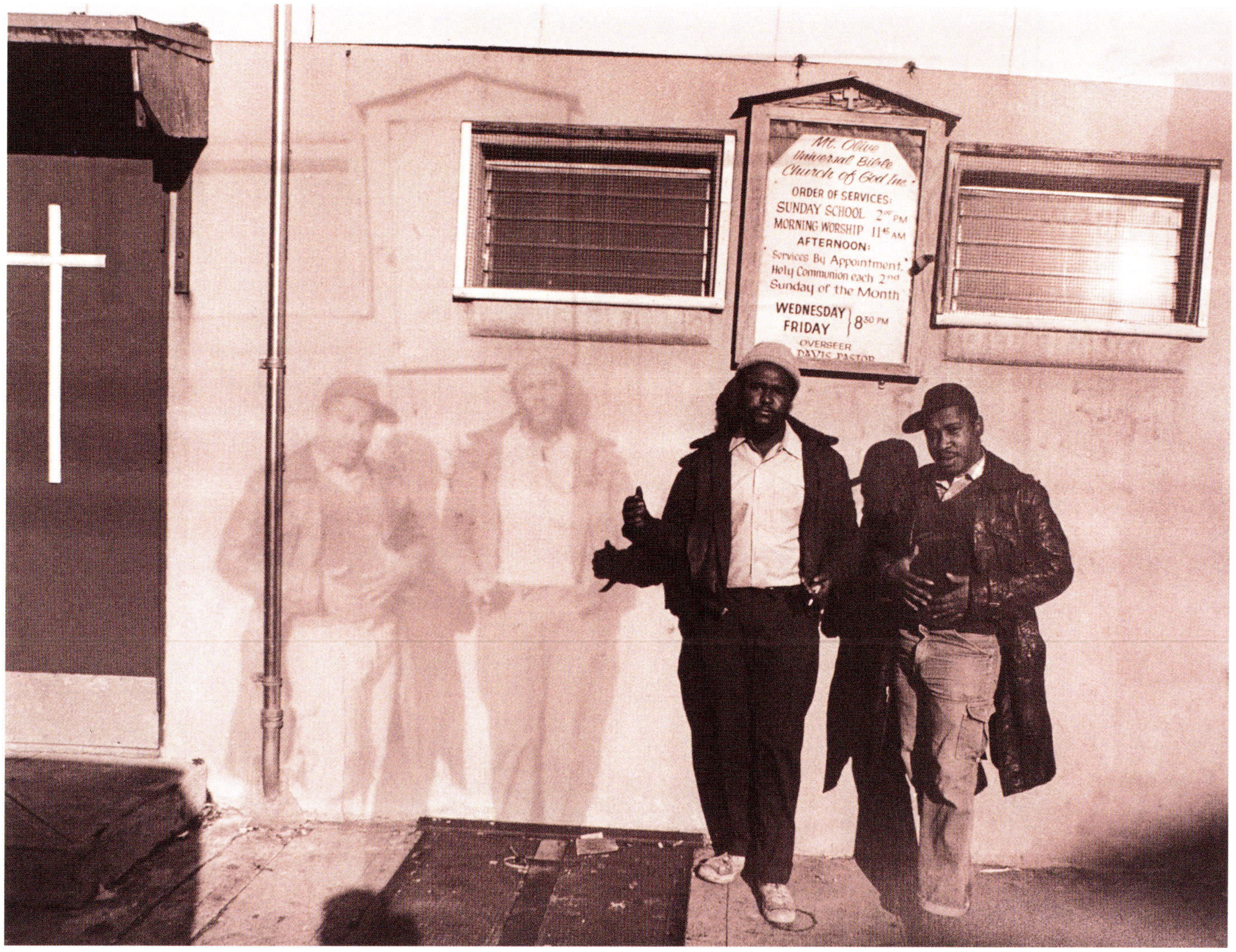

James Rushing

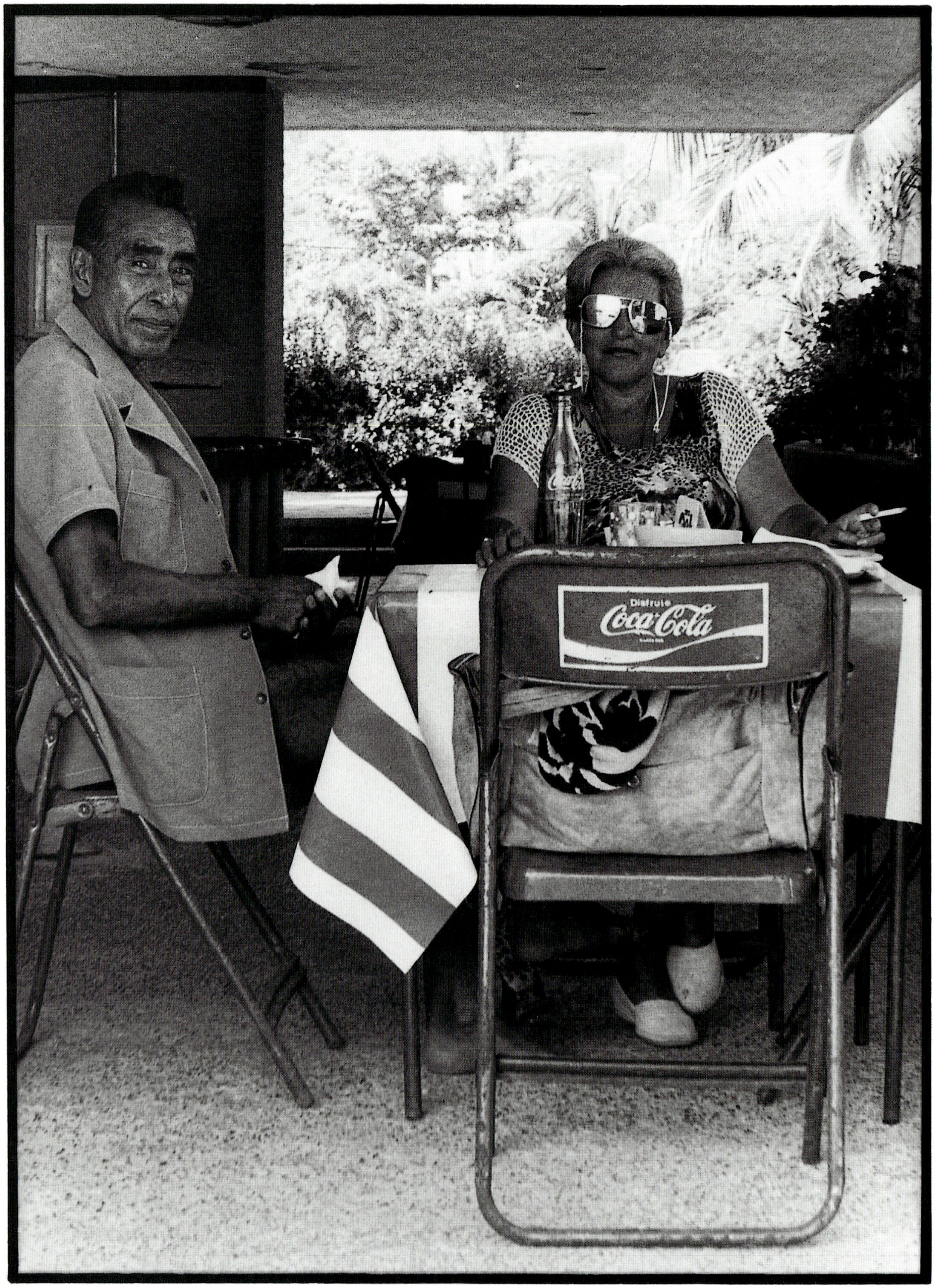

Kevin E. McWilliams

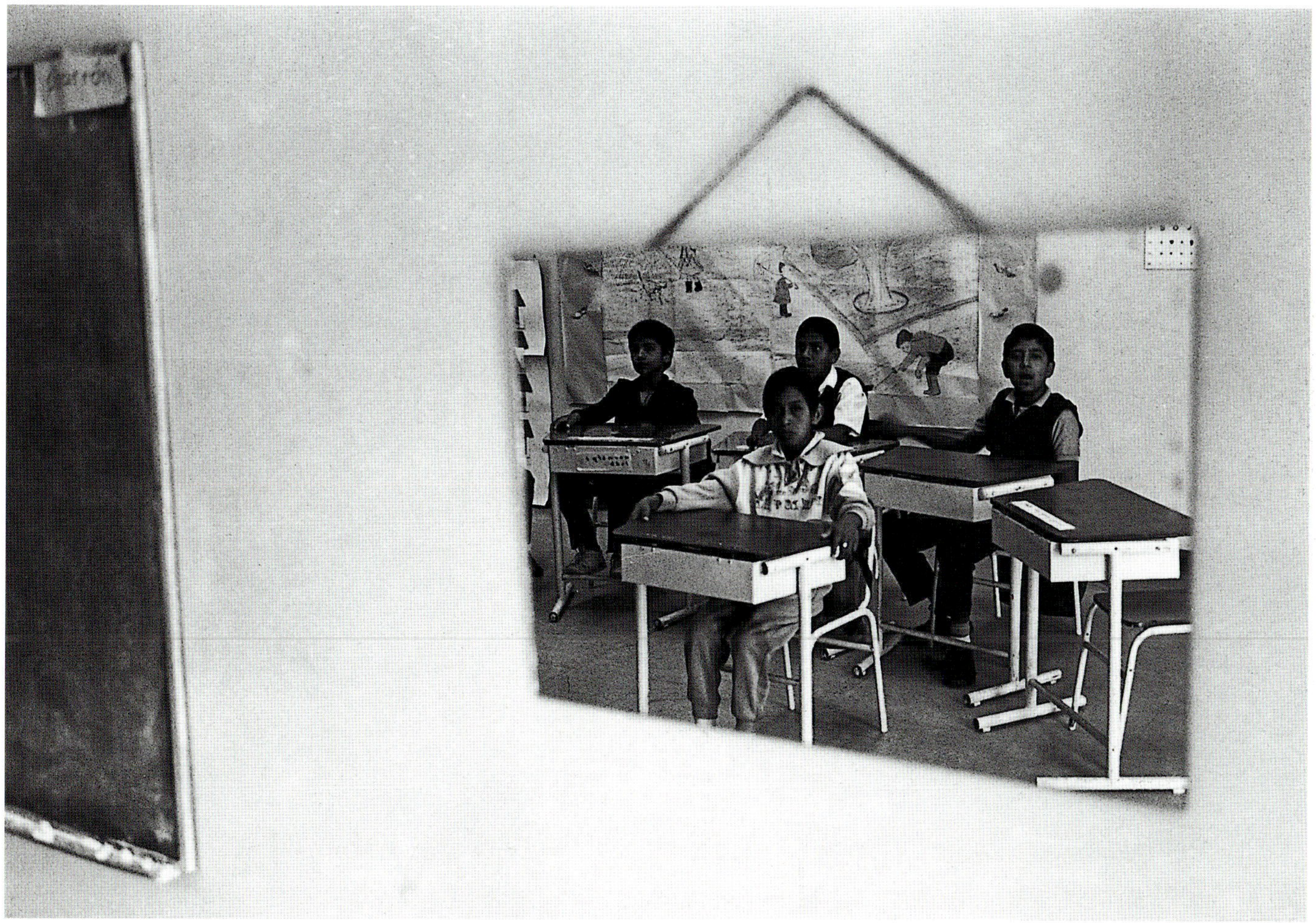

Libby Edelman

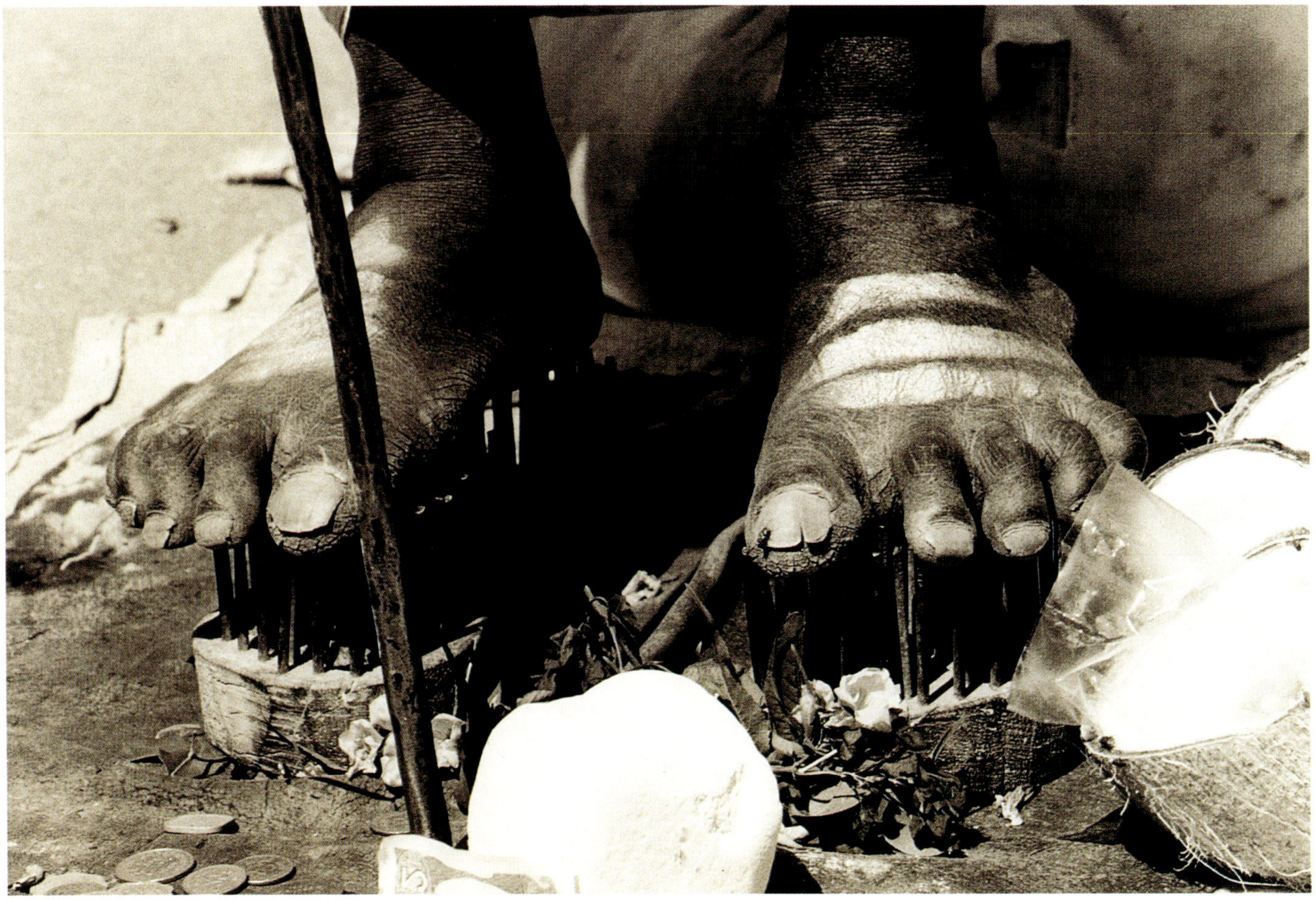

Greg Nielson

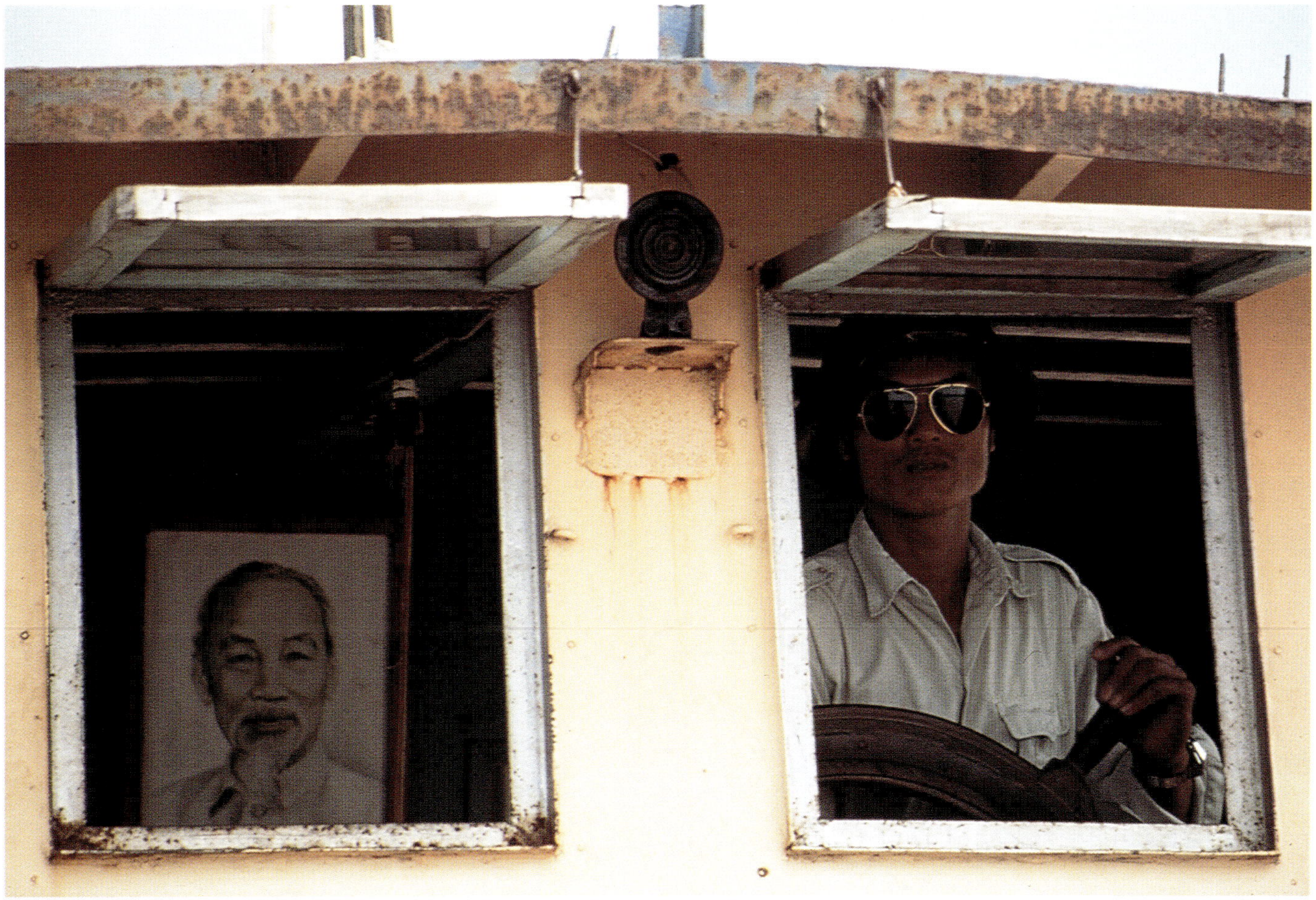

Donald Gurewitz

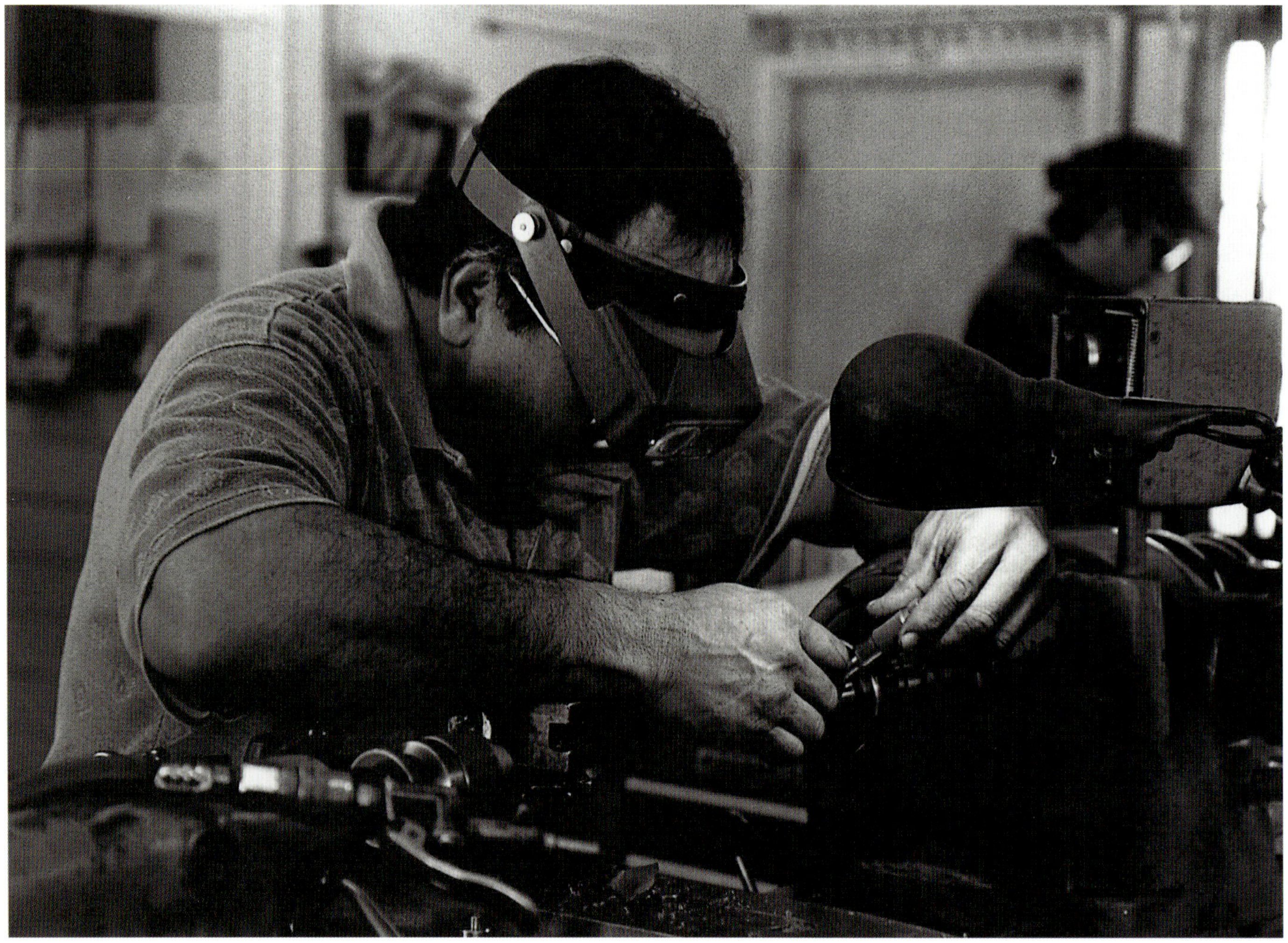

Stephen Yu

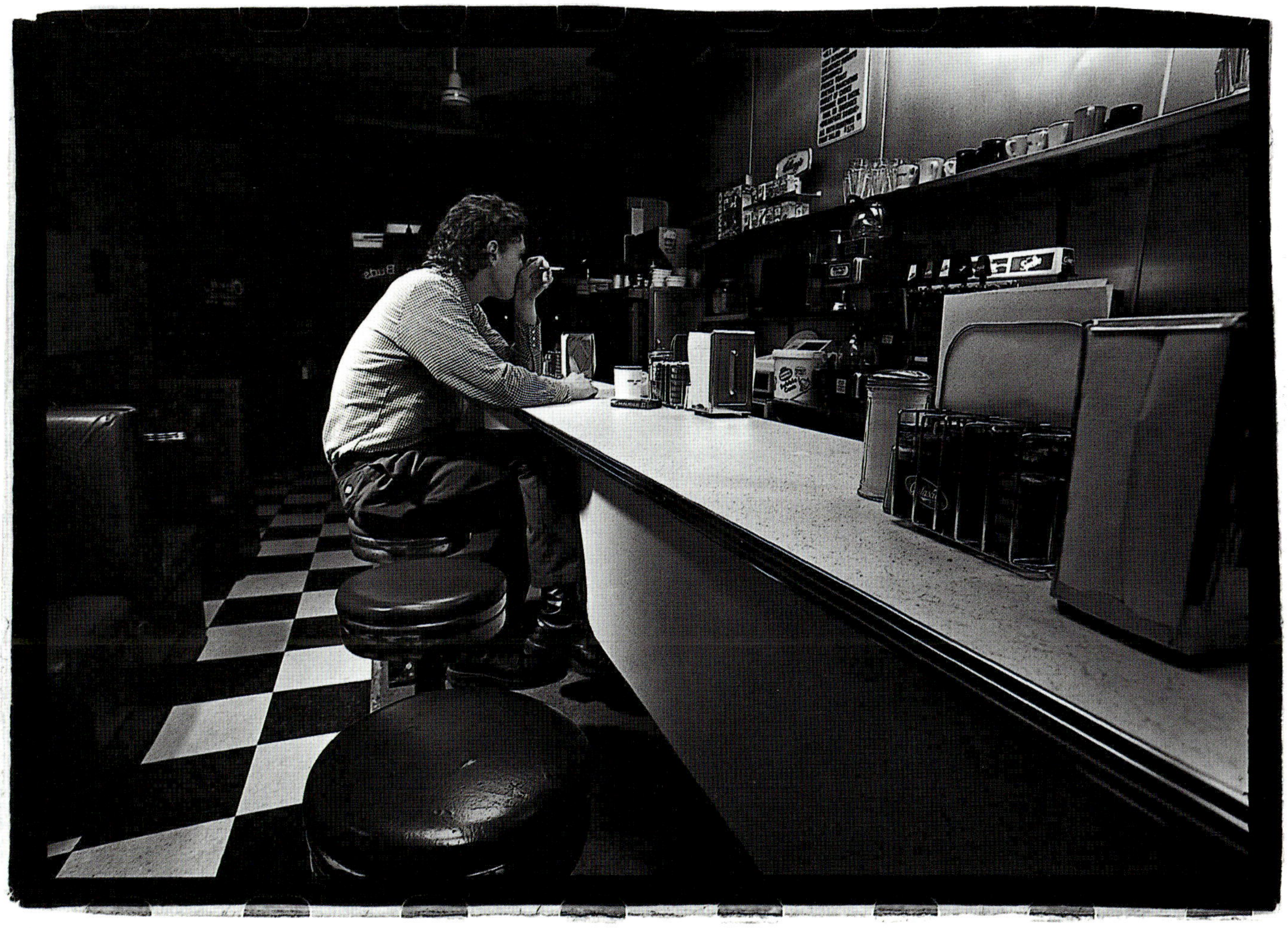

K.C. Armstrong

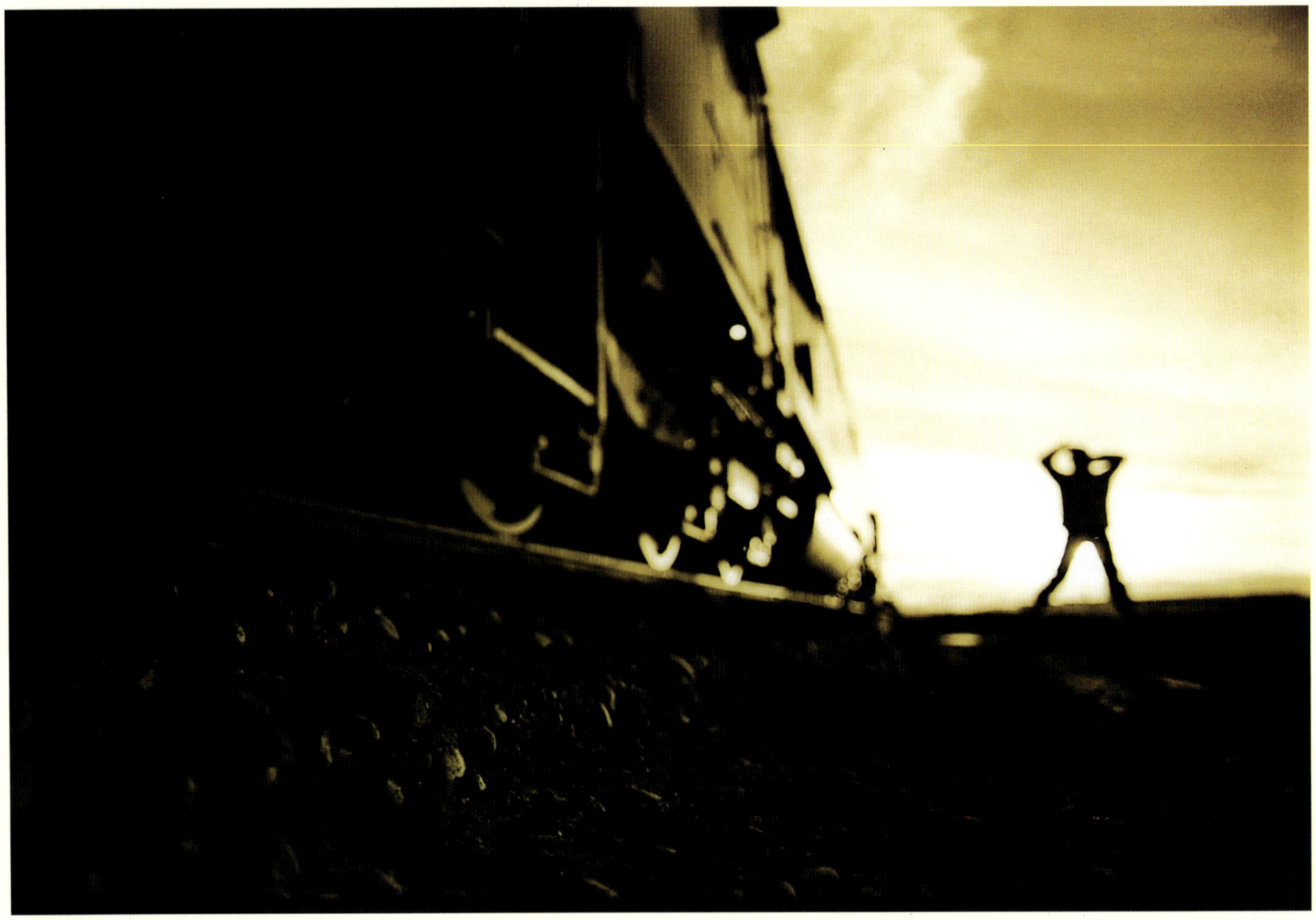

Stephen Wilde

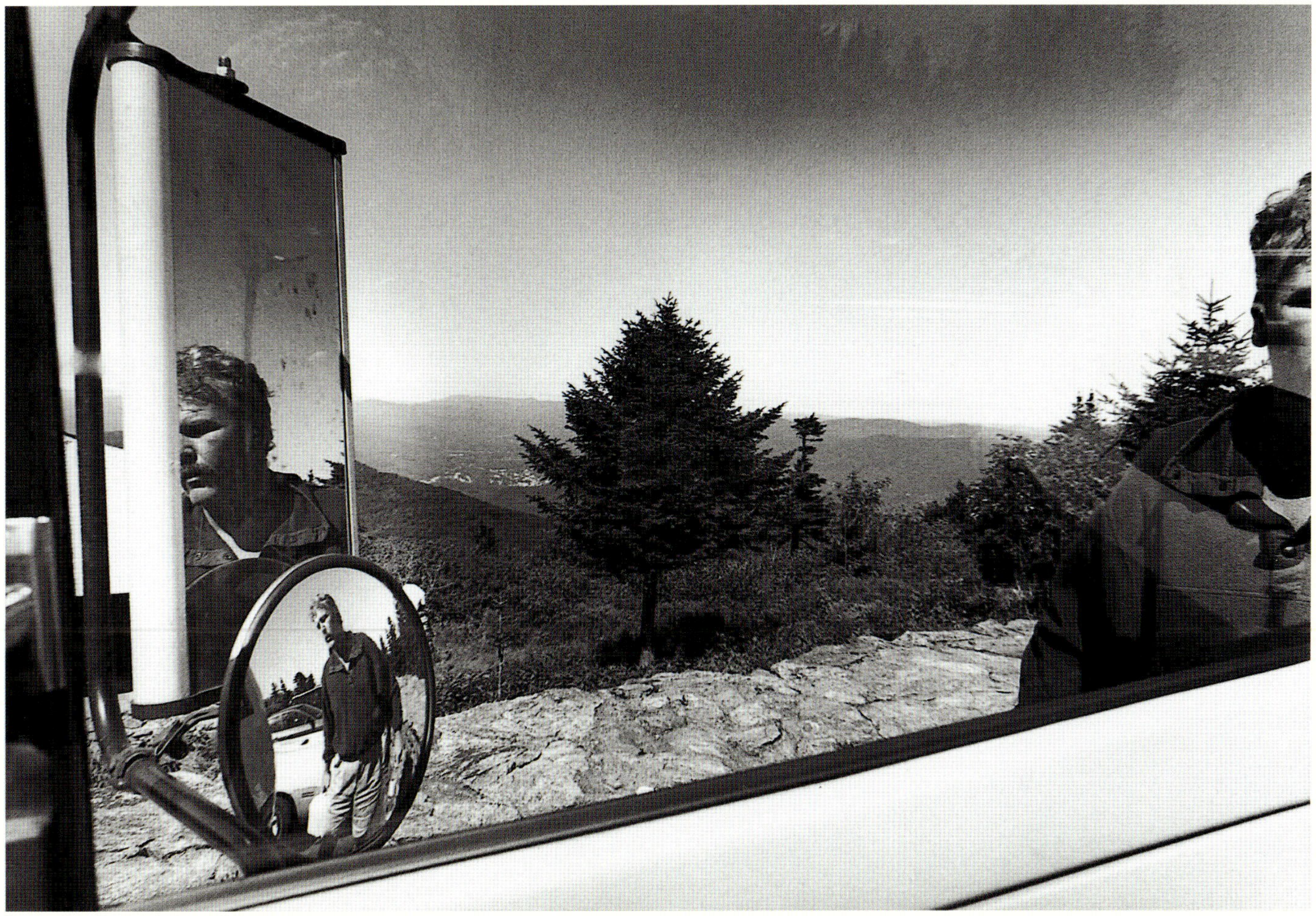

Davin R. M. Ellicson

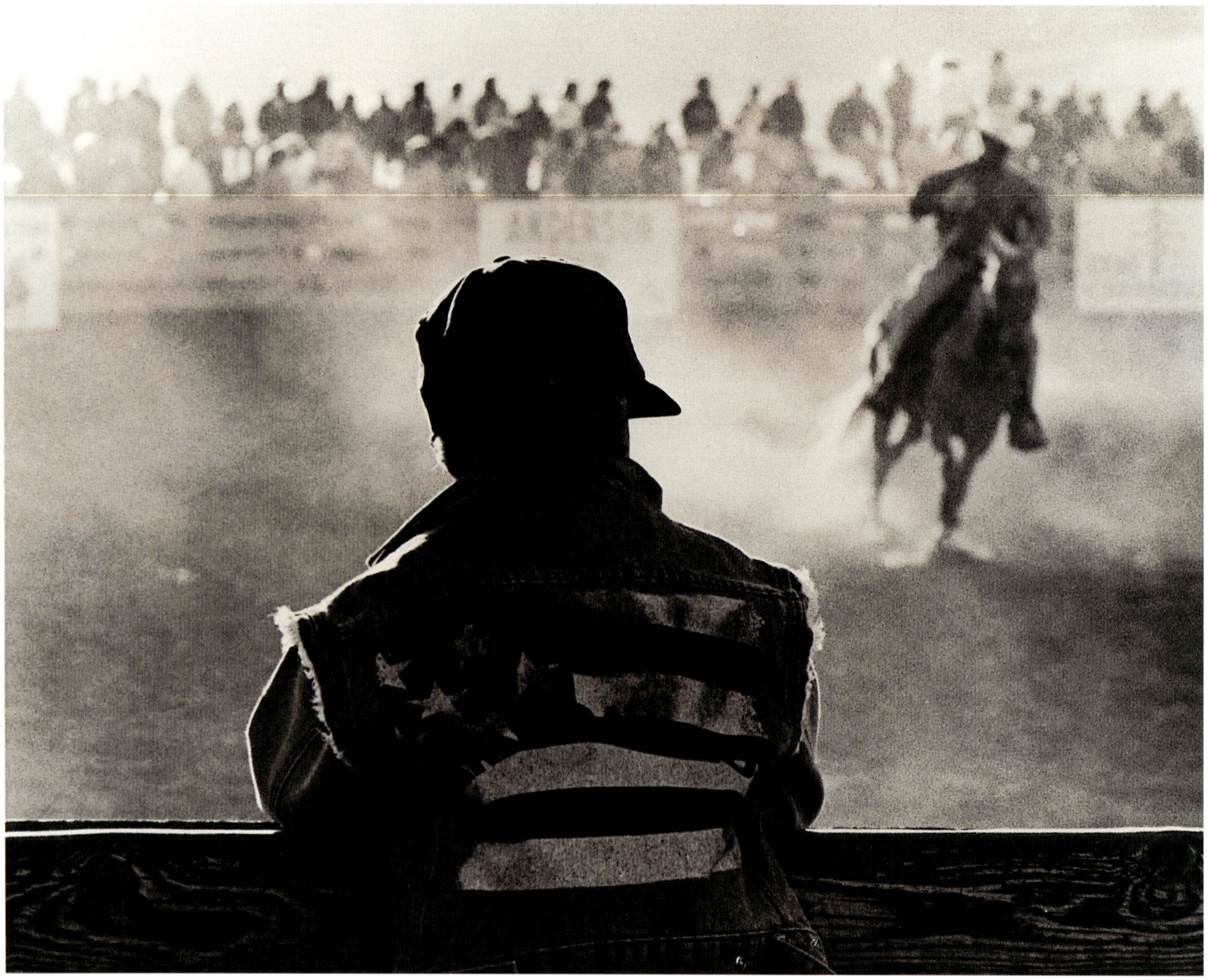

Christopher Clemente

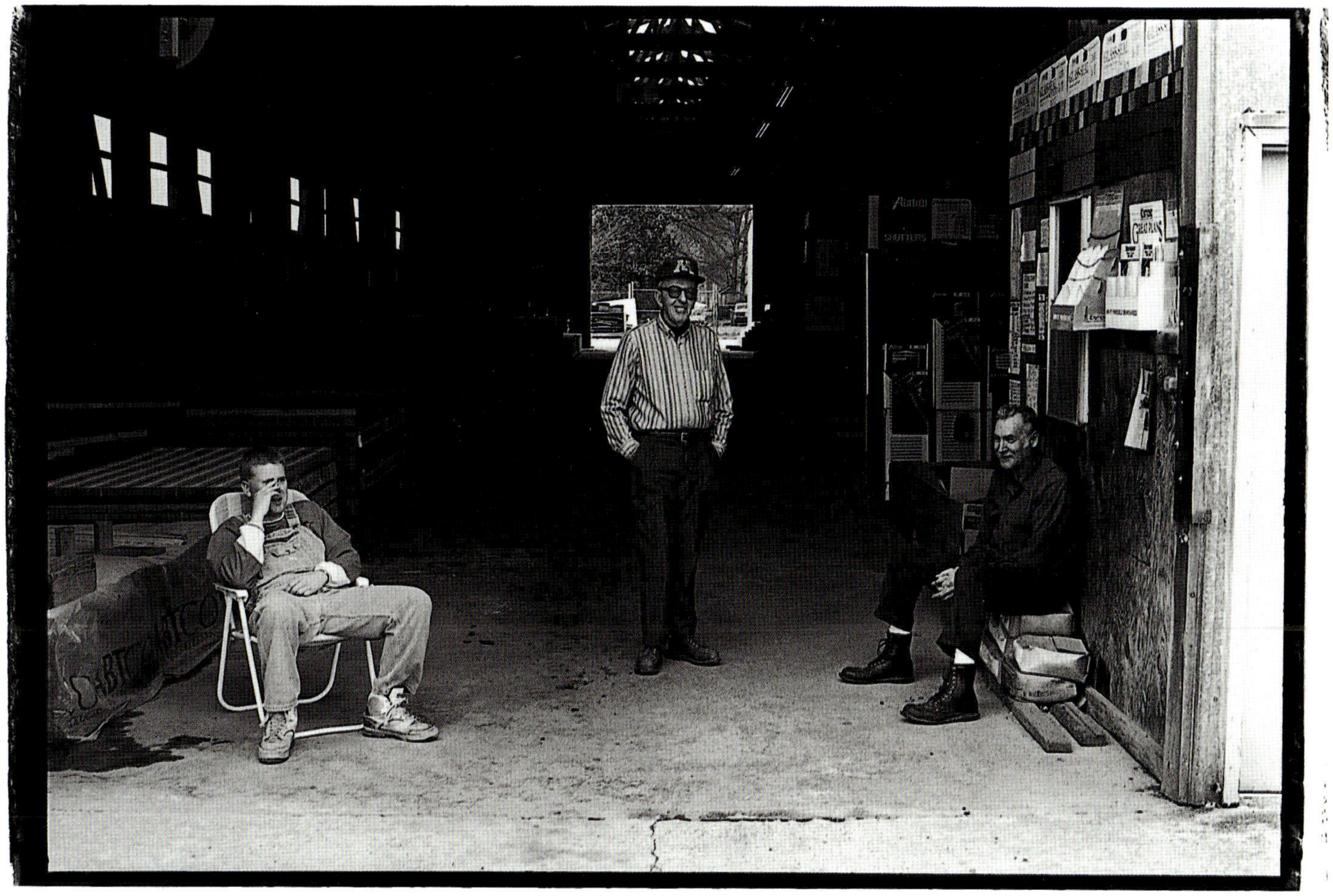

Richard Langone

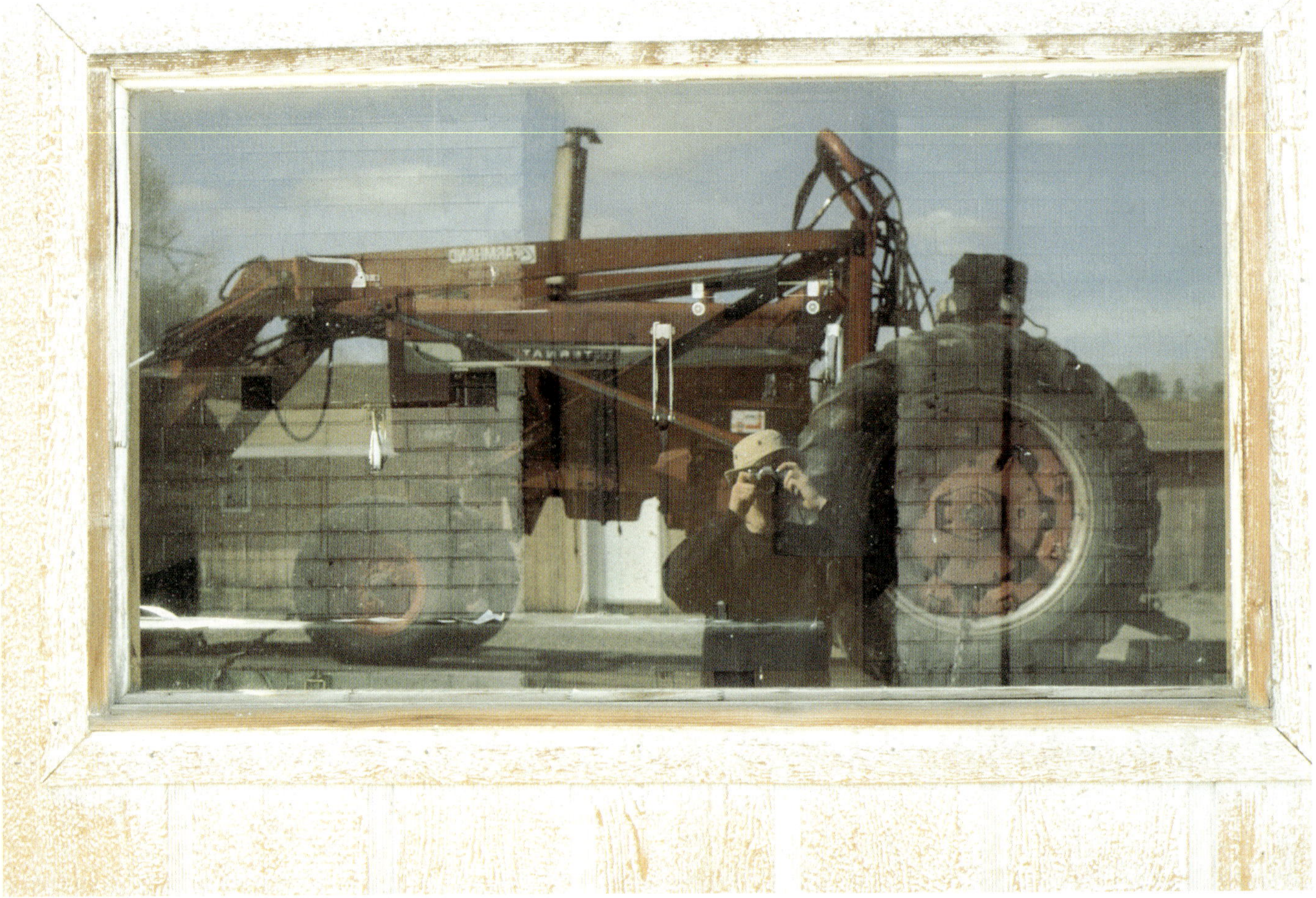

Trevor Nelson

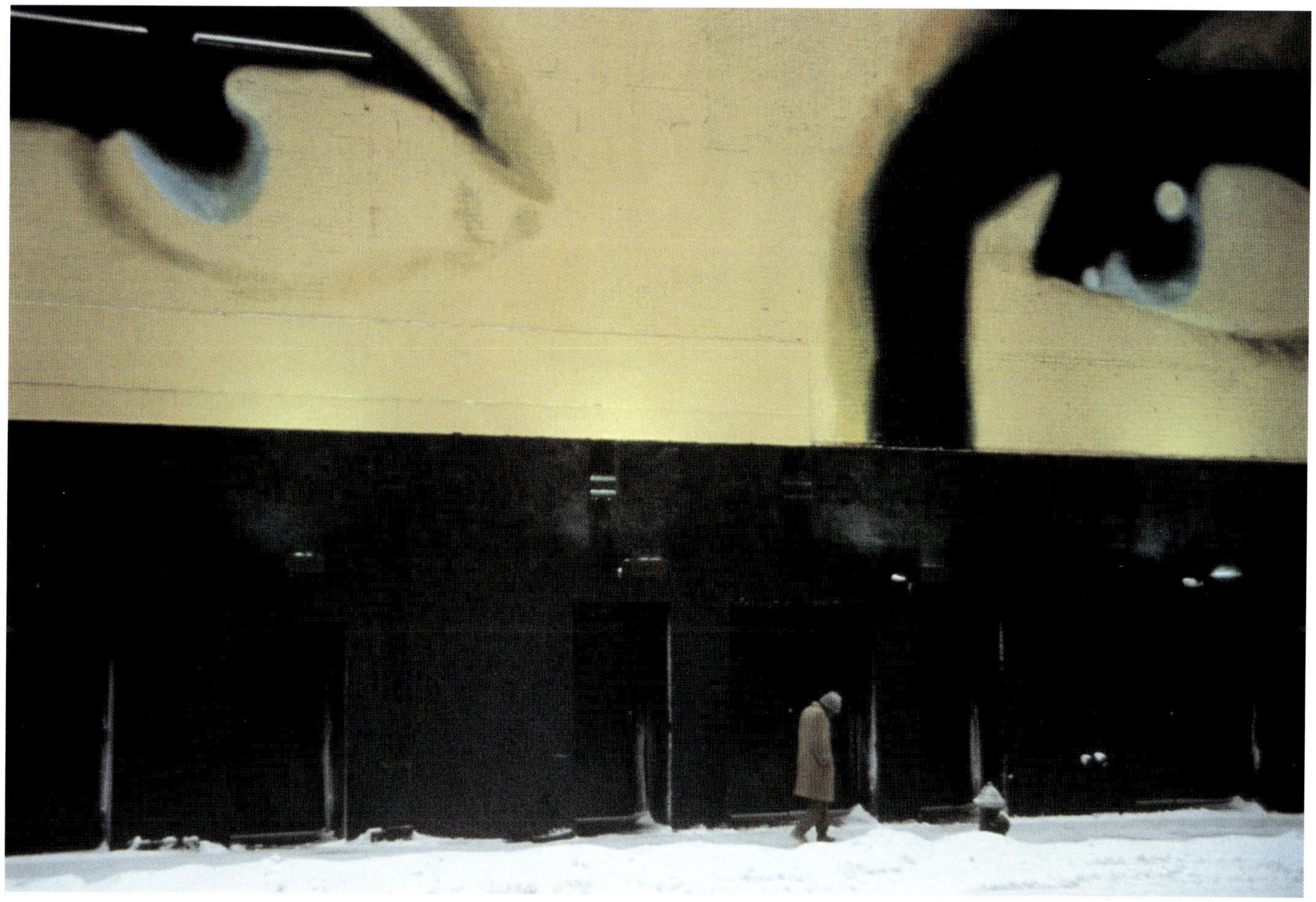

Emmanuel Caluag

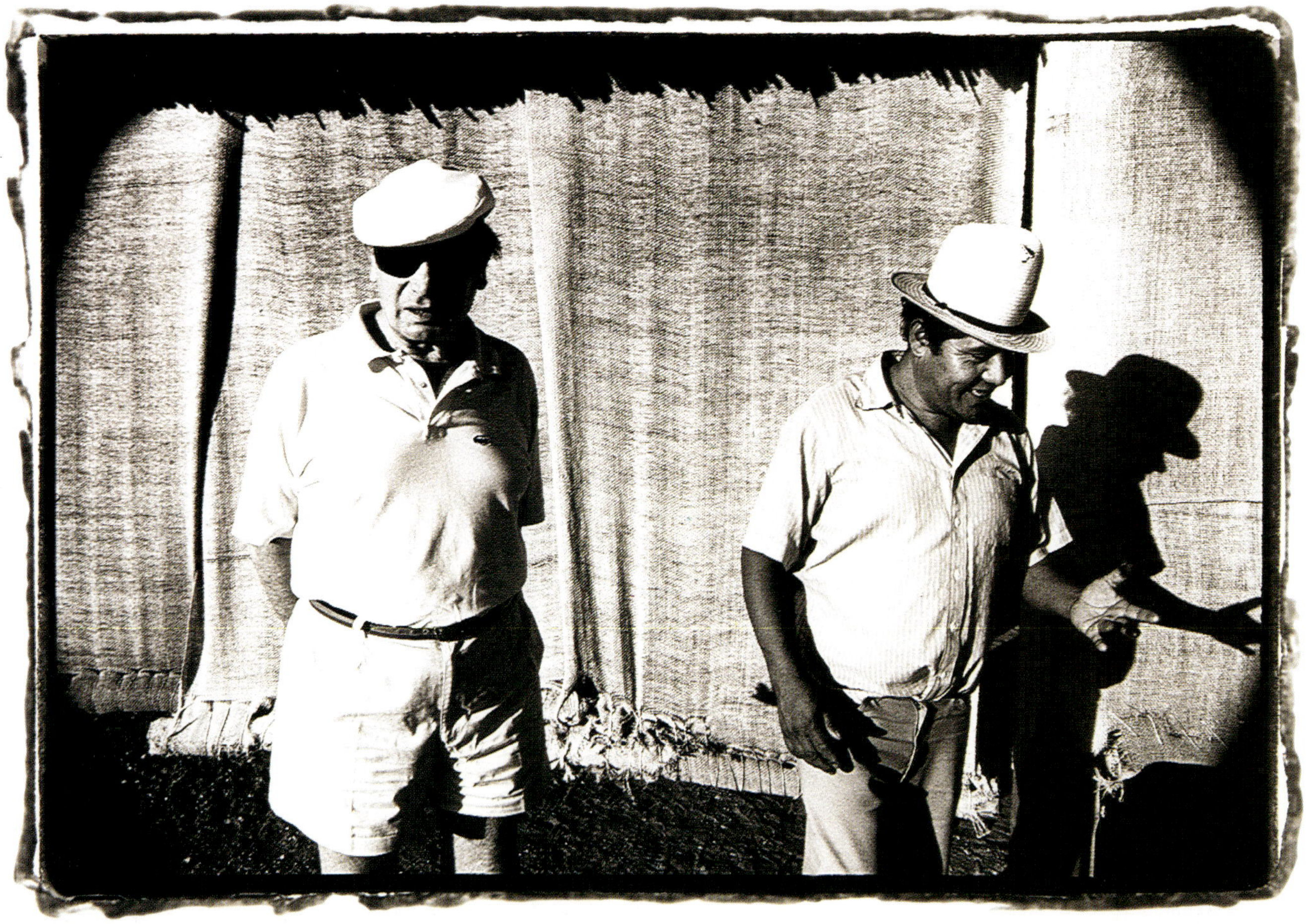

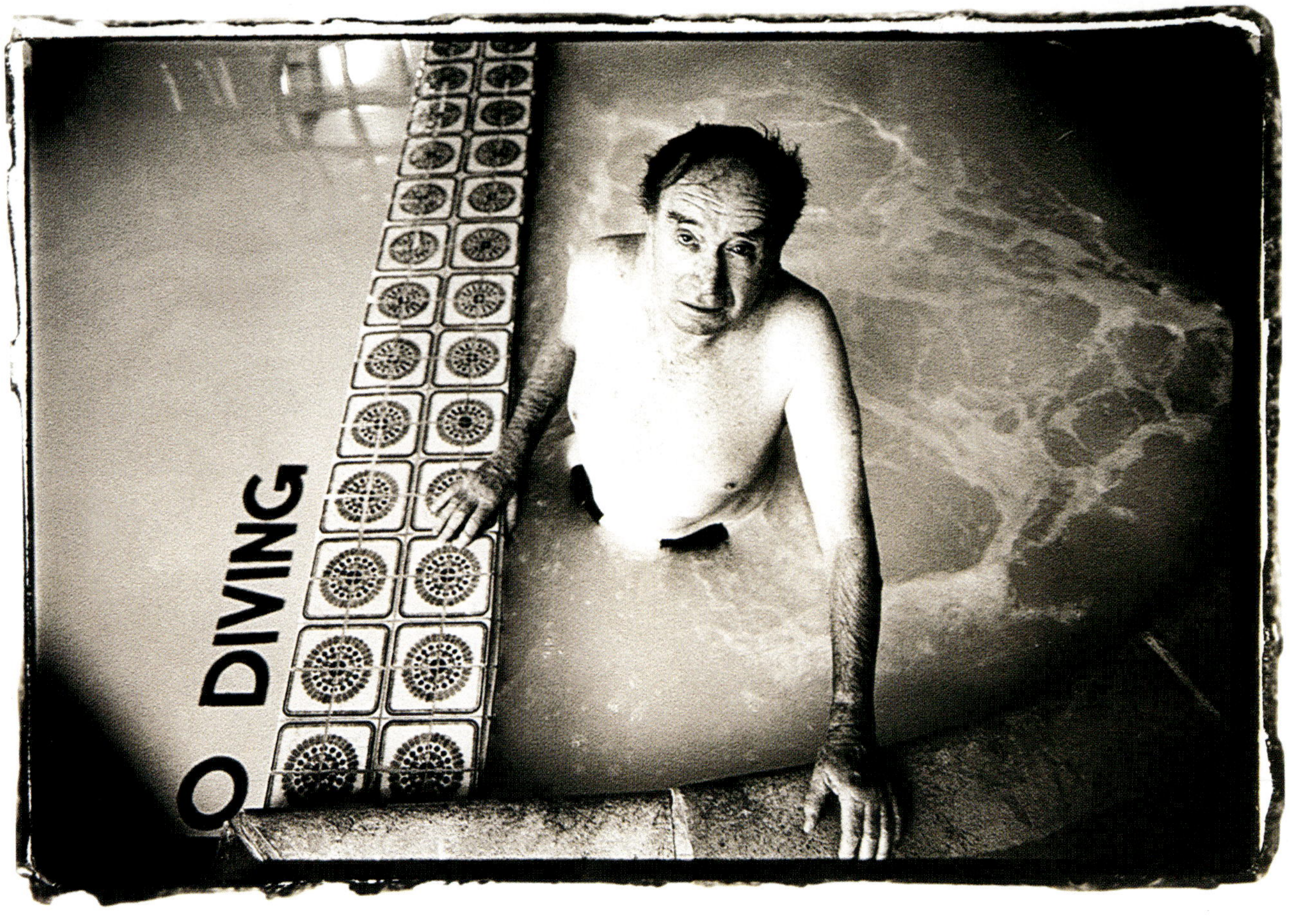

André Souroujon

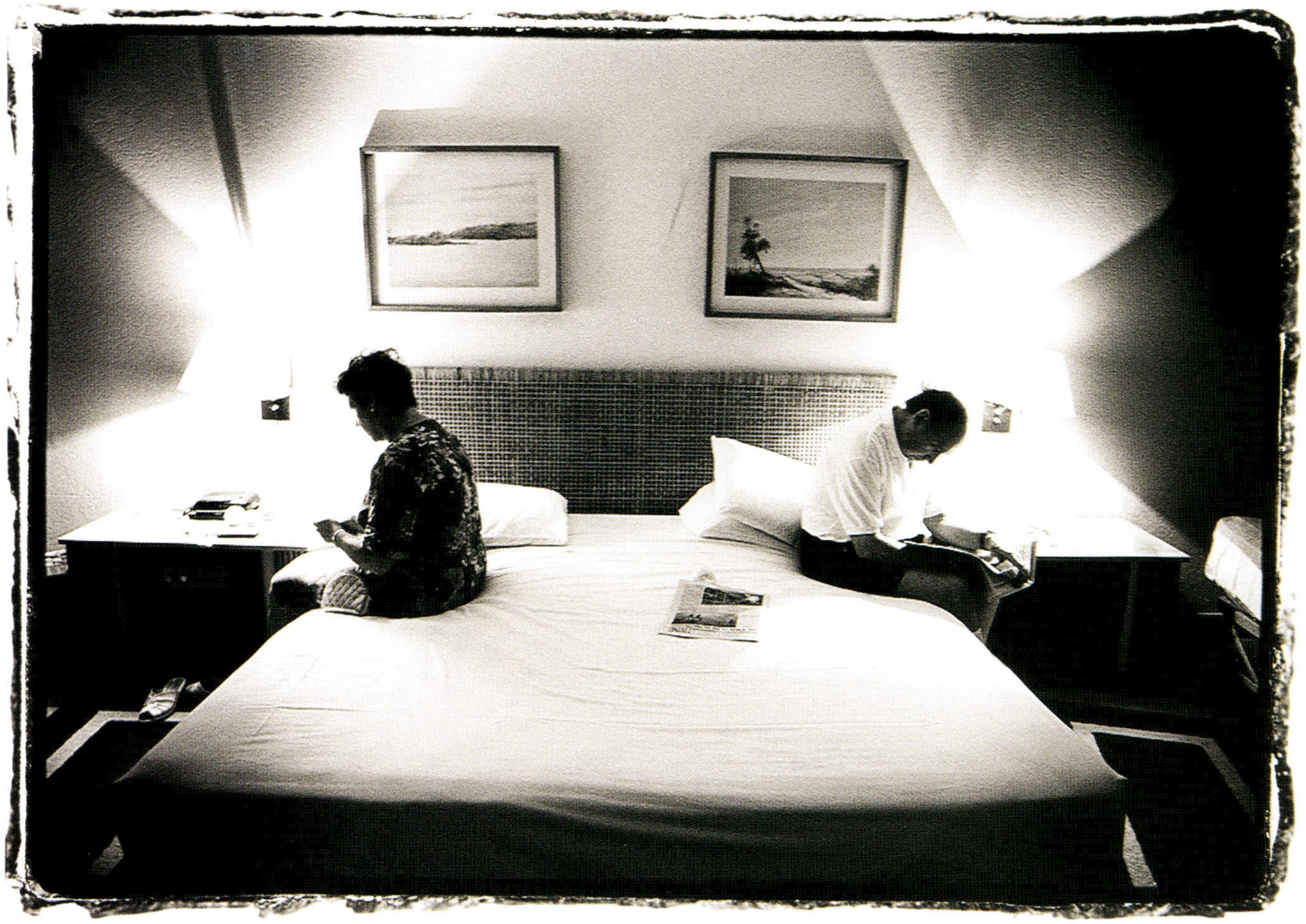

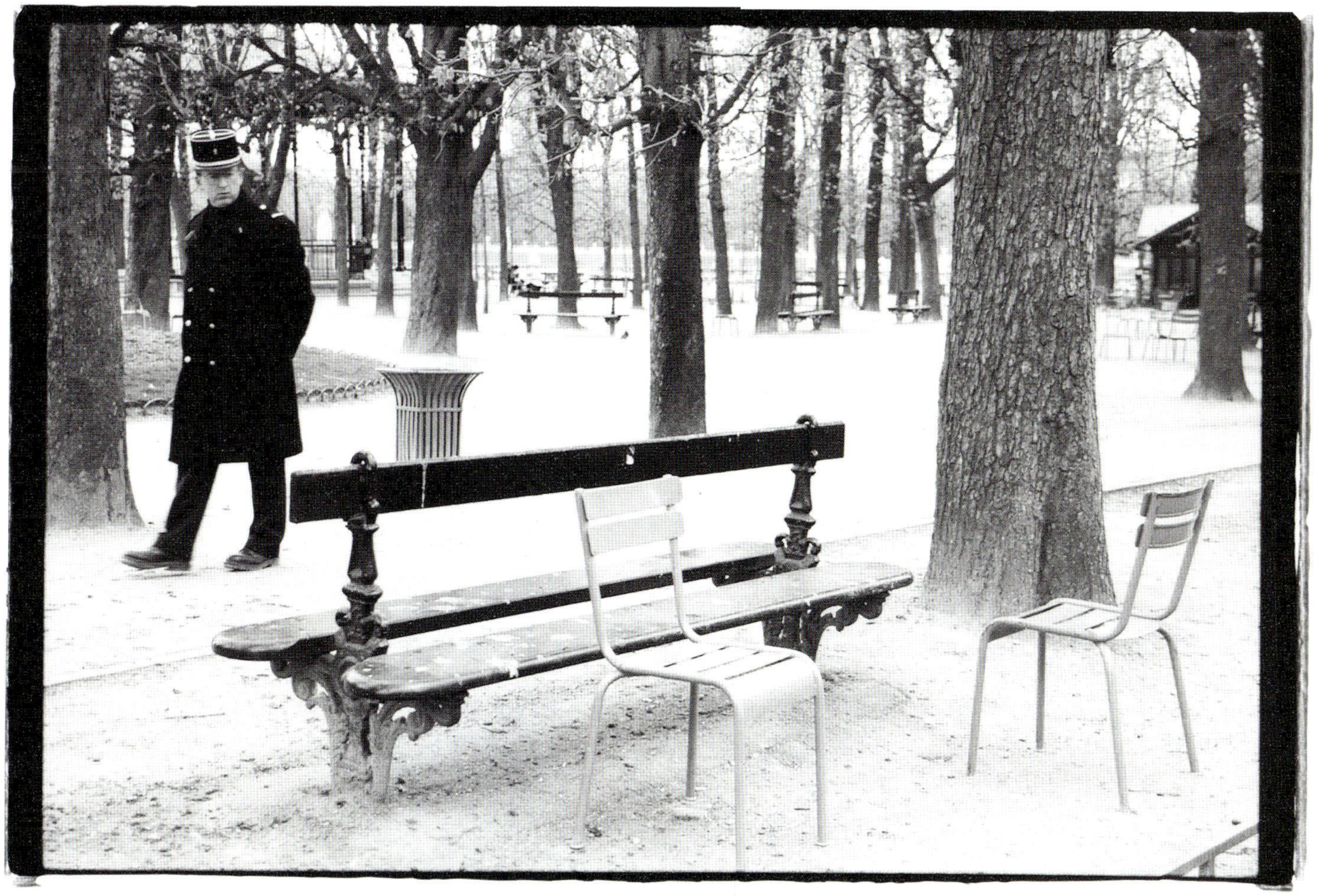

(TOP) *André Souroujon* ■ (BOTTOM) *Edie Pereira*

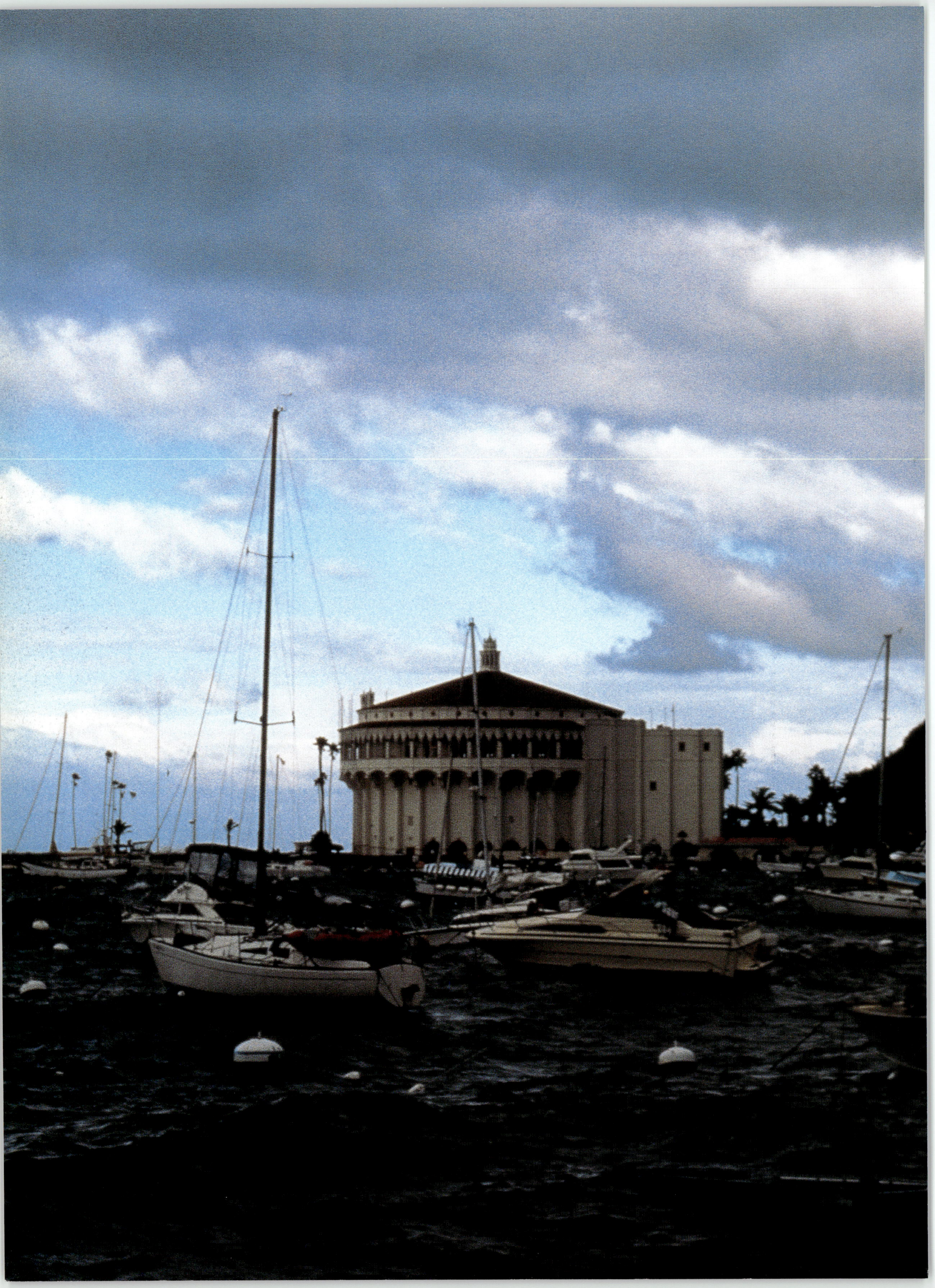

LANDSCAPES

LANDSCHAFTEN

PAYSAGES

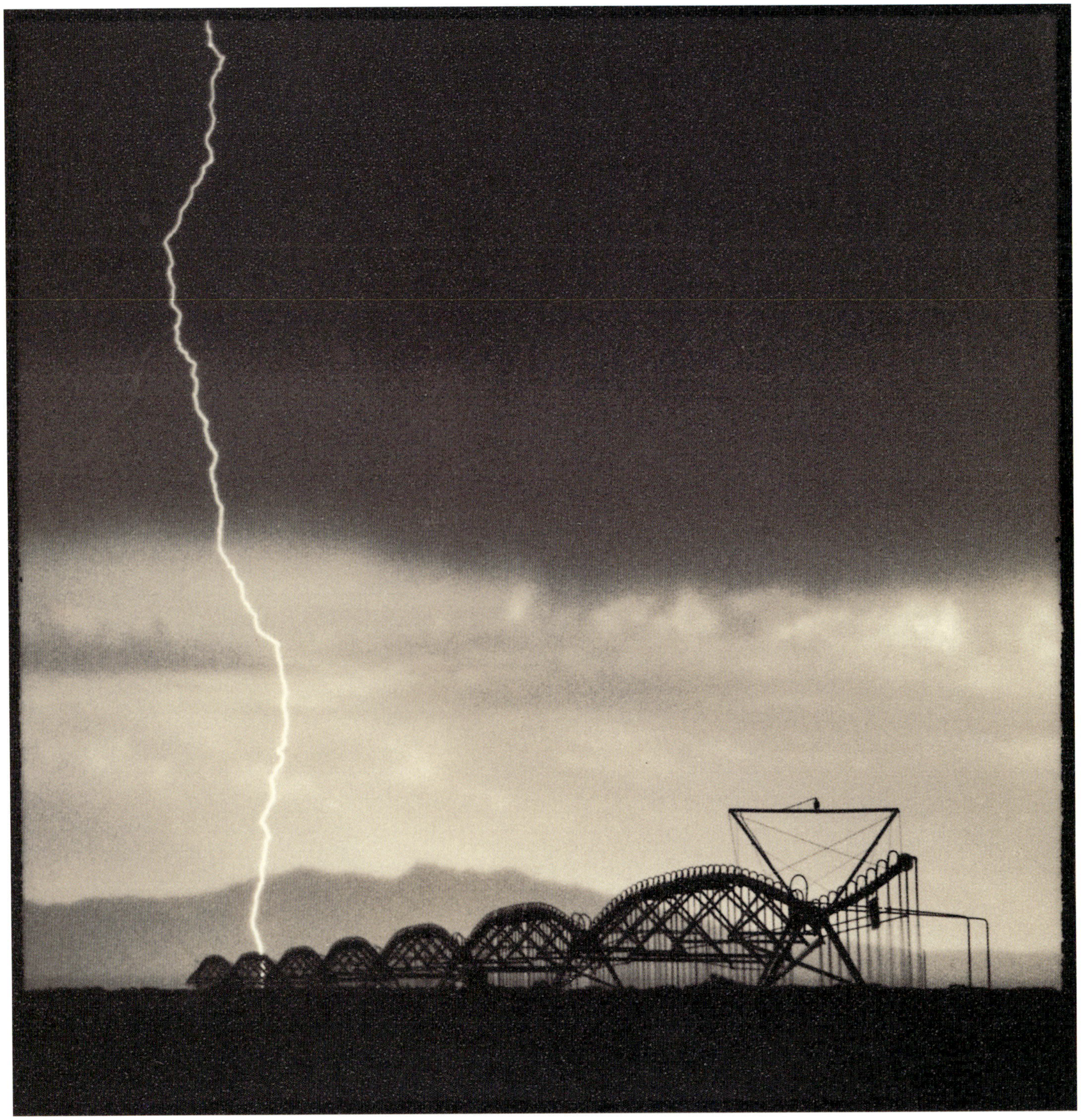

(PREVIOUS SPREAD) *William M. Mercadante* ■ (THIS PAGE) *Paul Kozal*

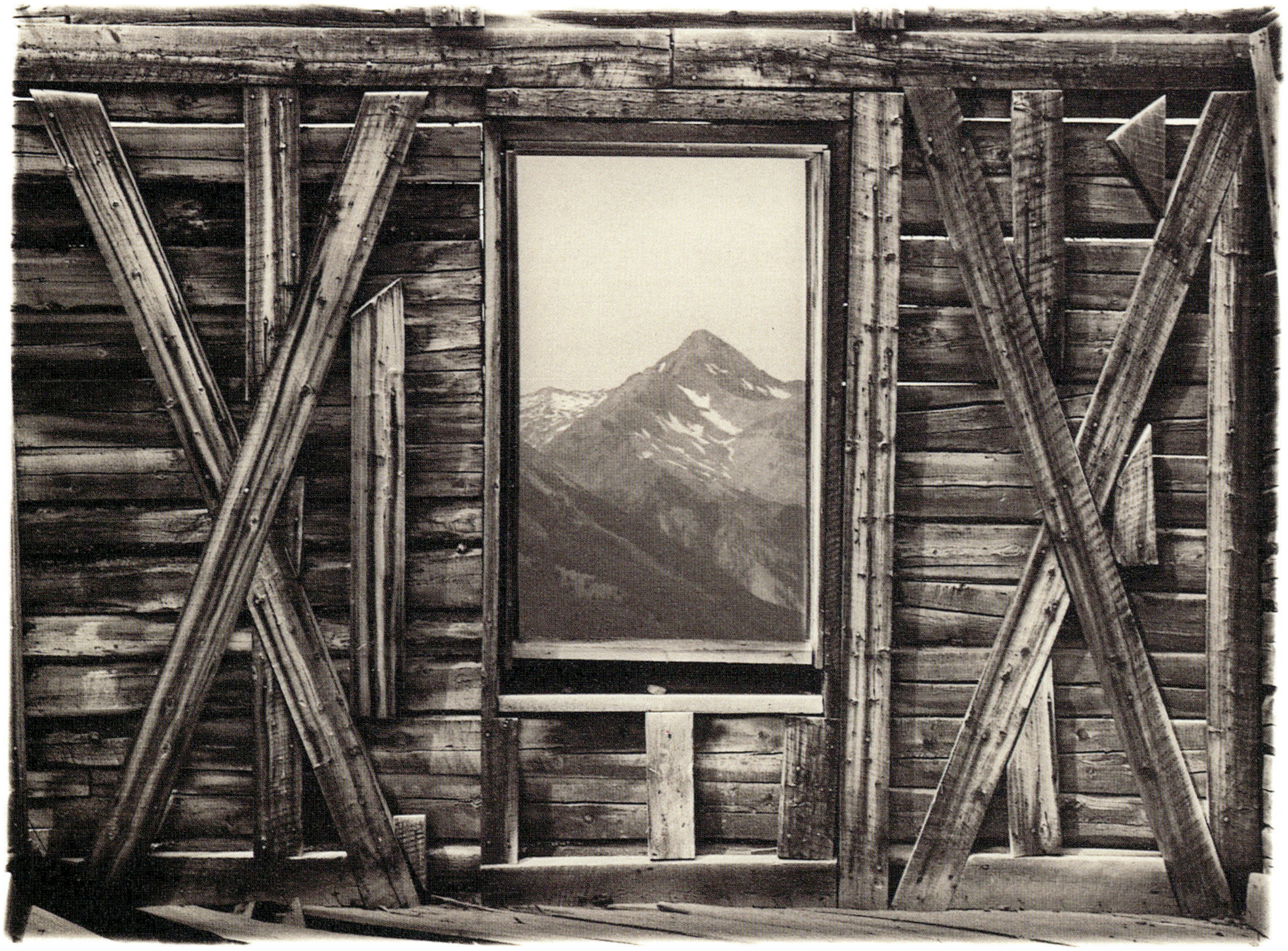

Paul Kozal

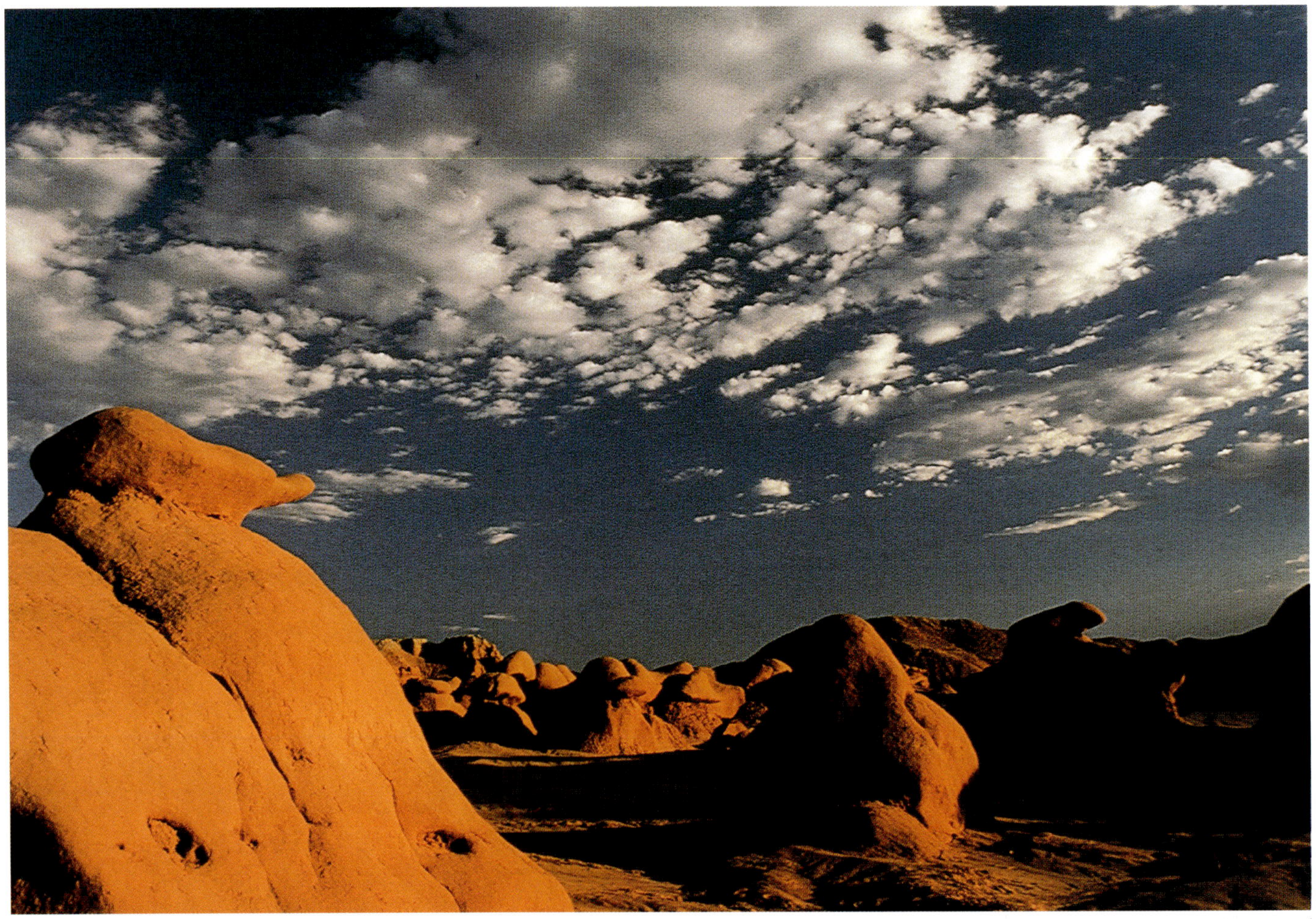

Ben Salvador

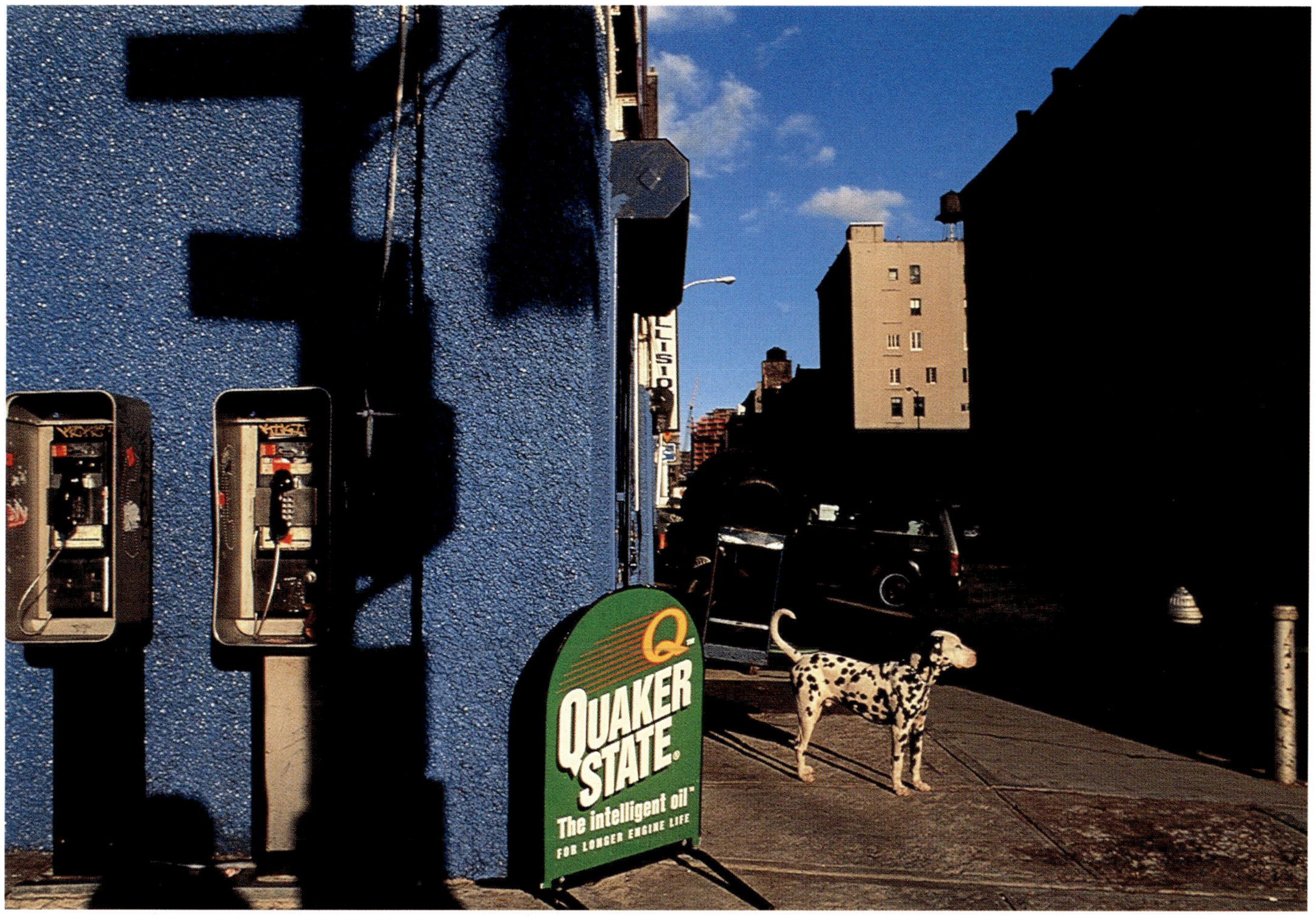

Susan Shamper

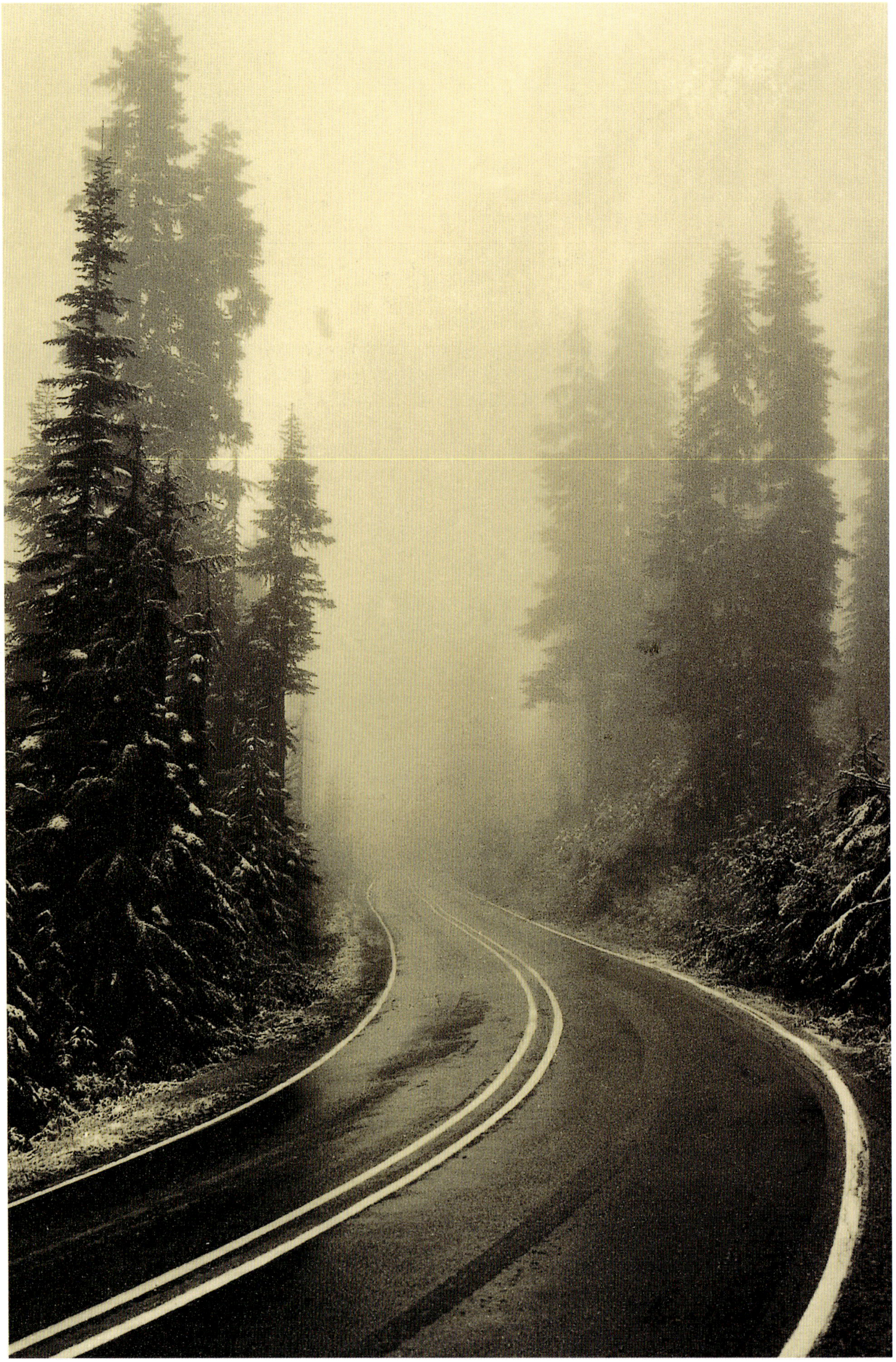

Paul Kozal

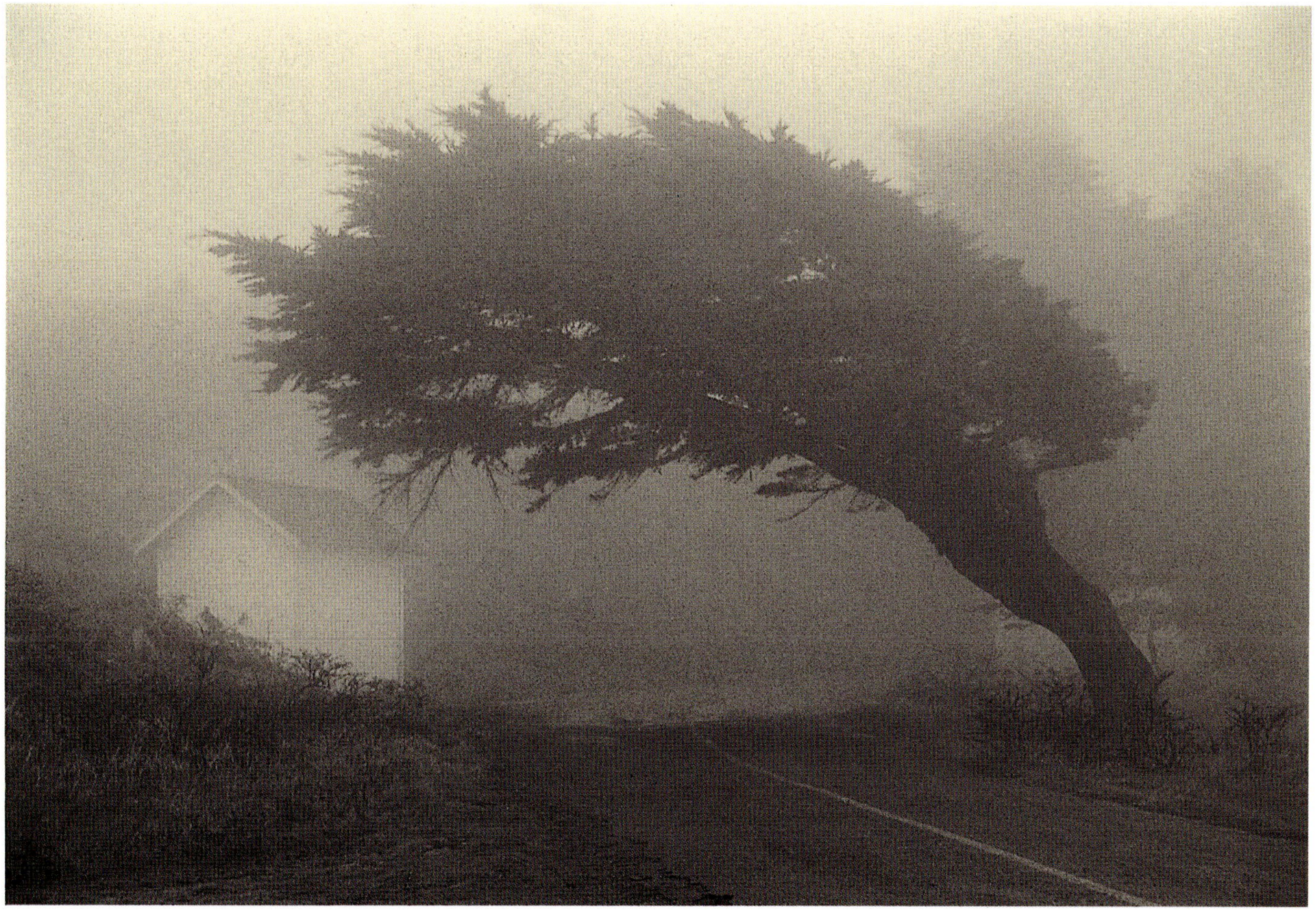

Paul Kozal

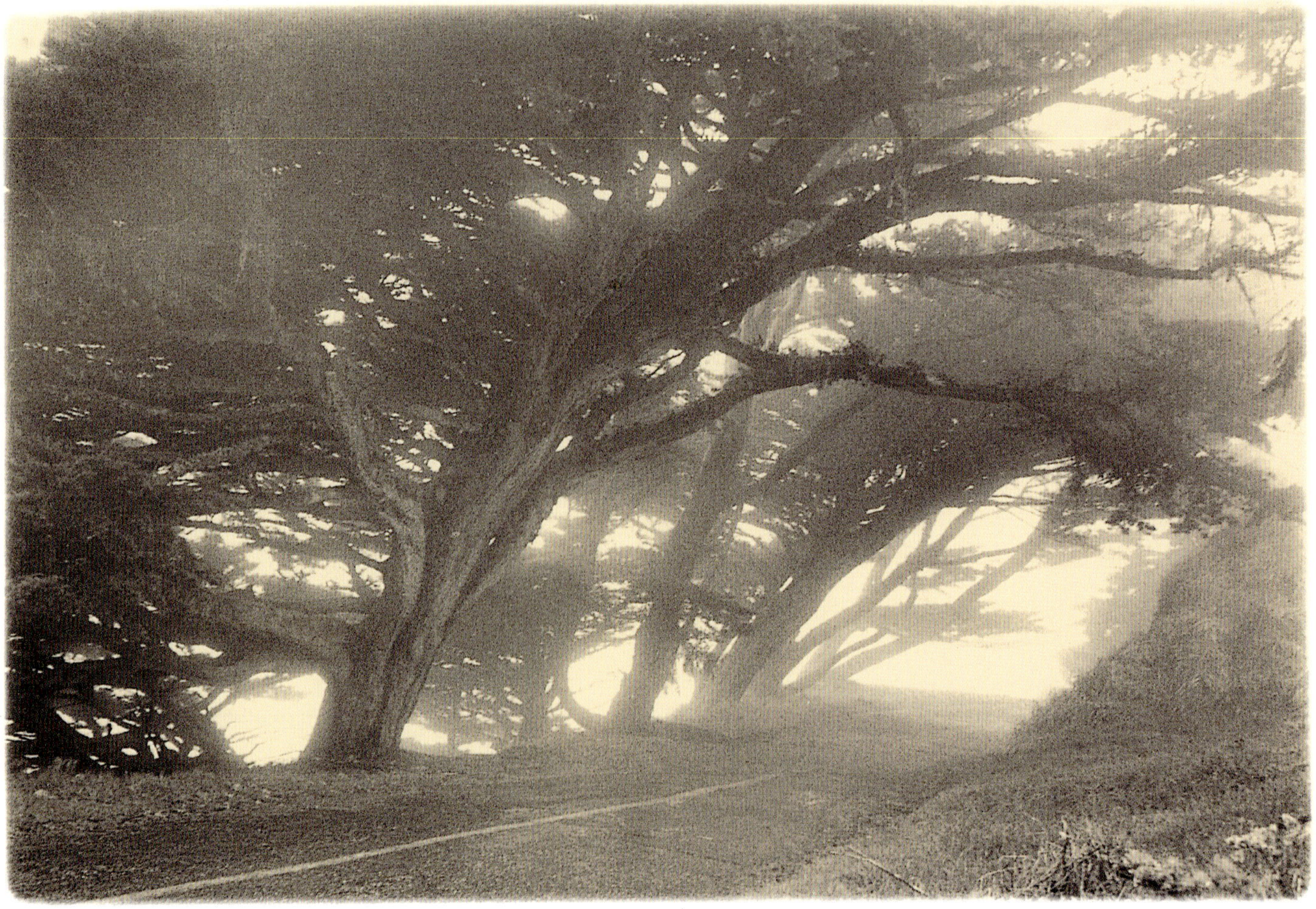

Paul Kozal

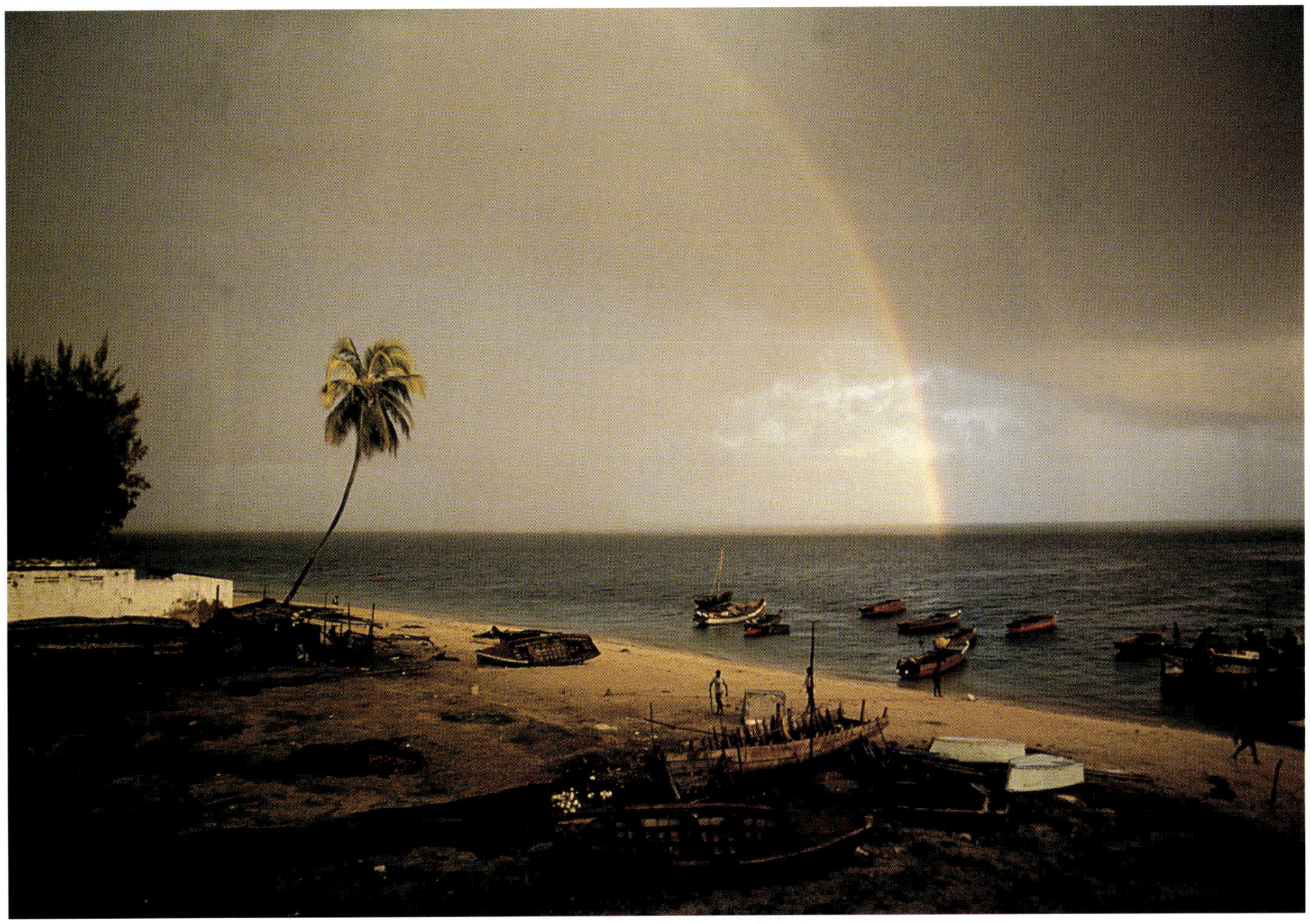

Patricia A. Jordan

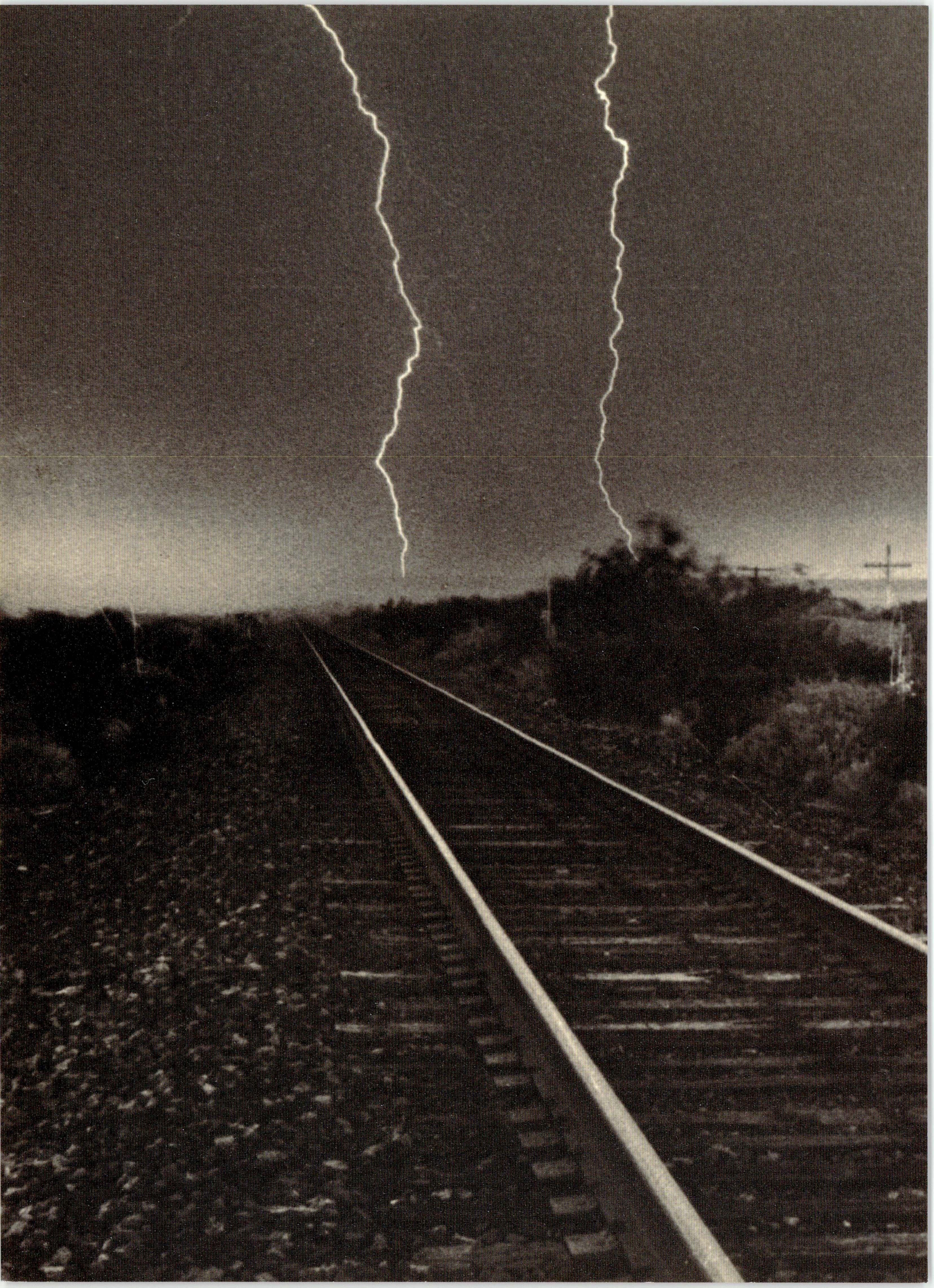

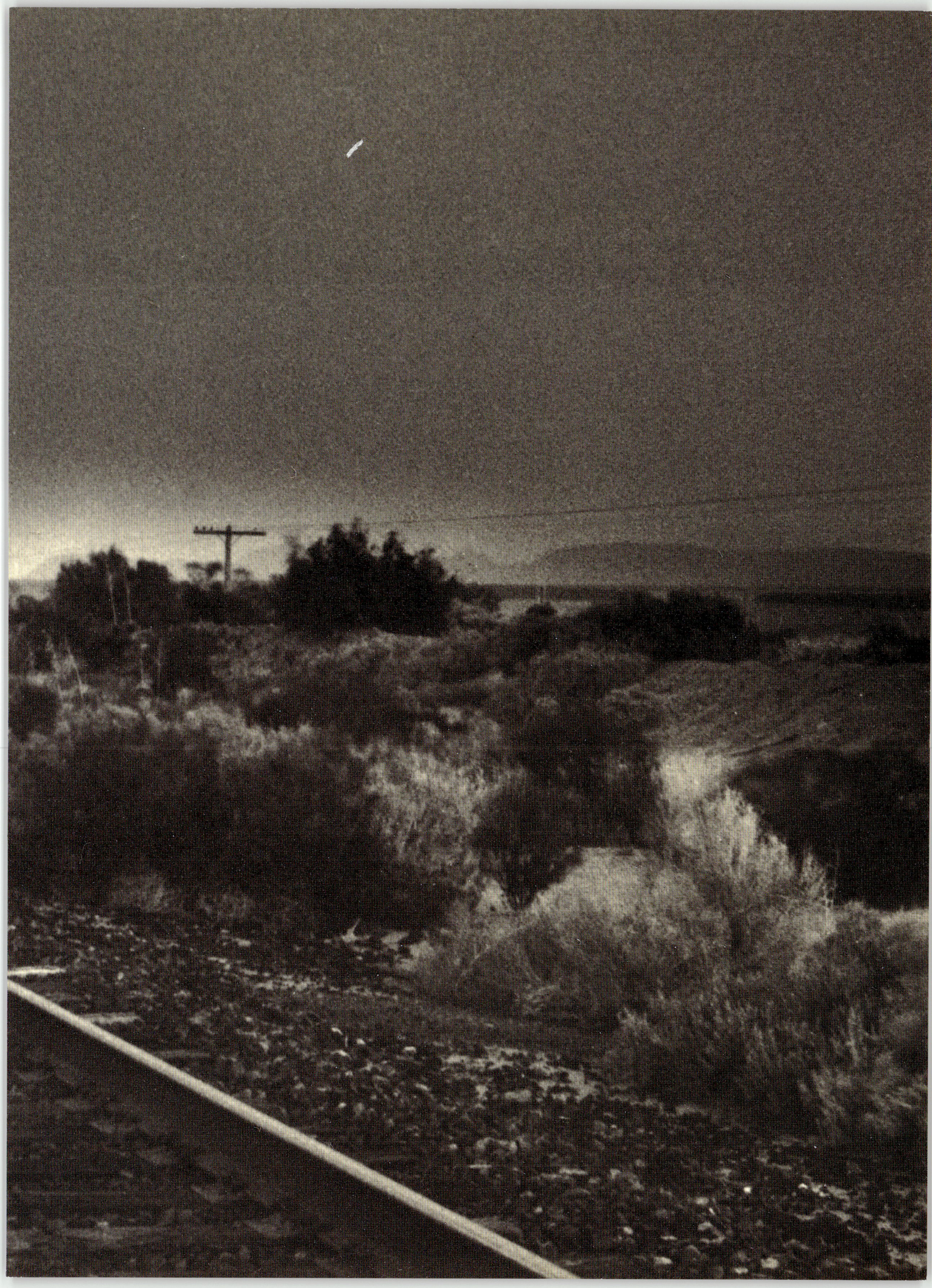

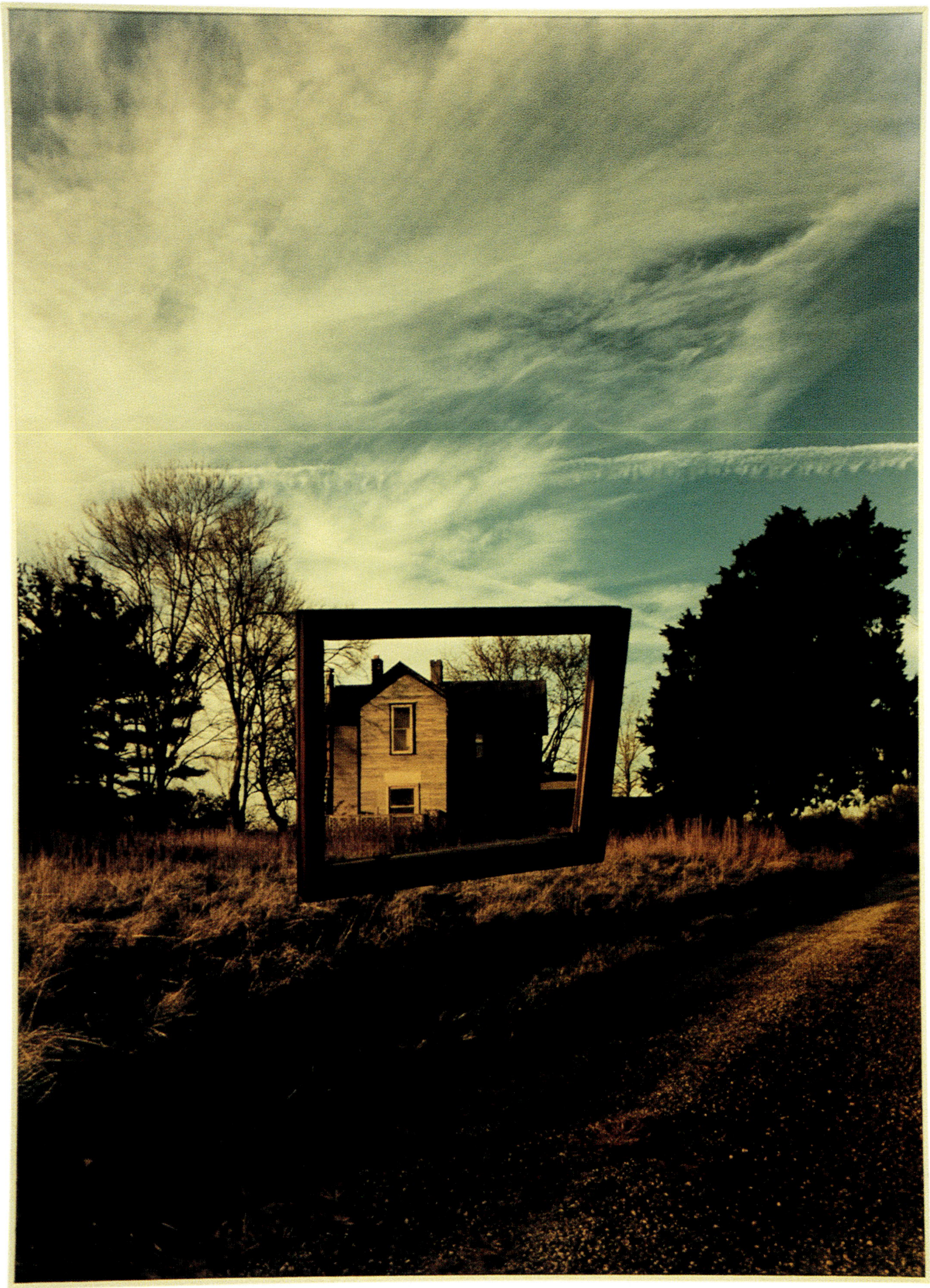

(PREVIOUS SPREAD) *Paul Kozal* ■ (THIS PAGE) *Brian David Hite*

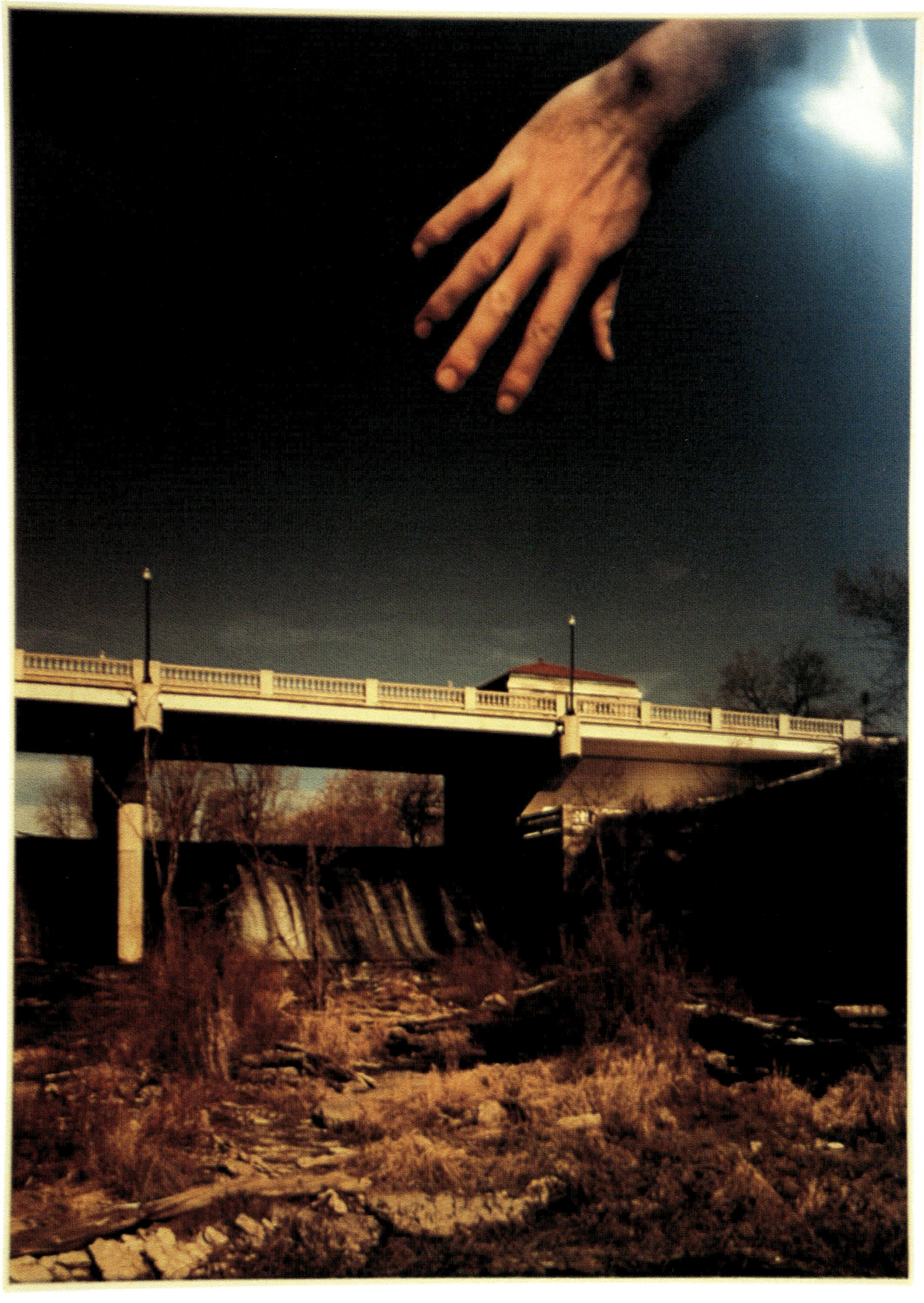

Brian David Hite

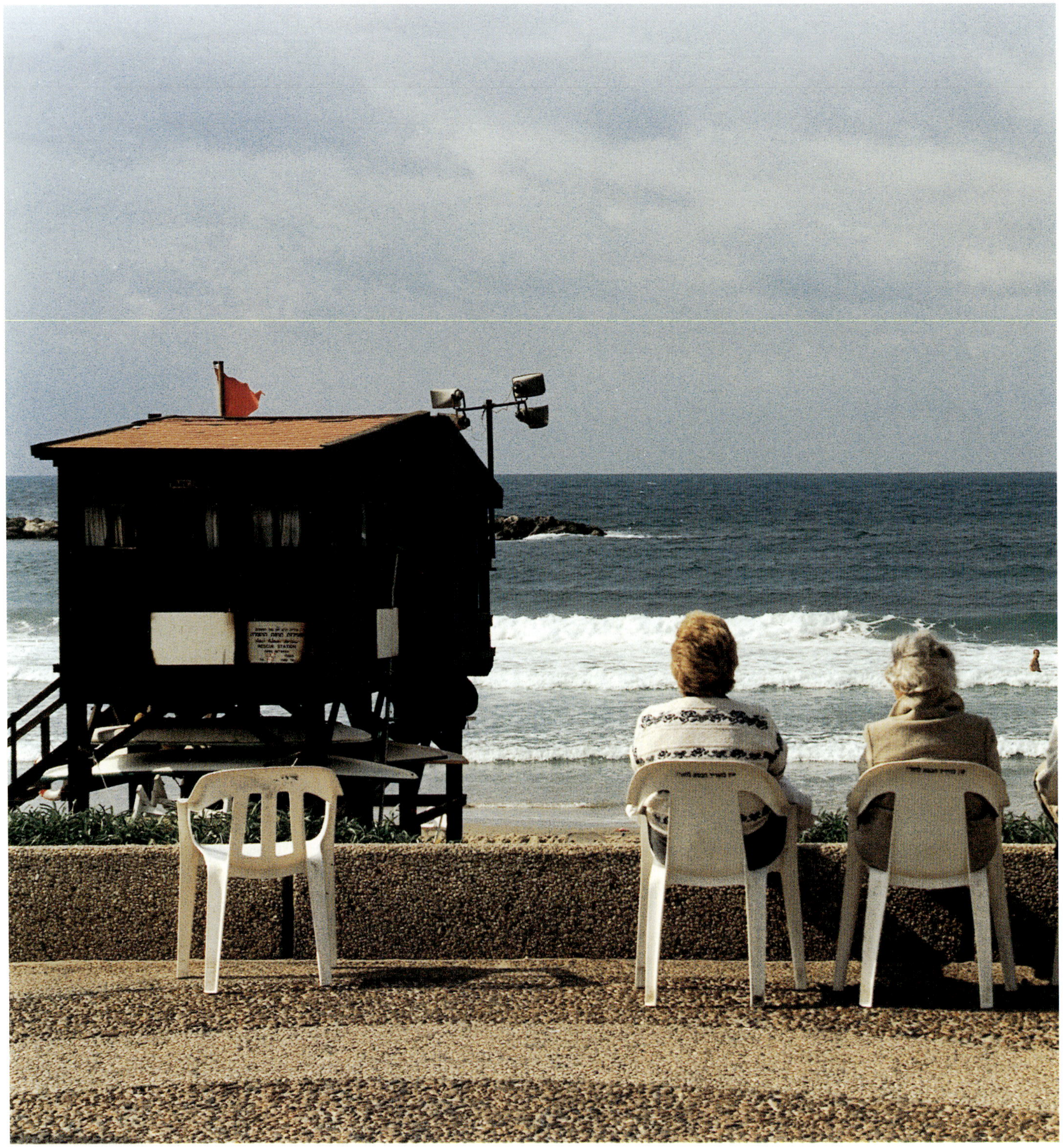

Joshua Even

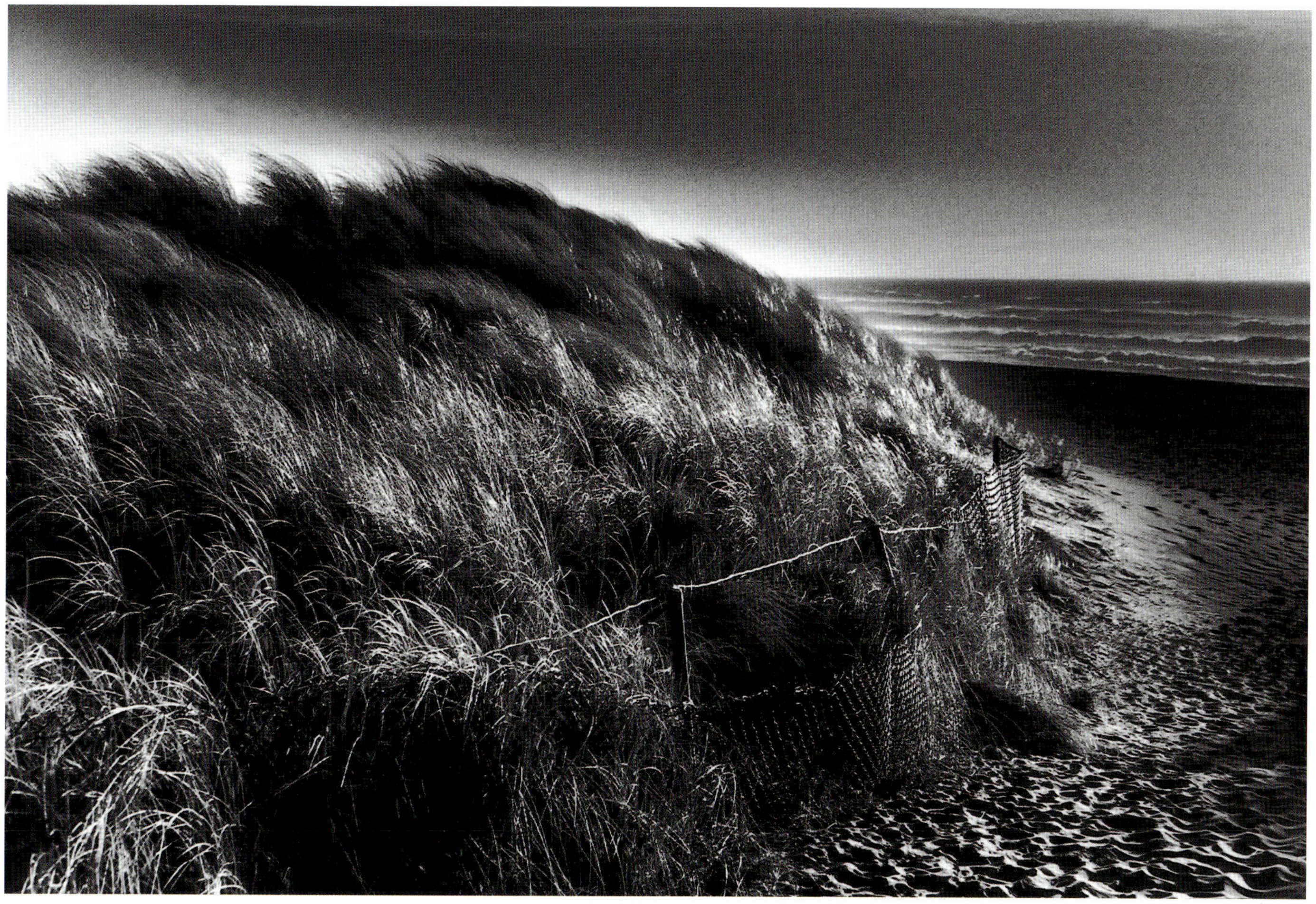

Aaron Landman

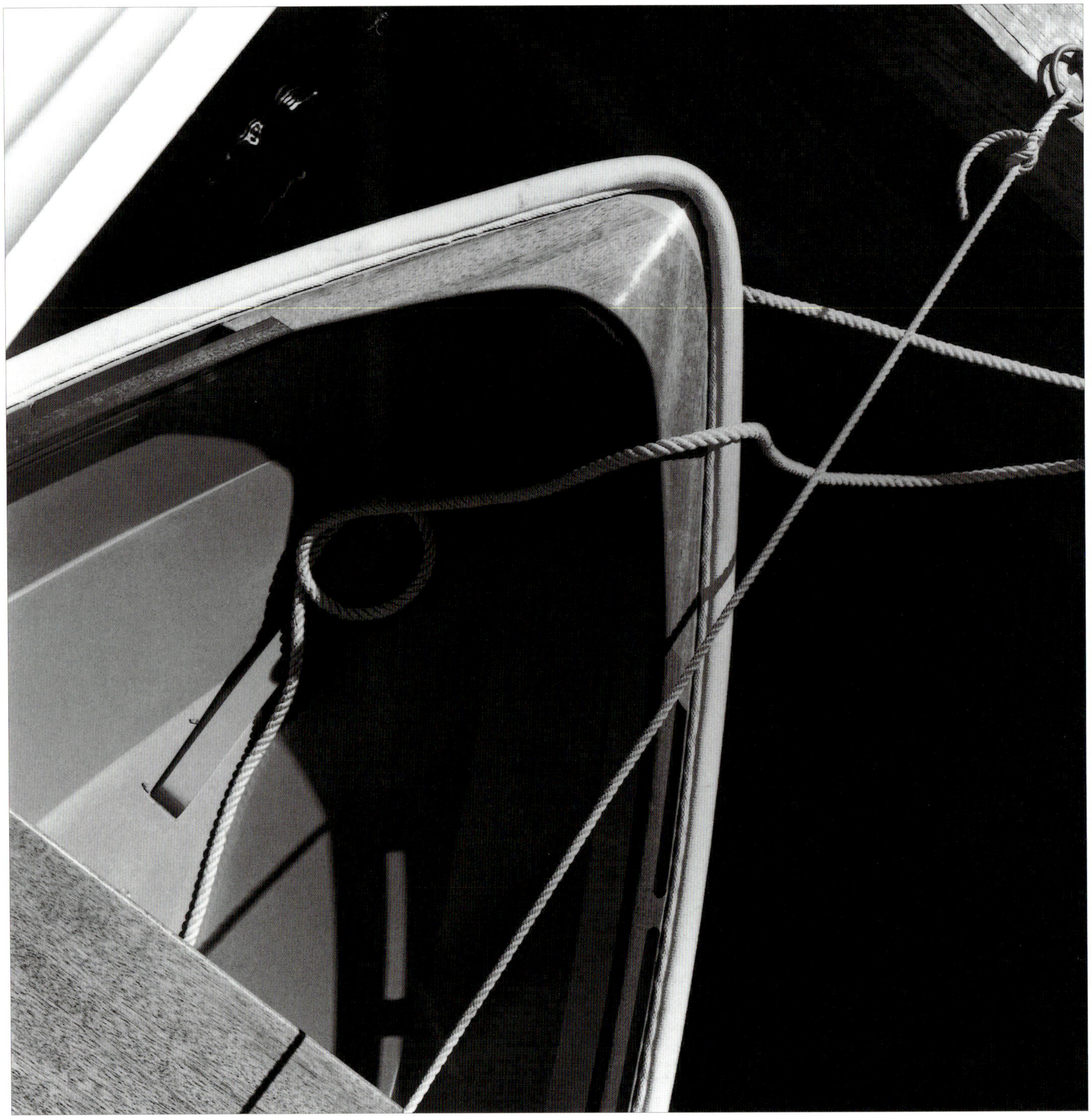

David Parker

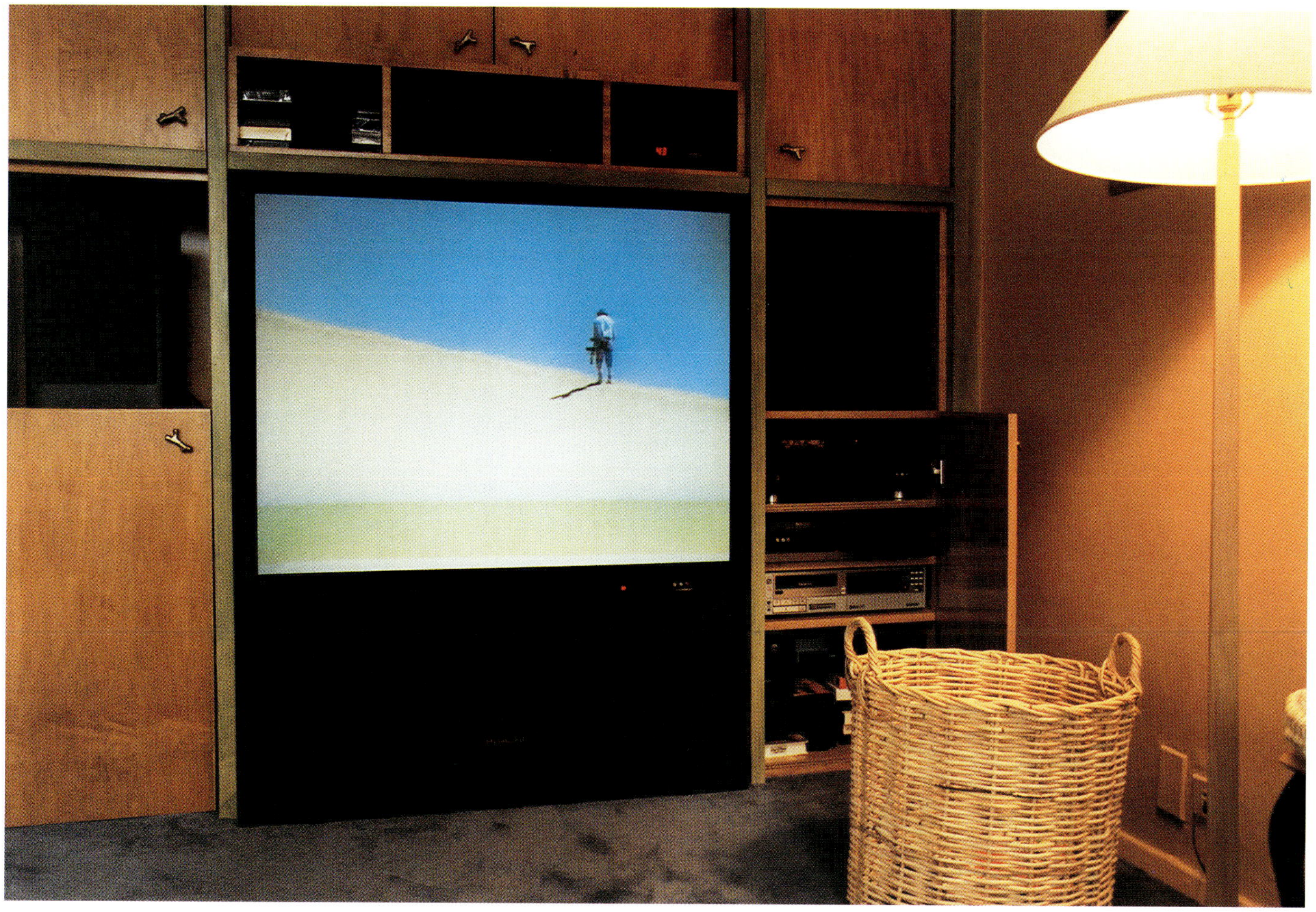

Joan Kane

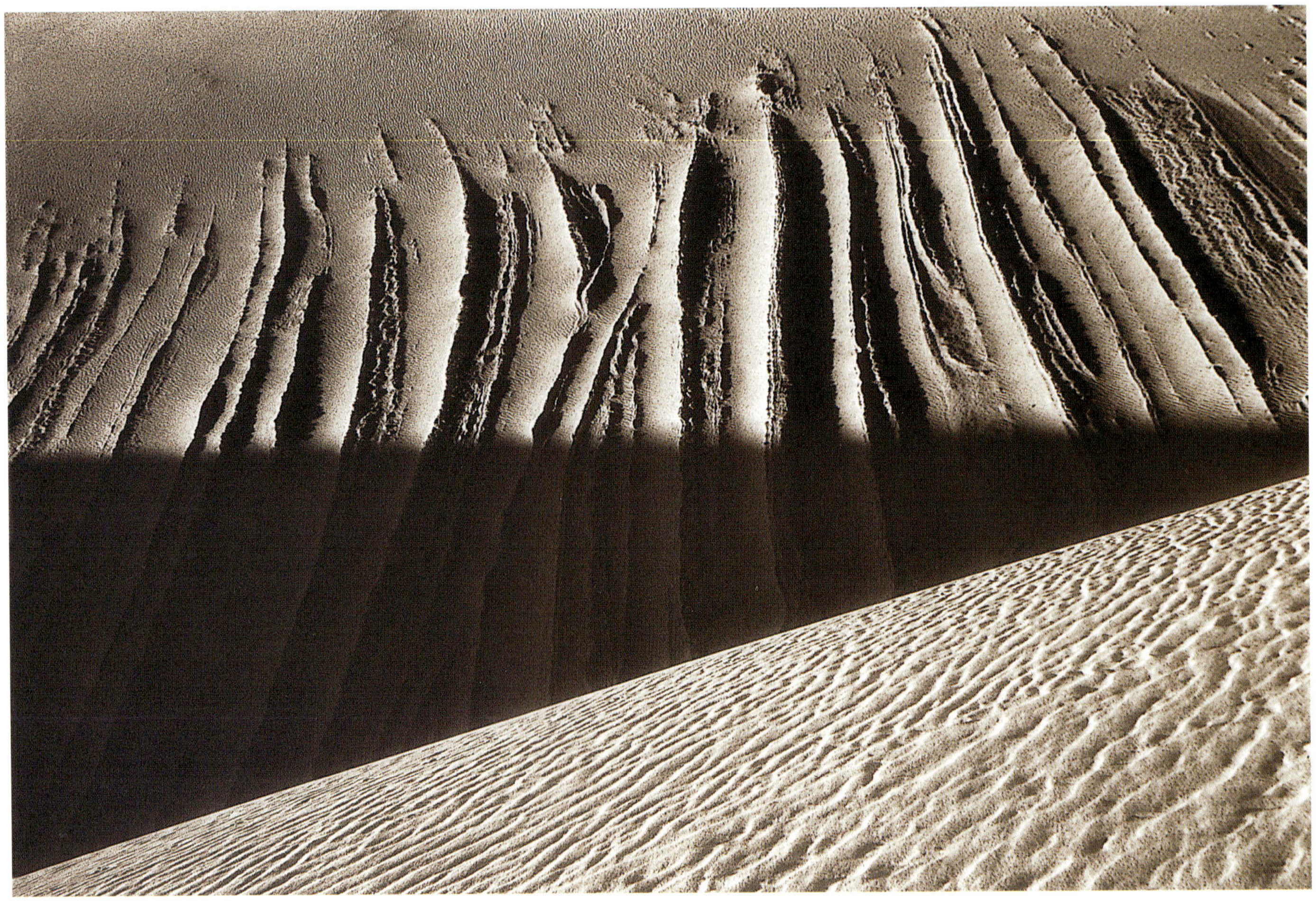

Paul Kozal

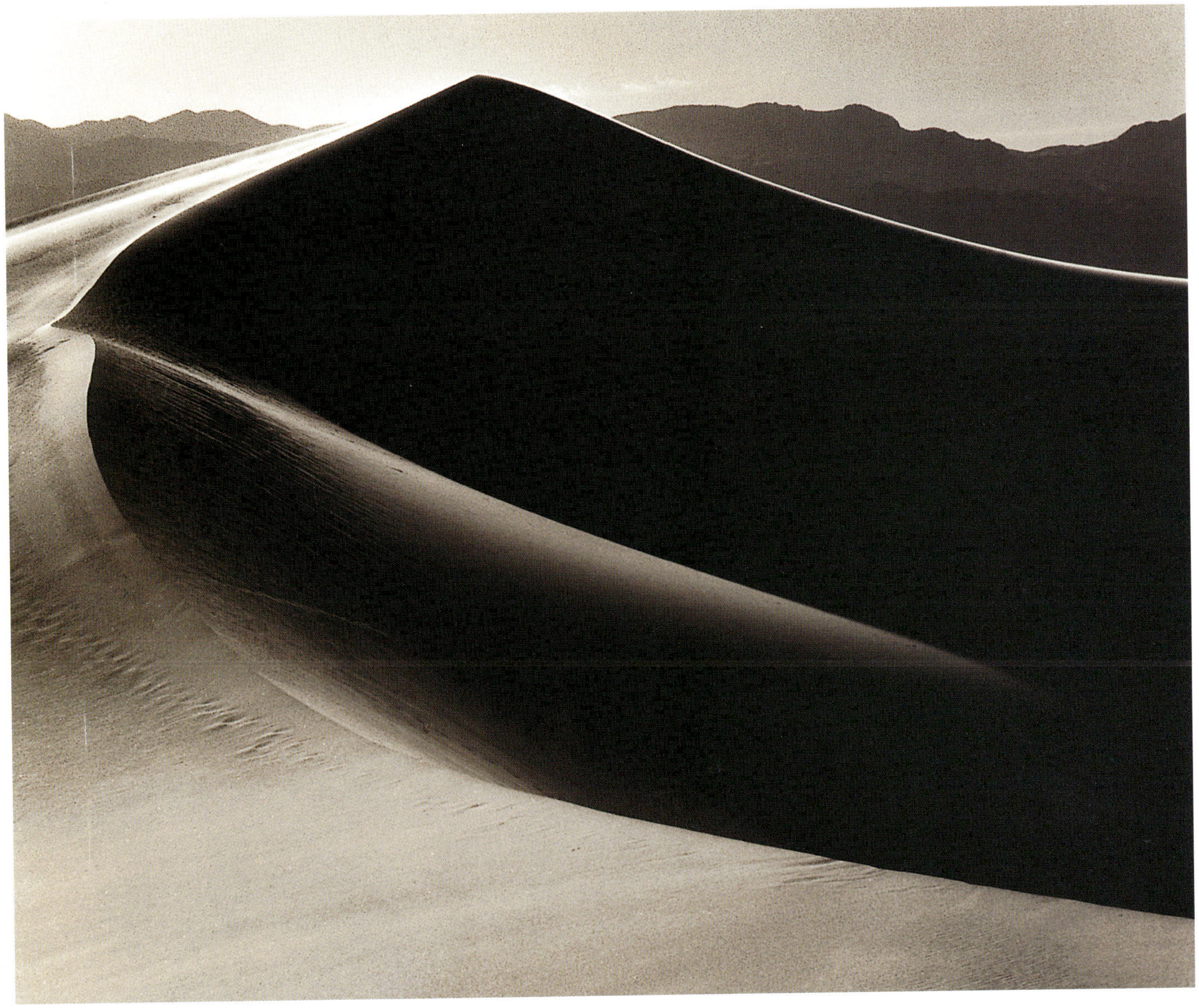

Paul Kozal

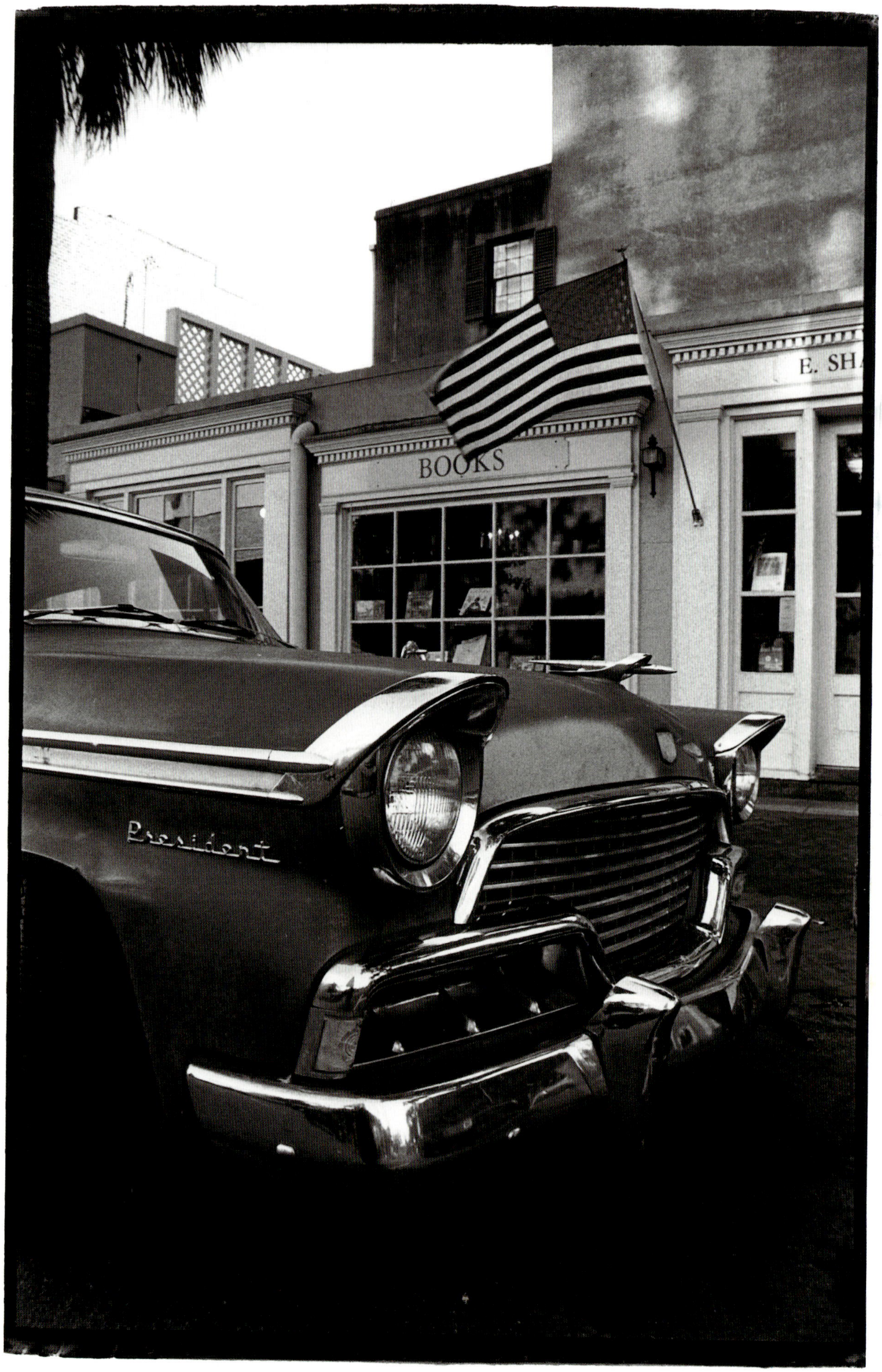

Richard Langone

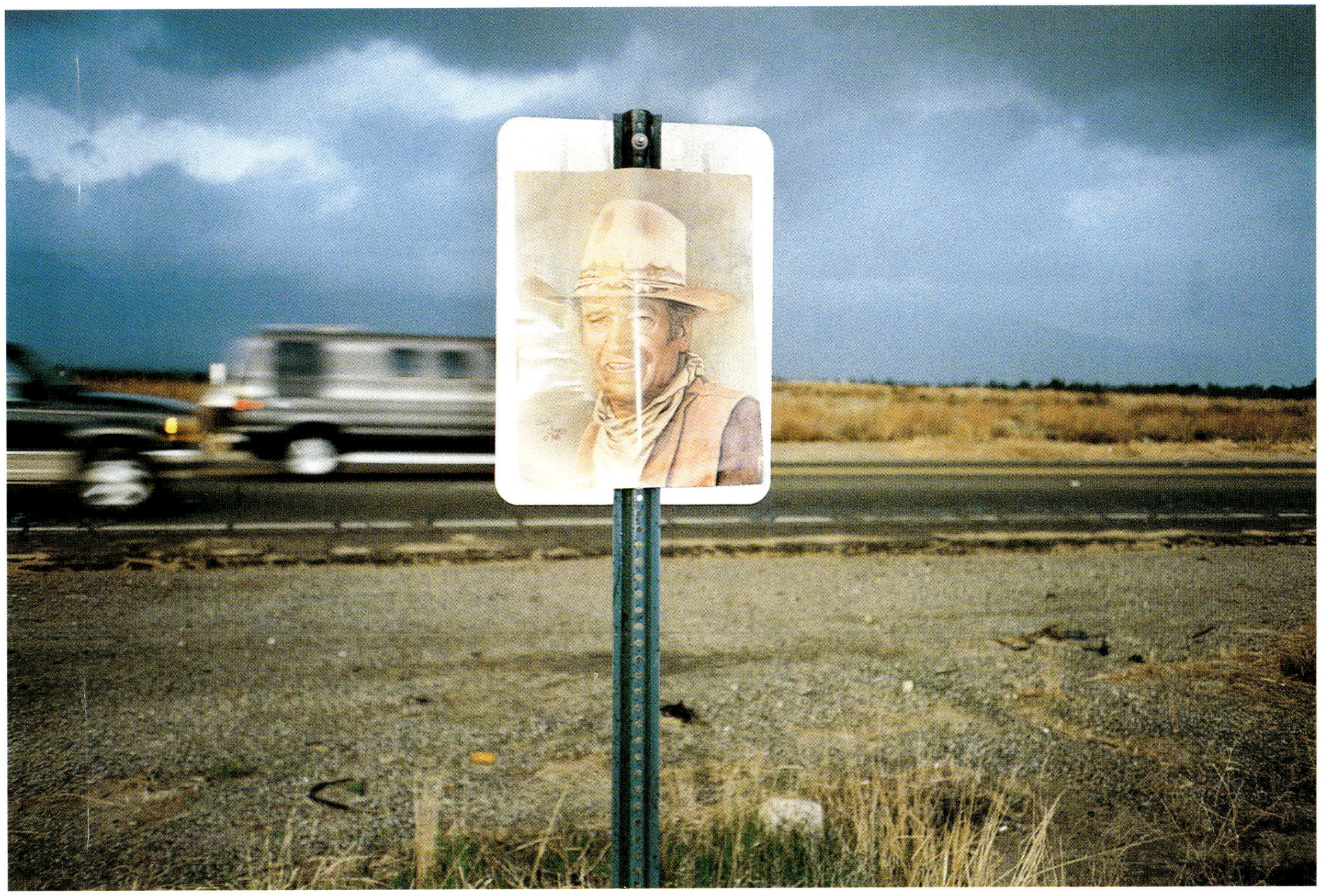

Robert Oliverio

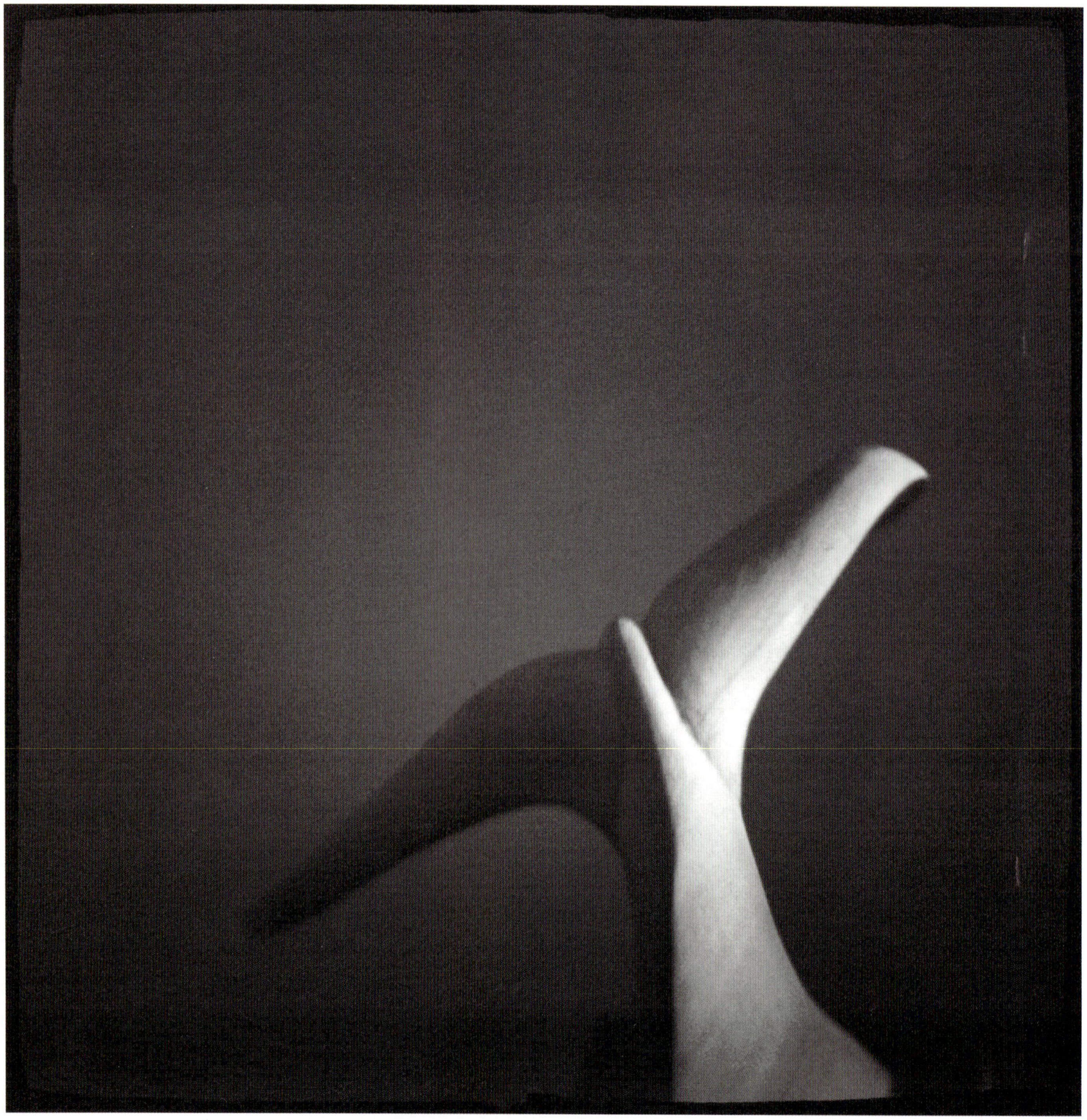

Jason Costanzo

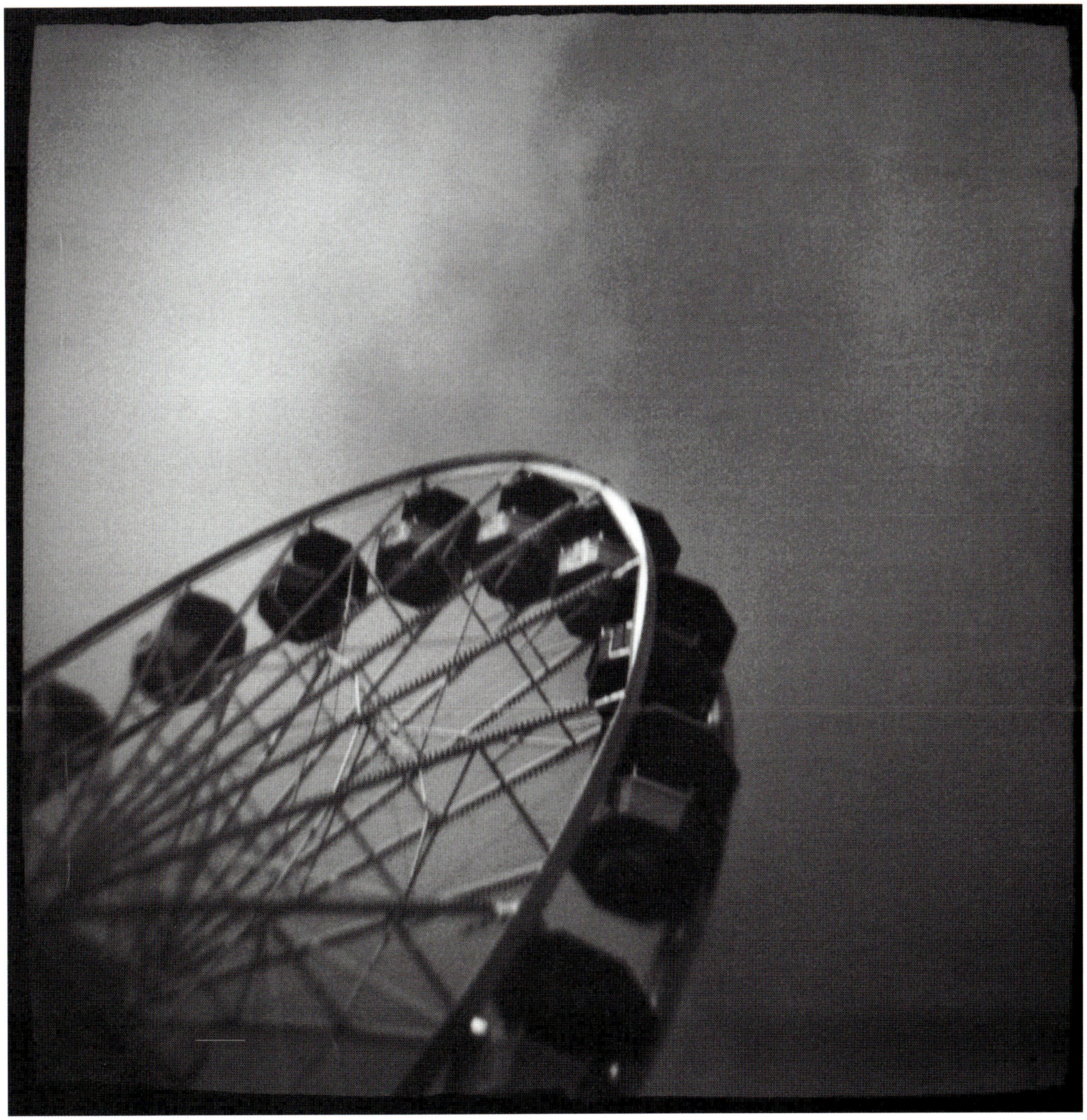

Jason Costanzo

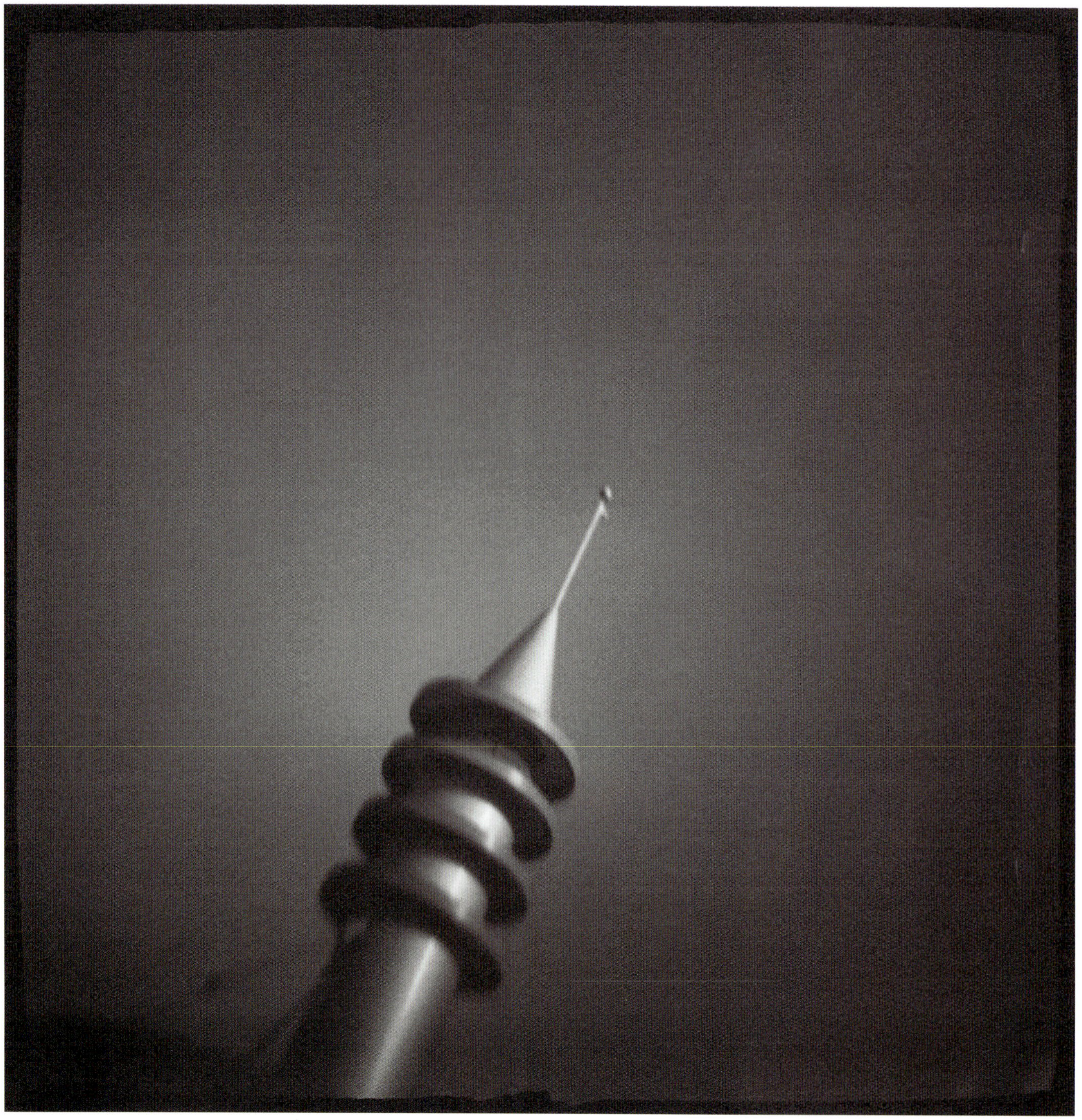

Jason Costanzo

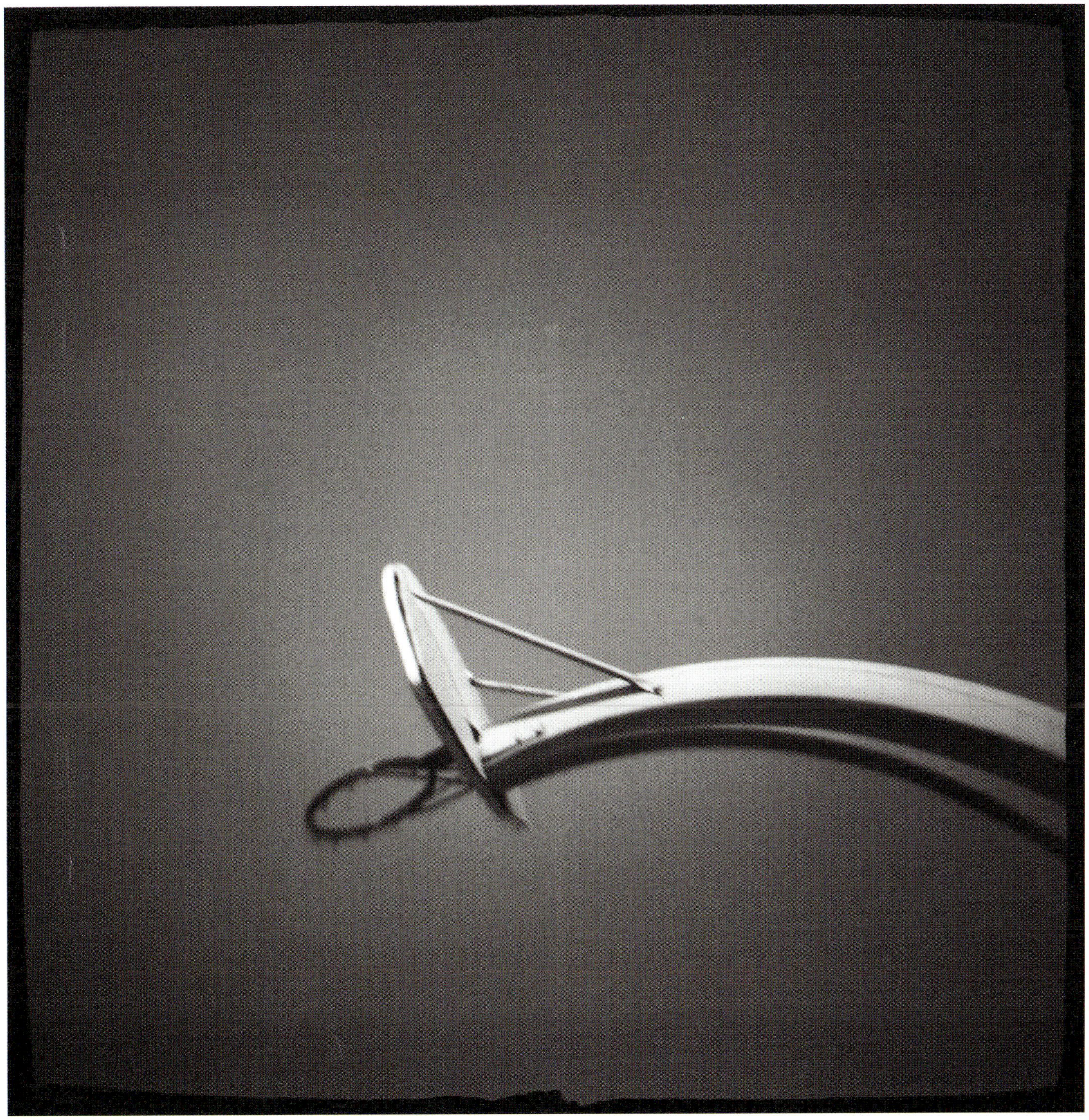

Jason Costanzo

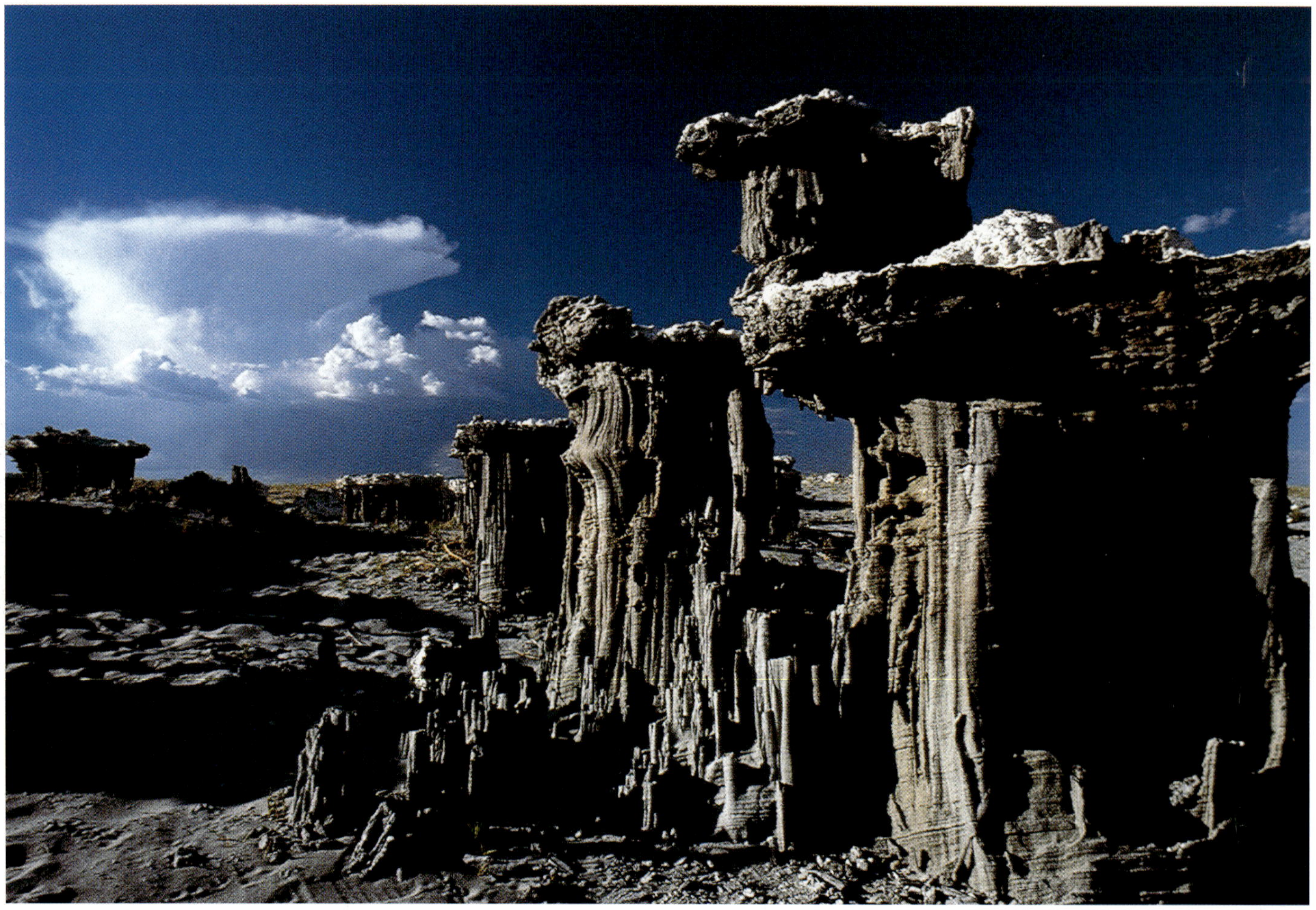

Ben Salvador

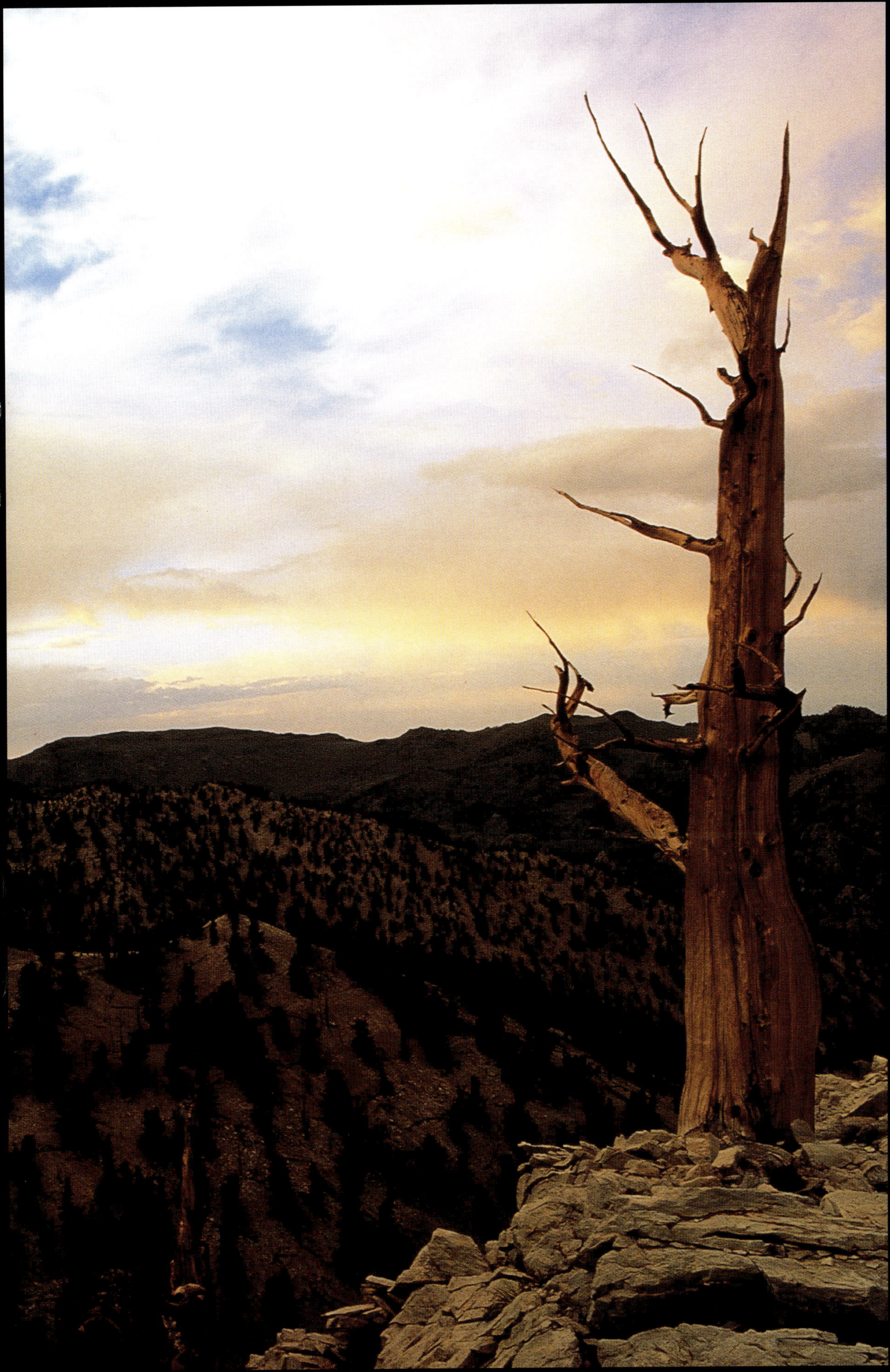

Voytek Otok

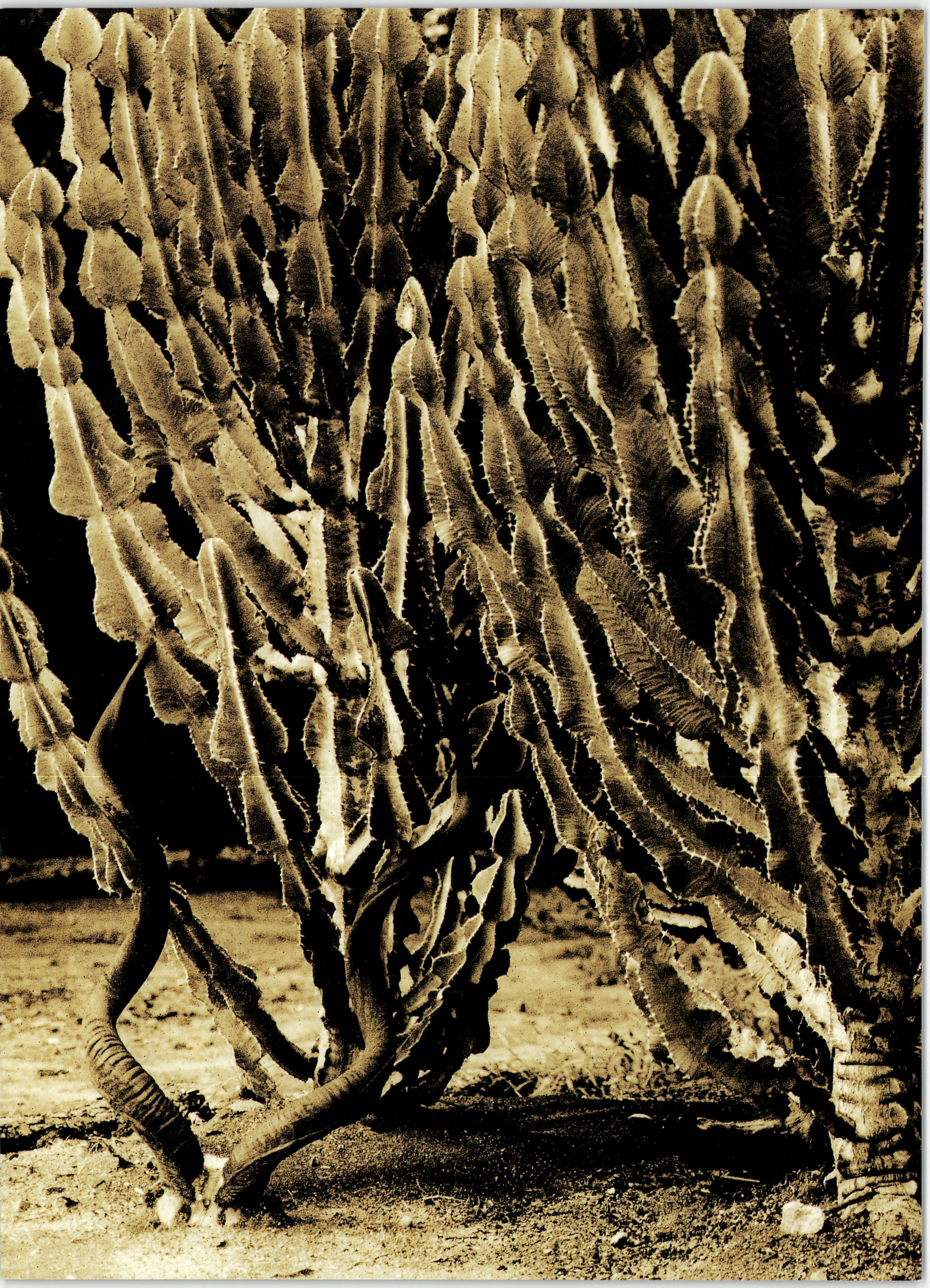

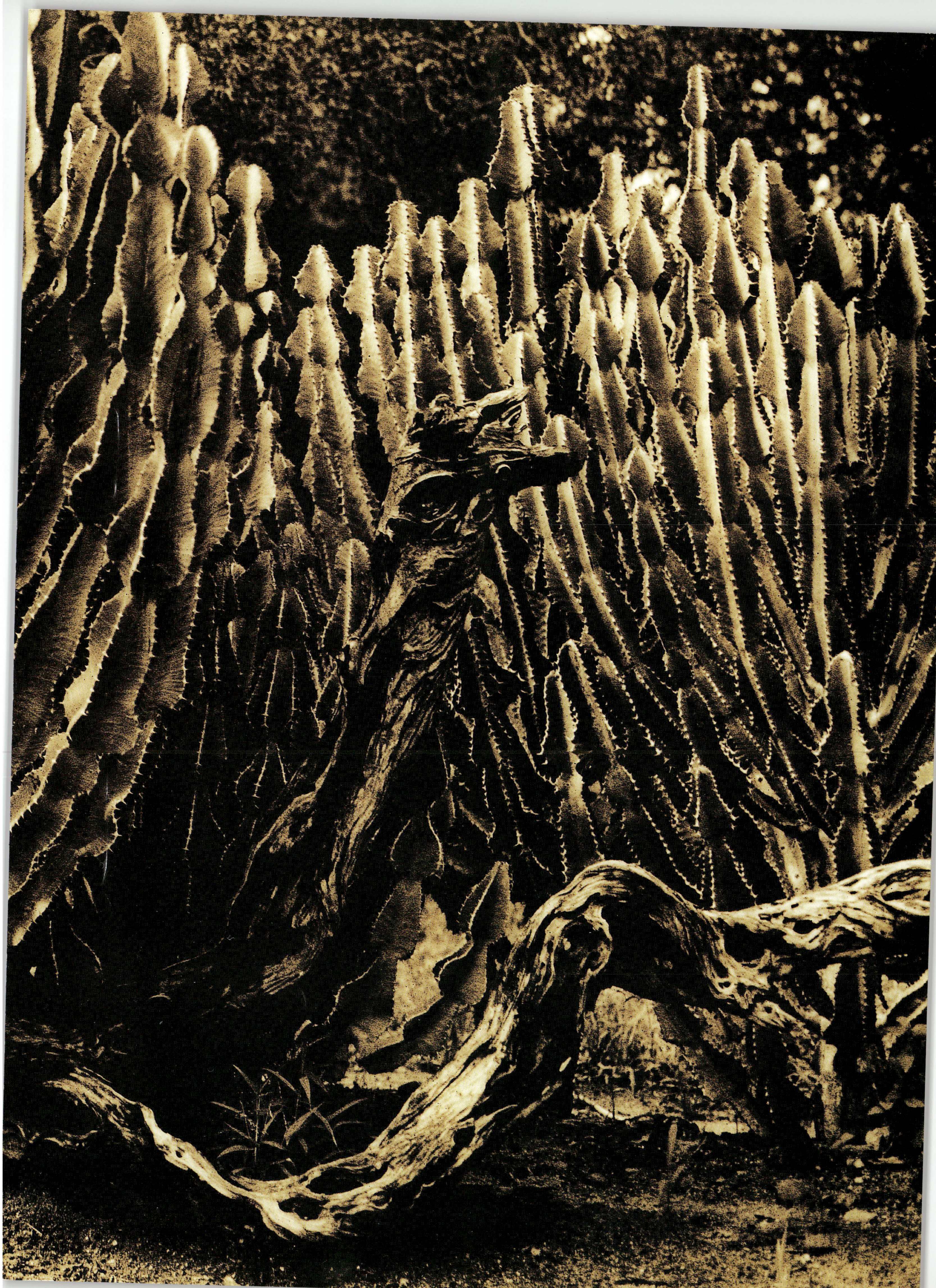

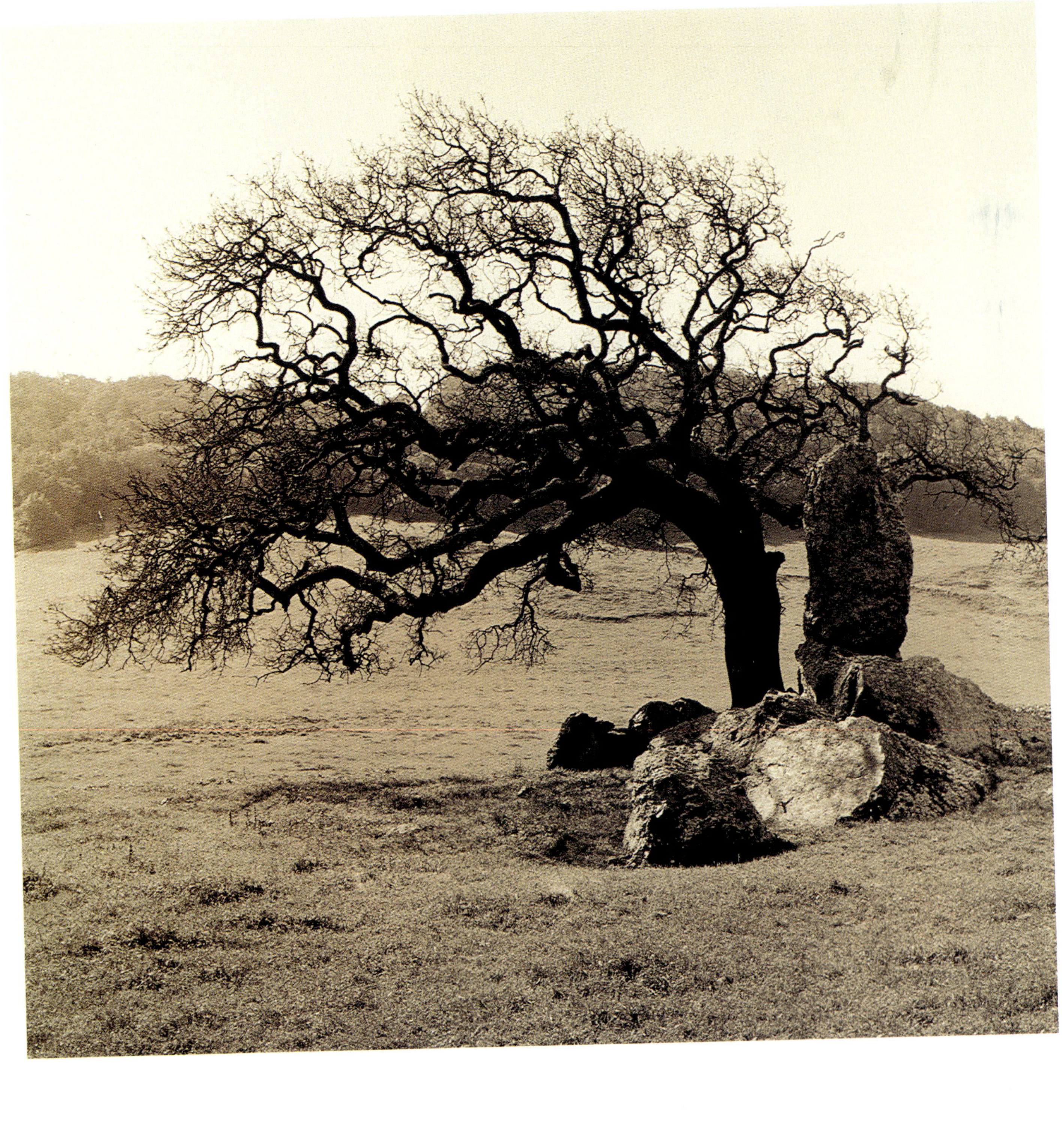

(PREVIOUS SPREAD) *Malinda Kilmer* ■ (THIS PAGE) *Darriel Caston*

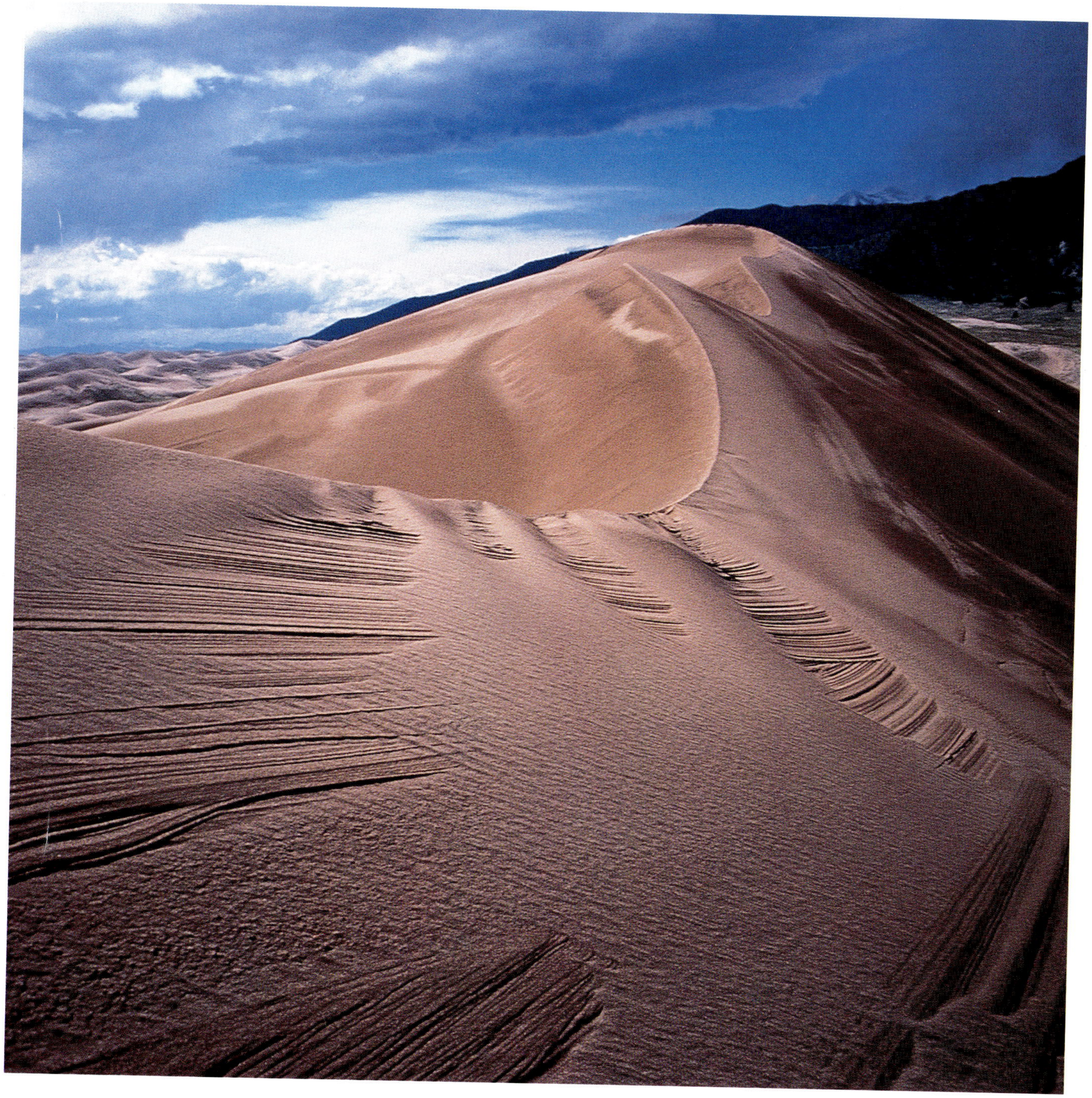

Ryan Skorecki

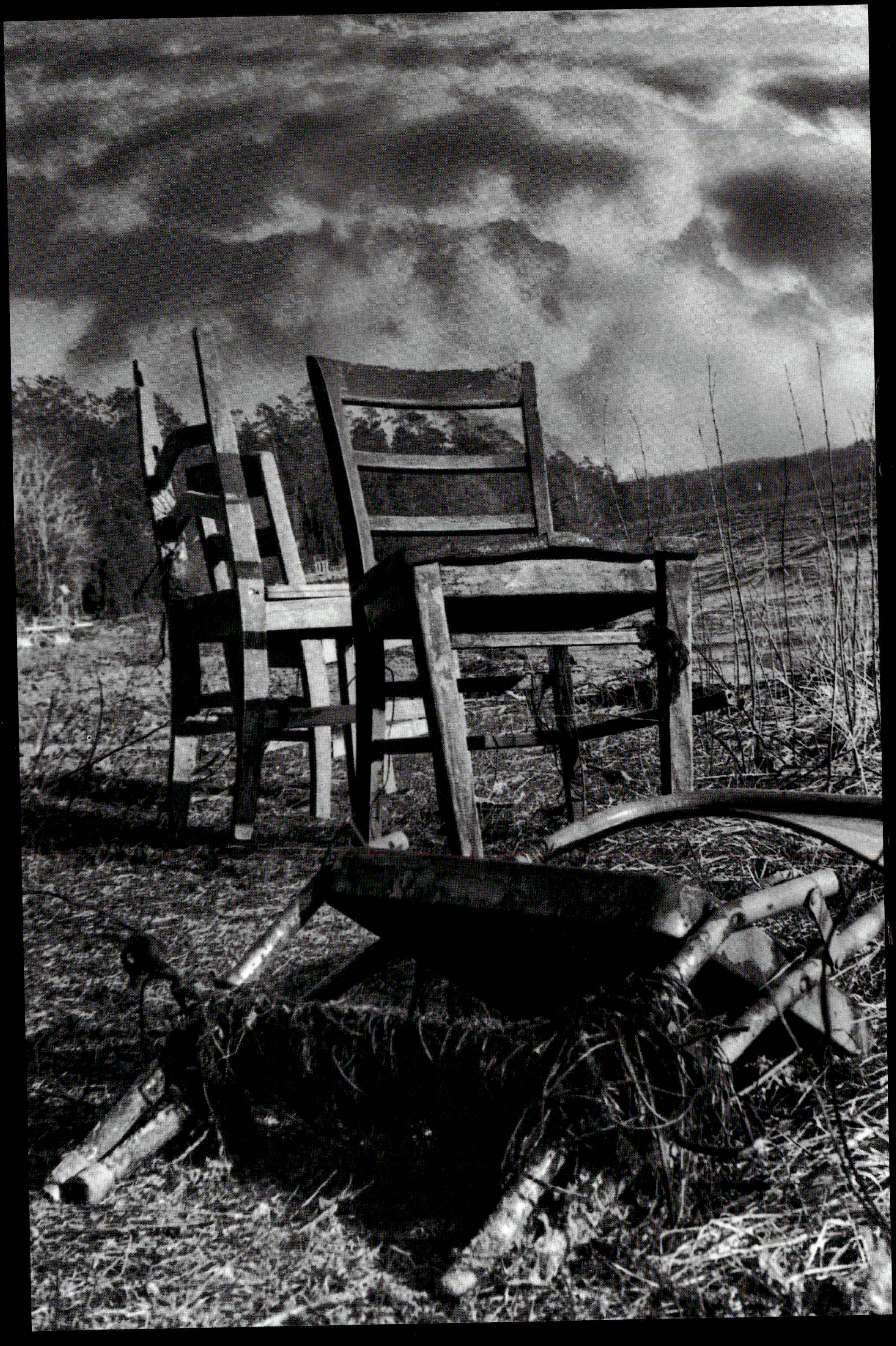

Clara Teufel

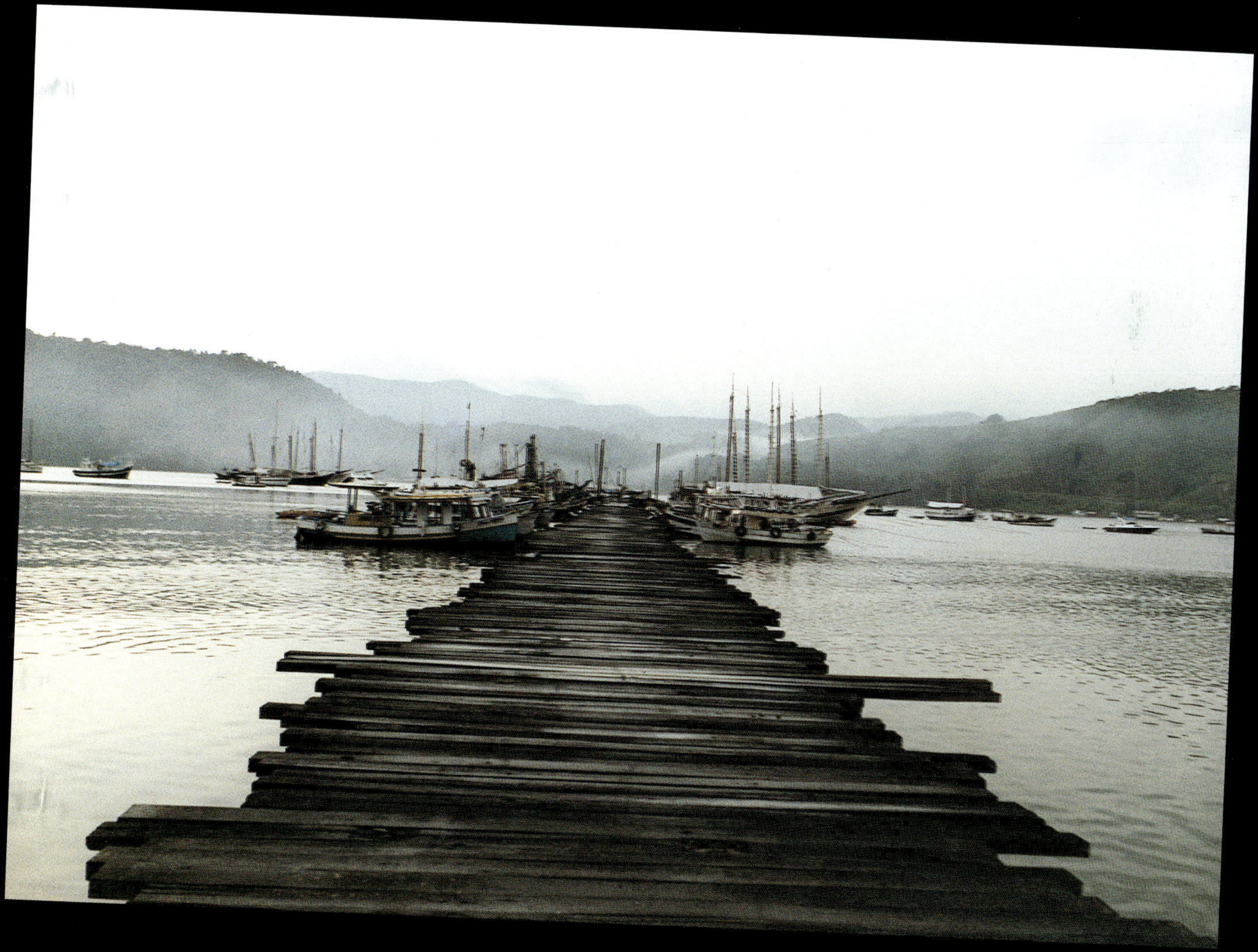

Sonia Christine Barrozo

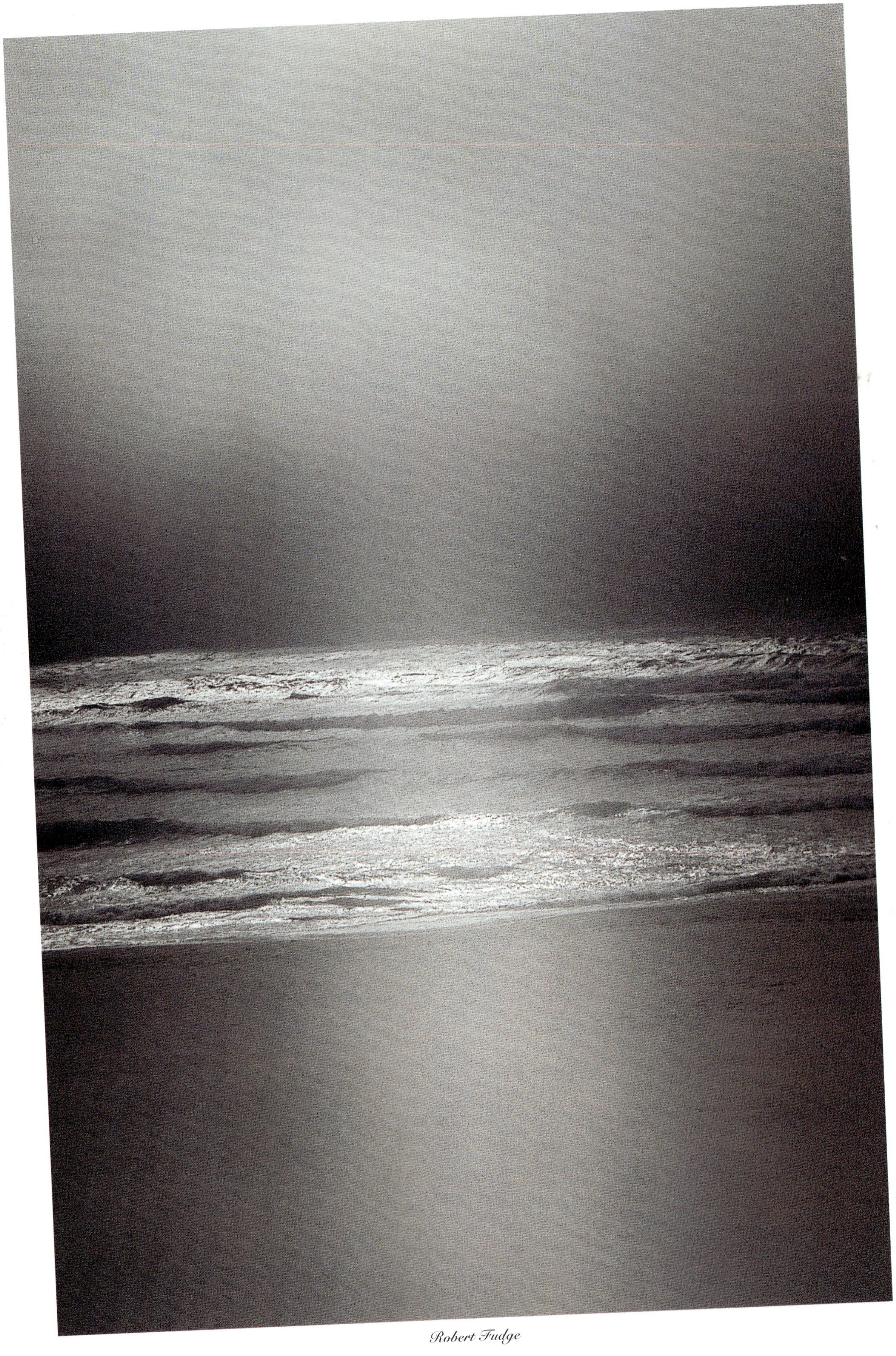

Robert Fudge

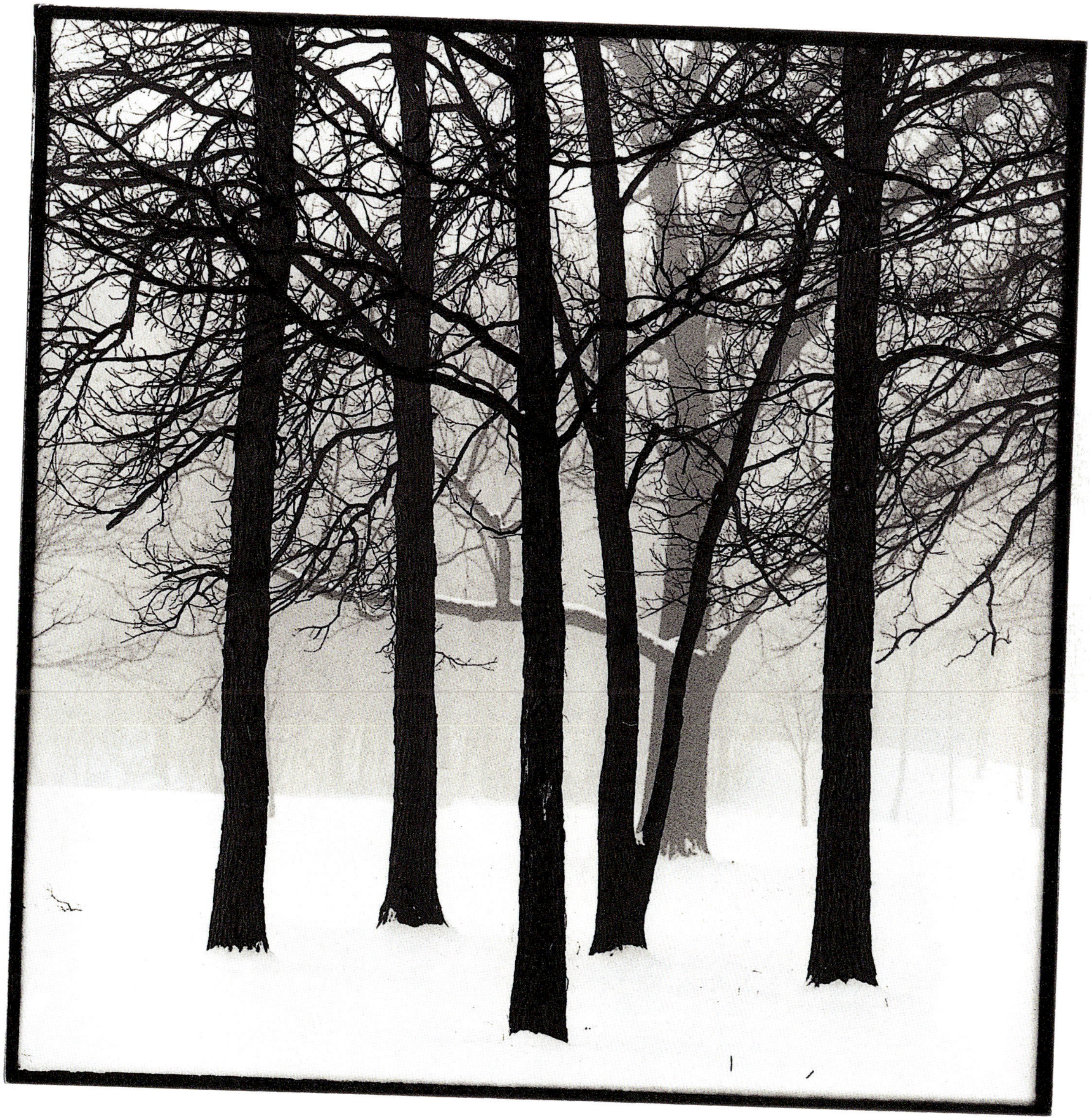

Paul Kozal

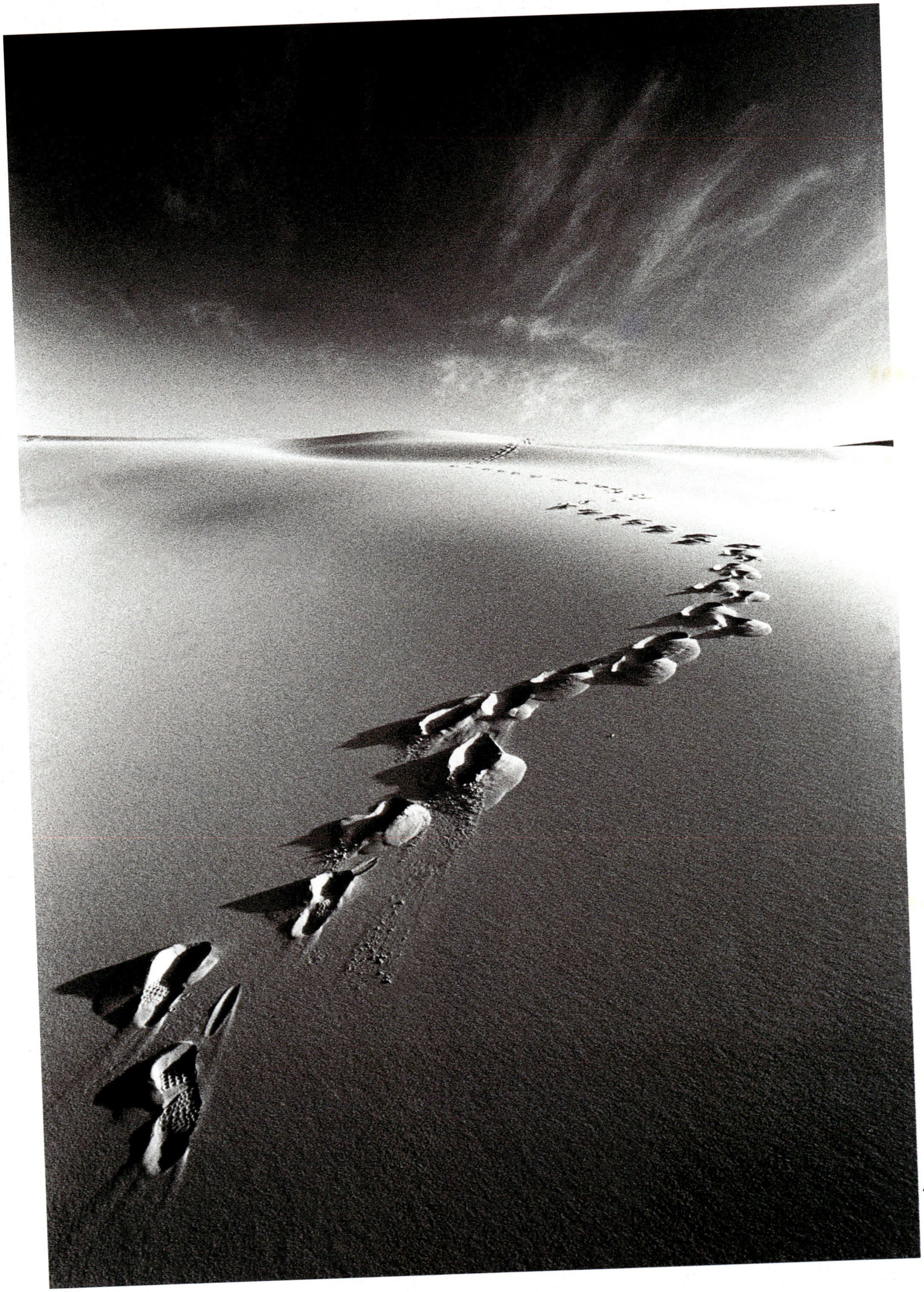

Lorne Resnick

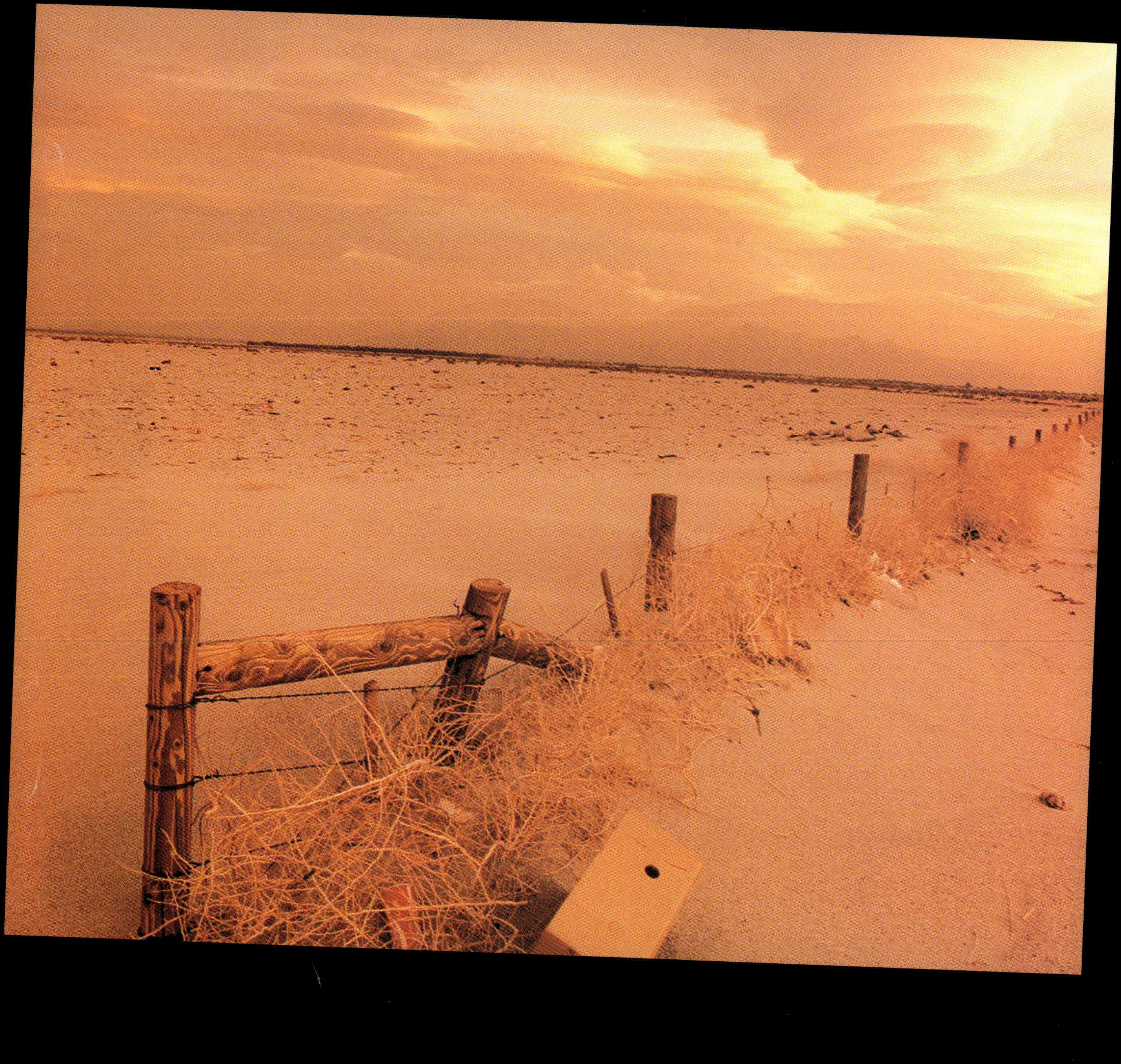

Nathan Teutle

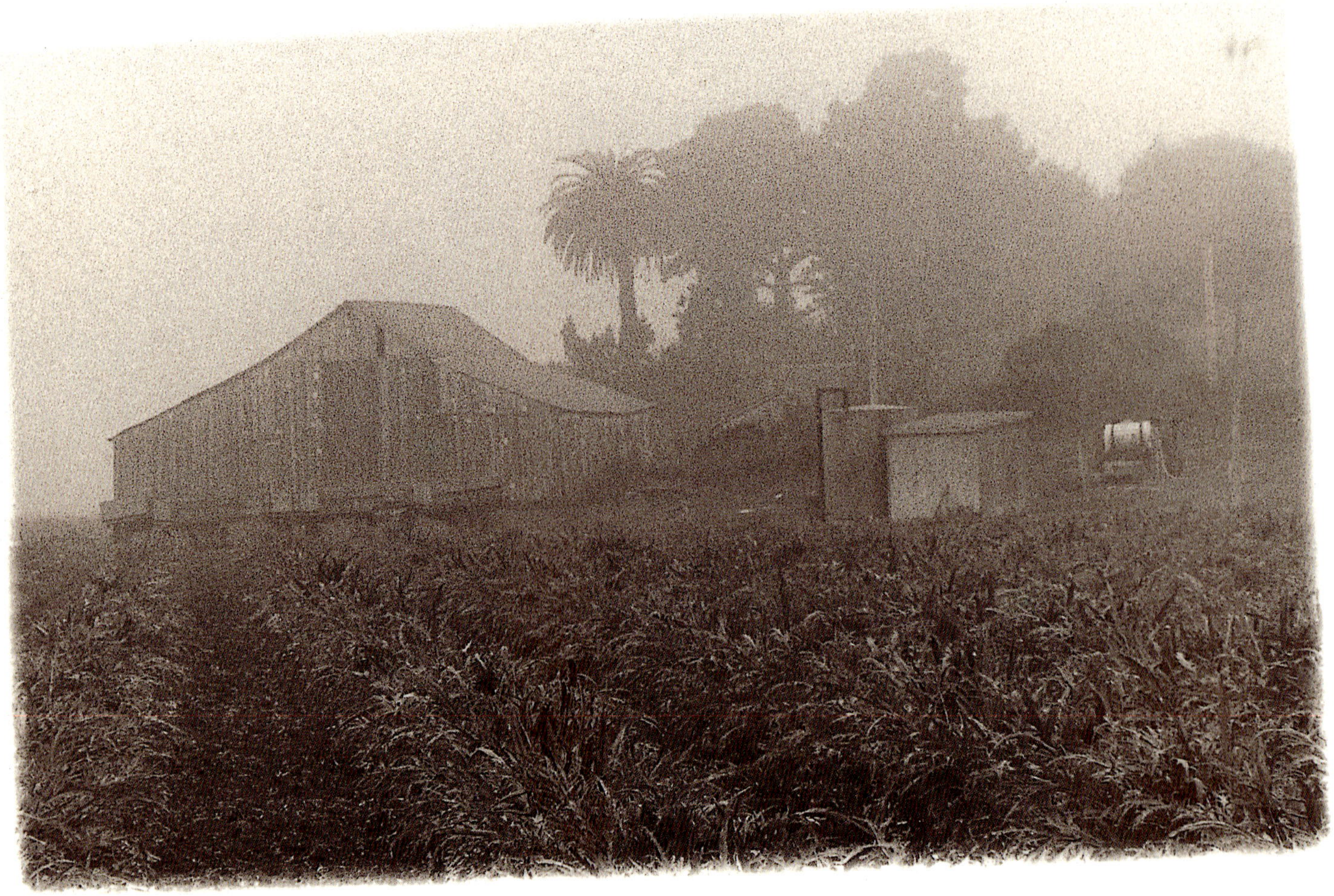

Paul Kozal

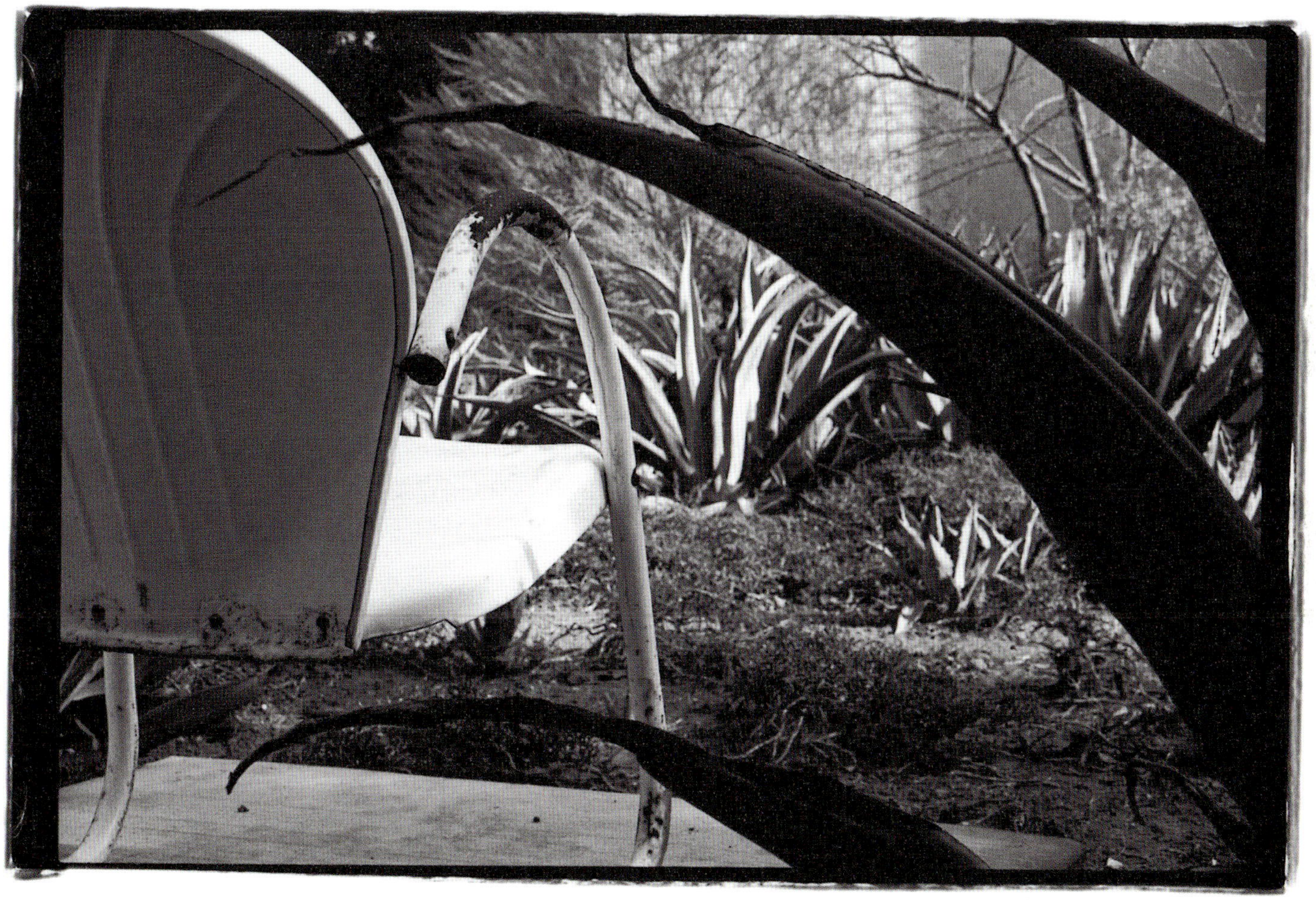

Edie Pereira

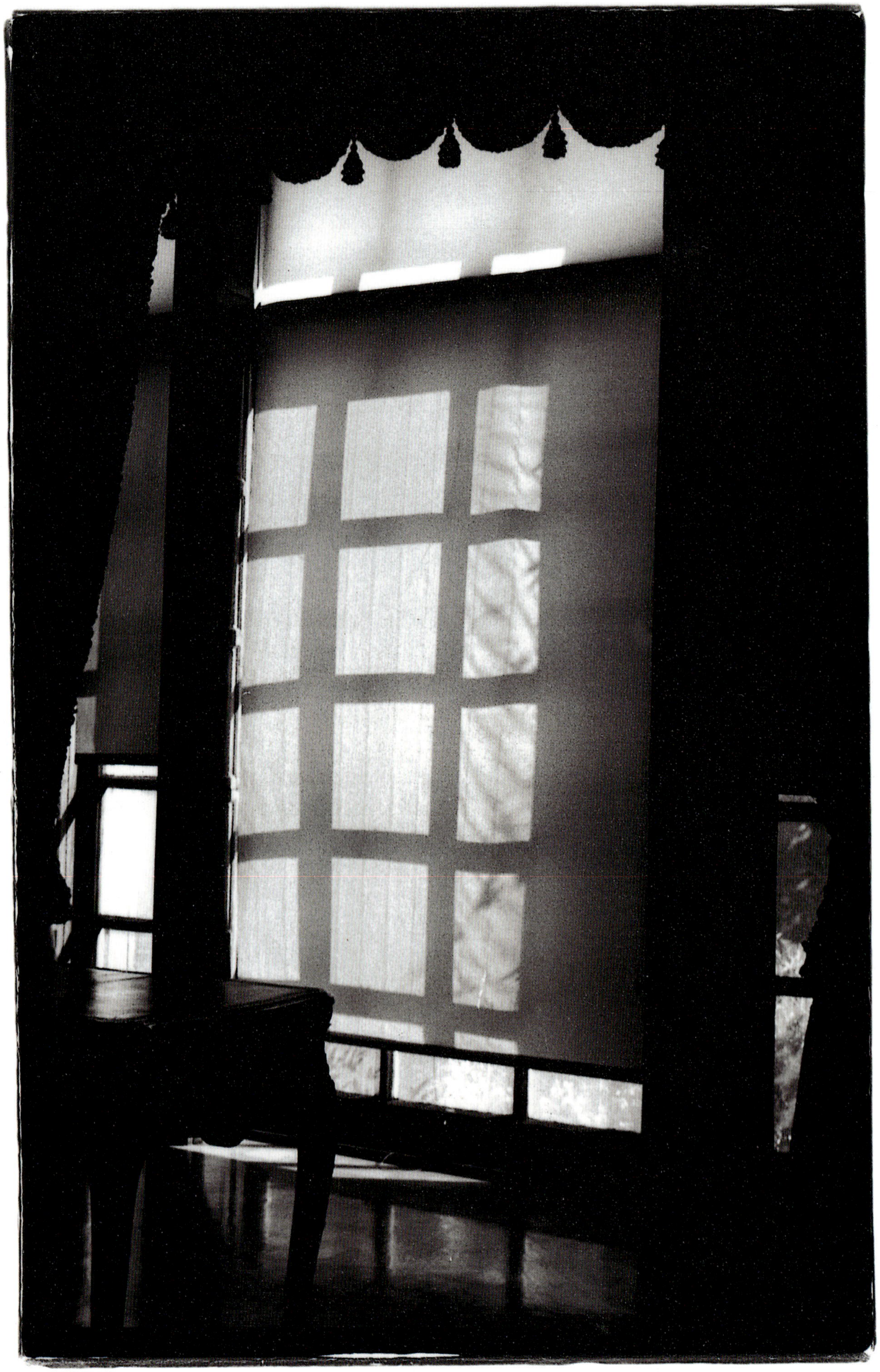

Edie Pereira

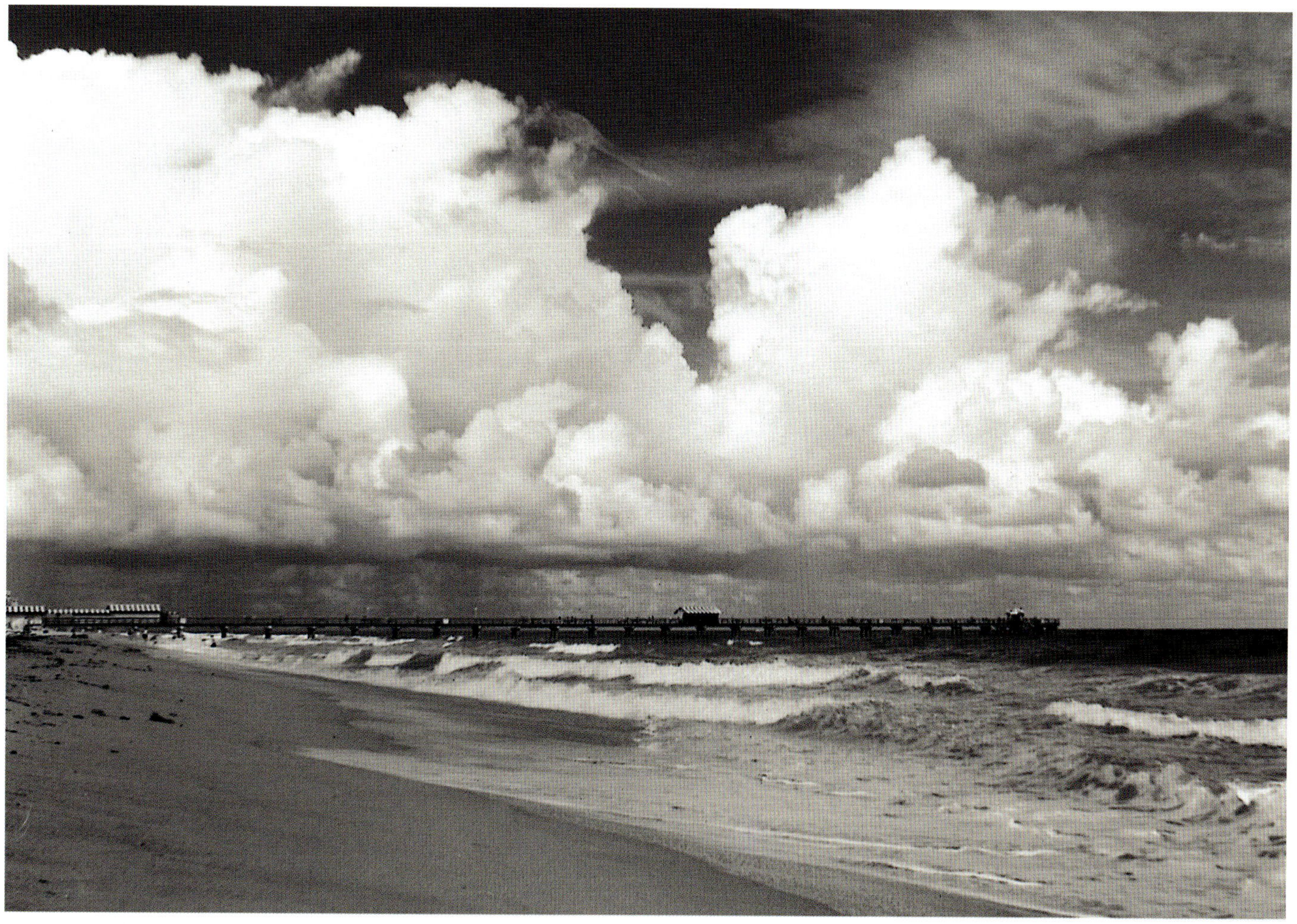

Mathew Courtney

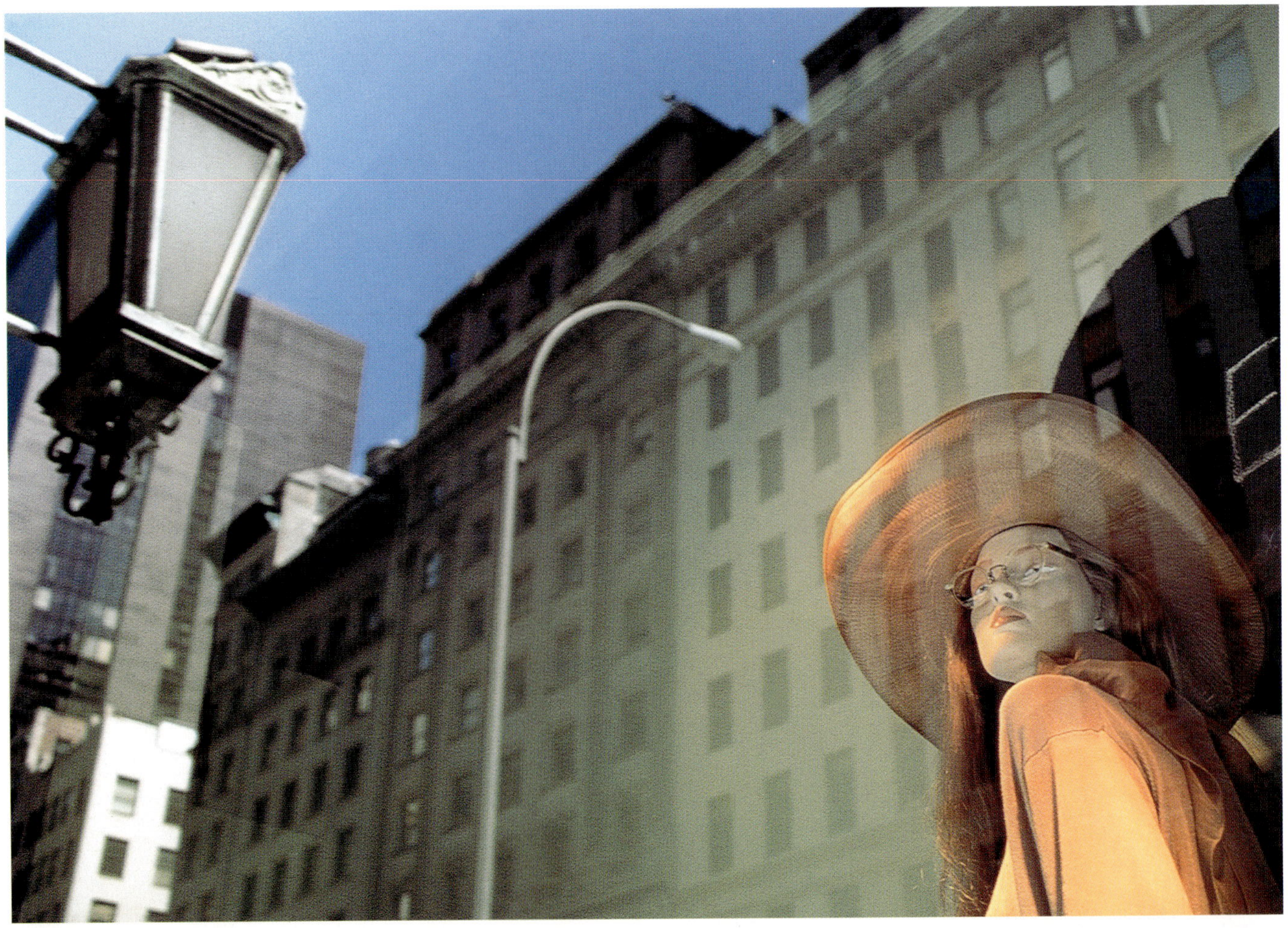

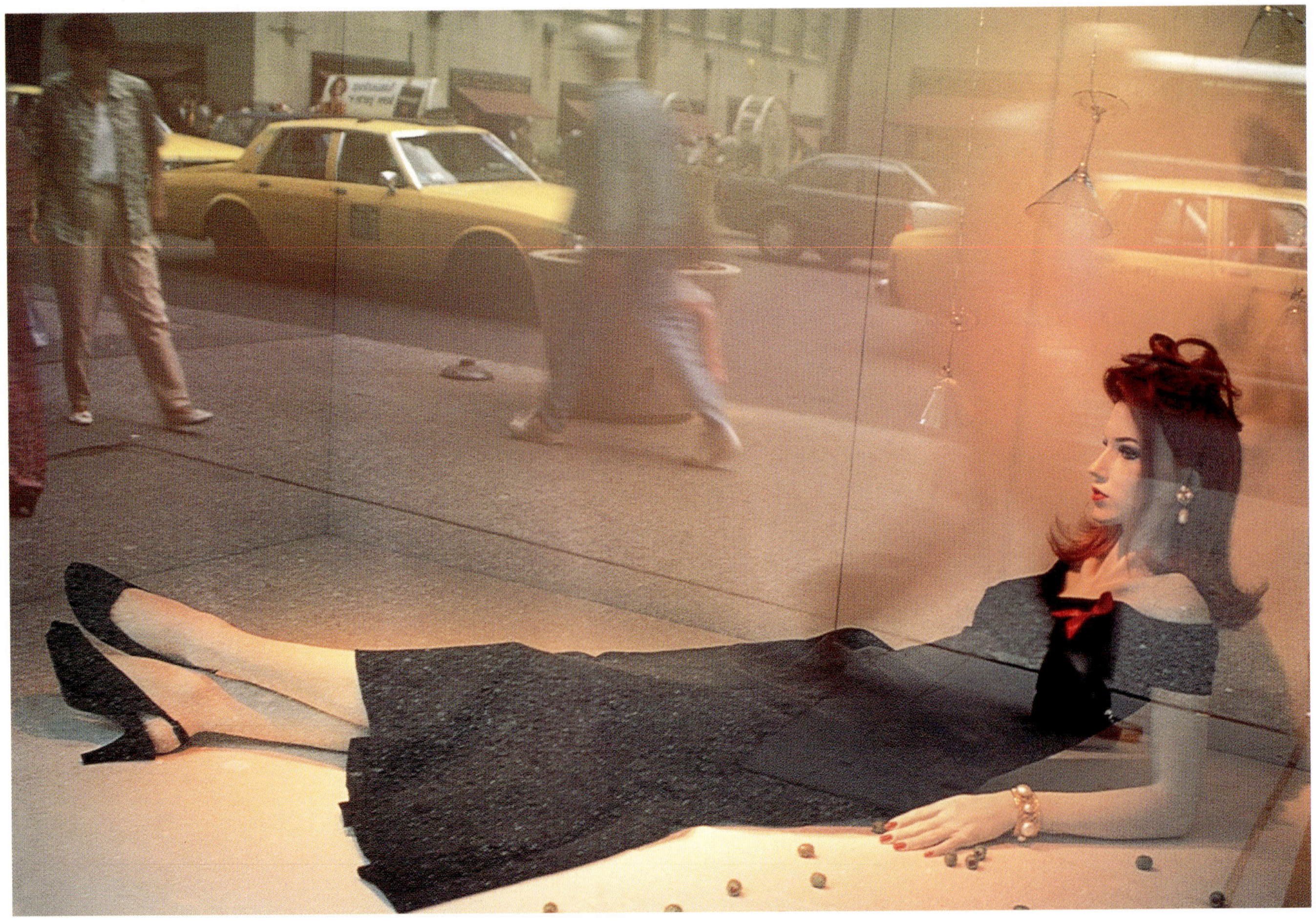

Babs Armour

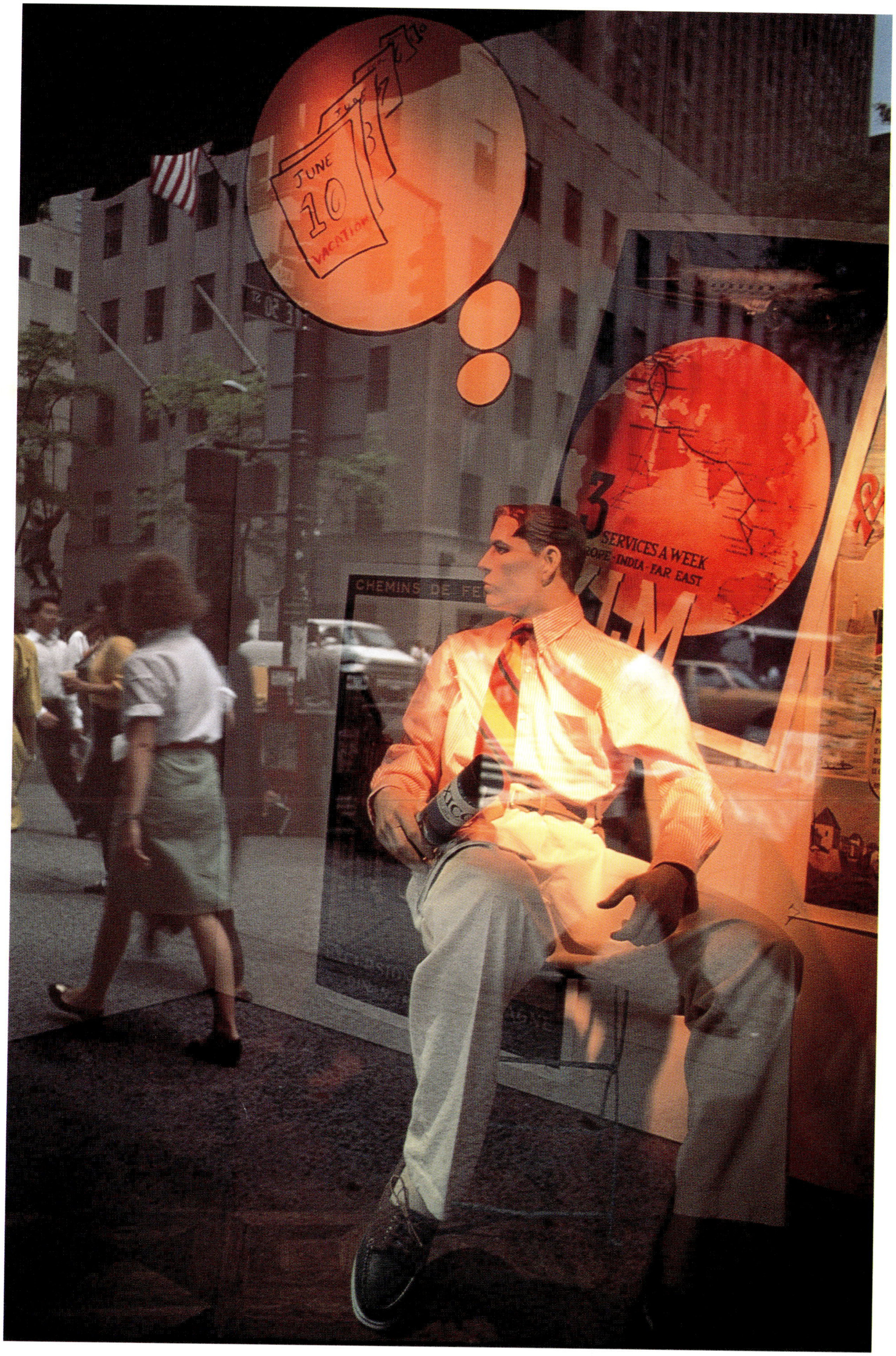

Babs Armour

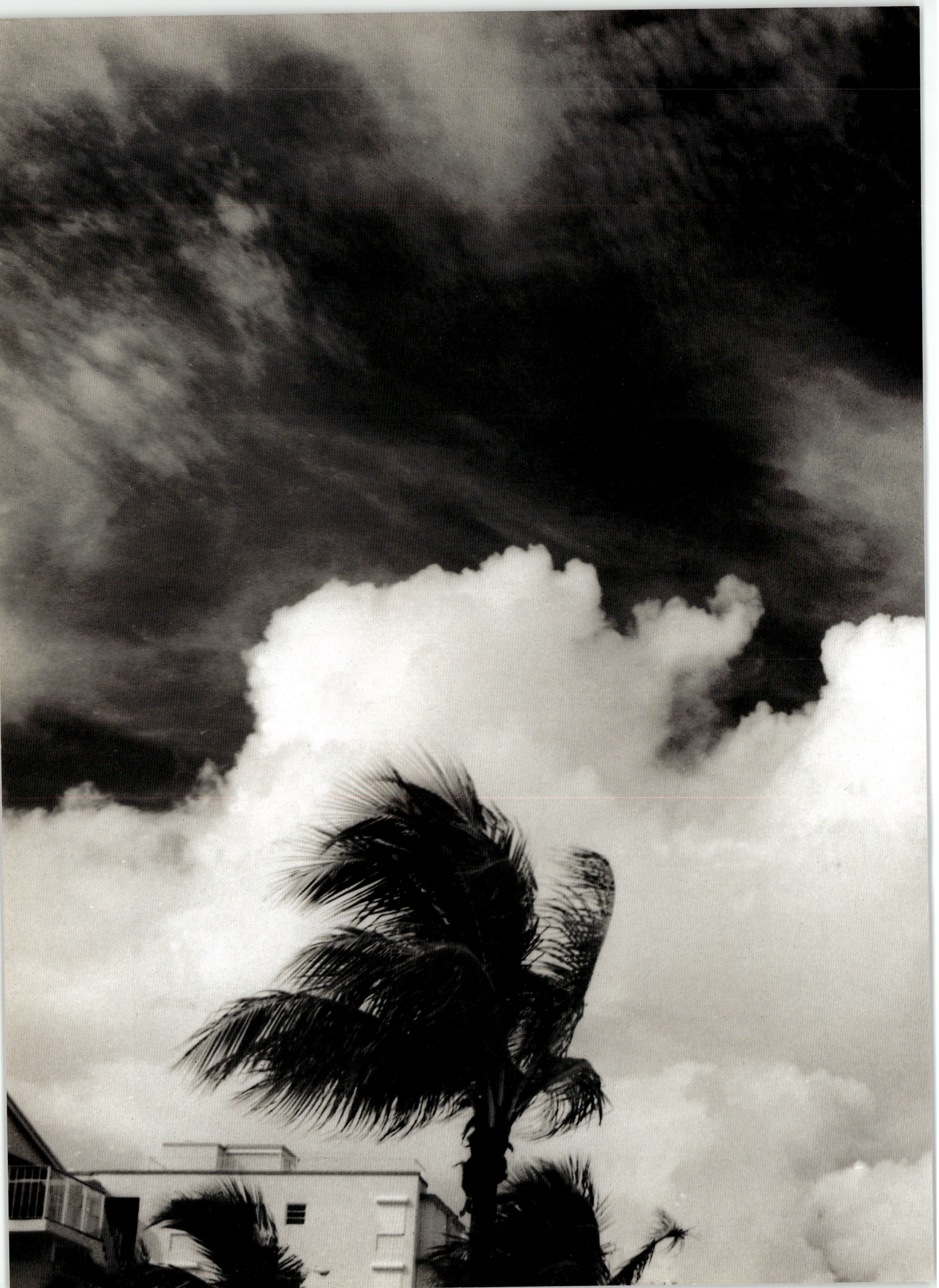

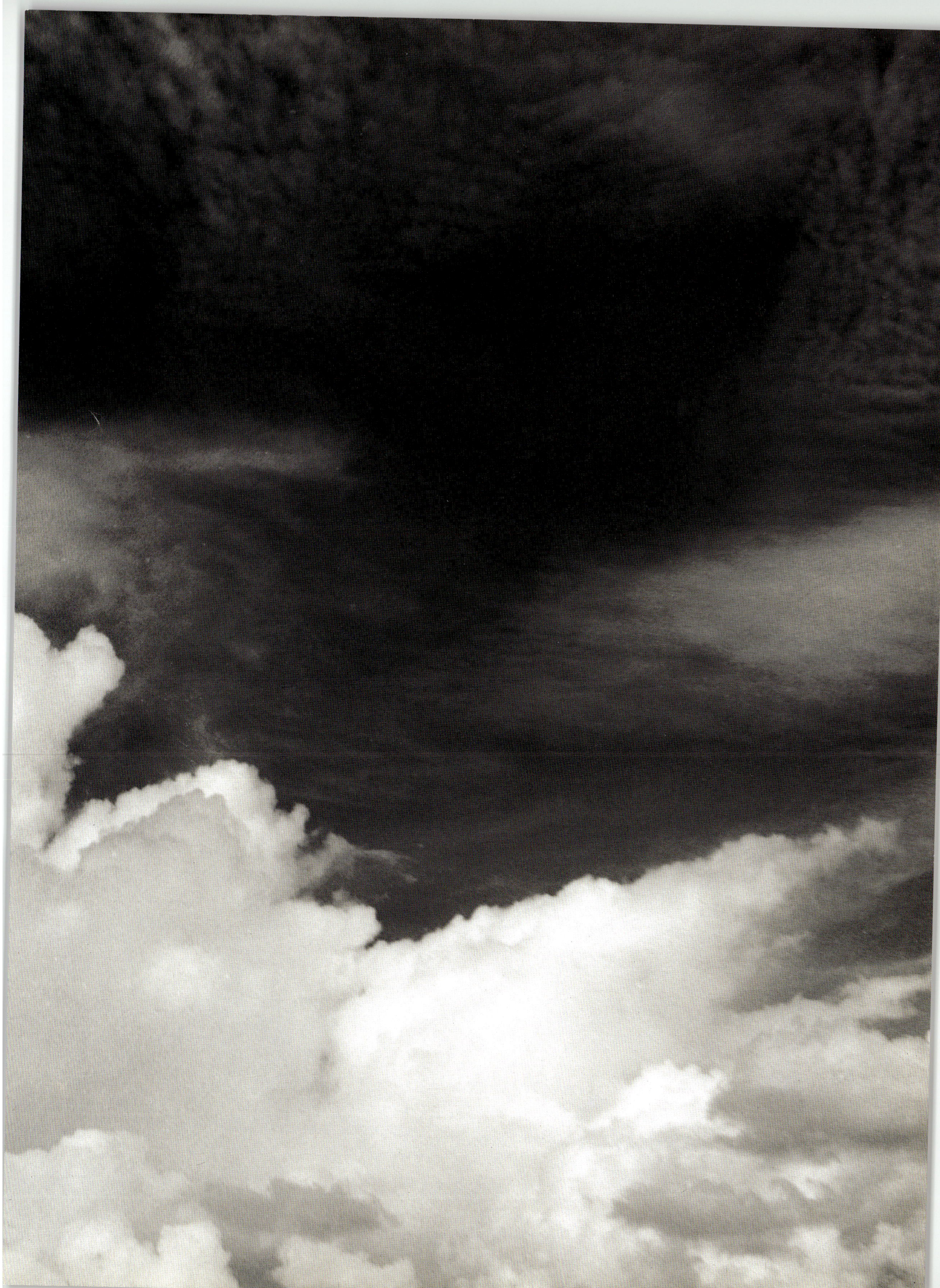

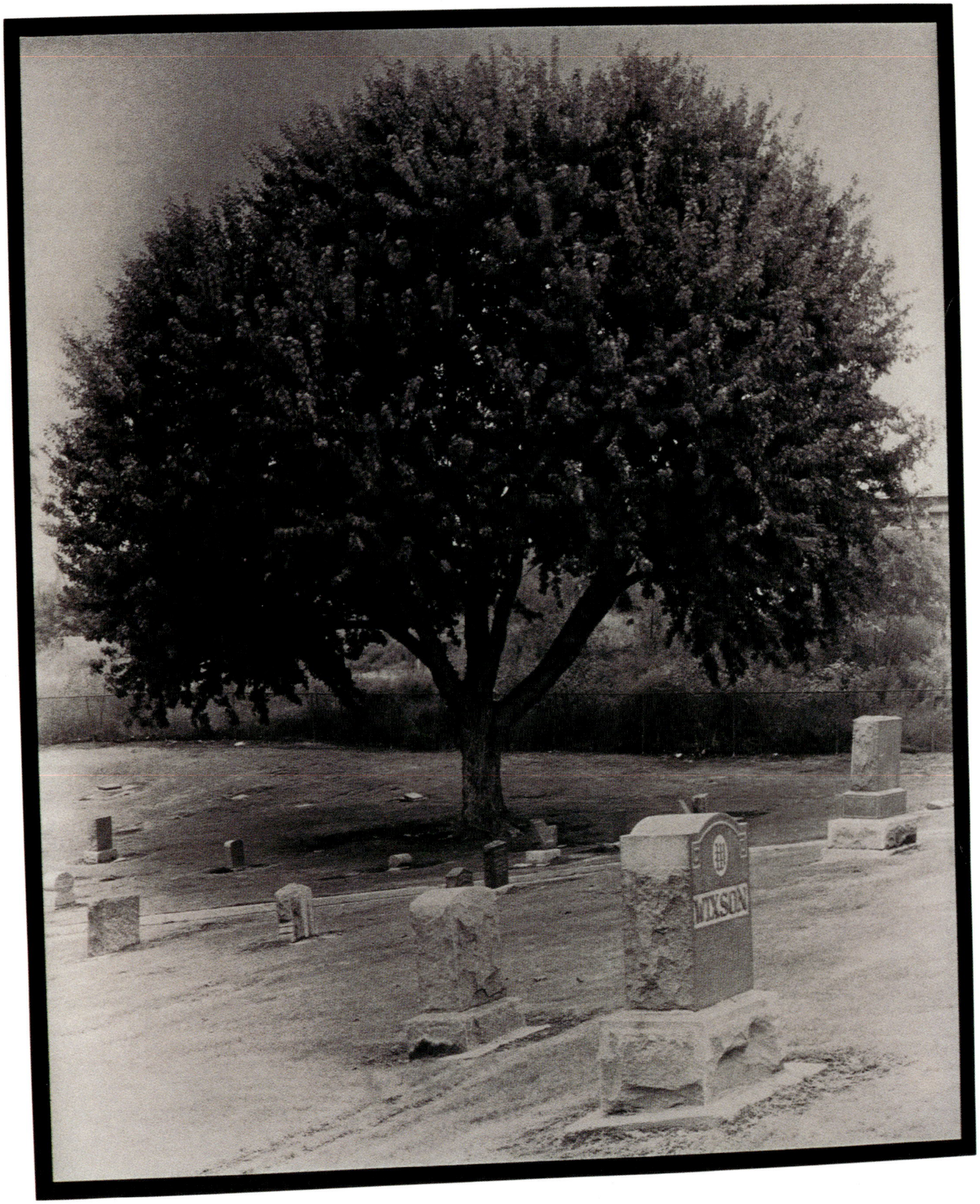

(PREVIOUS SPREAD) *Matthew Courtney* ■ (THIS PAGE) *Anthony Lawson*

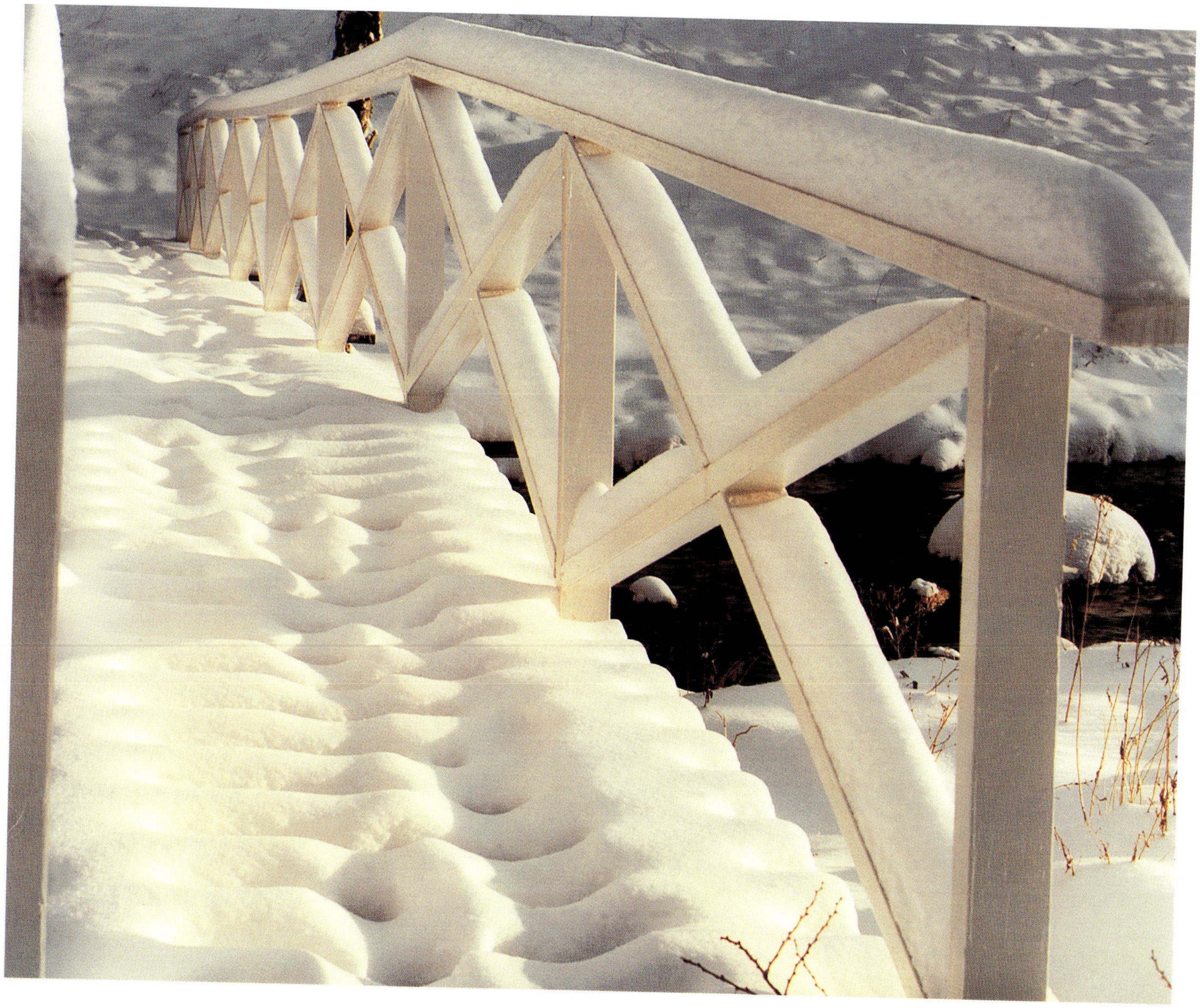

Michael Totaro'

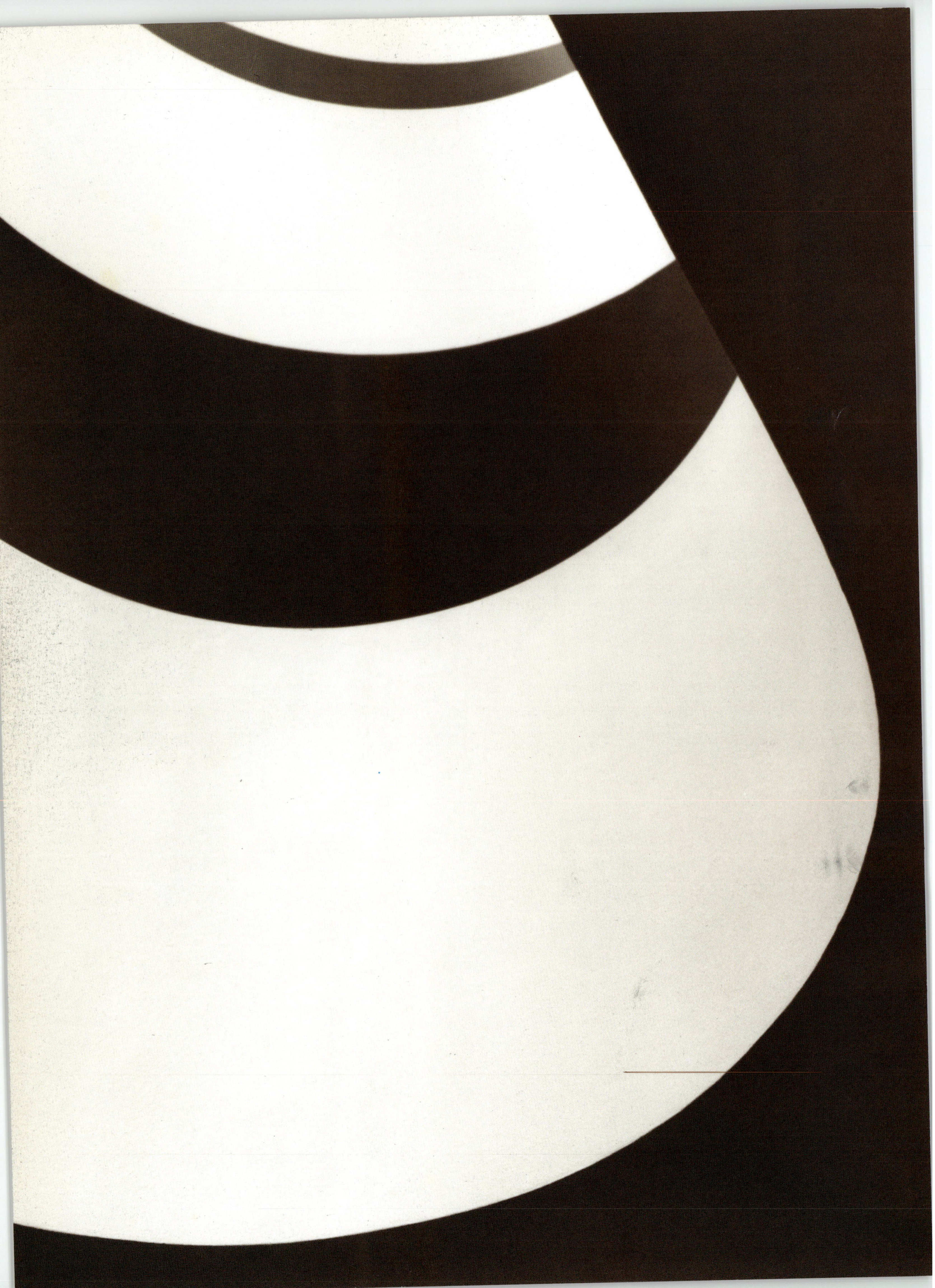

ARCHITECTURE

ARCHITEKTUR

ARCHITECTURE

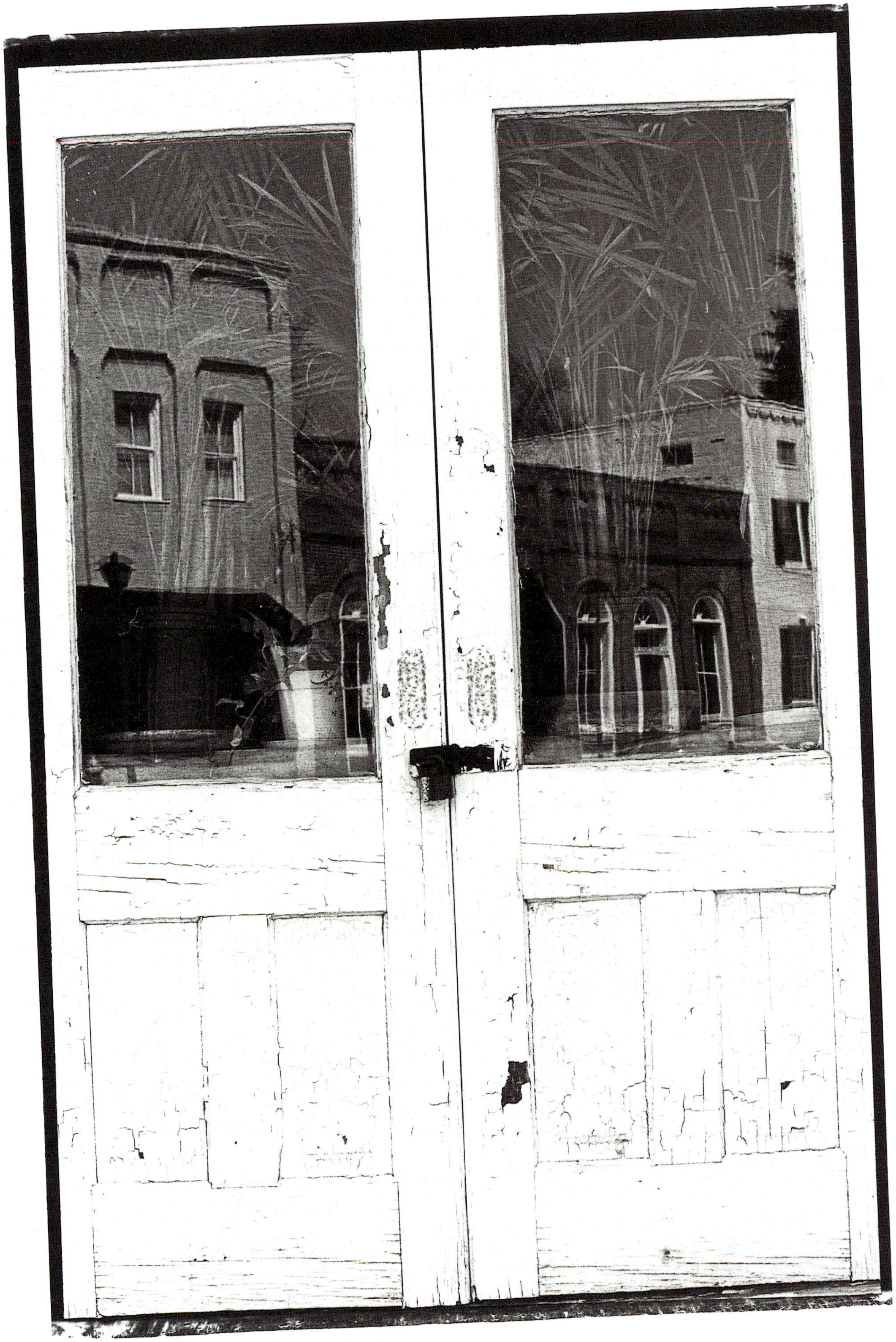

(PREVIOUS SPREAD) *Paul Kozal* ■ (THIS PAGE) *Richard Langone*

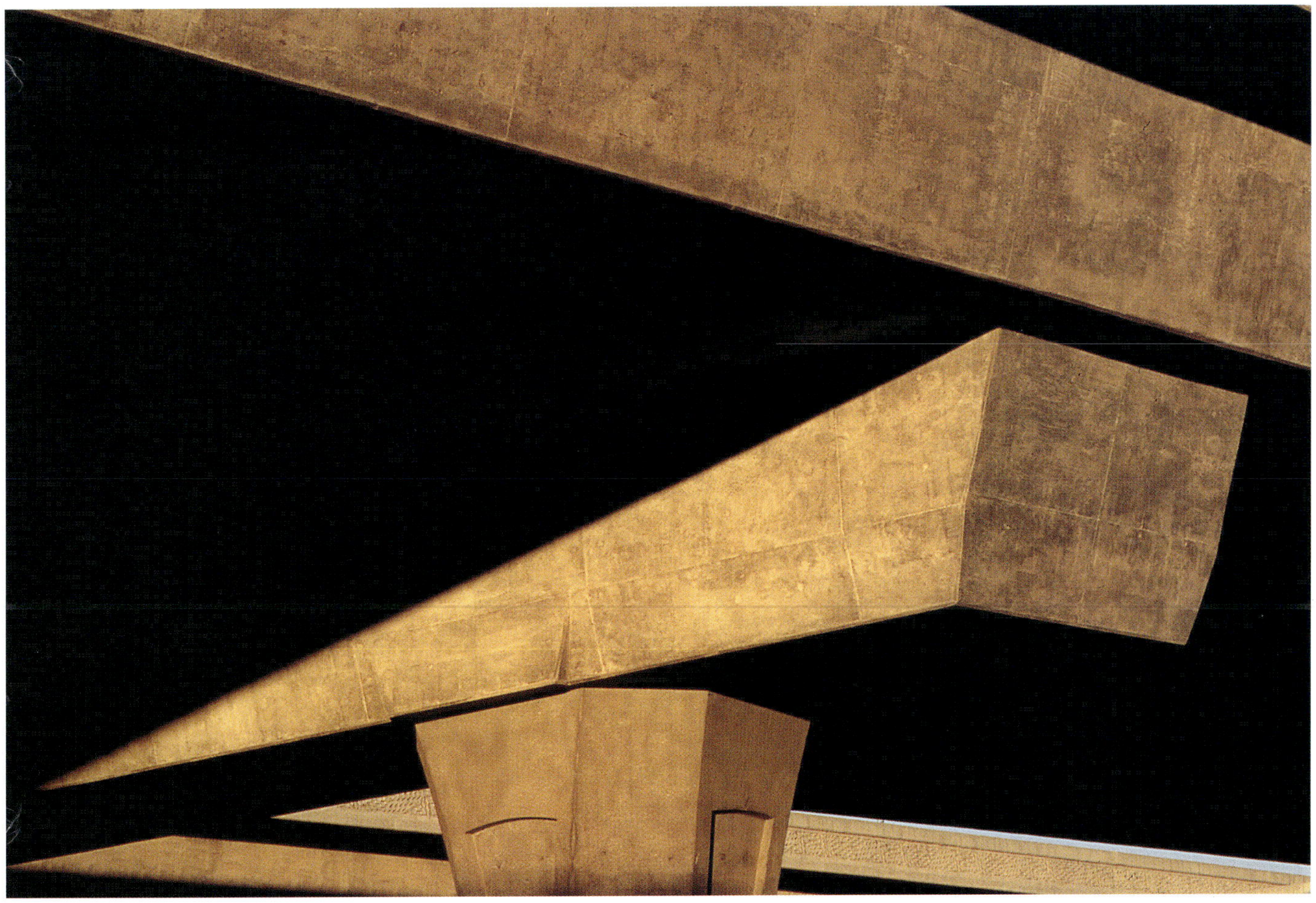

Timothy N. Gilbert

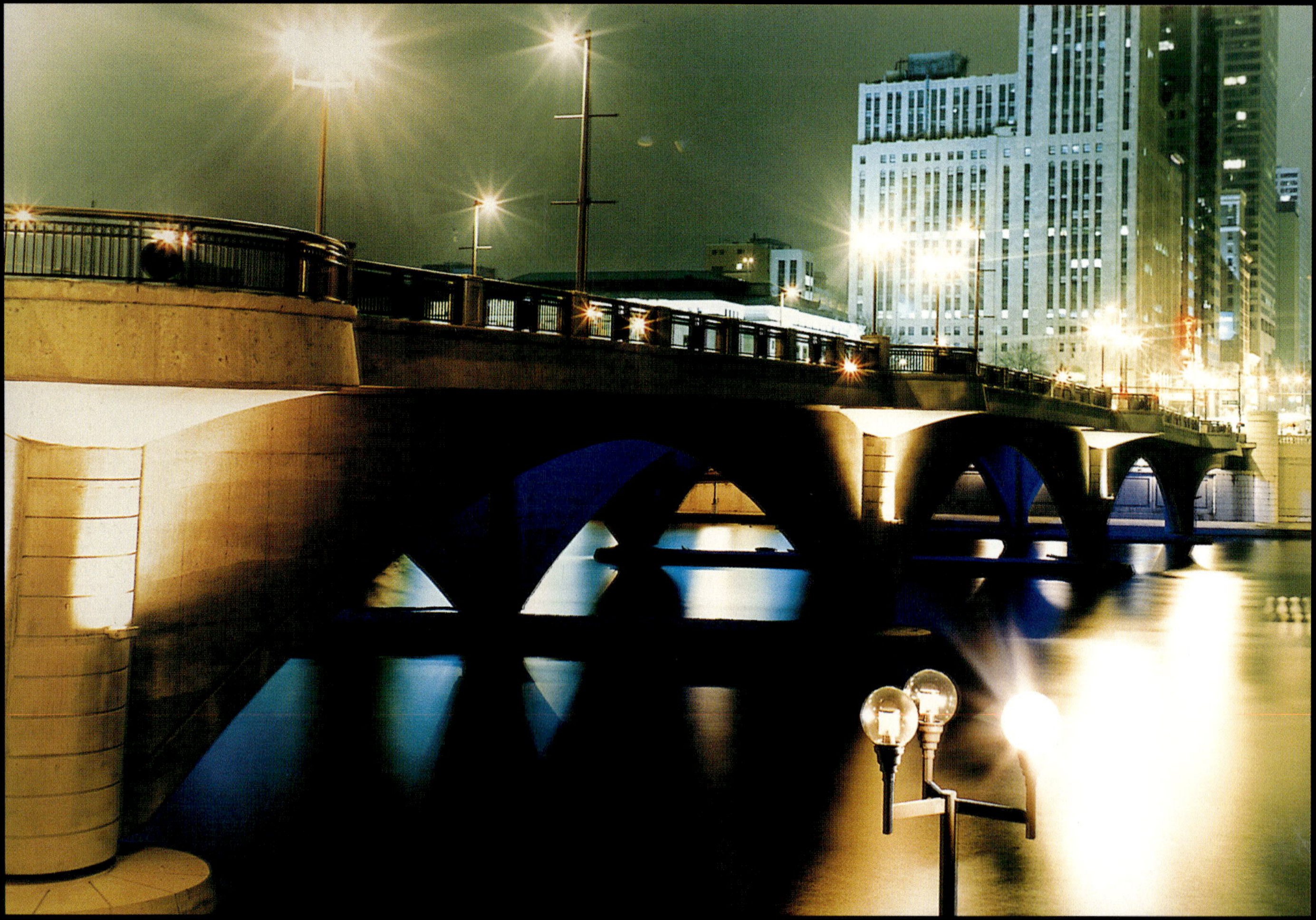

Christopher Lovenguth

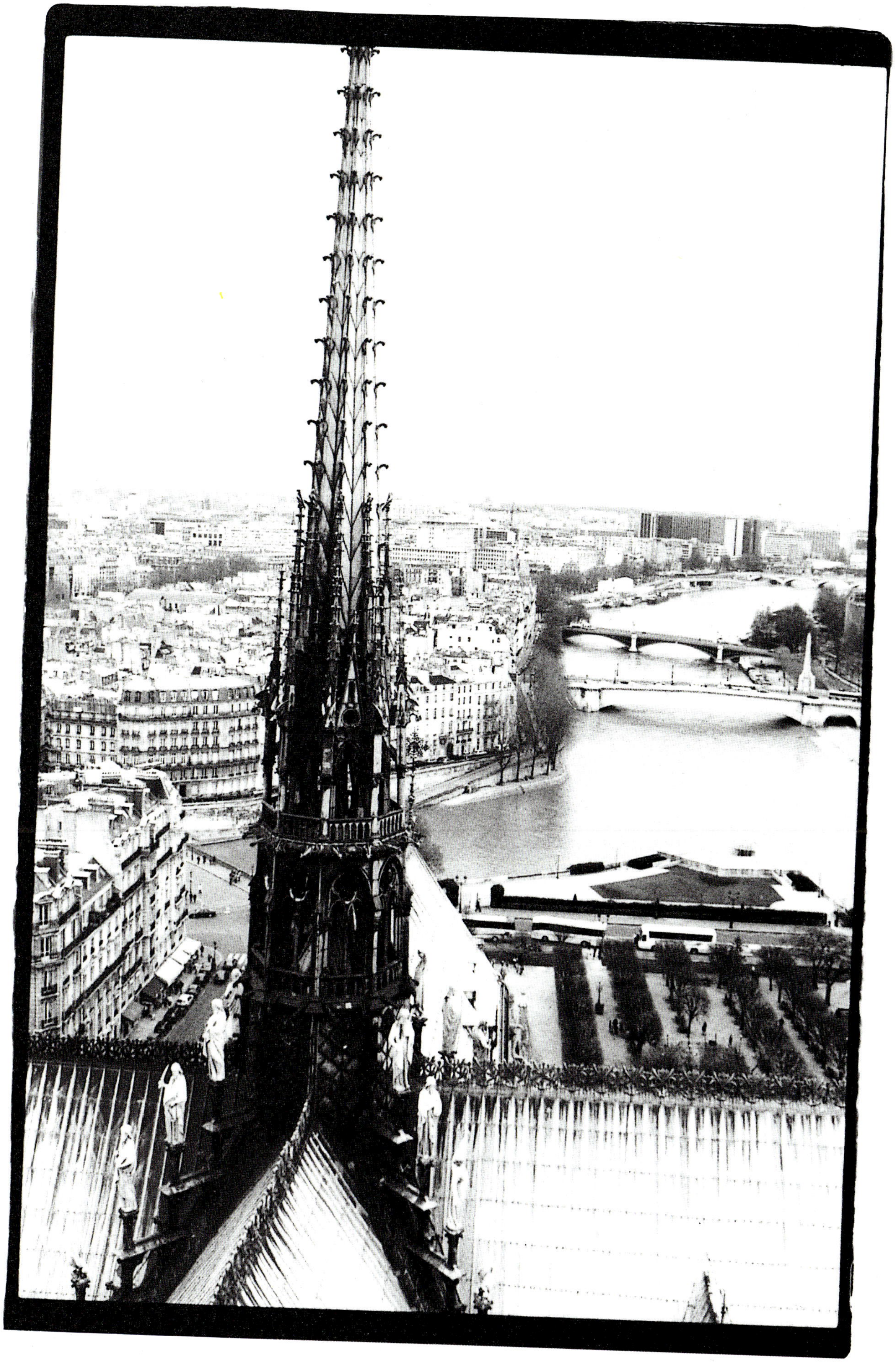

Edie Pereira

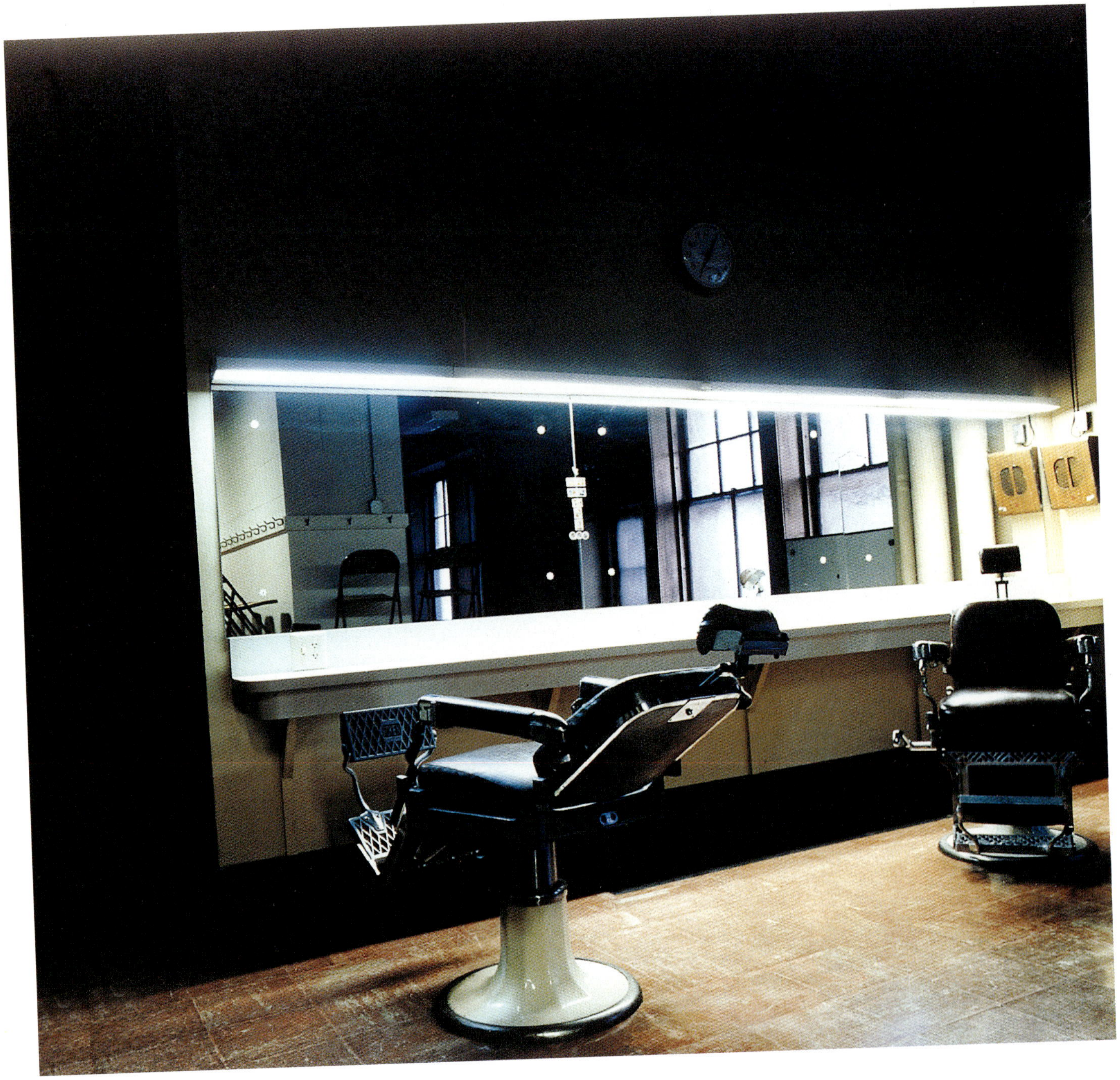

Jane Evans

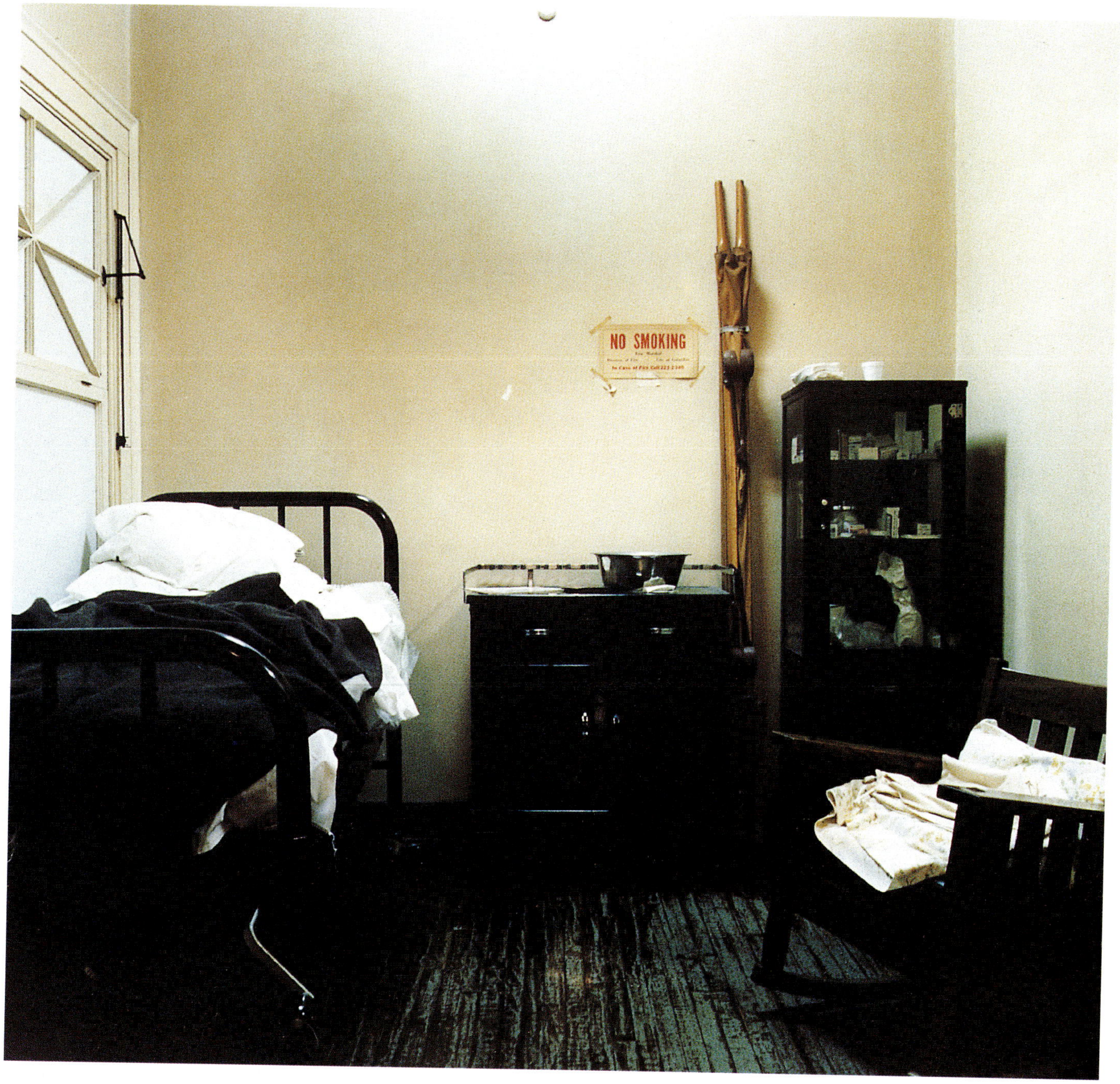

Jane Evans

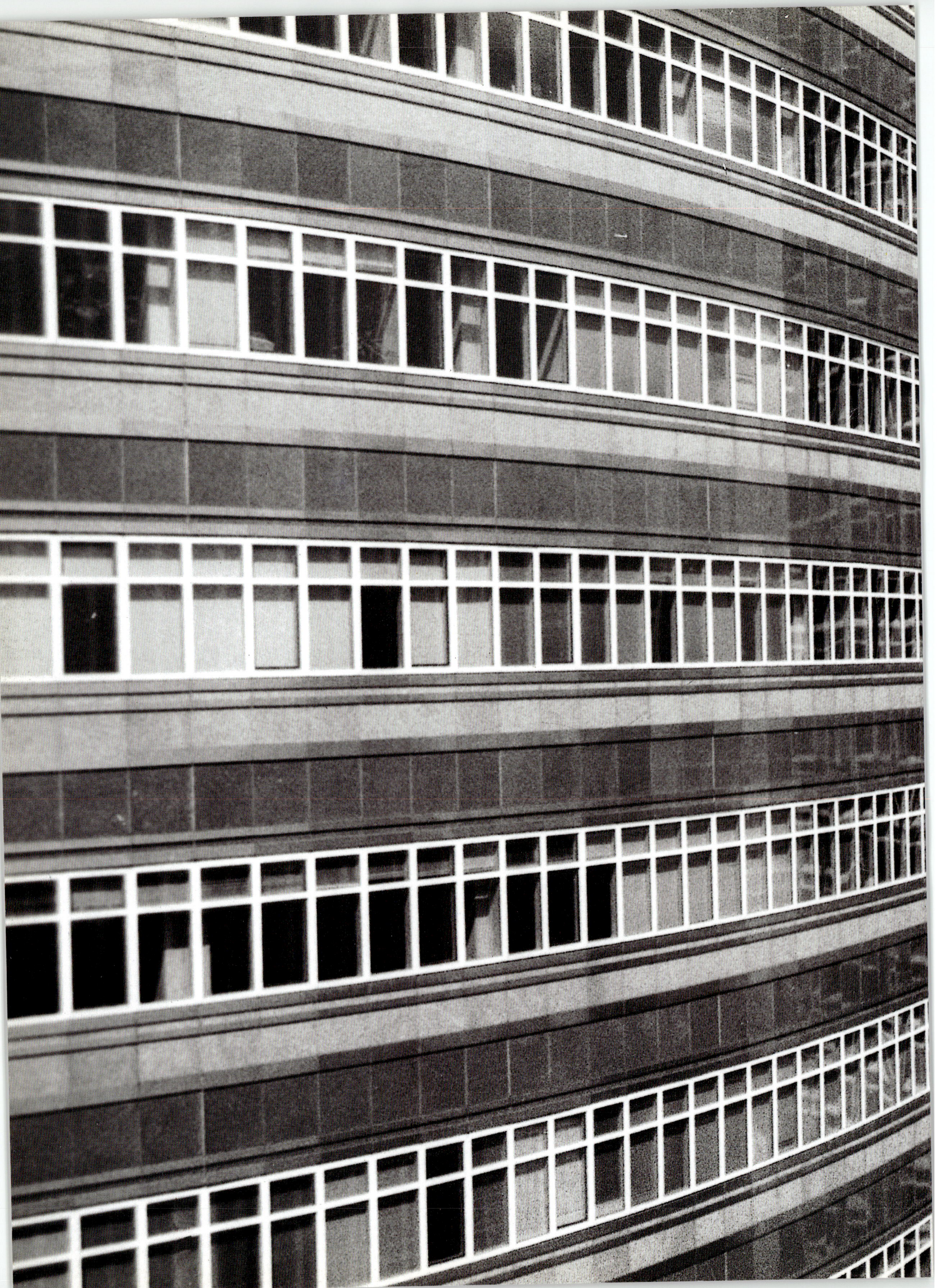

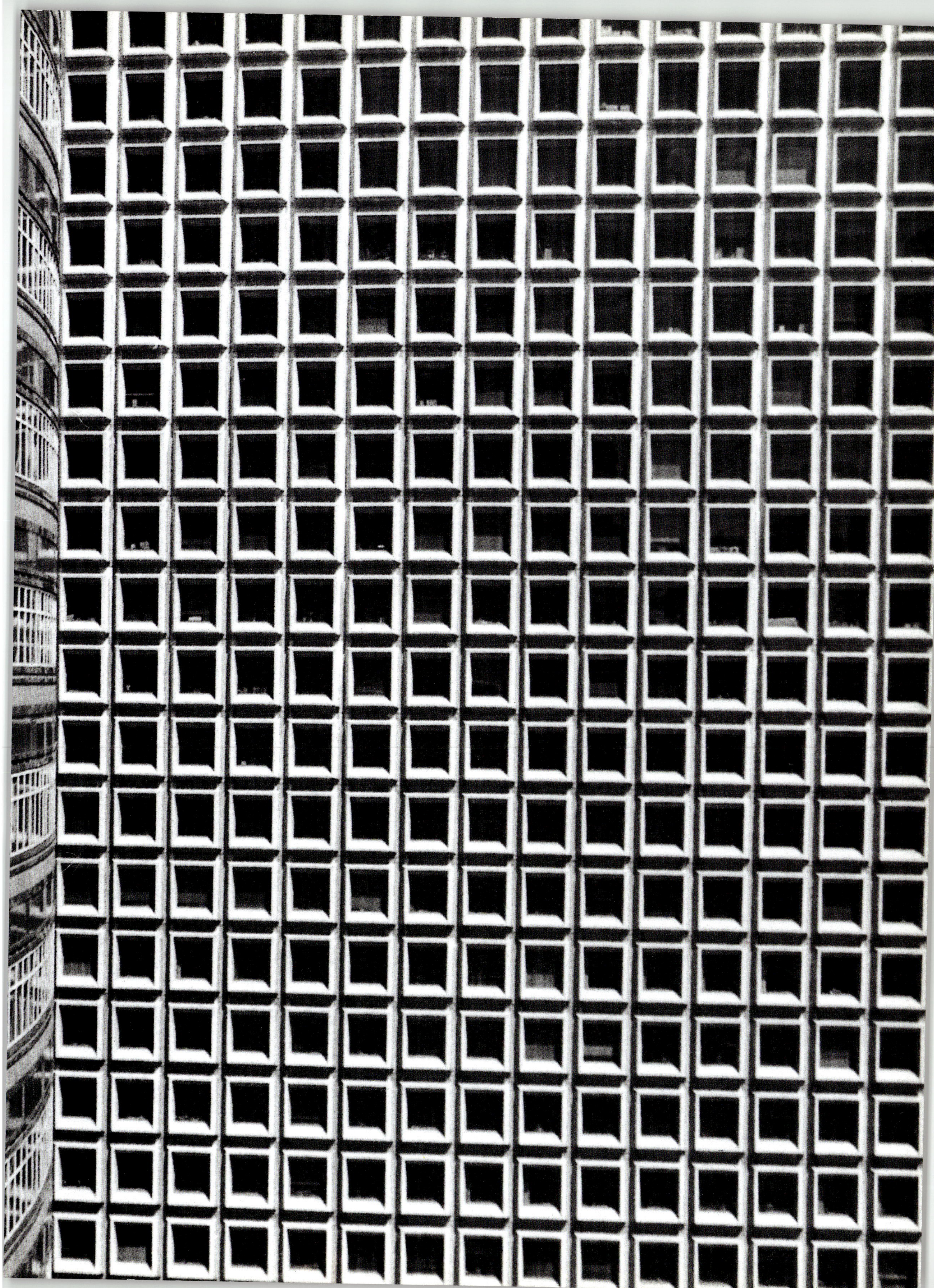

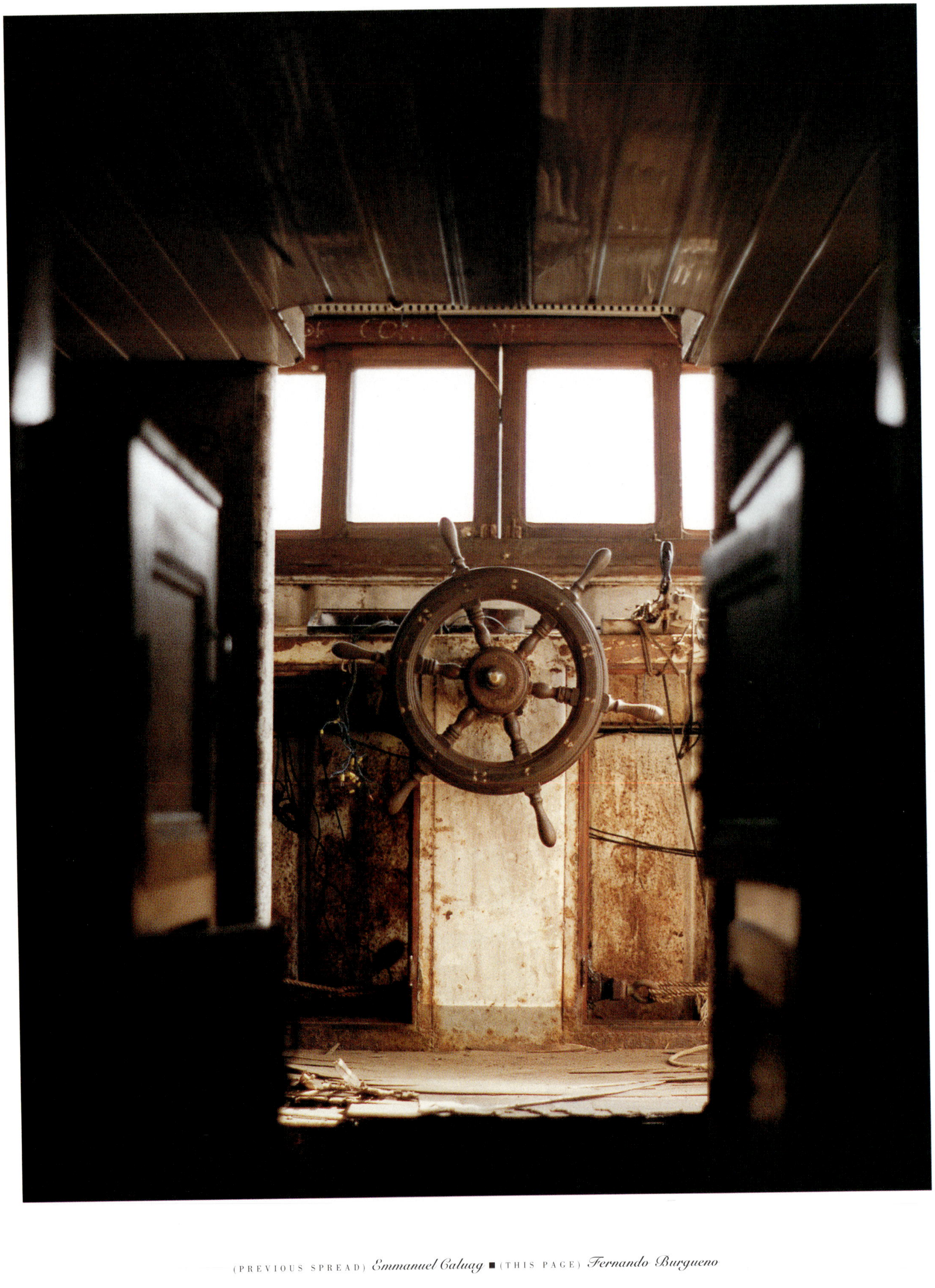

(PREVIOUS SPREAD) *Emmanuel Caluag* ■ (THIS PAGE) *Fernando Burgueno*

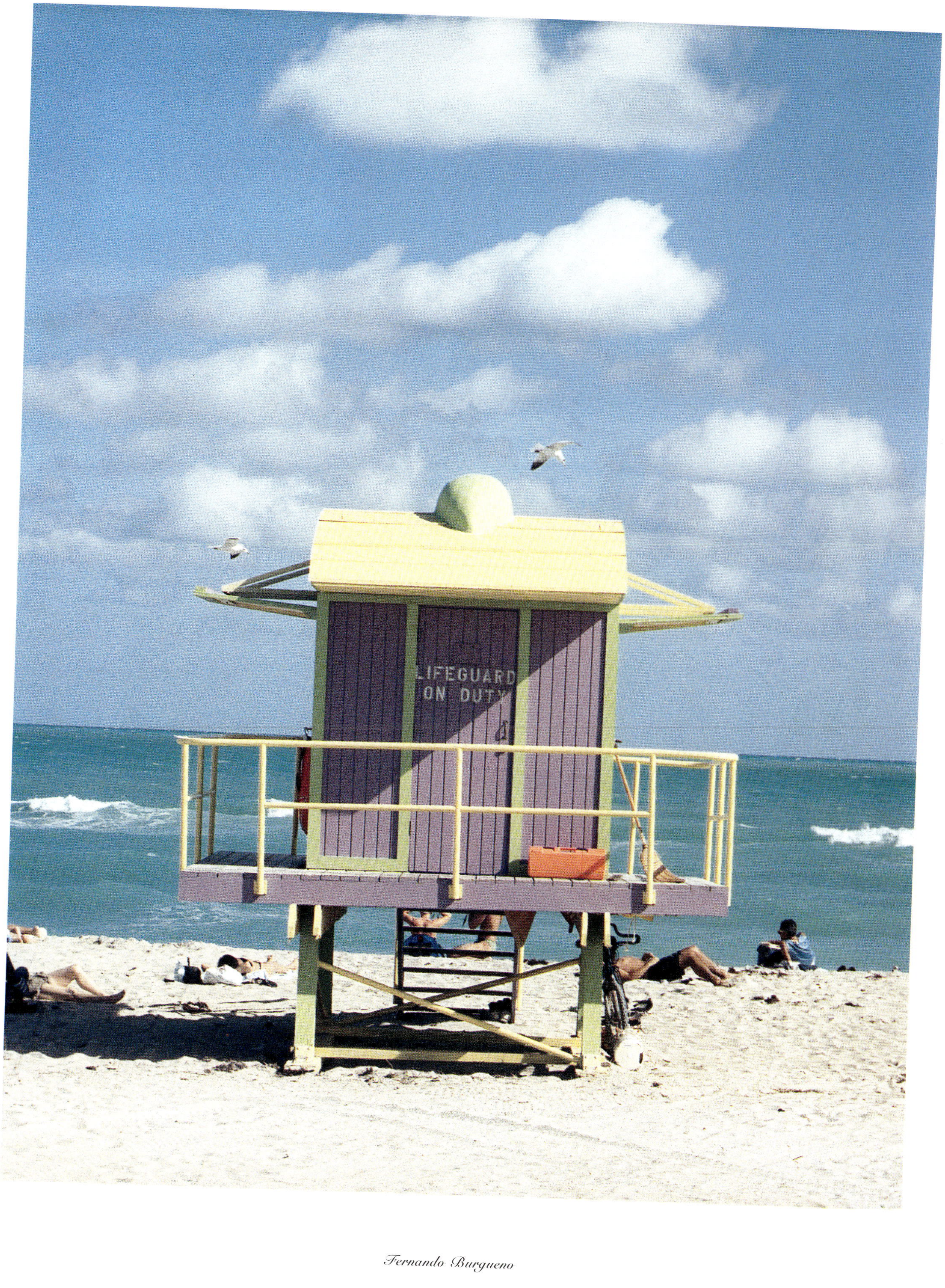

Fernando Burgueno

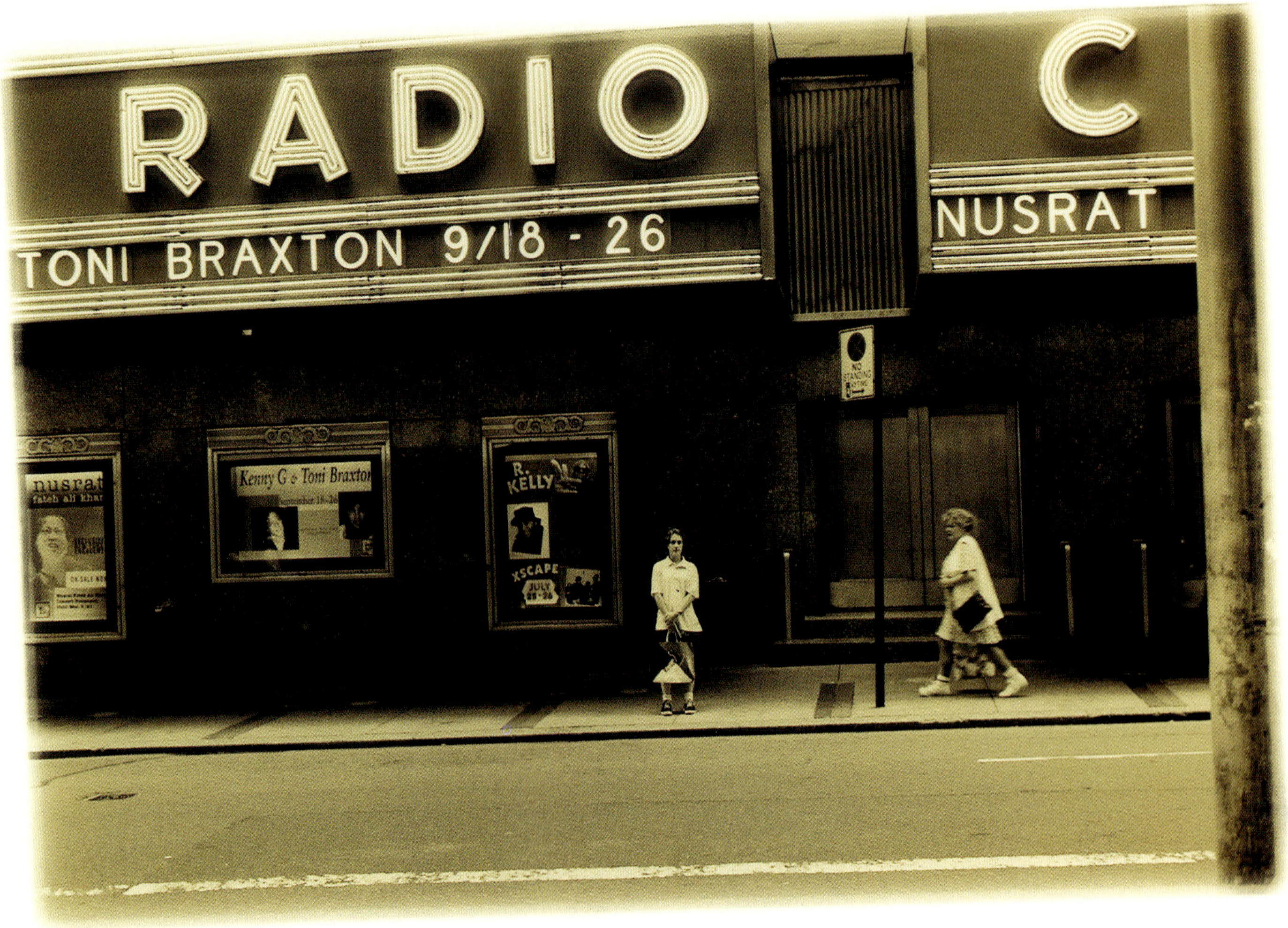

Gregory R. Kihlstrom

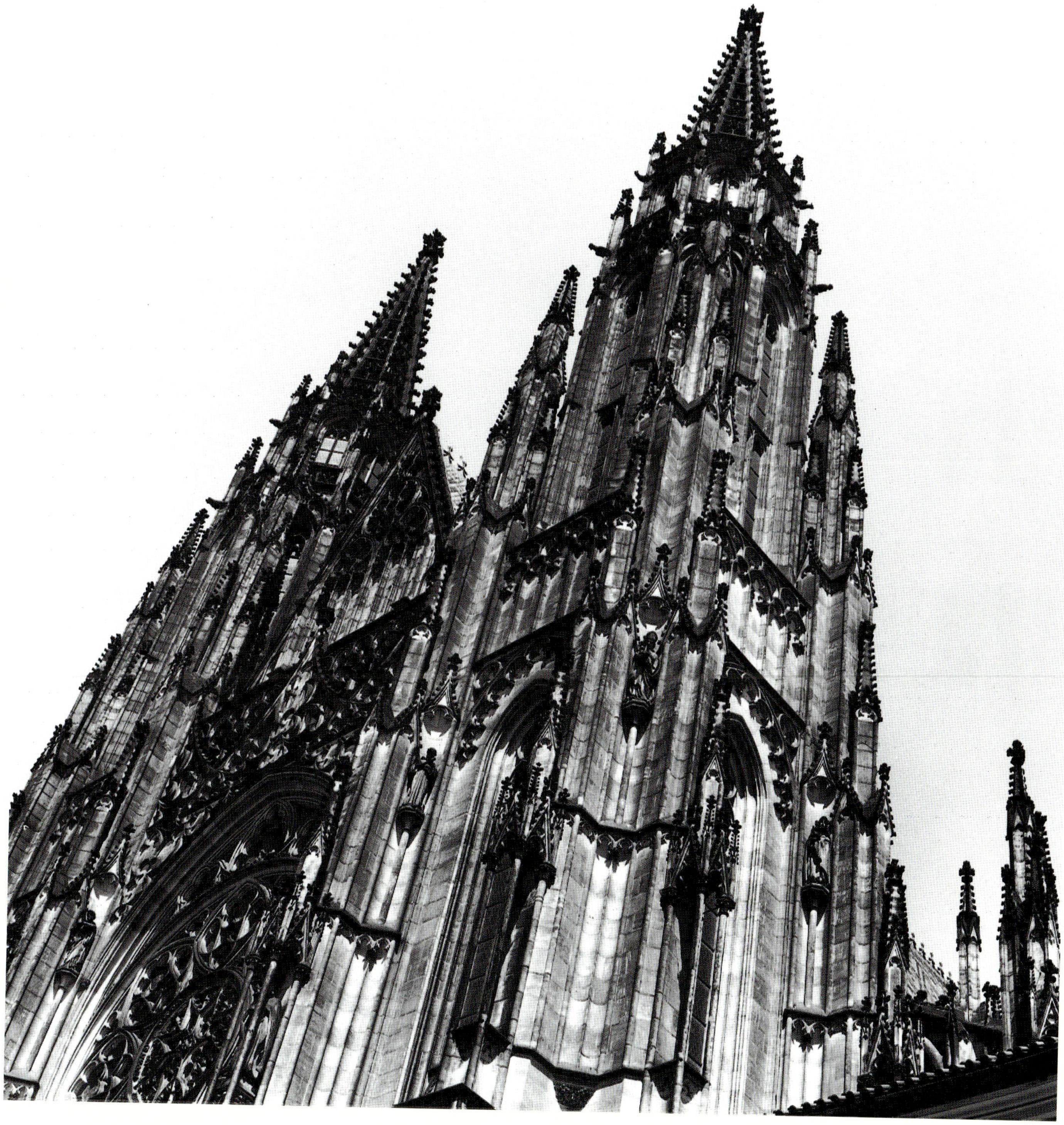

Jan Rosol

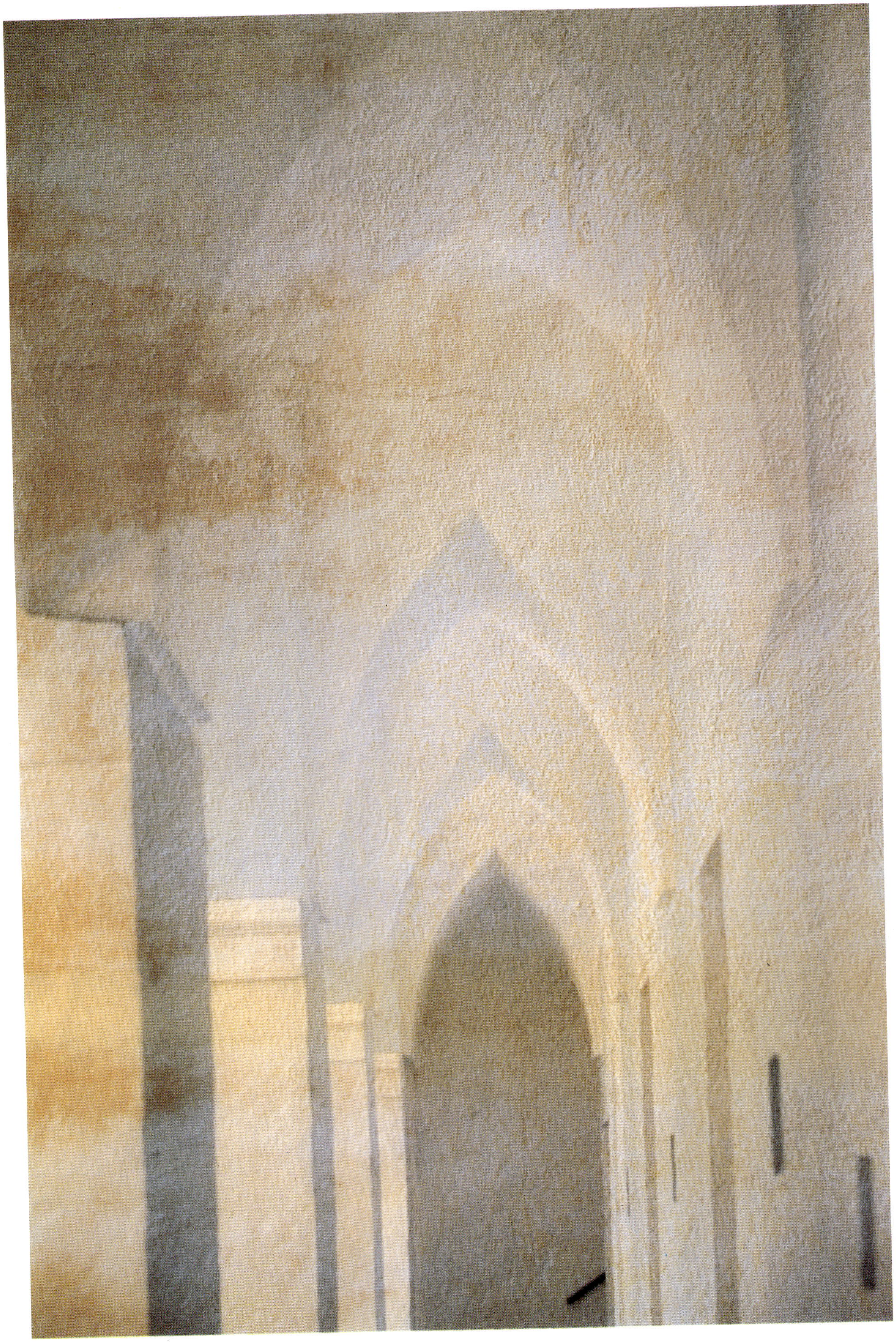

Claudio Gangi

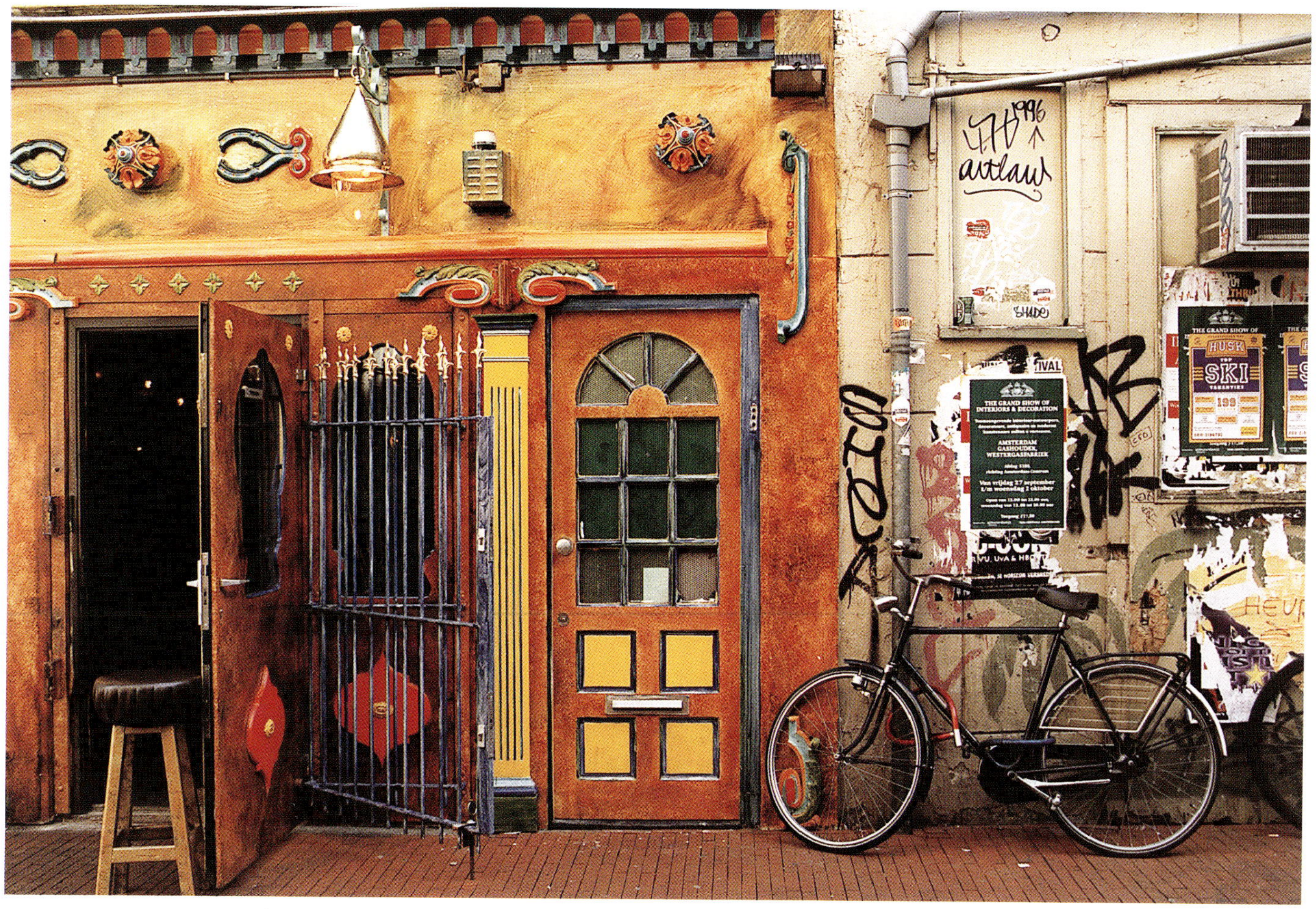
THE GRAND SHOW OF
INTERIORS & DECORATION
AMSTERDAM
GASHOUDER,
WESTERGASFABRIEK
Van vrijdag 27 september
t/m woensdag 2 oktober
THE GRAND SHOW OF
HUSK
SKI
VAKANTIES

Joshua Even

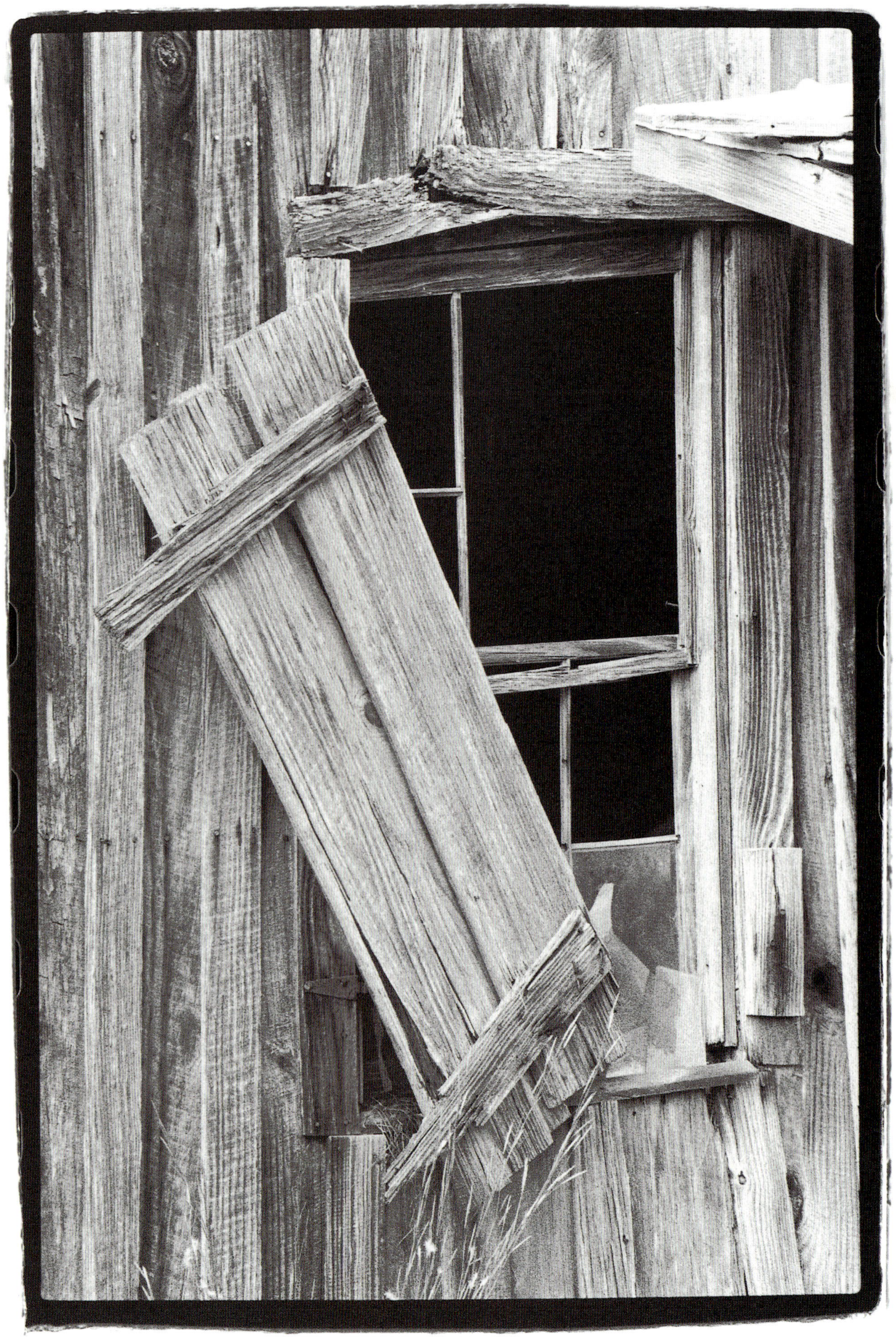

Ron McDonald

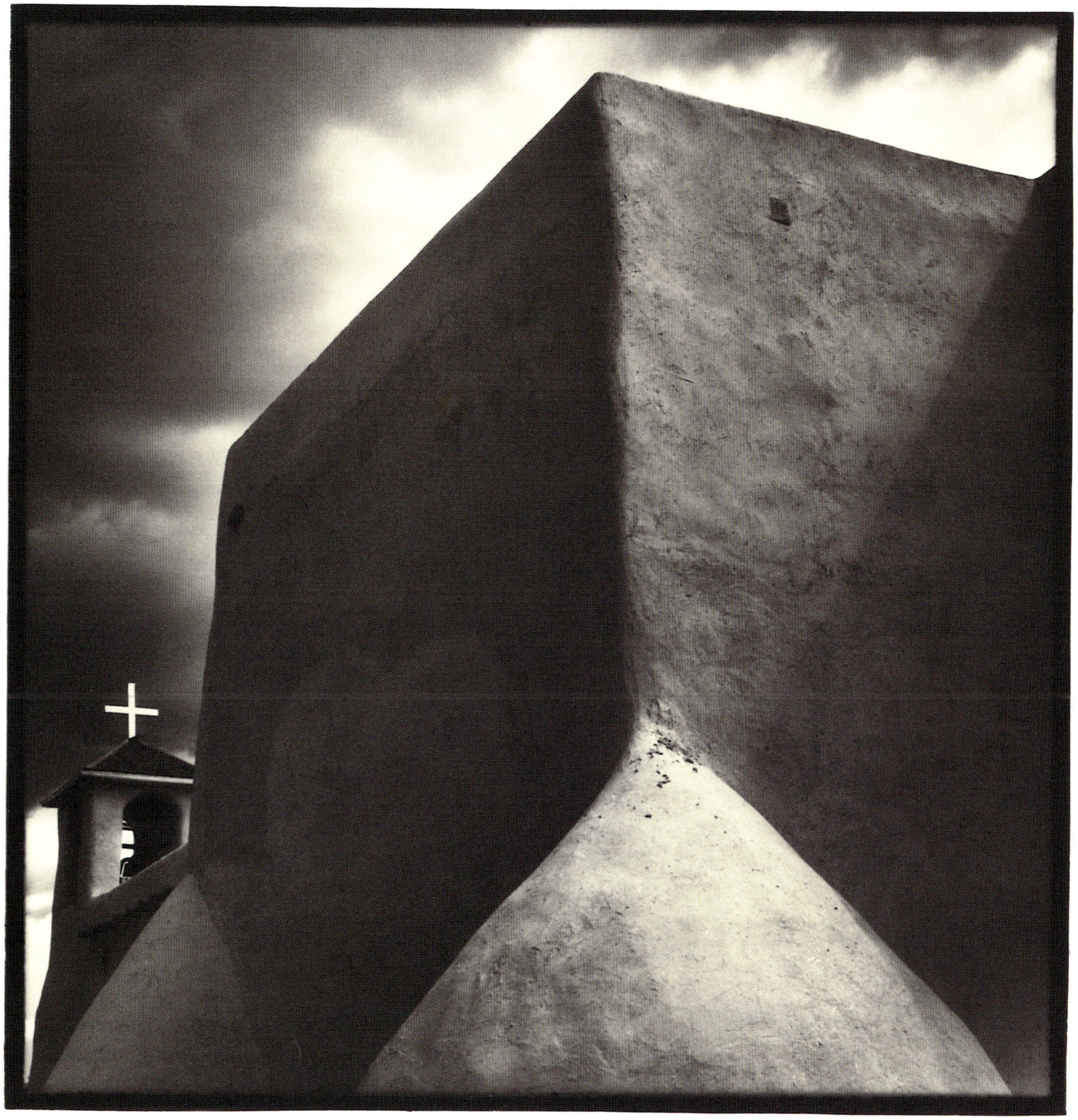

Paul Kozal

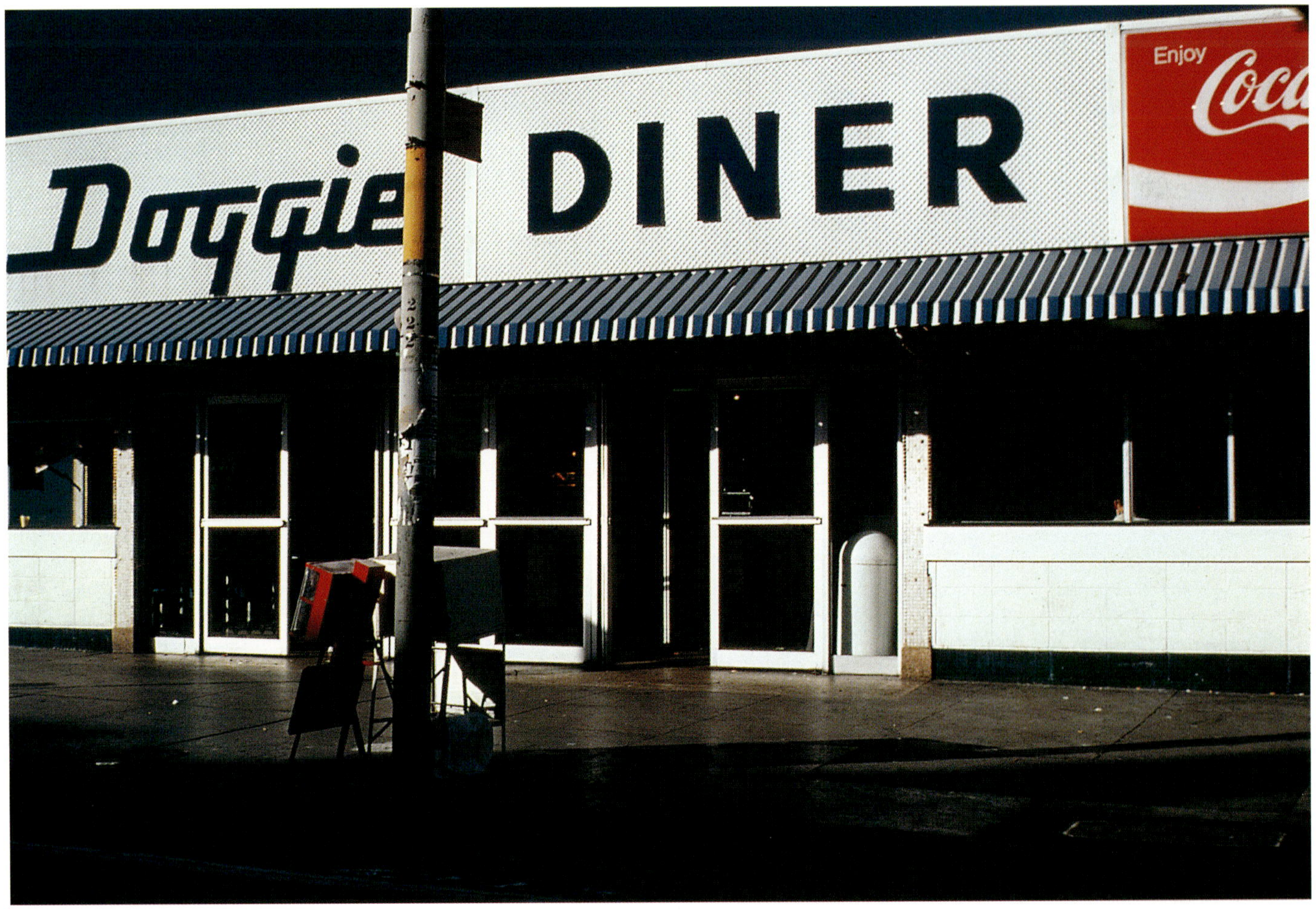

John Cameron

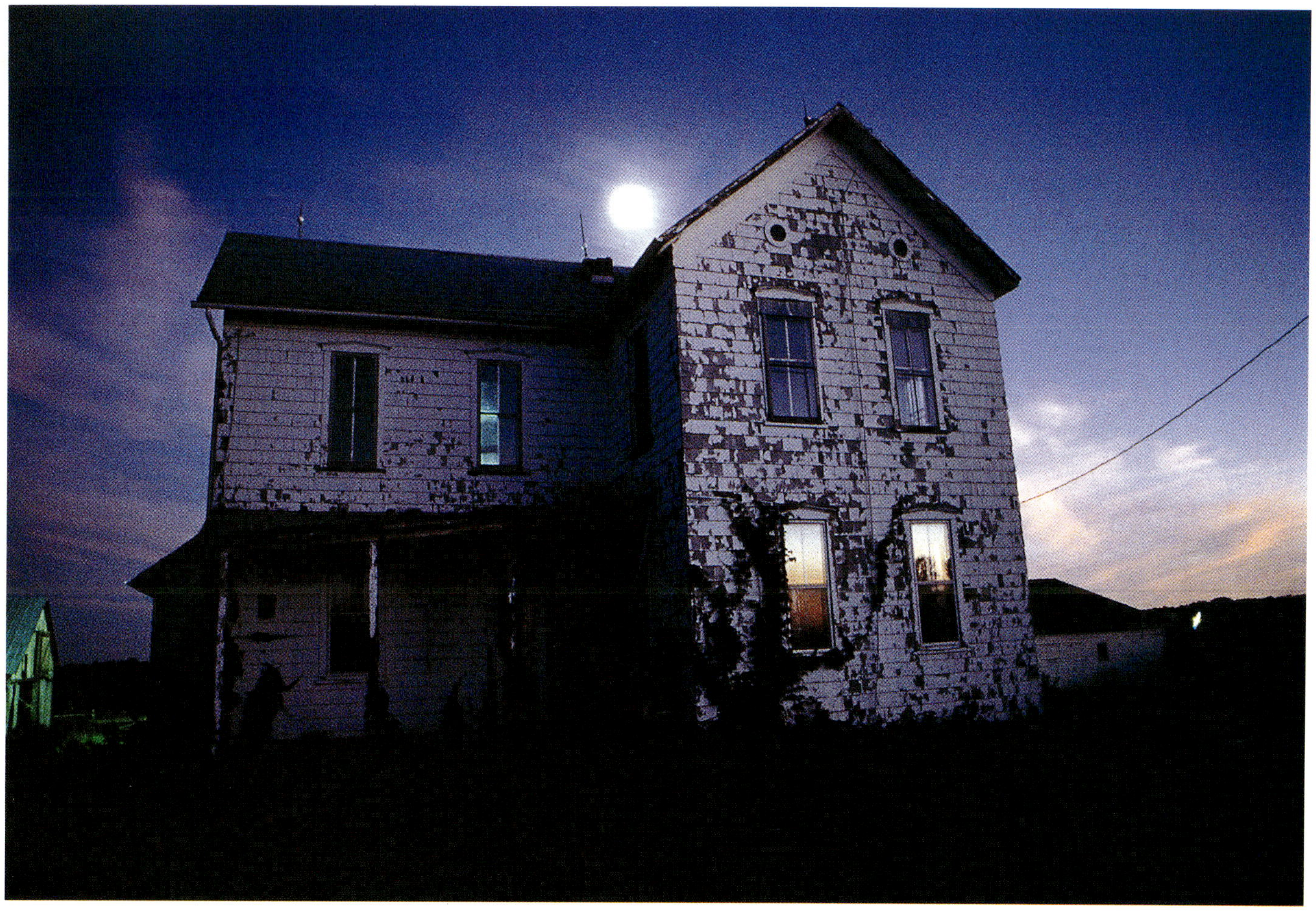

Russell Kroll

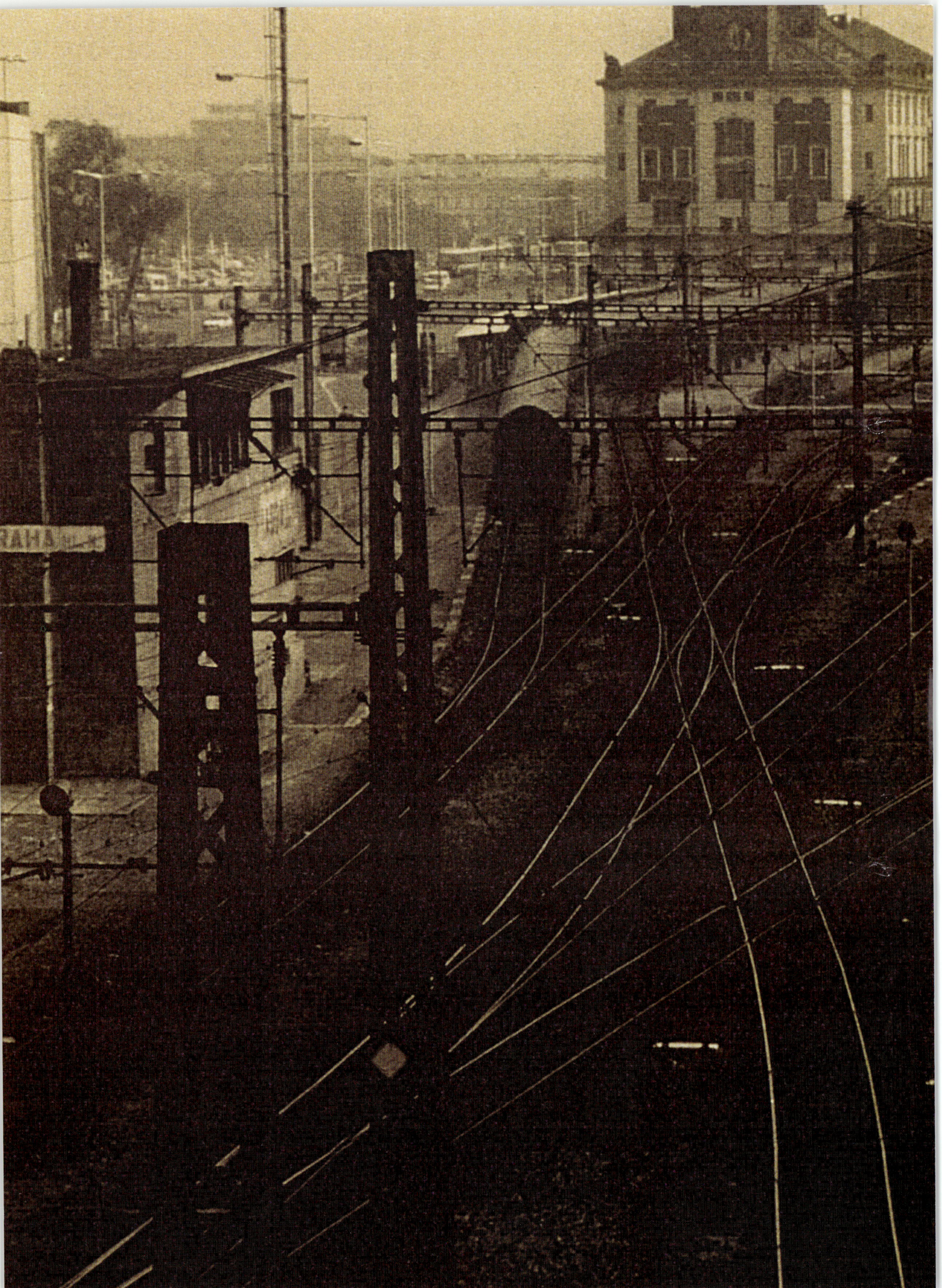
RAHA

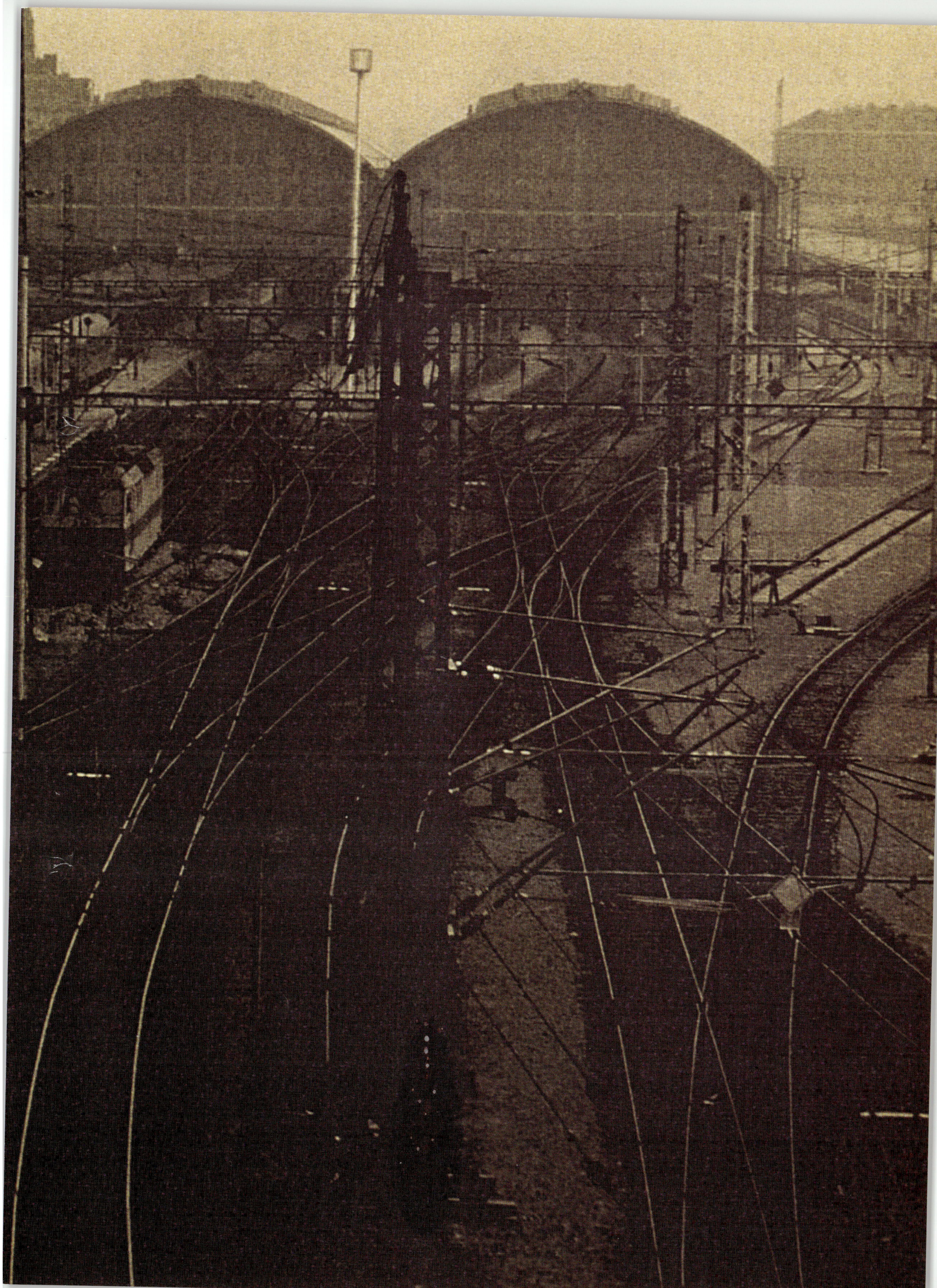

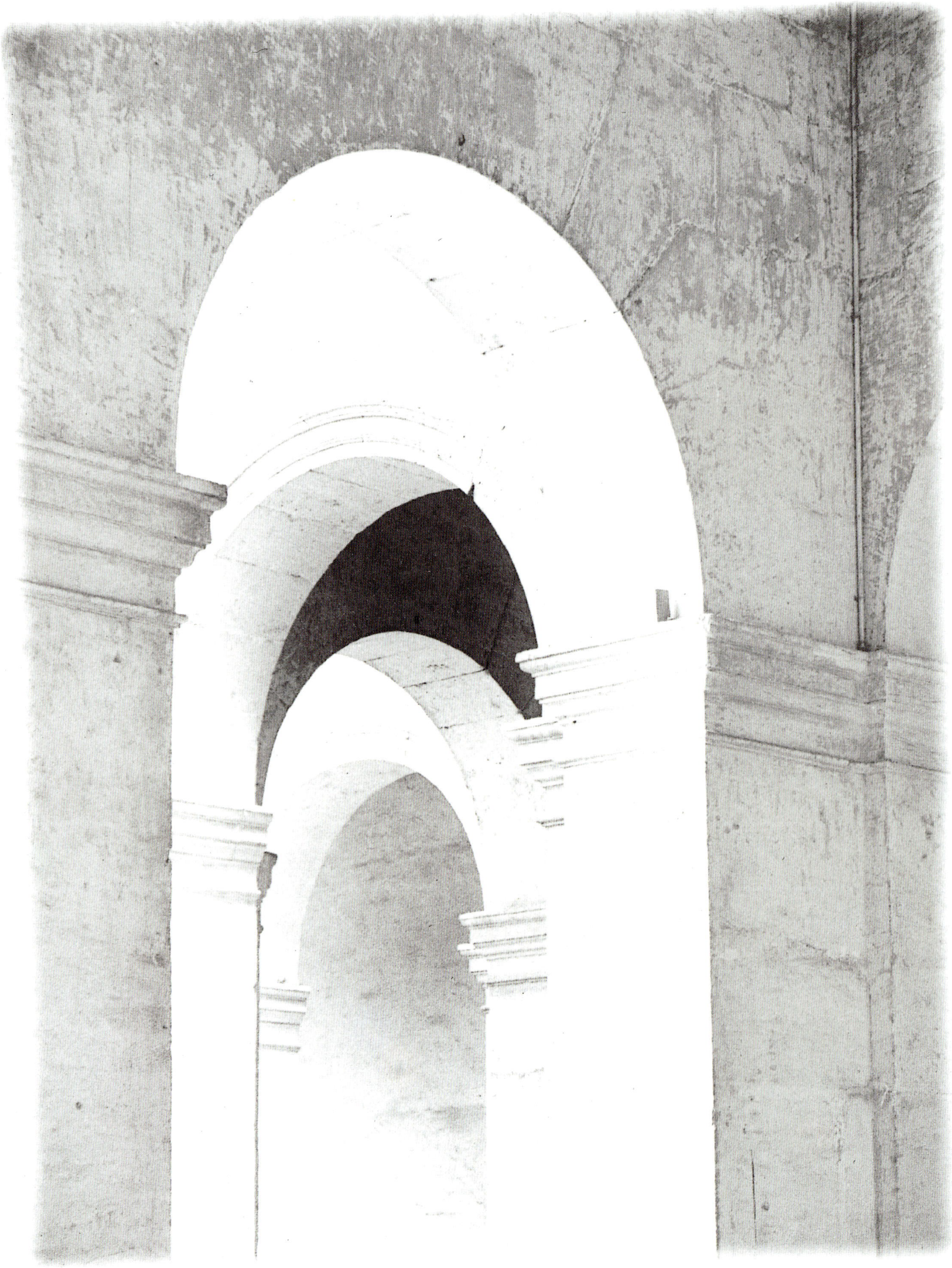

(PREVIOUS SPREAD) *Terése Makar* ■ (THIS PAGE) *Paul Kozal*

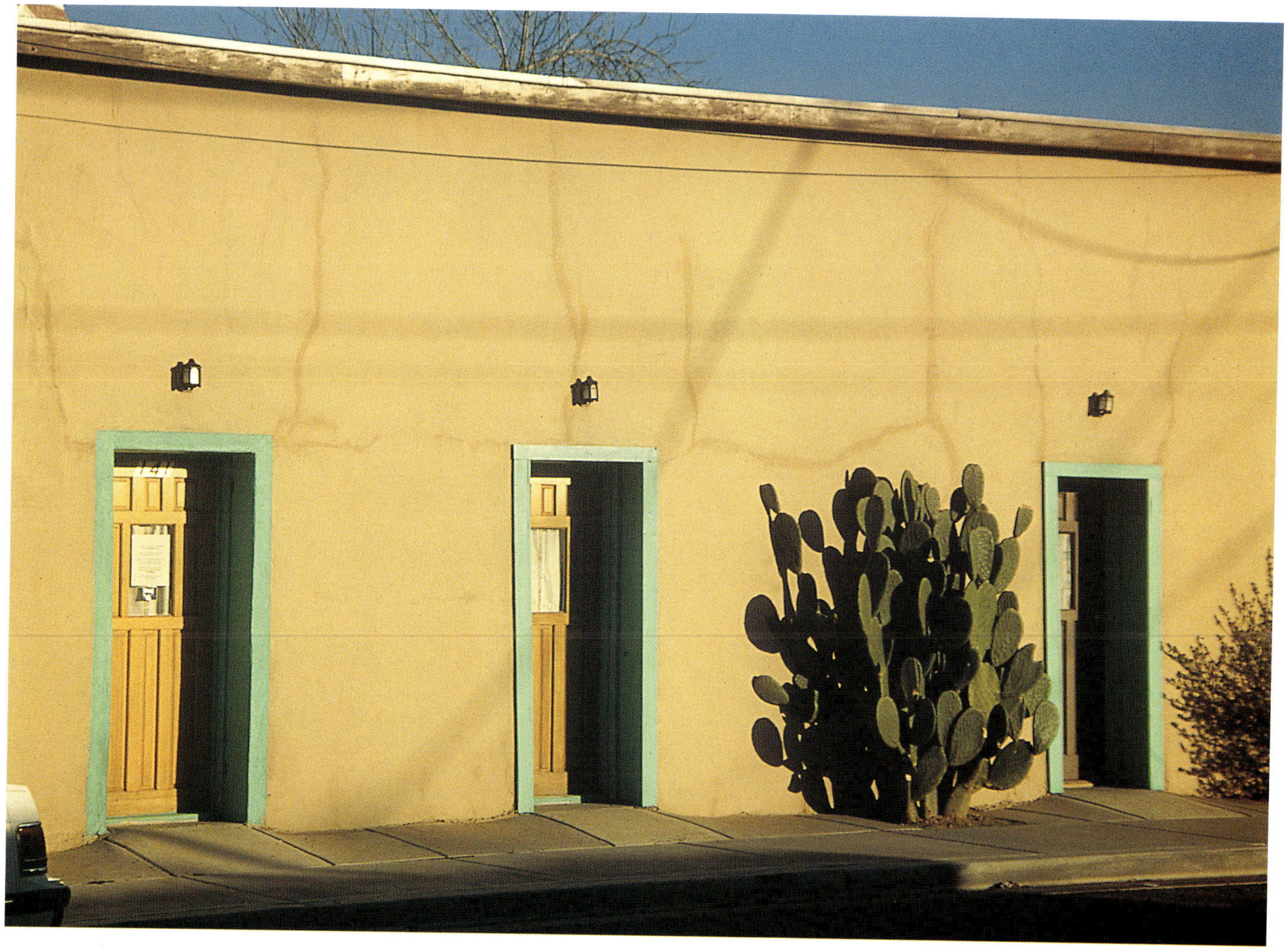

John K. Crawford

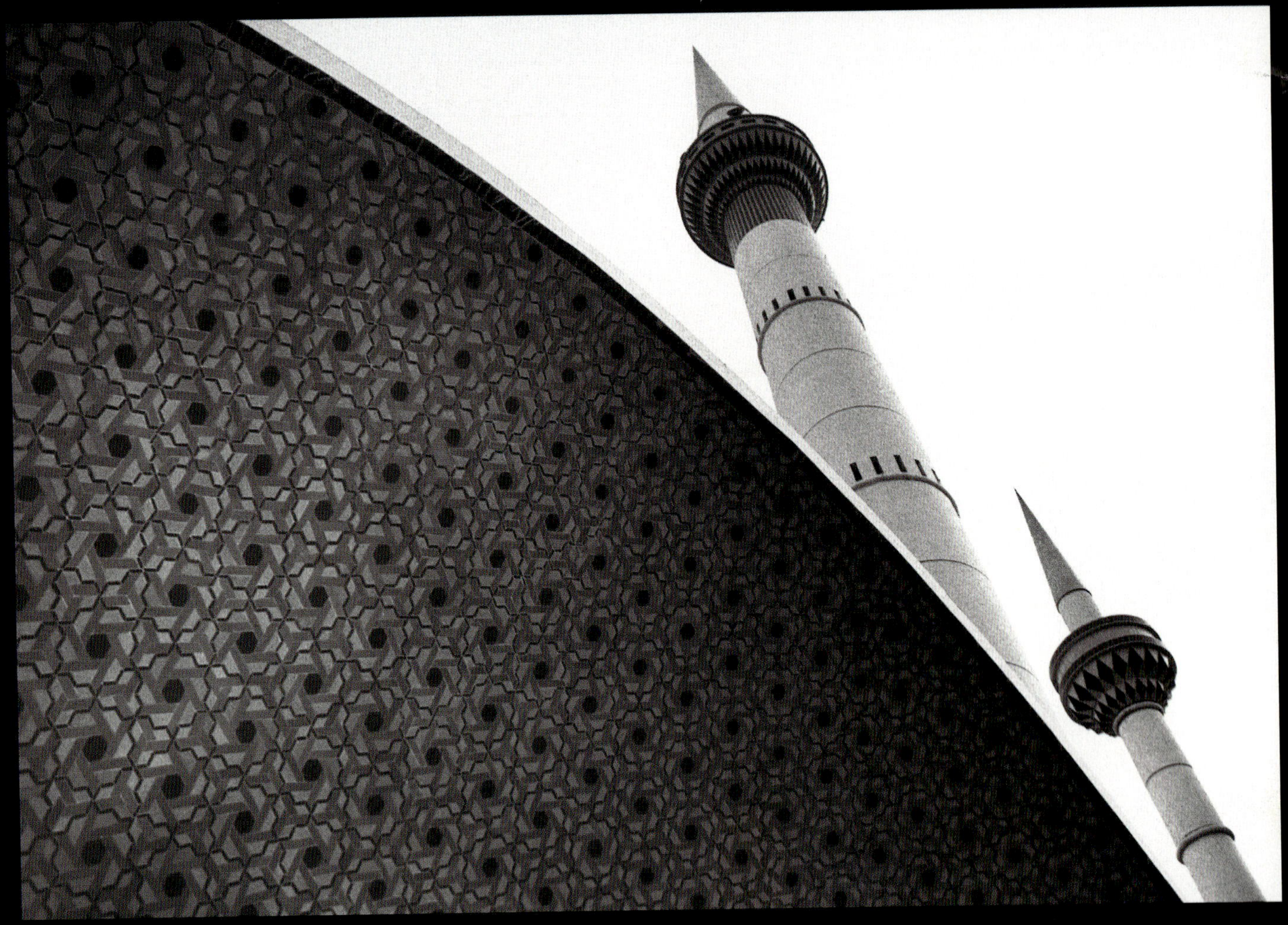

Amina Baig

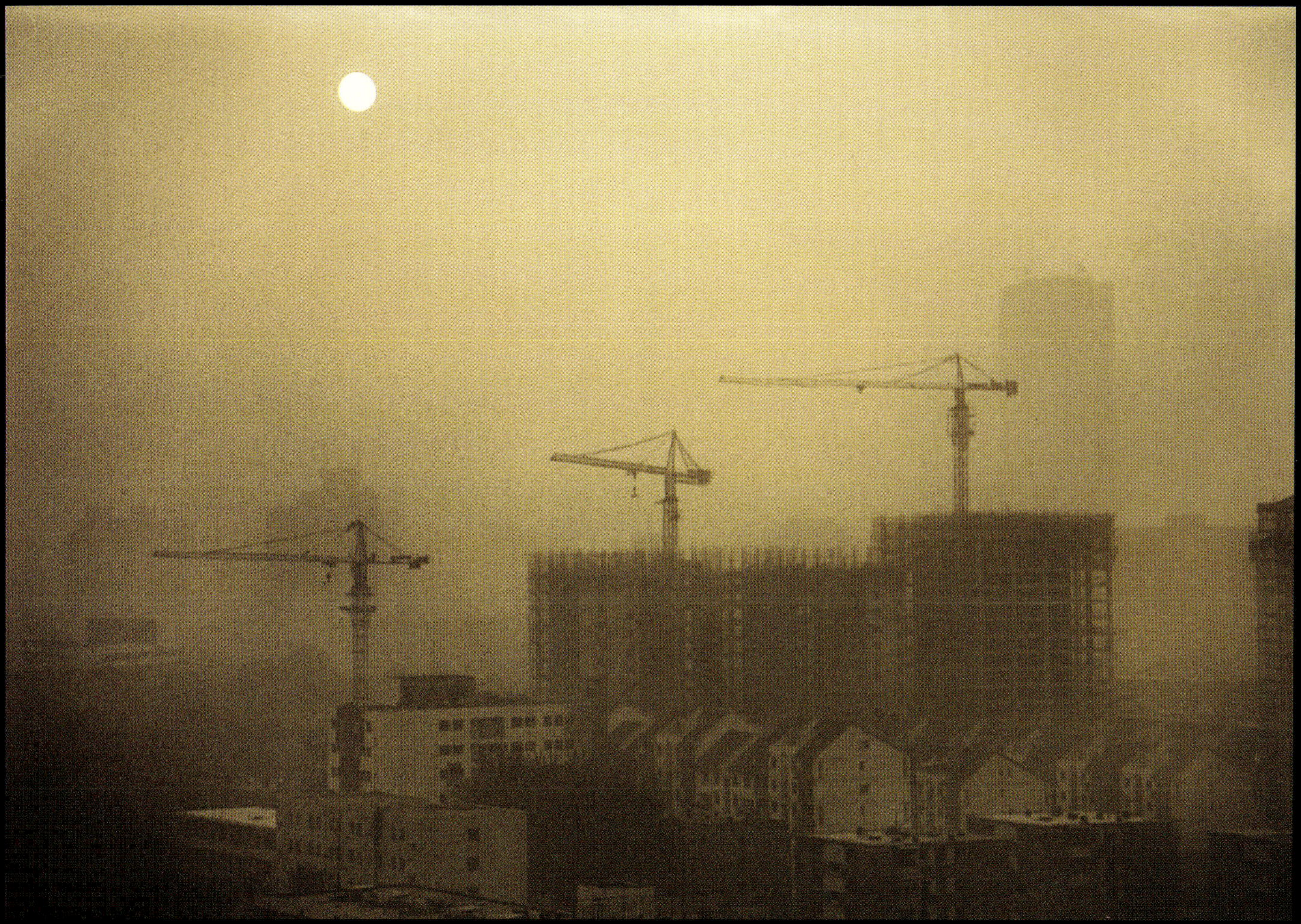

Paul Kozal

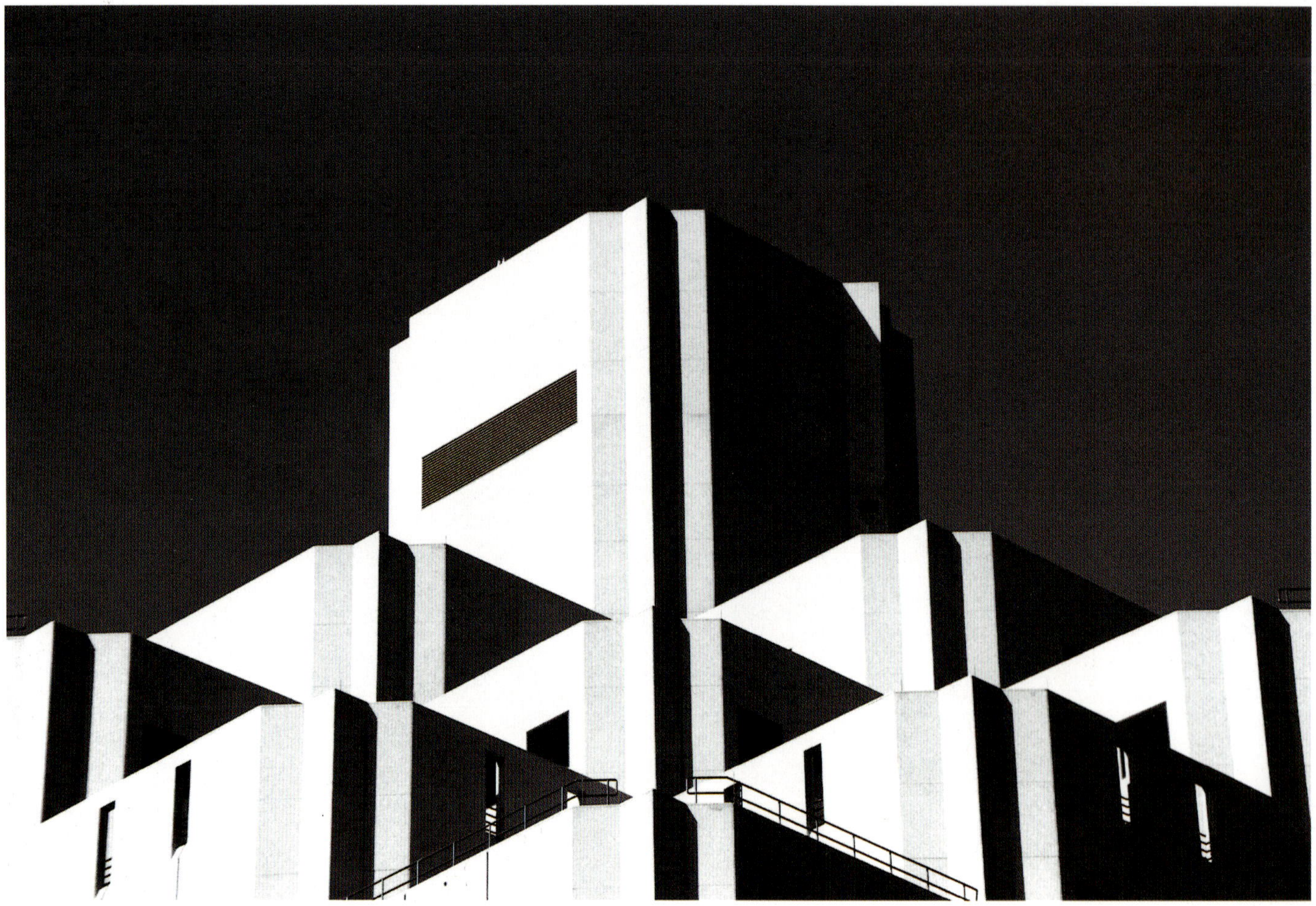

Michael Guzman

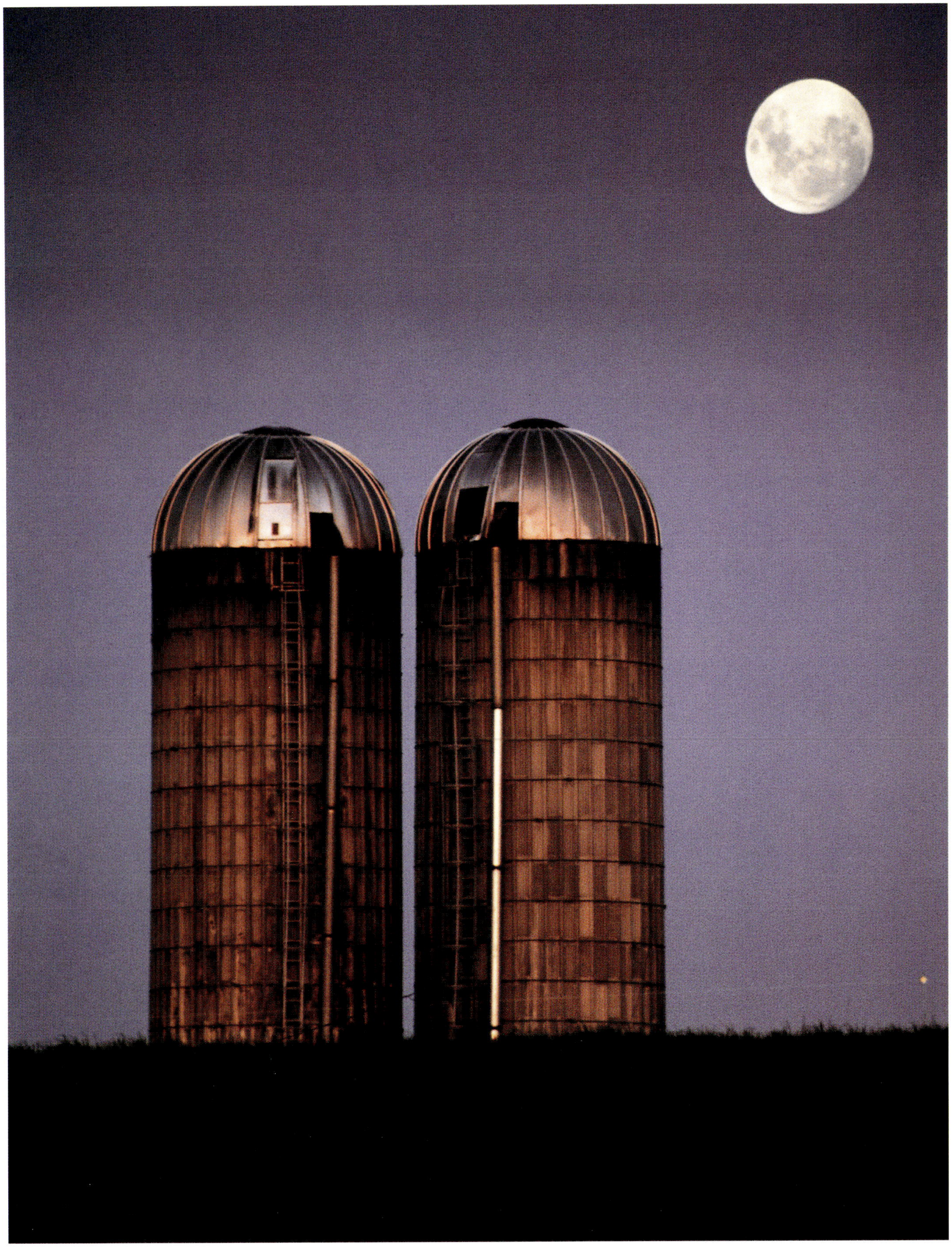

Jason Williams

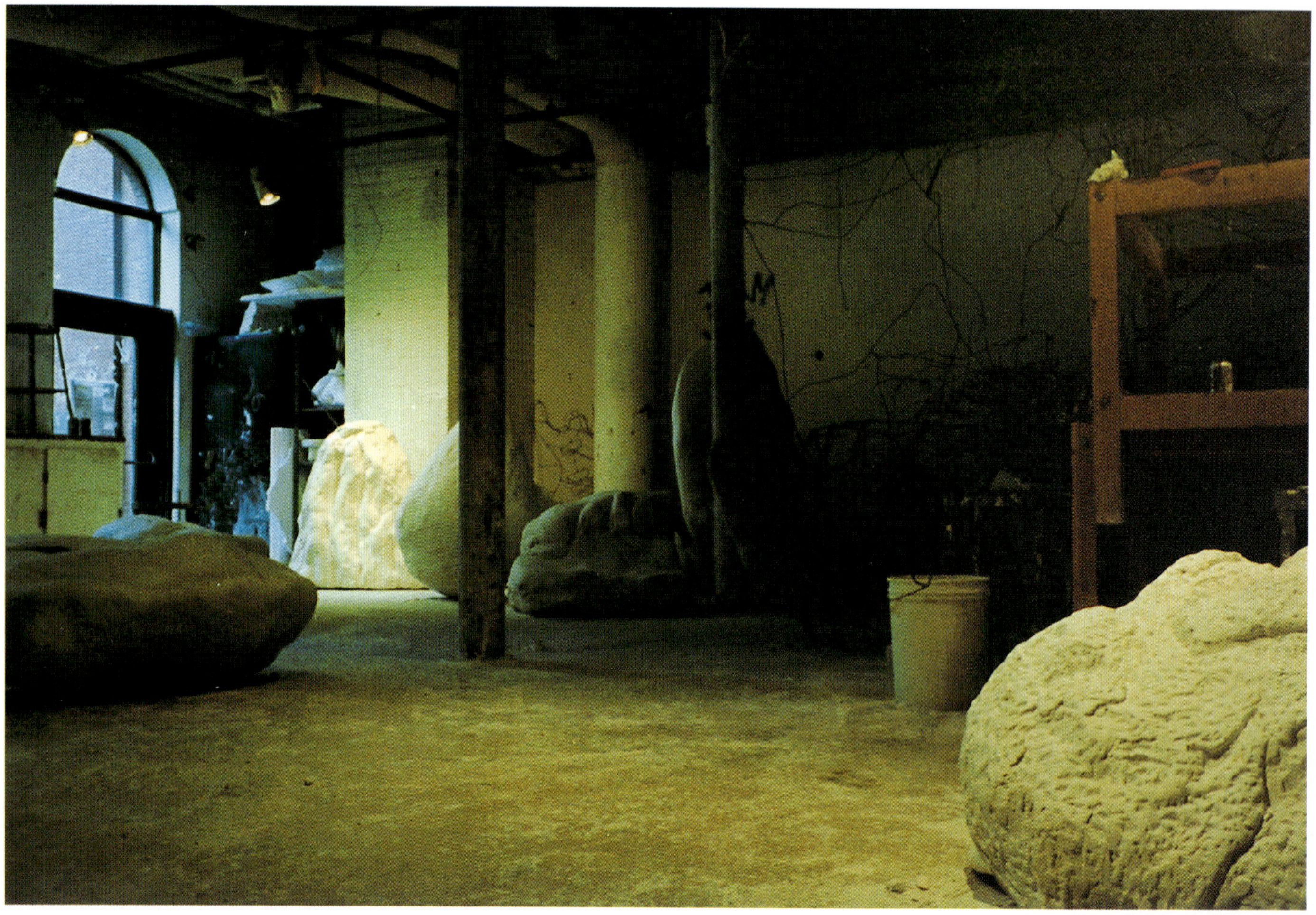

Christopher Lovenguth

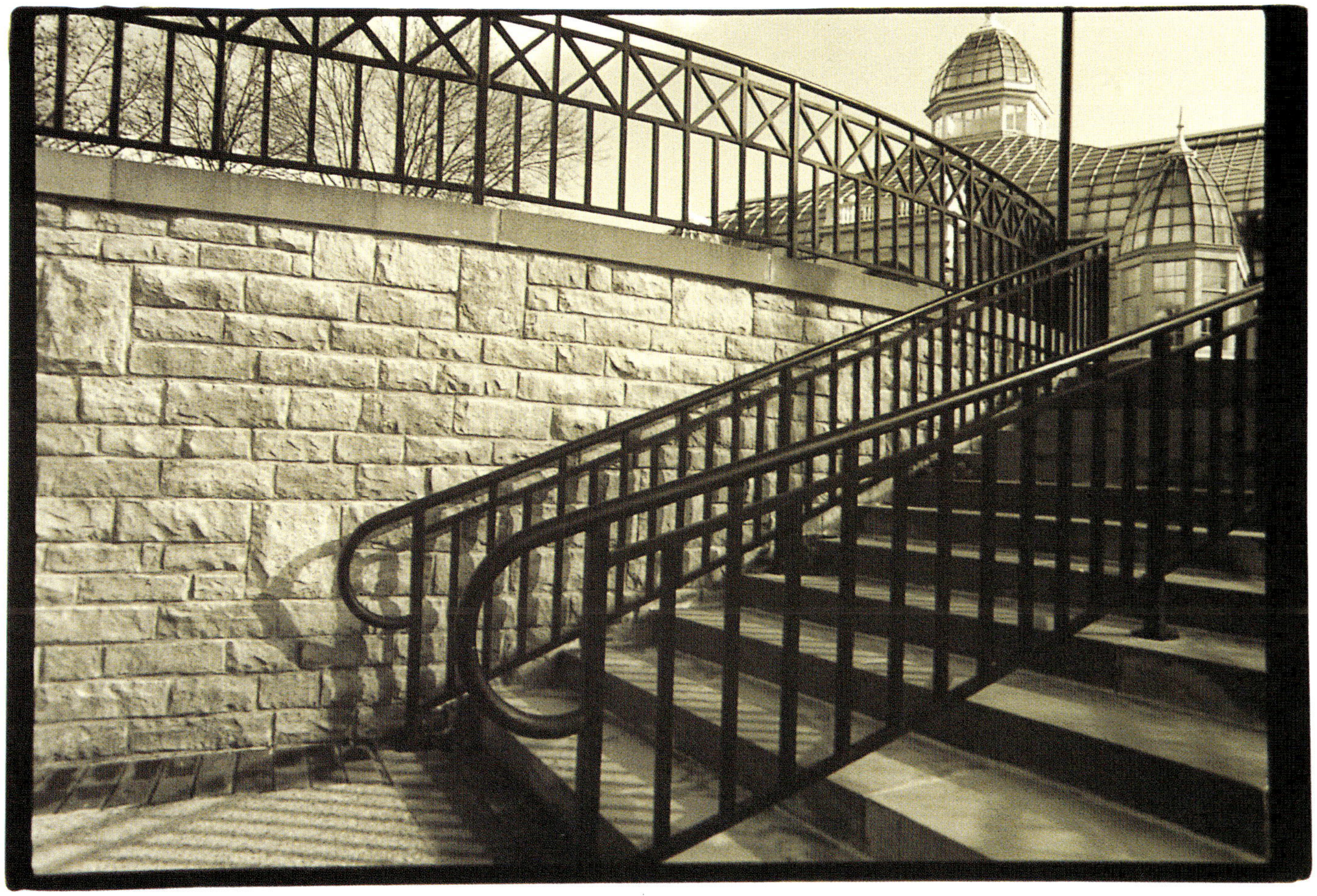

Brian David Hite

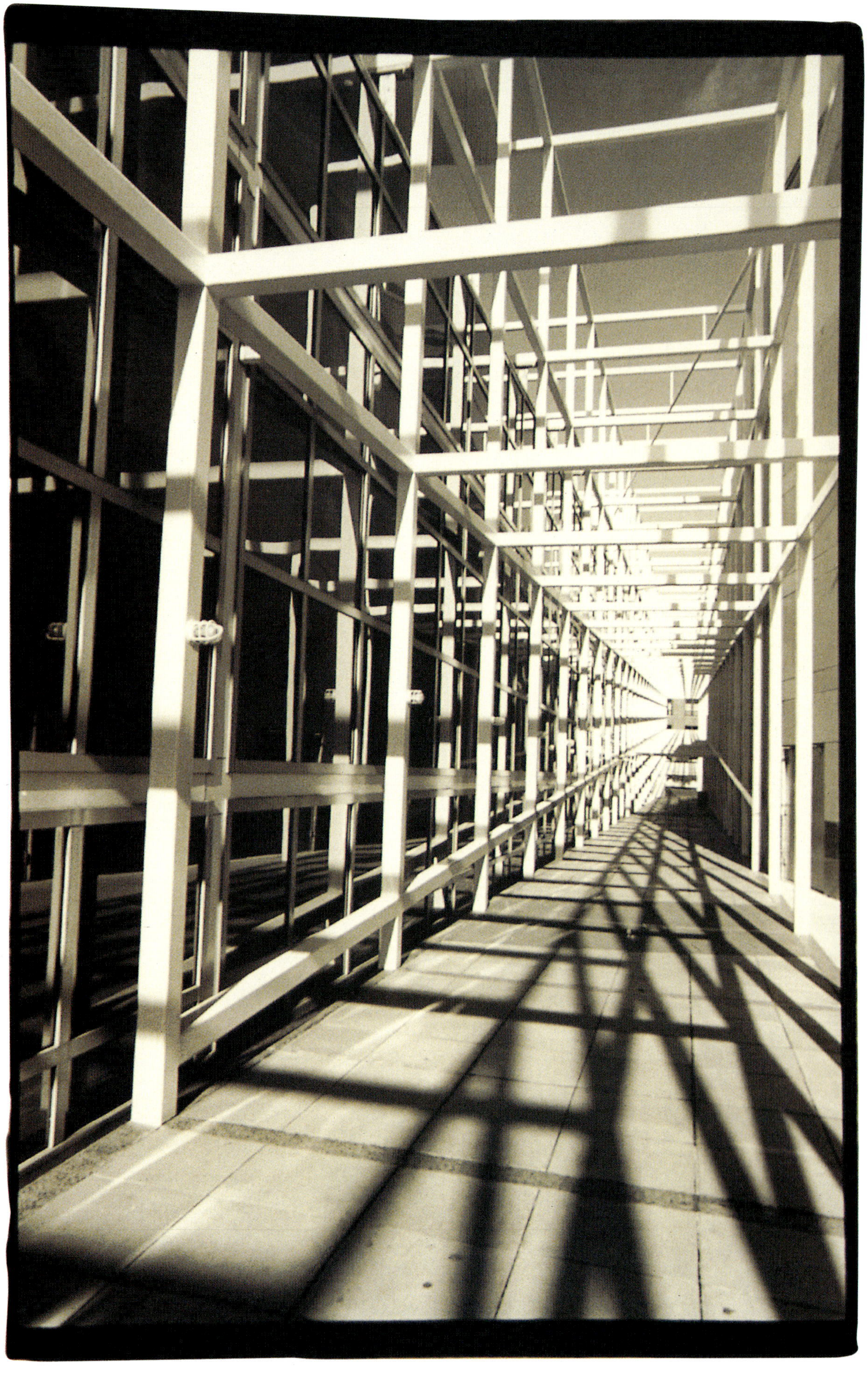

Brian David Hite

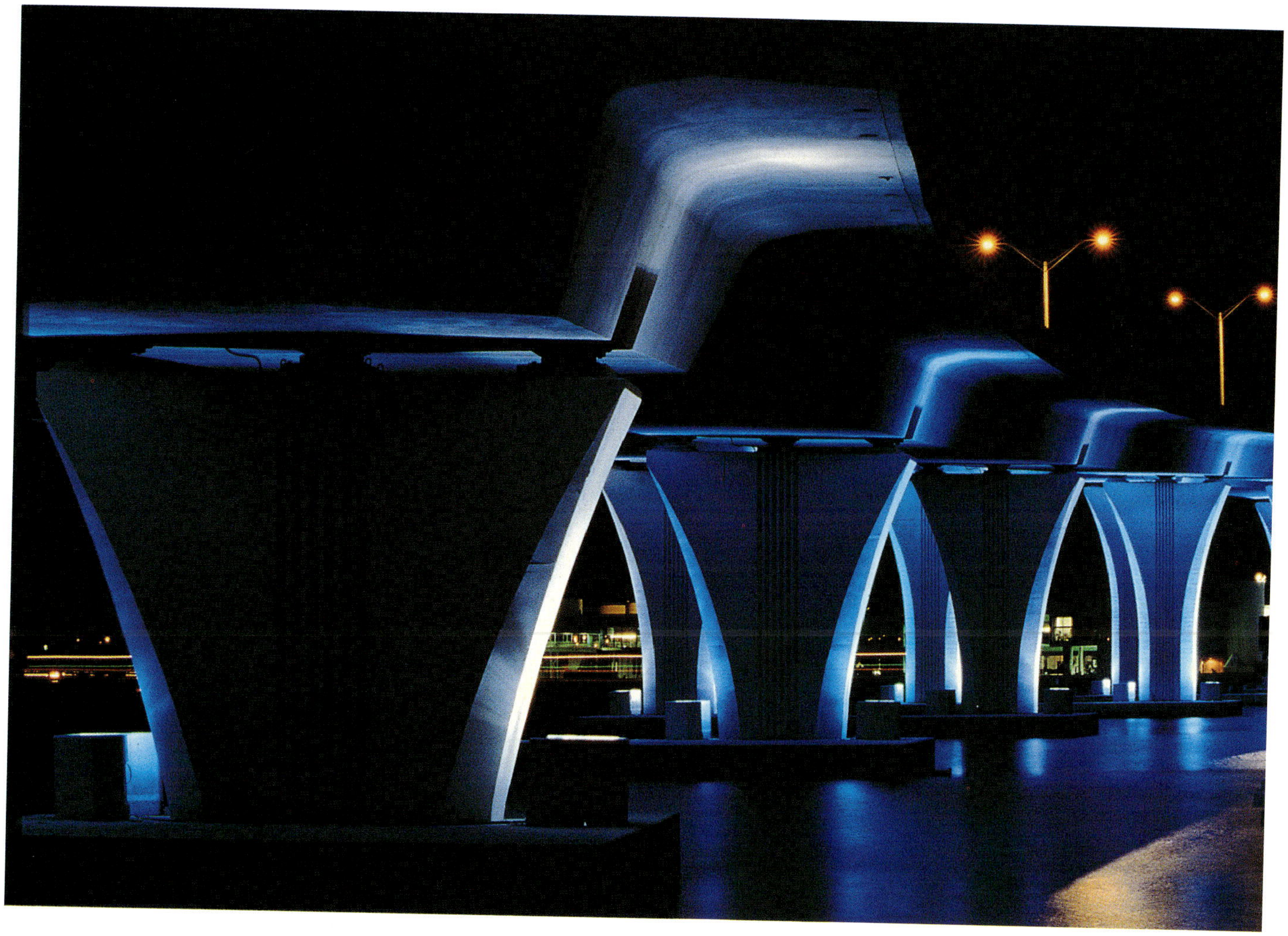

Stuart Brown

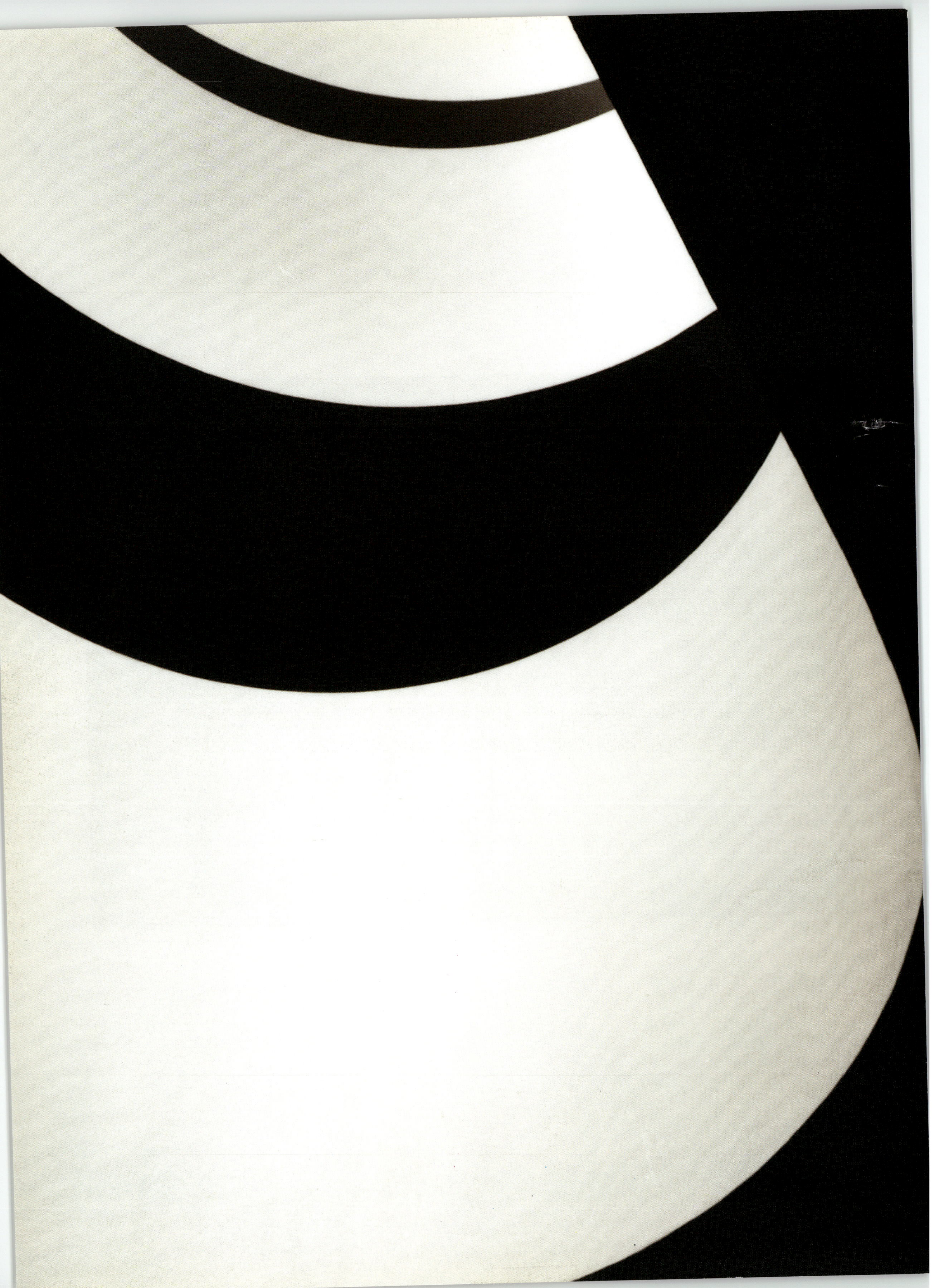

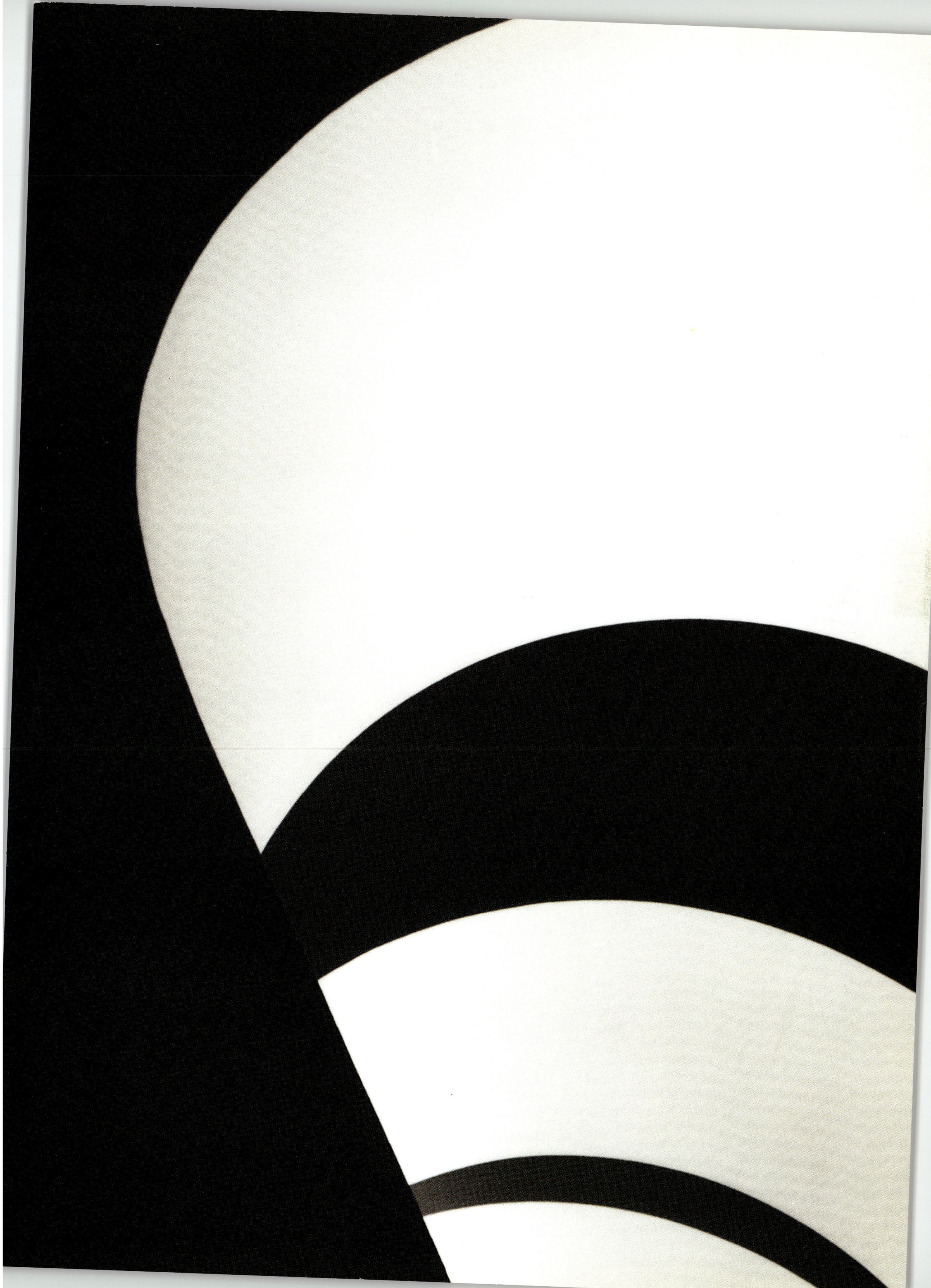

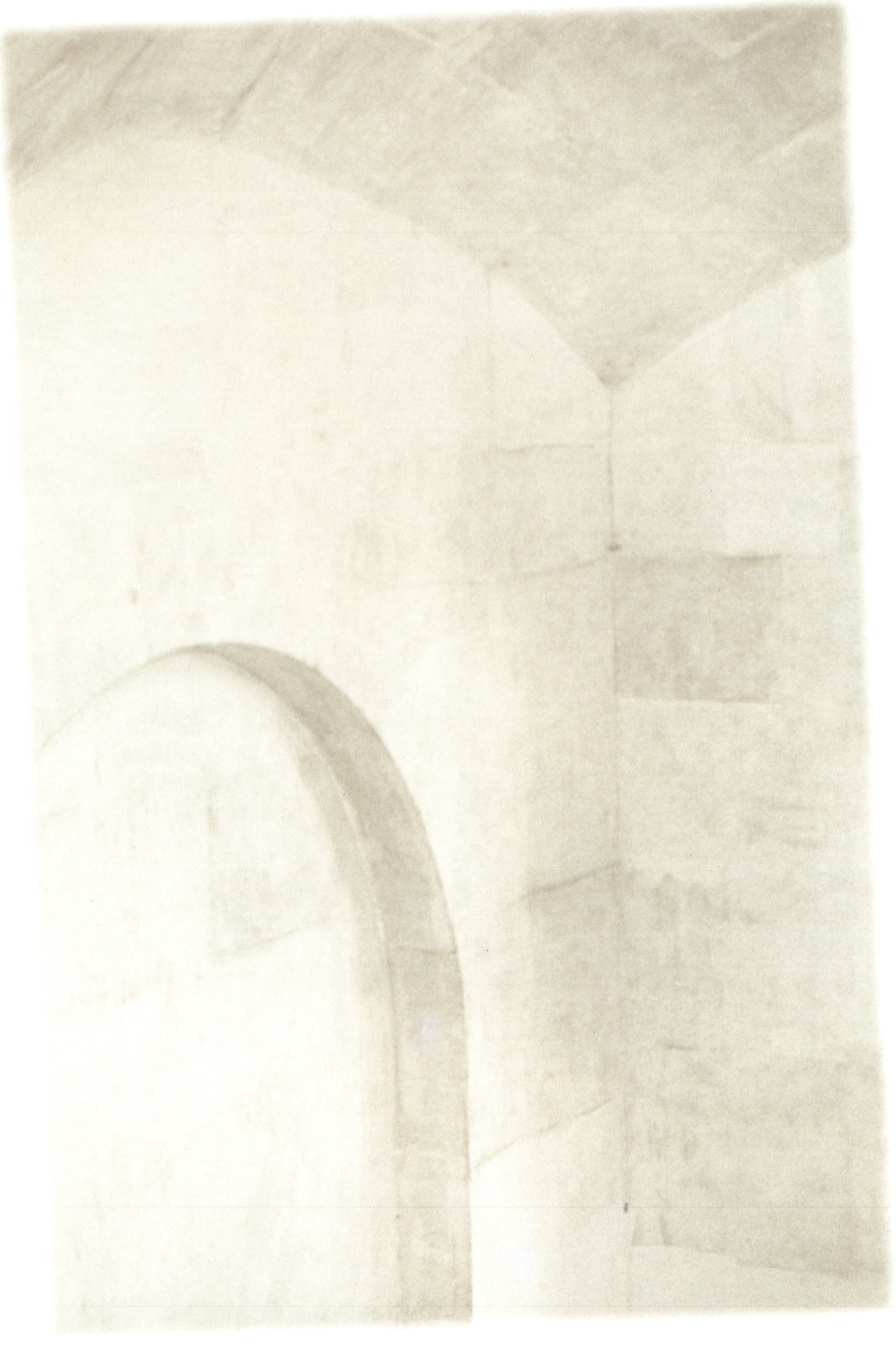

(PREVIOUS SPREAD & THIS PAGE) *Paul Kozal*

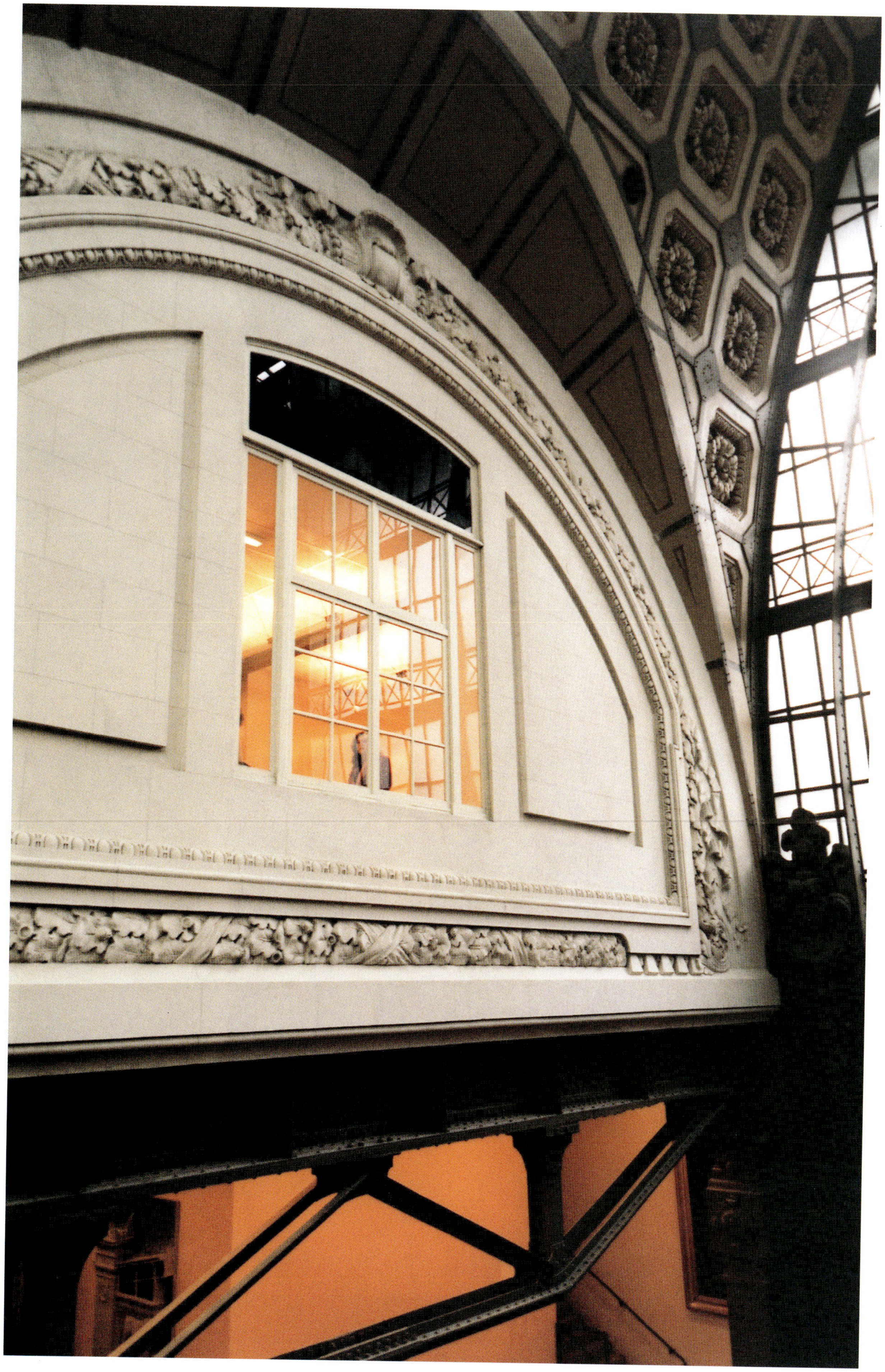

Gregory Morton

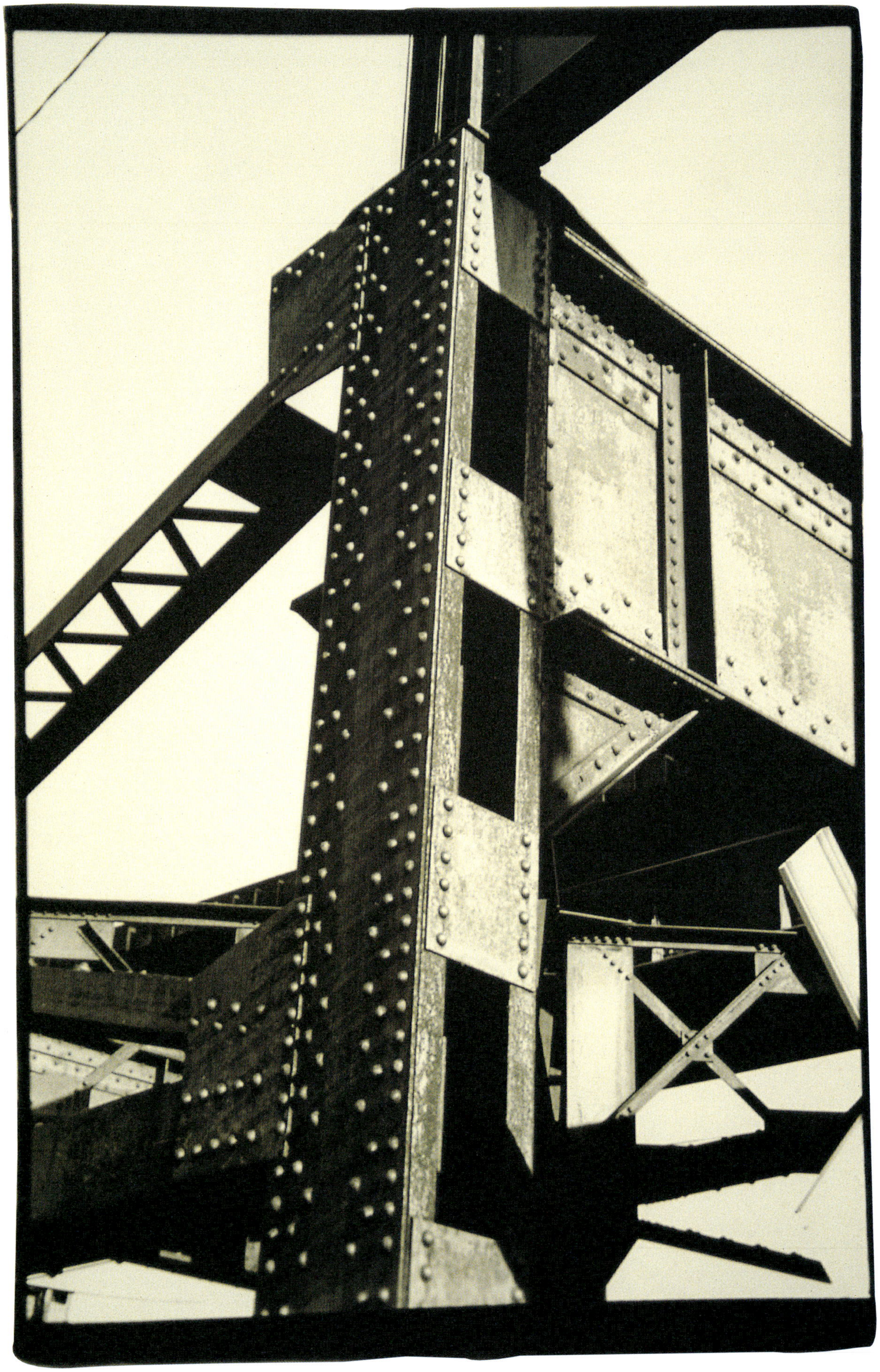

Brian David Hite

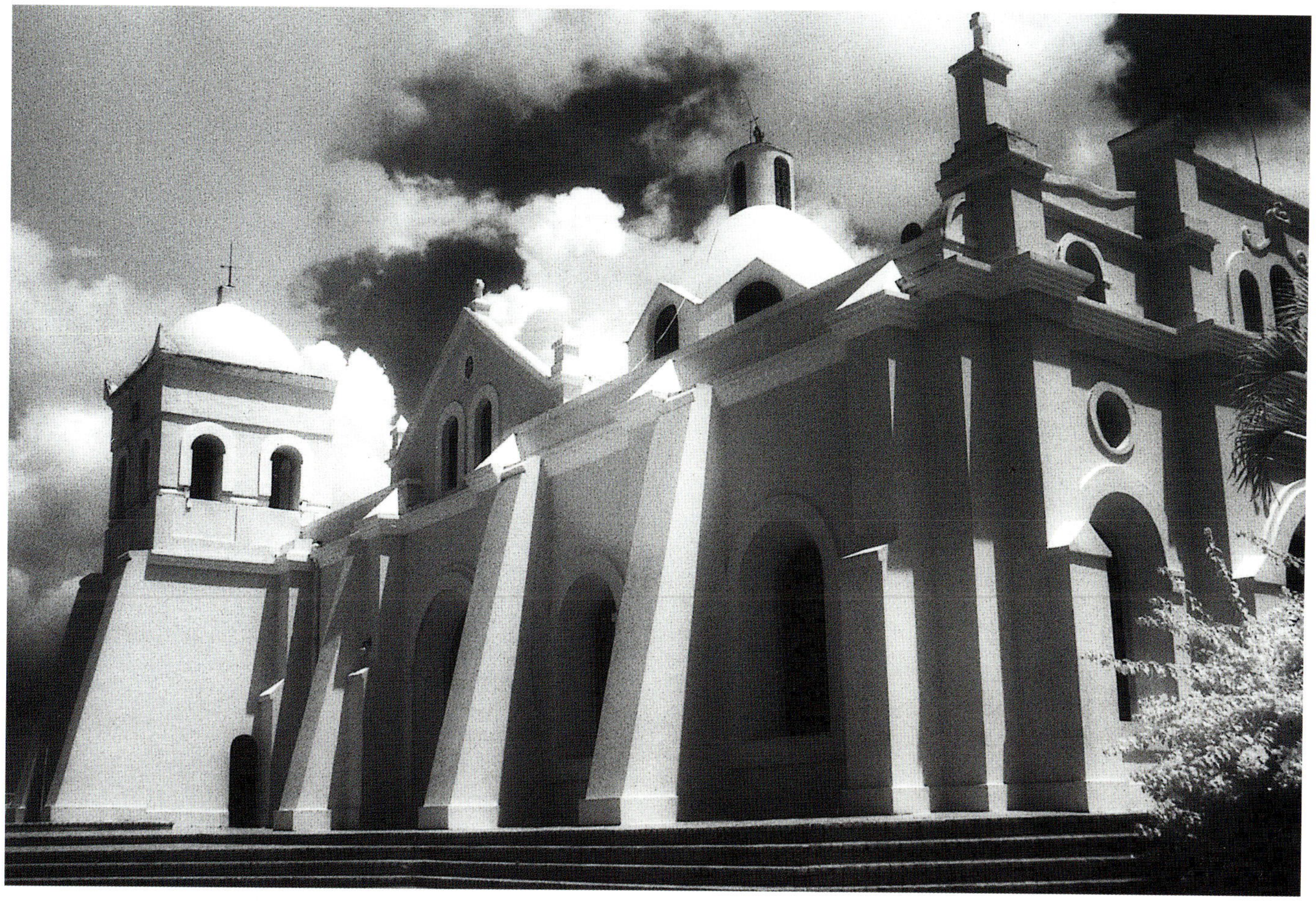

Juan Jose Nunez Estevez

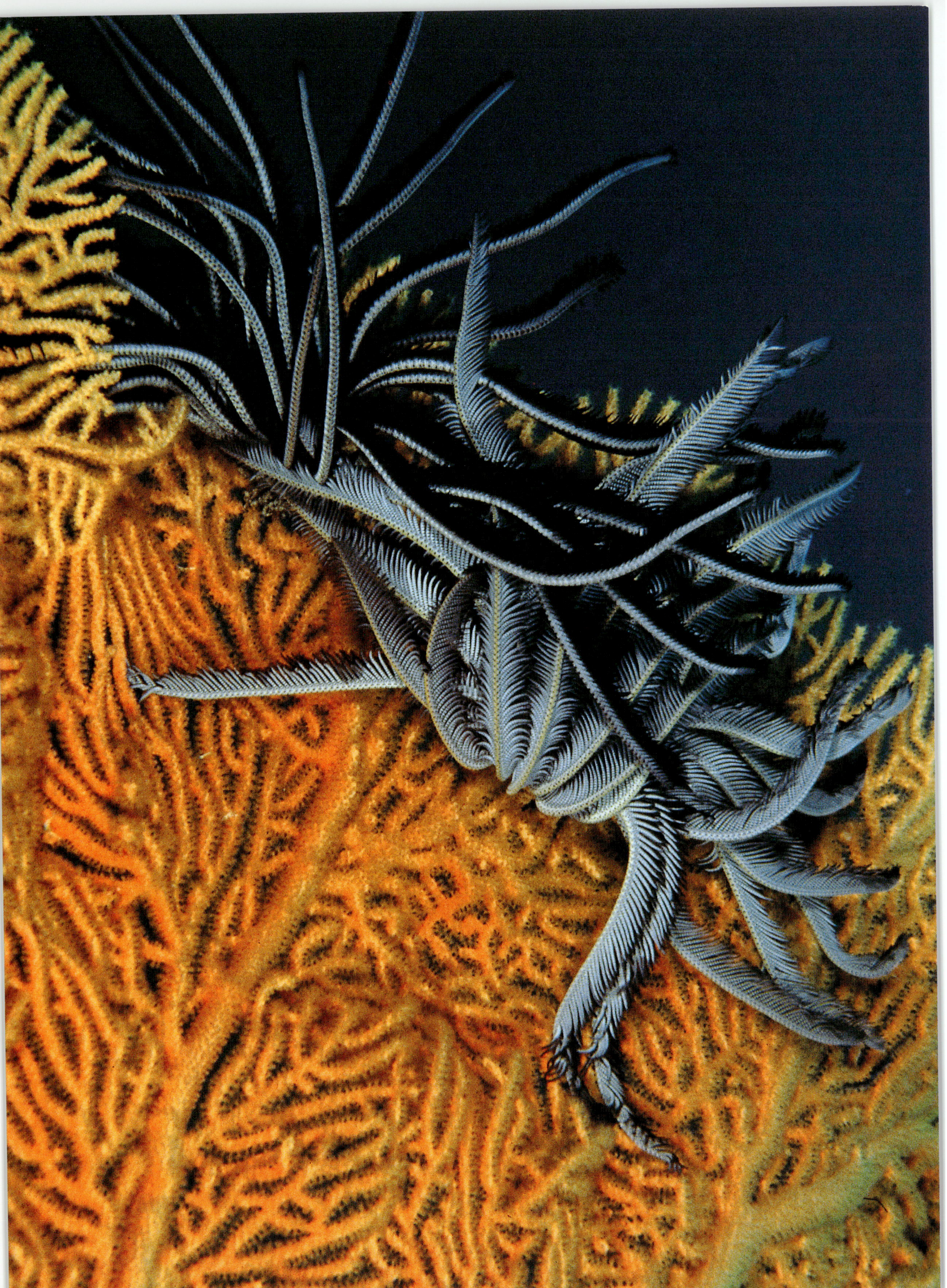

WILDLIFE

TIERE

ANIMAUX

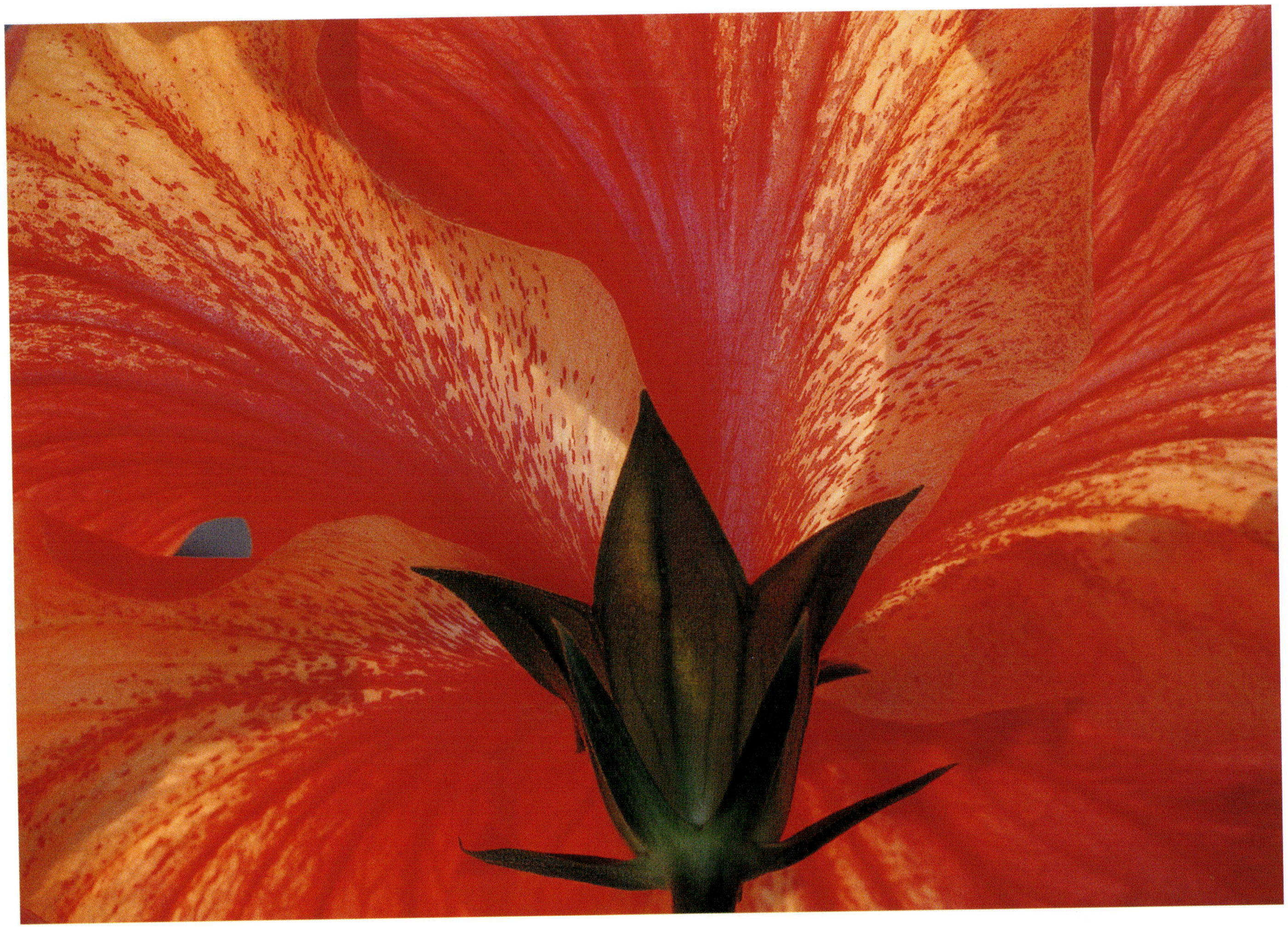

(PREVIOUS SPREAD) *Patricia A. Jordan* ■ (THIS PAGE) *Hèlena Fierlinger*

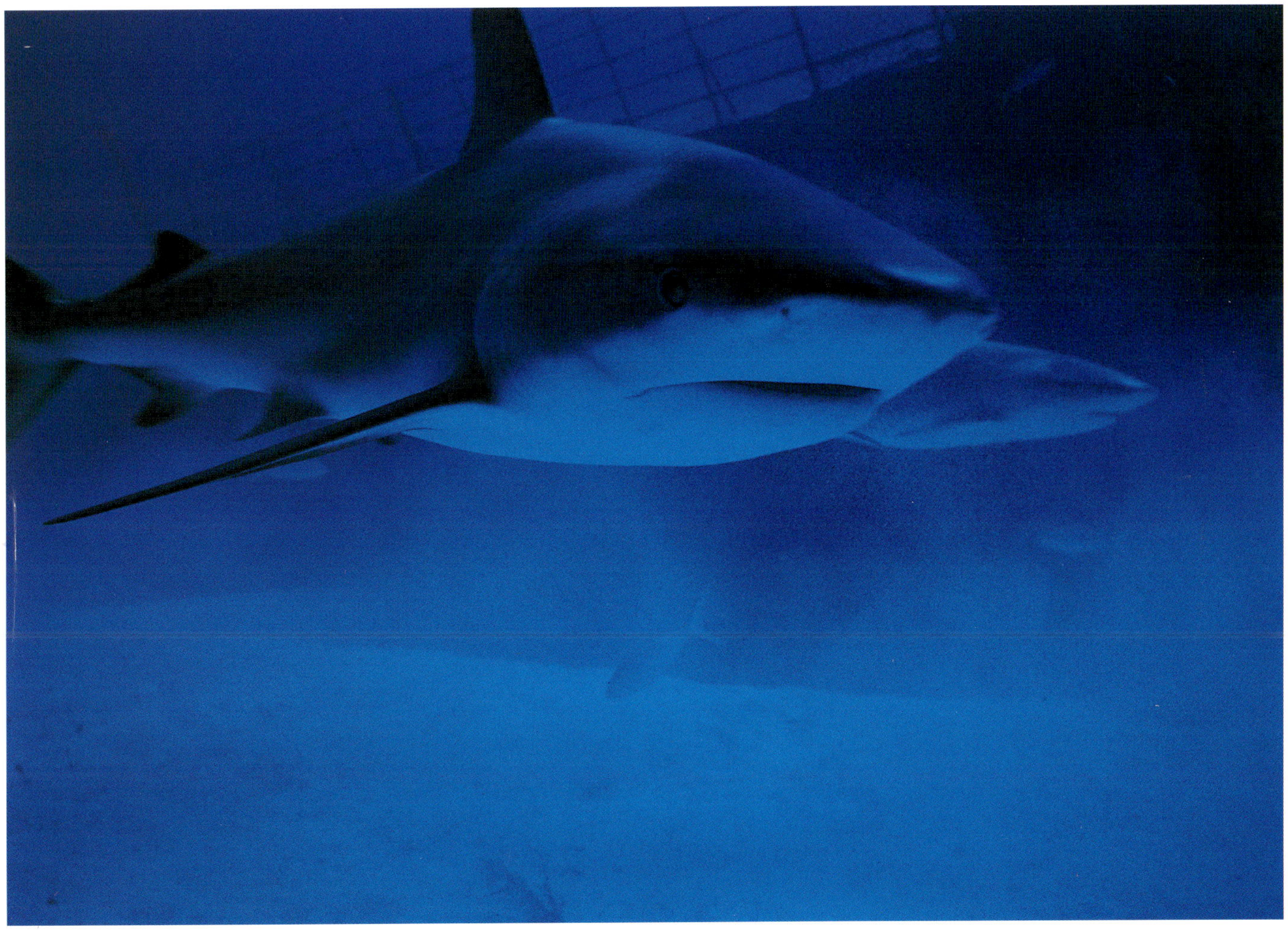

Jordan Weinstein

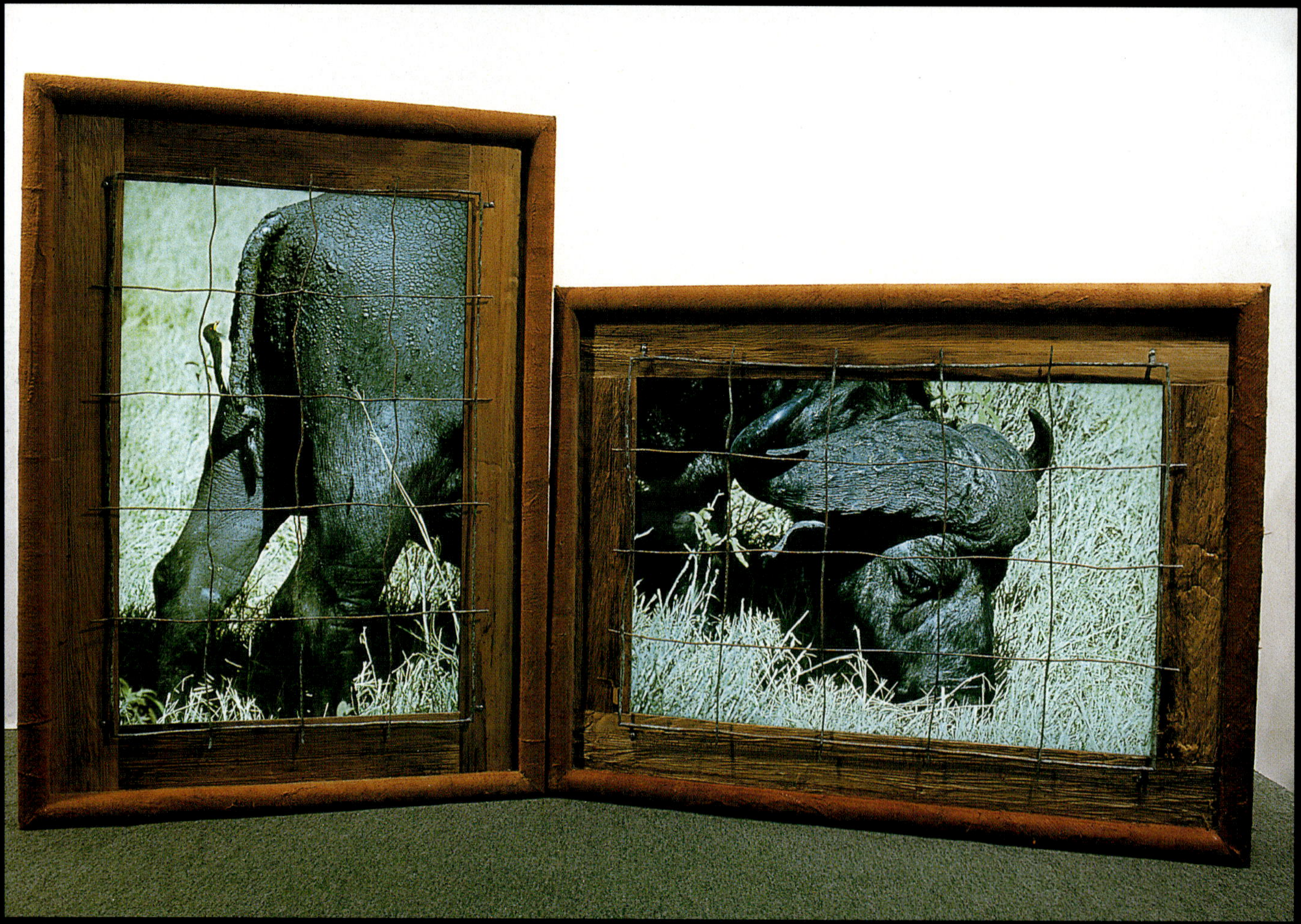

Mark Scheflen

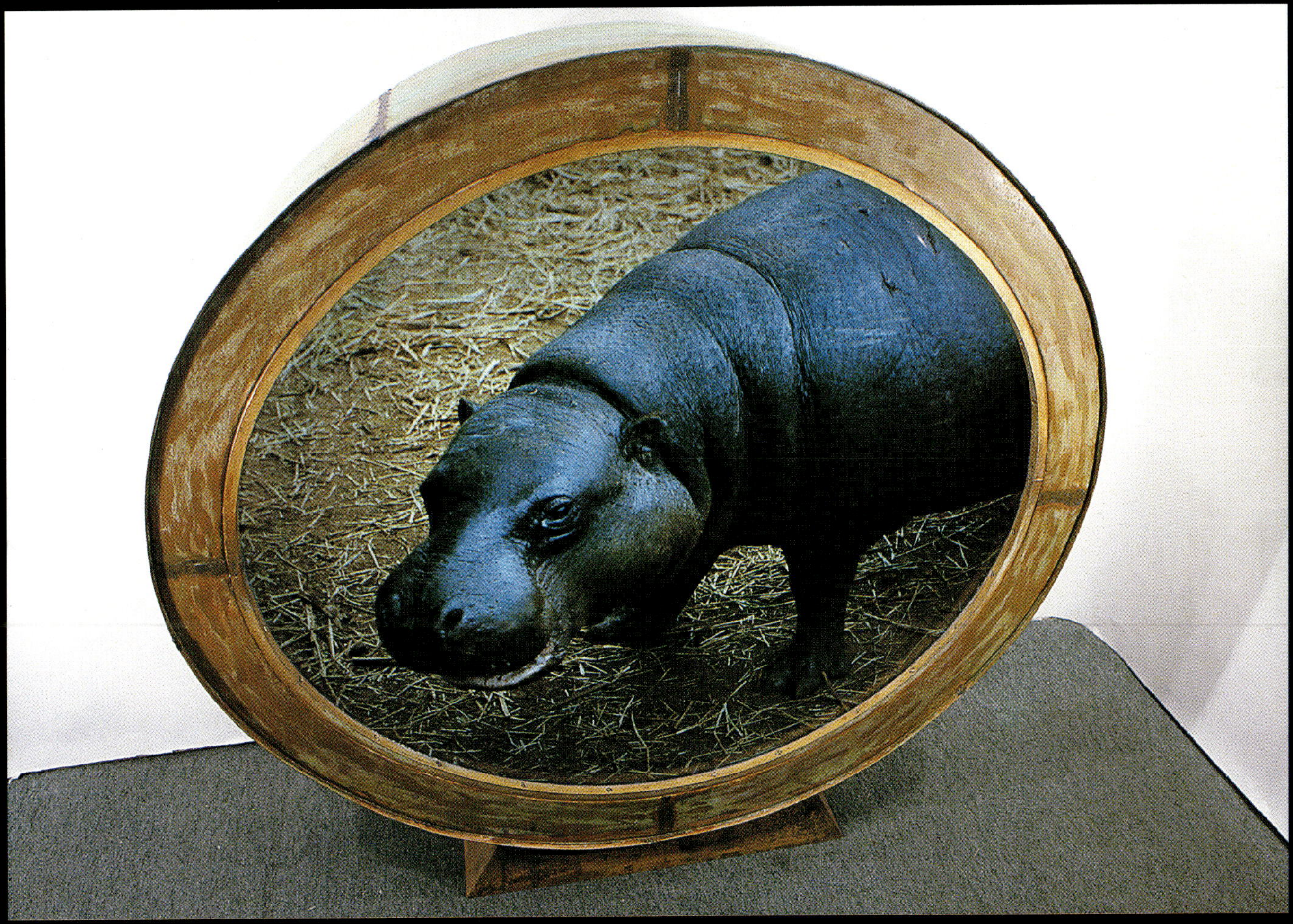

Mark Scheflen

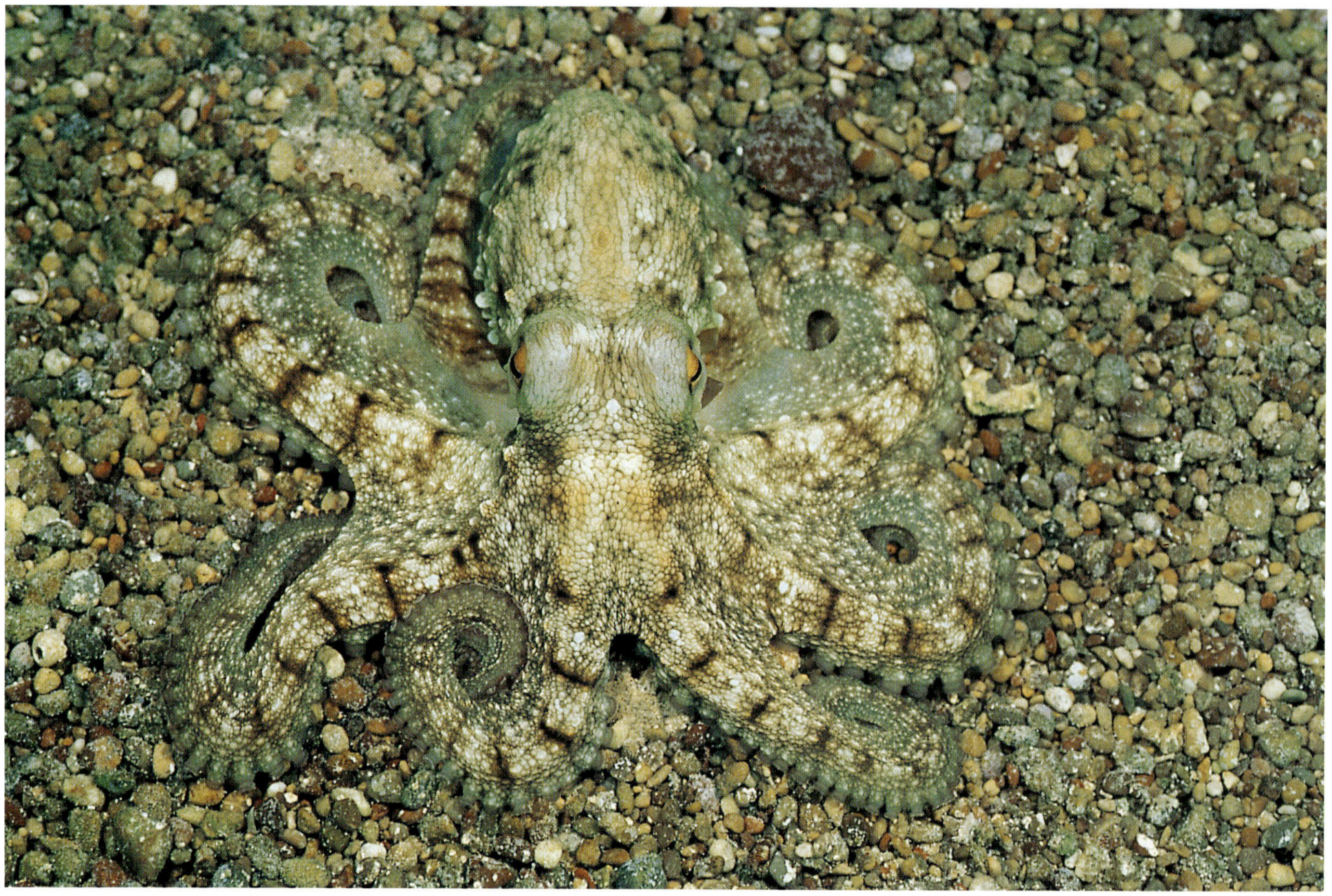

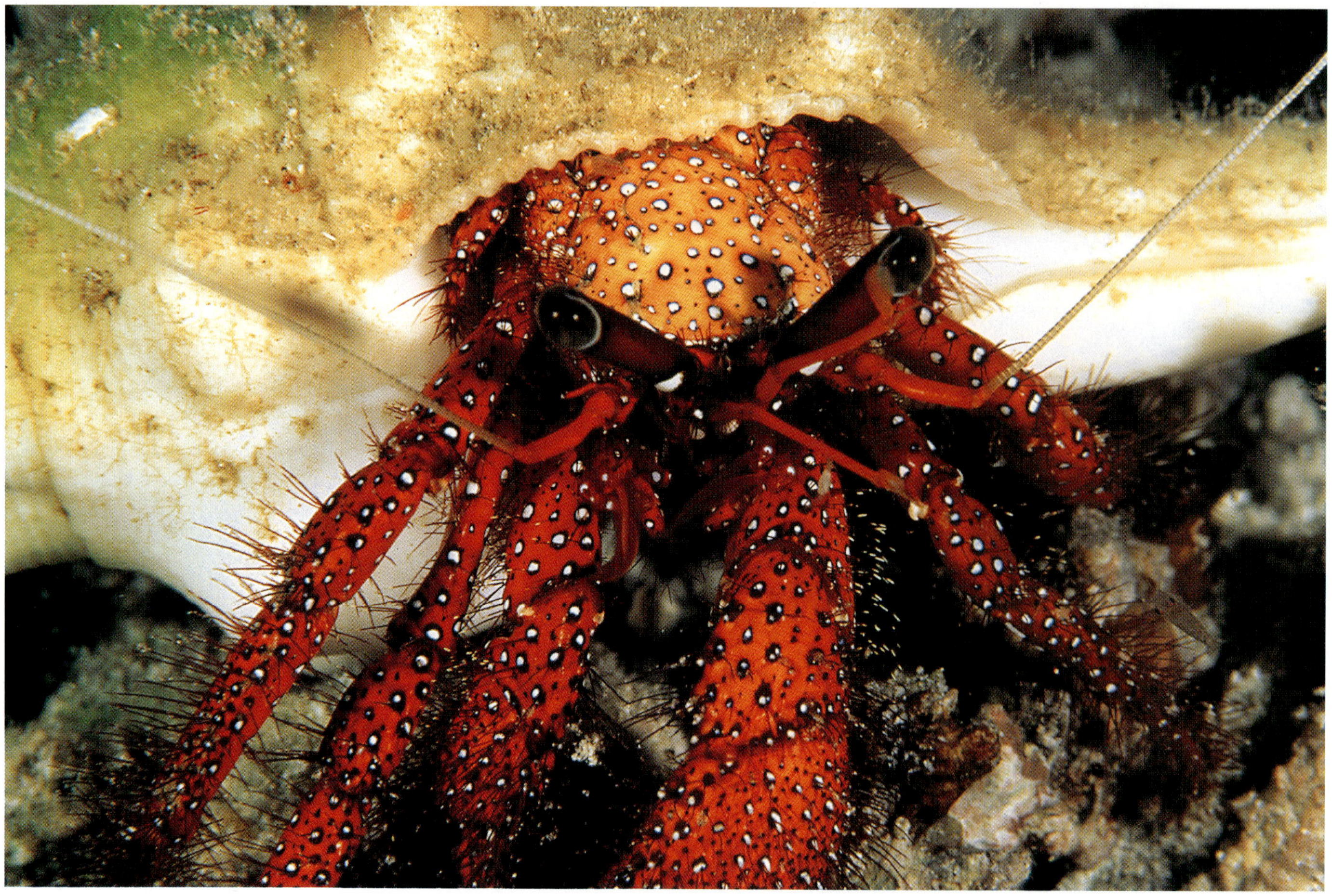

Constantinos Petrinos

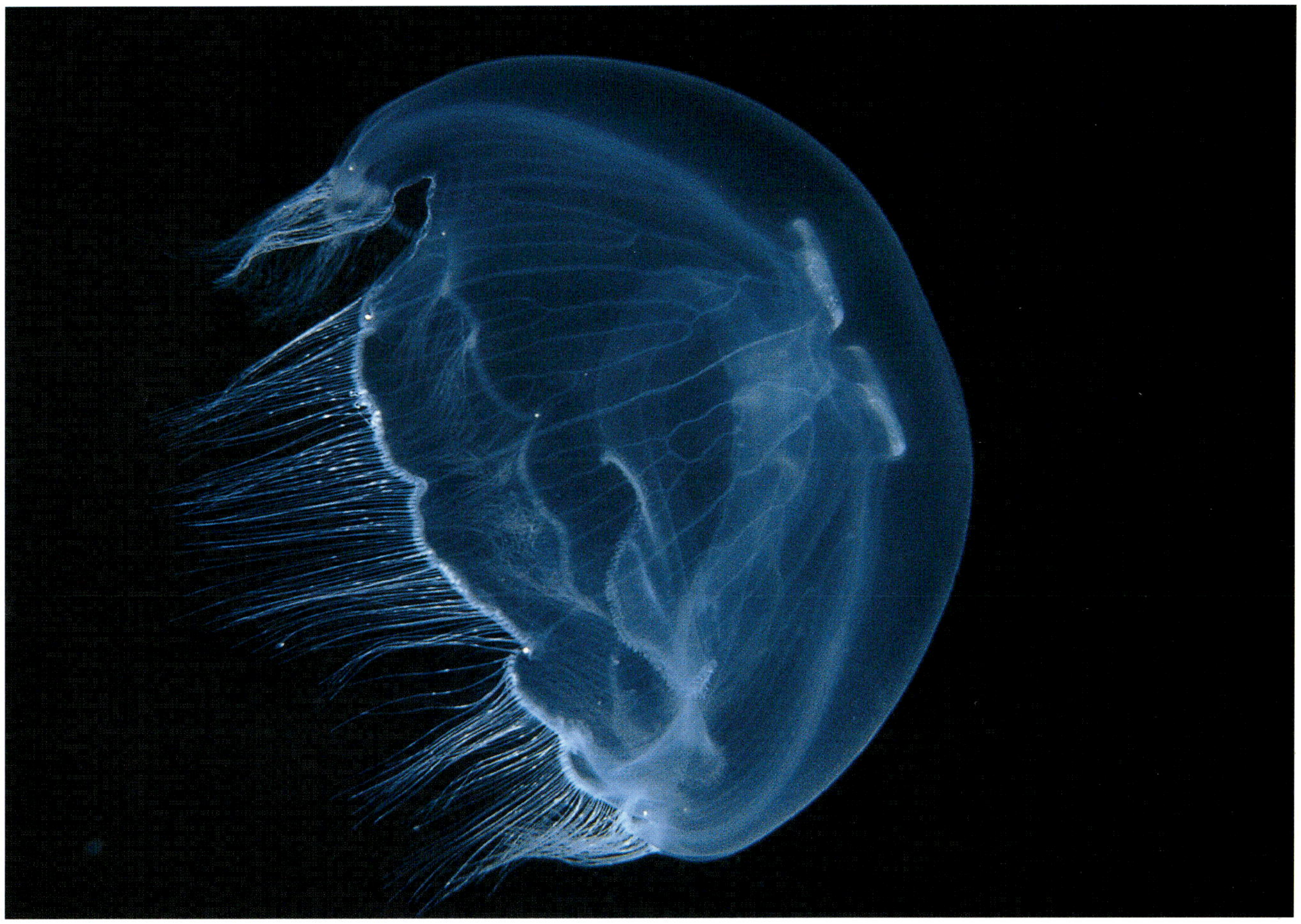

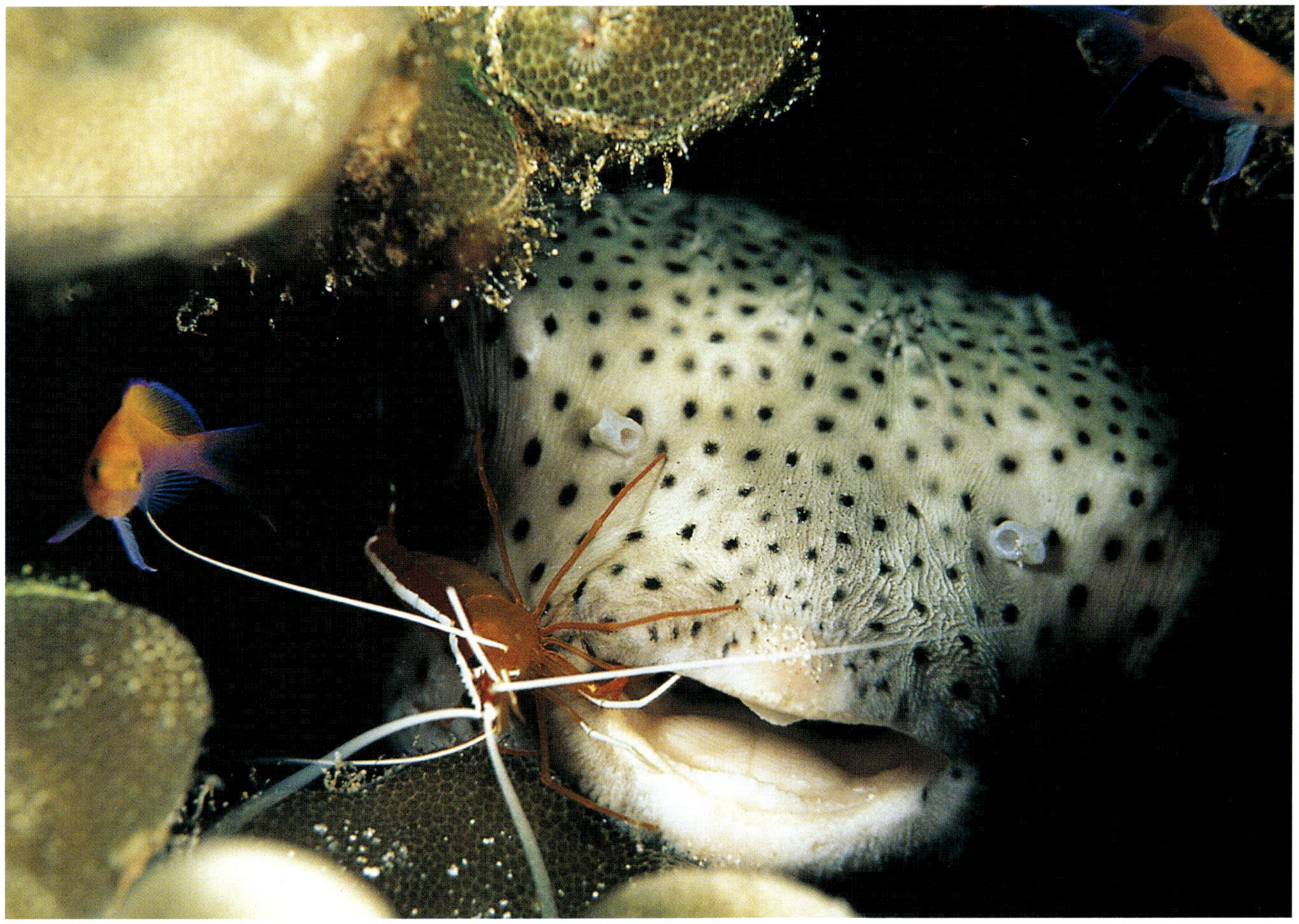

Patricia A. Jordan

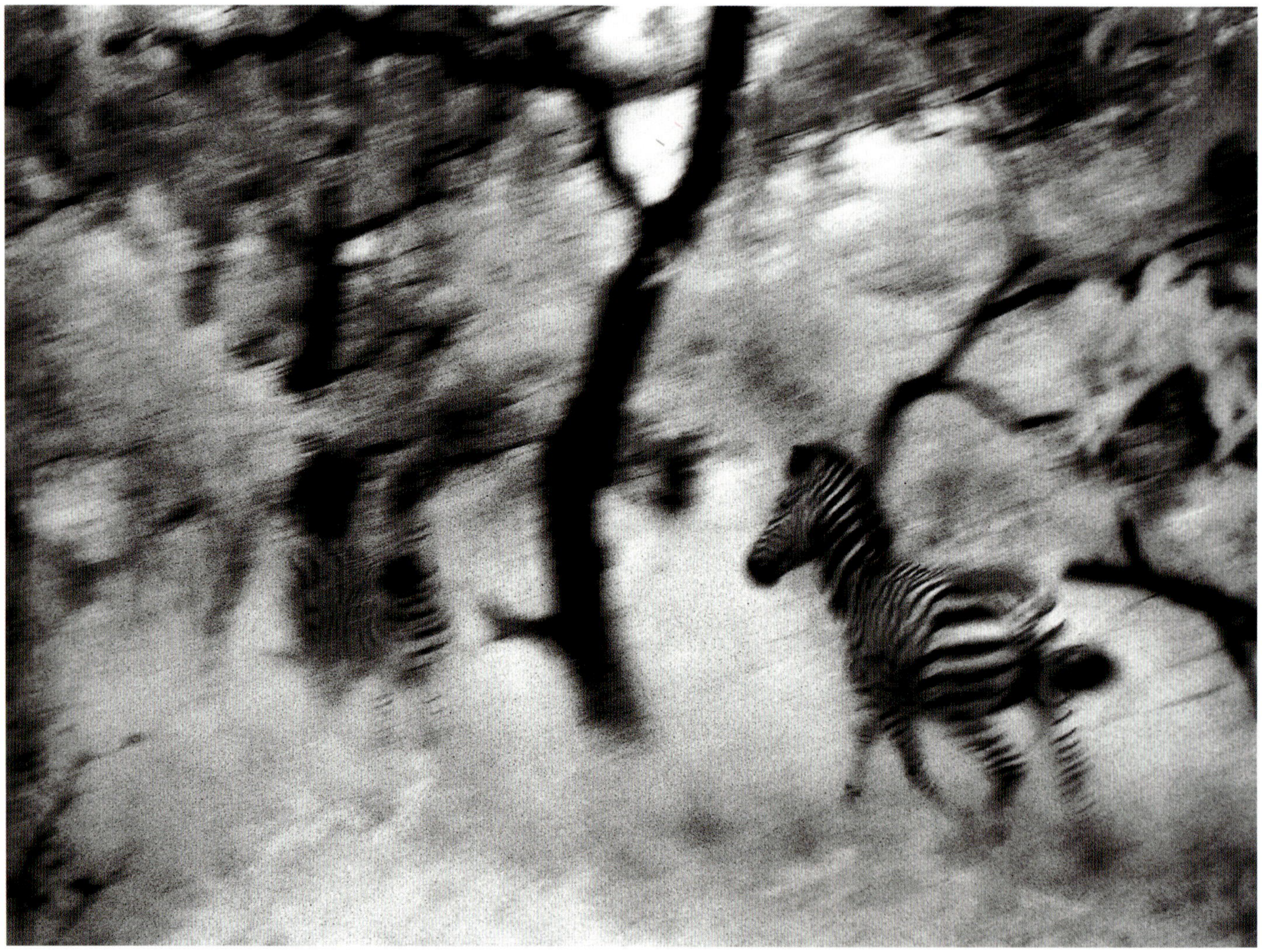

Malinda Kilmer

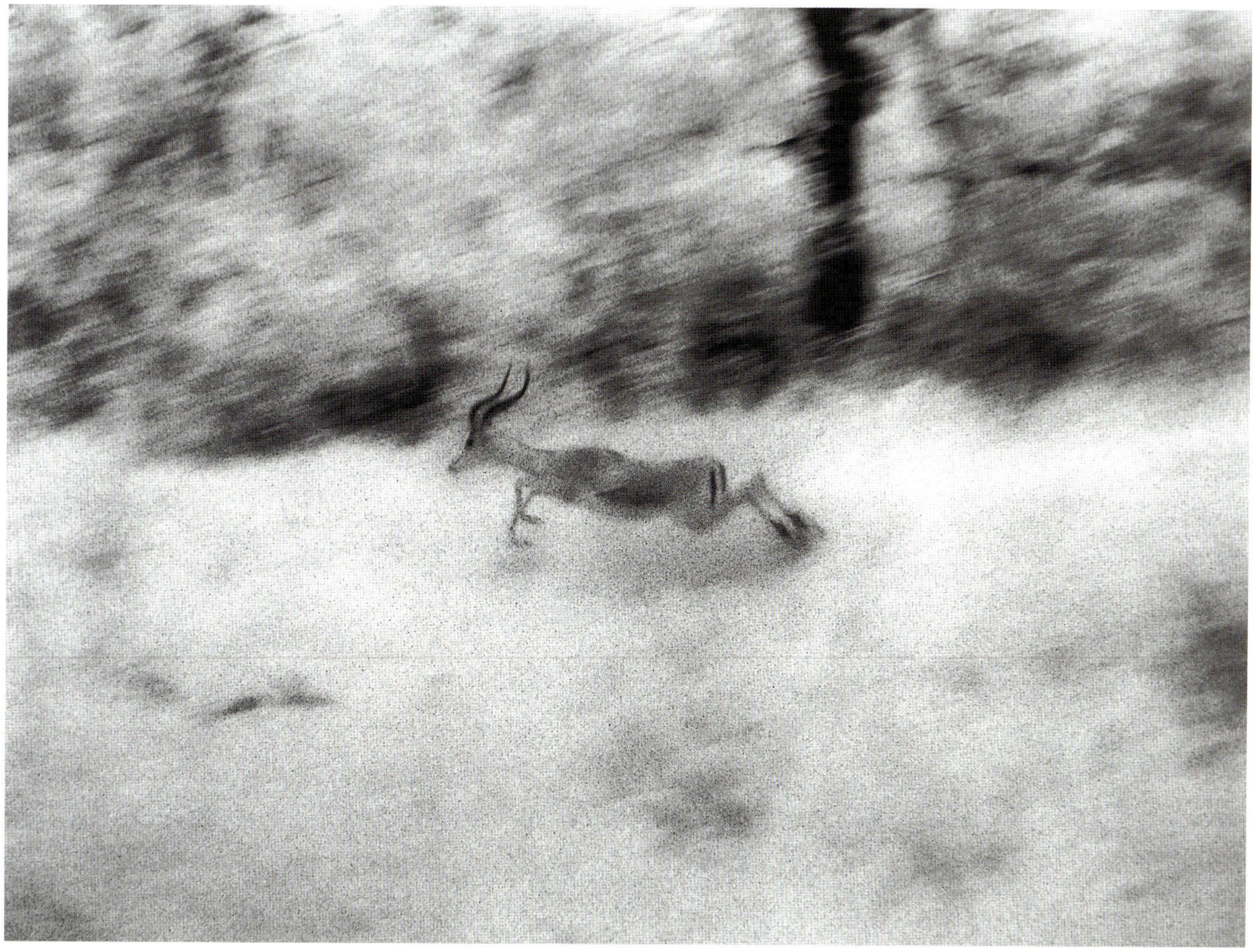

Malinda Kilmer

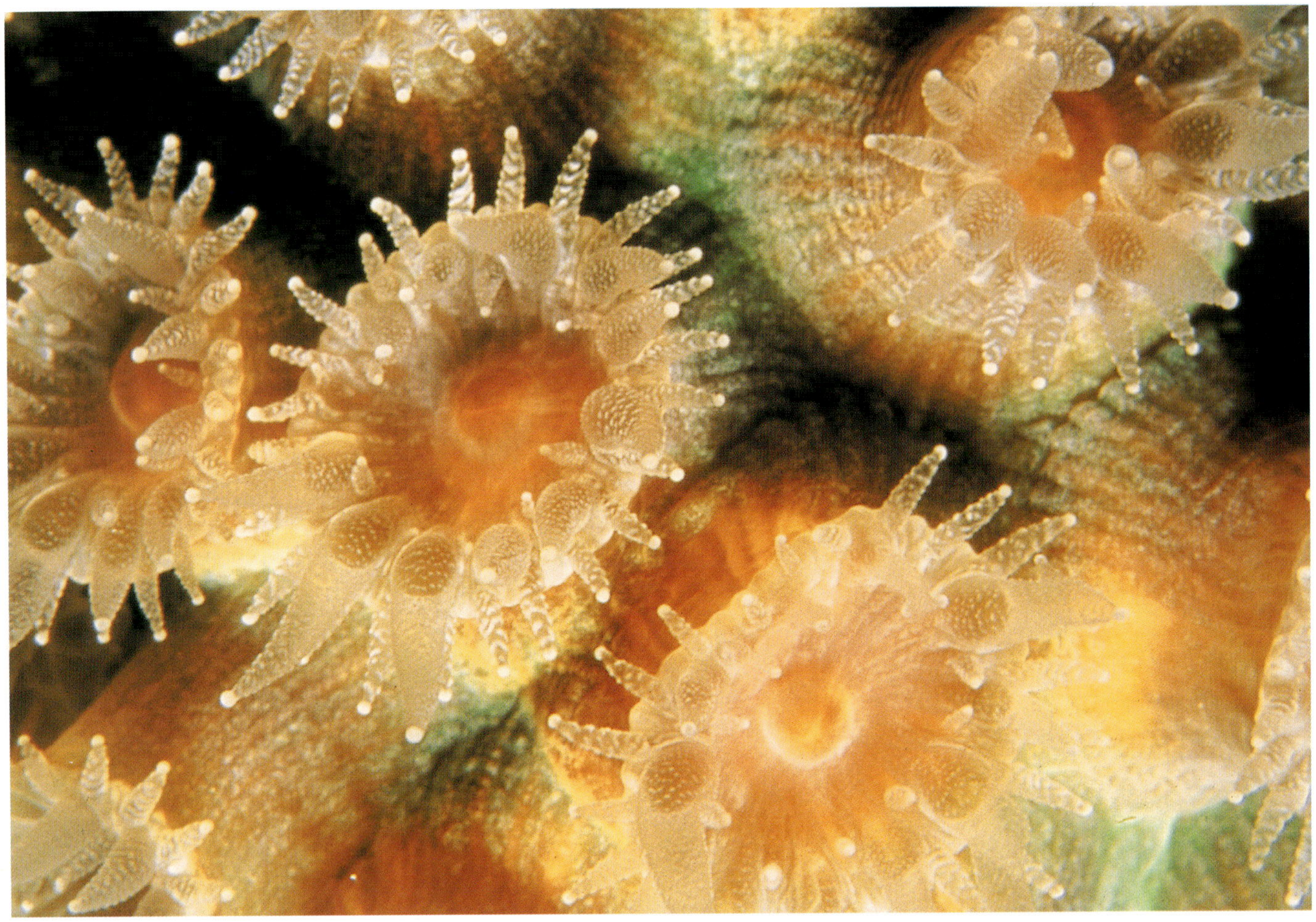

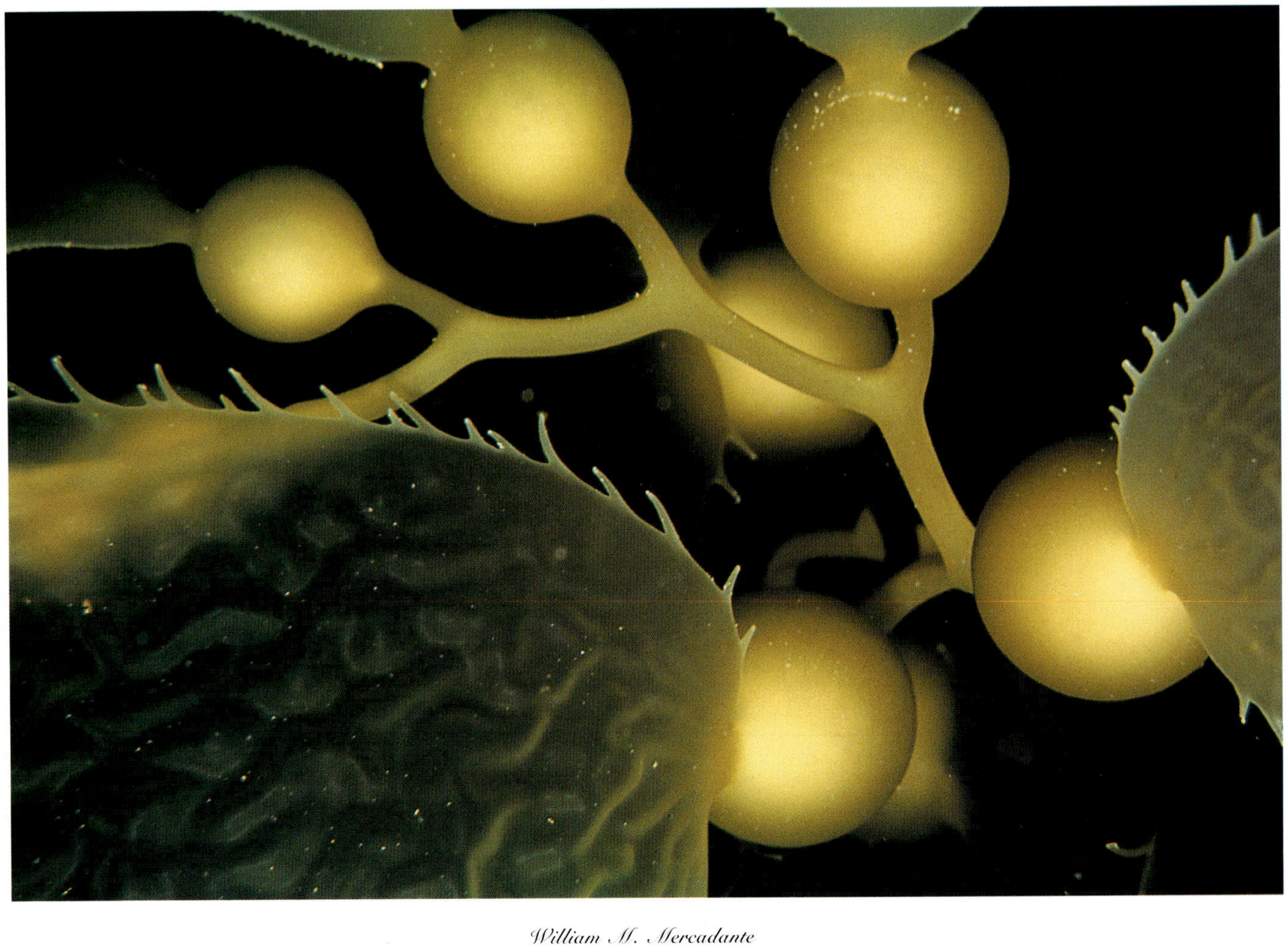

William M. Mercadante

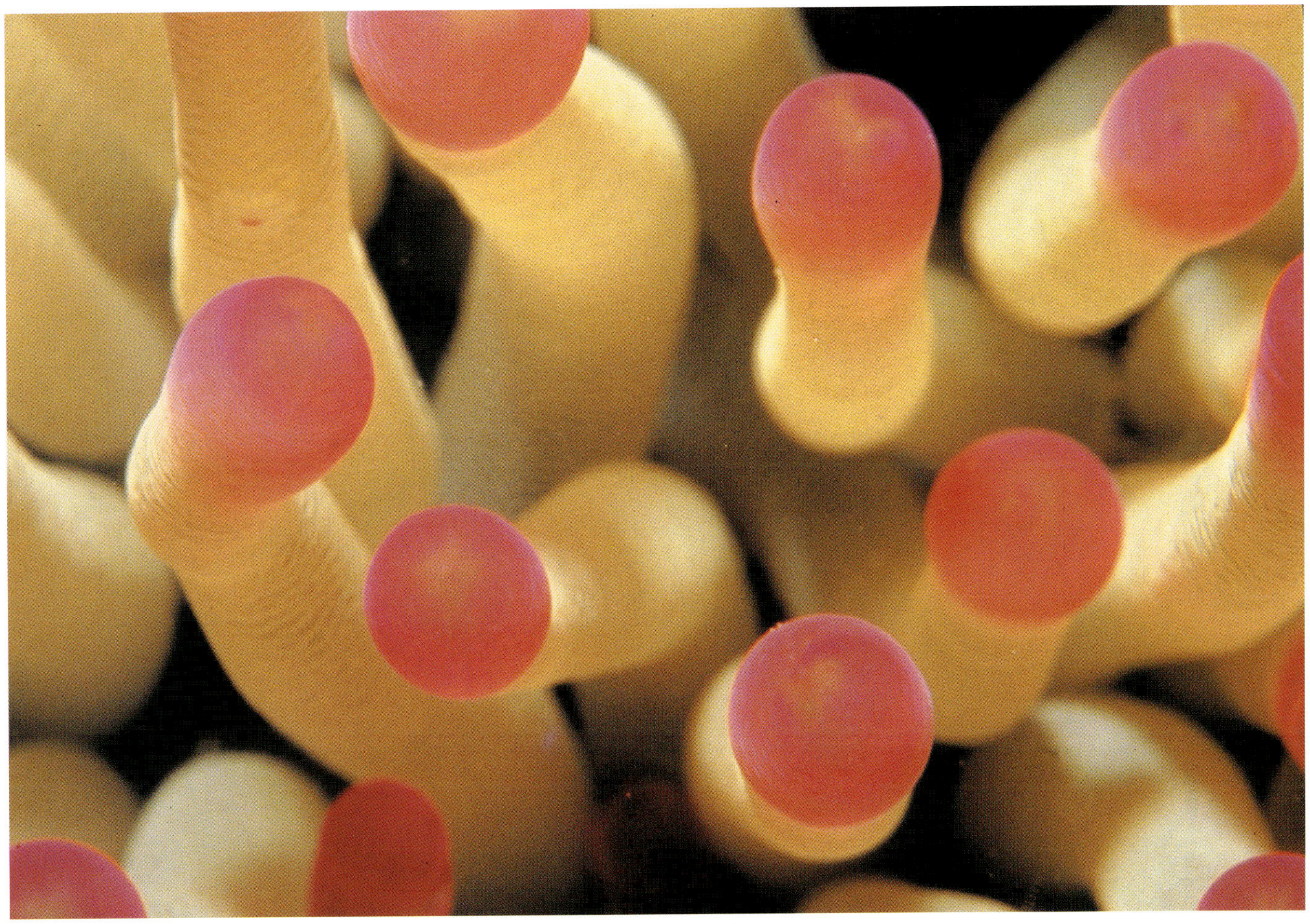

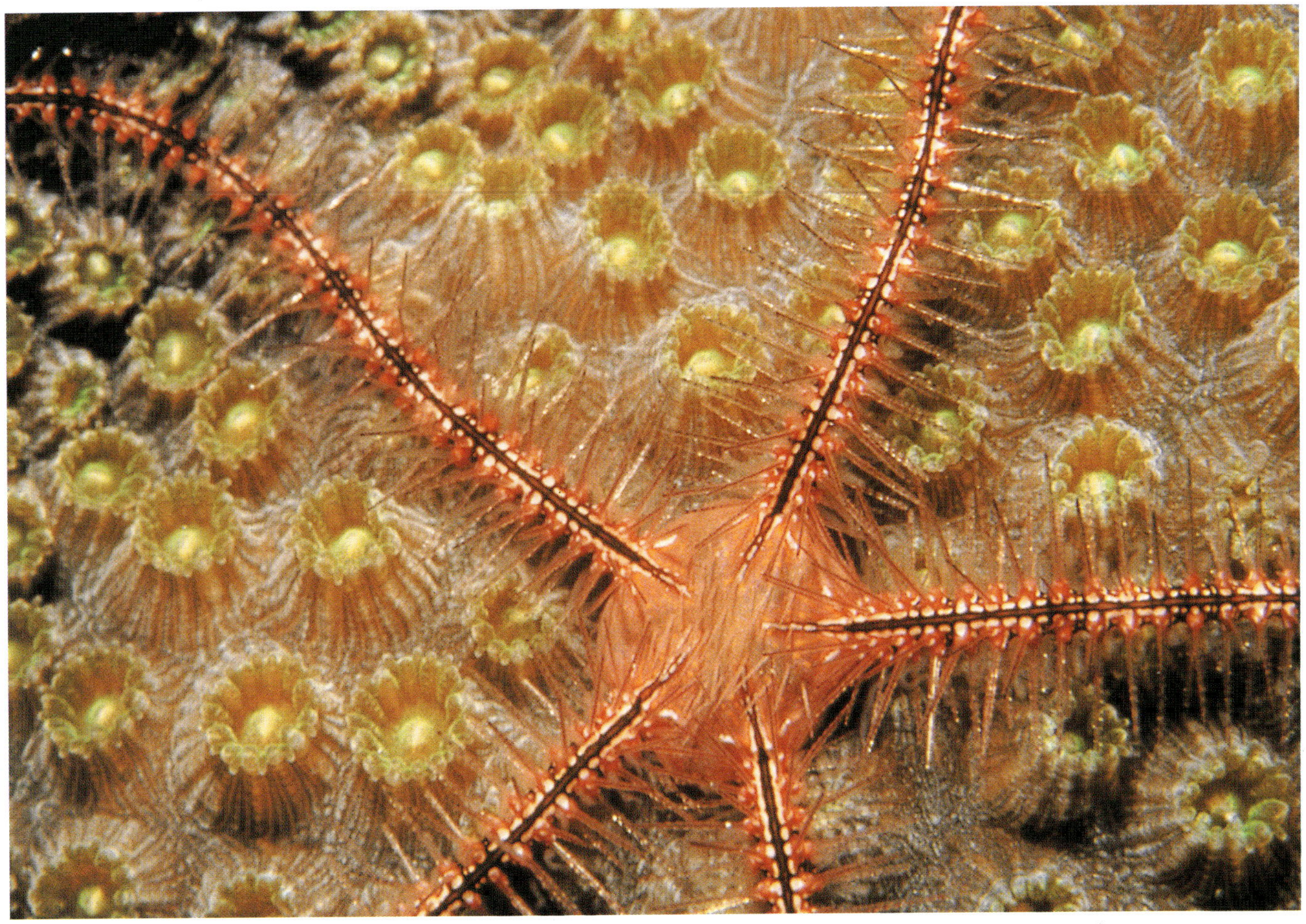

William M. Mercadante

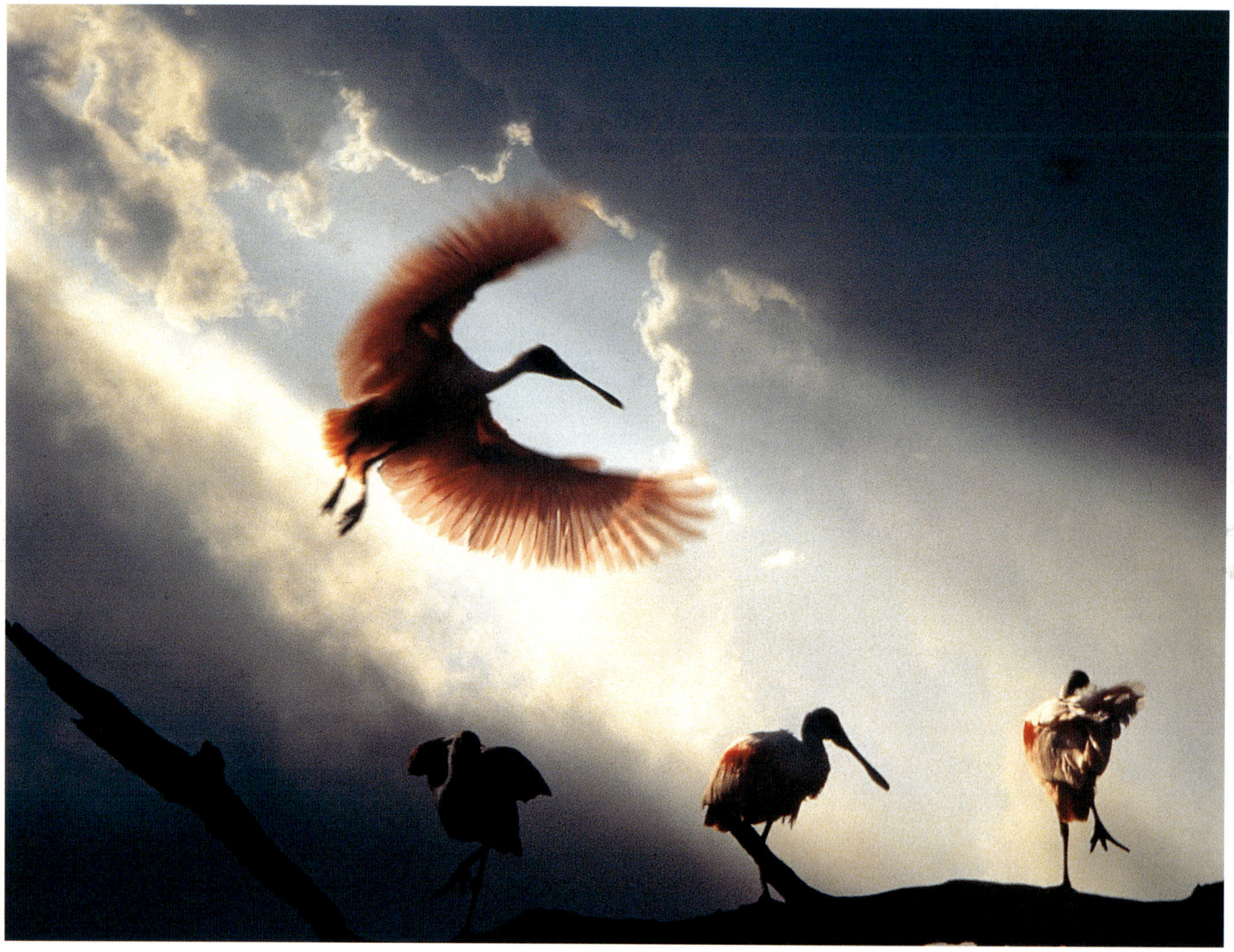

Jianzhang Xu

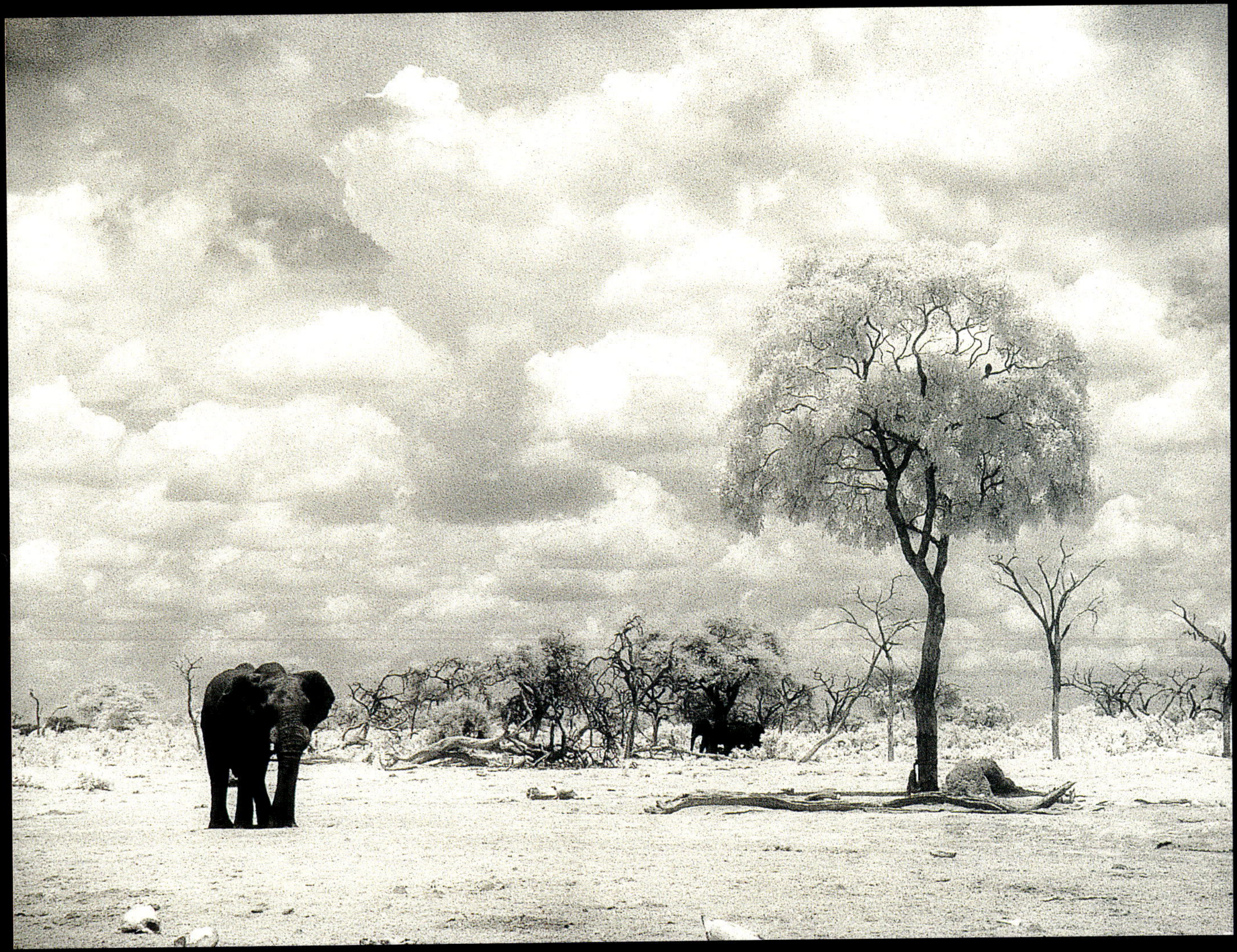

Lorne Resnick

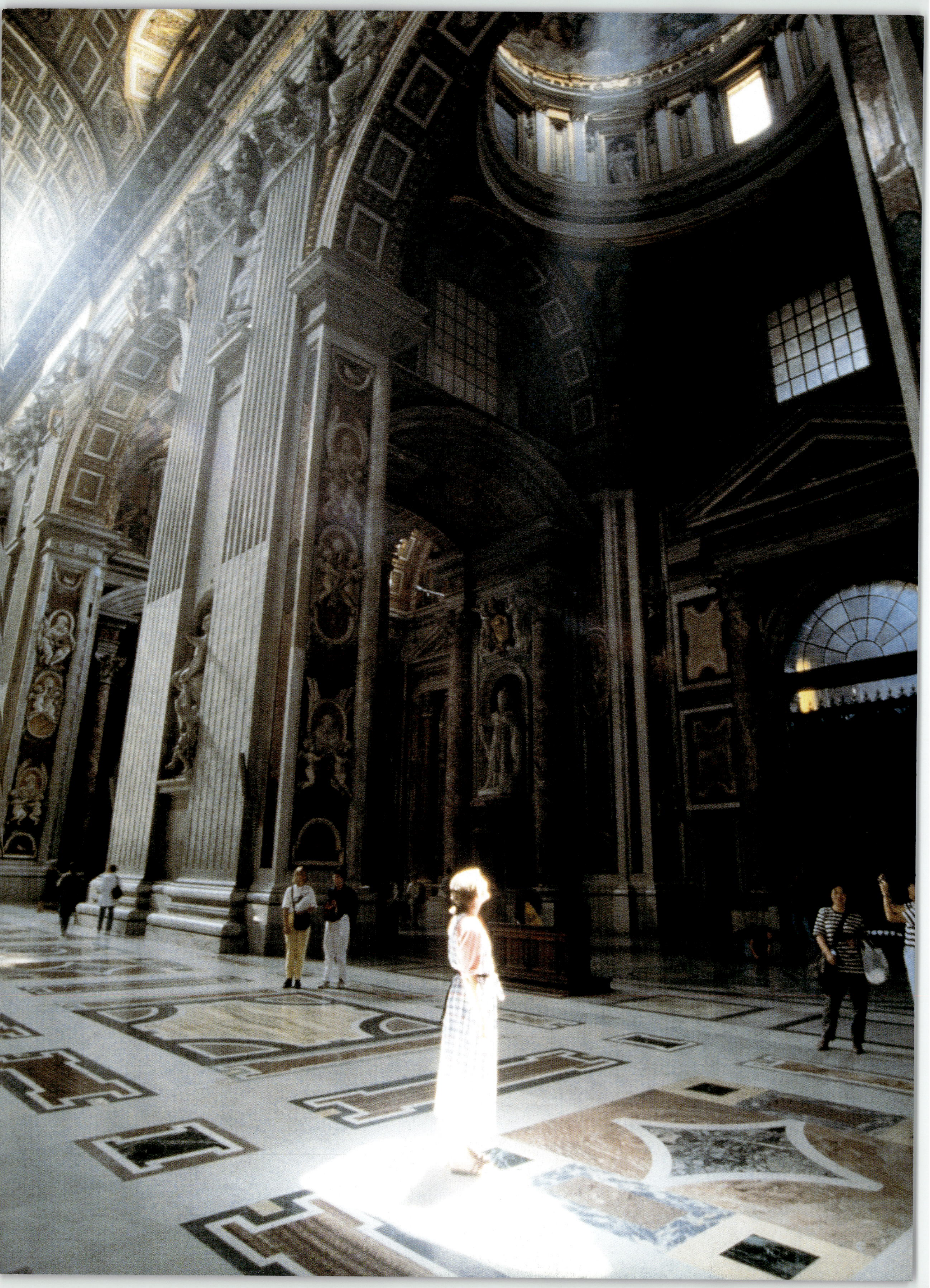

TRAVEL

REISEN

VOYAGE

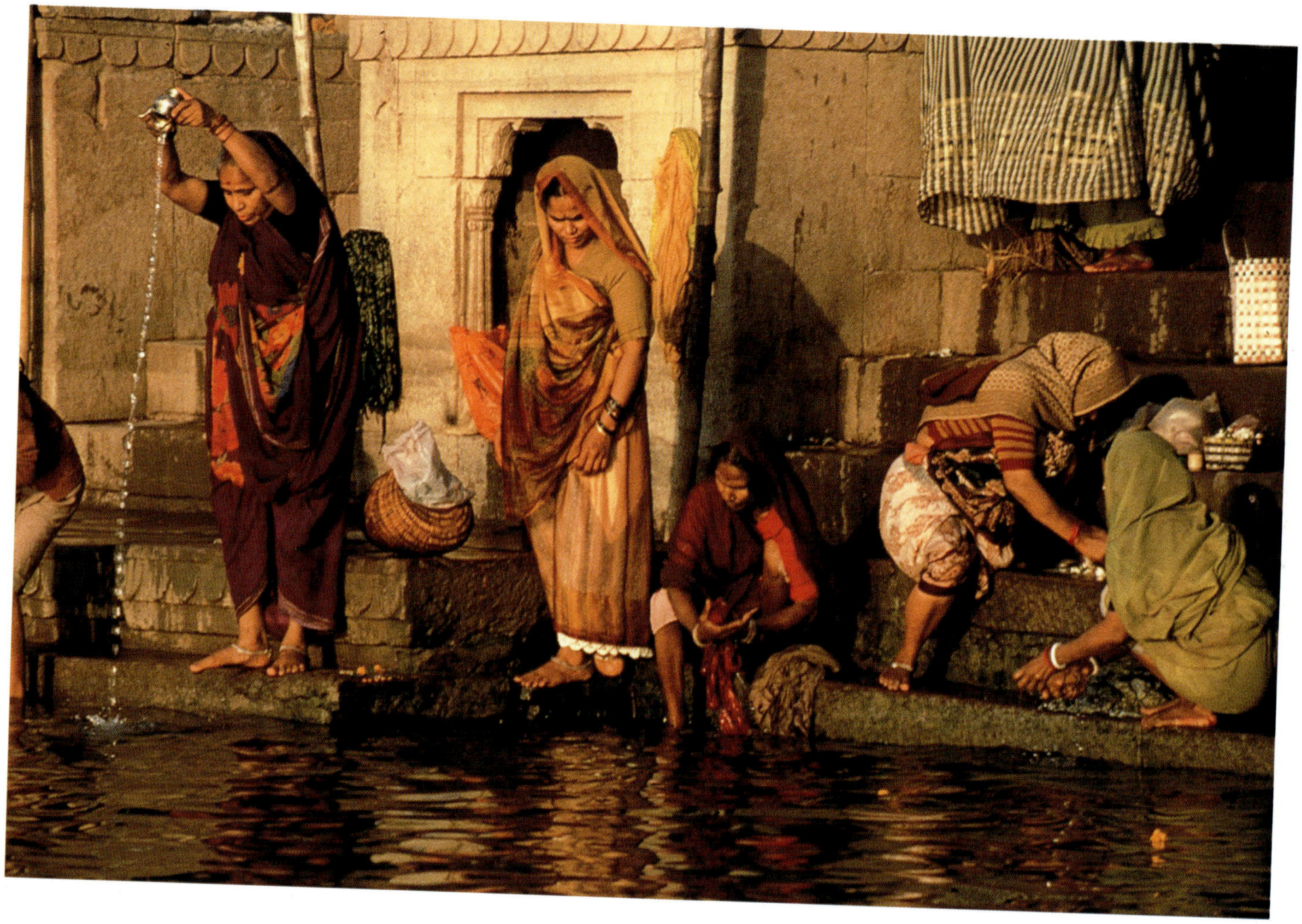

(PREVIOUS SPREAD) *Jianzhang Xu* ■ (THIS PAGE) *Donald Gurewitz*

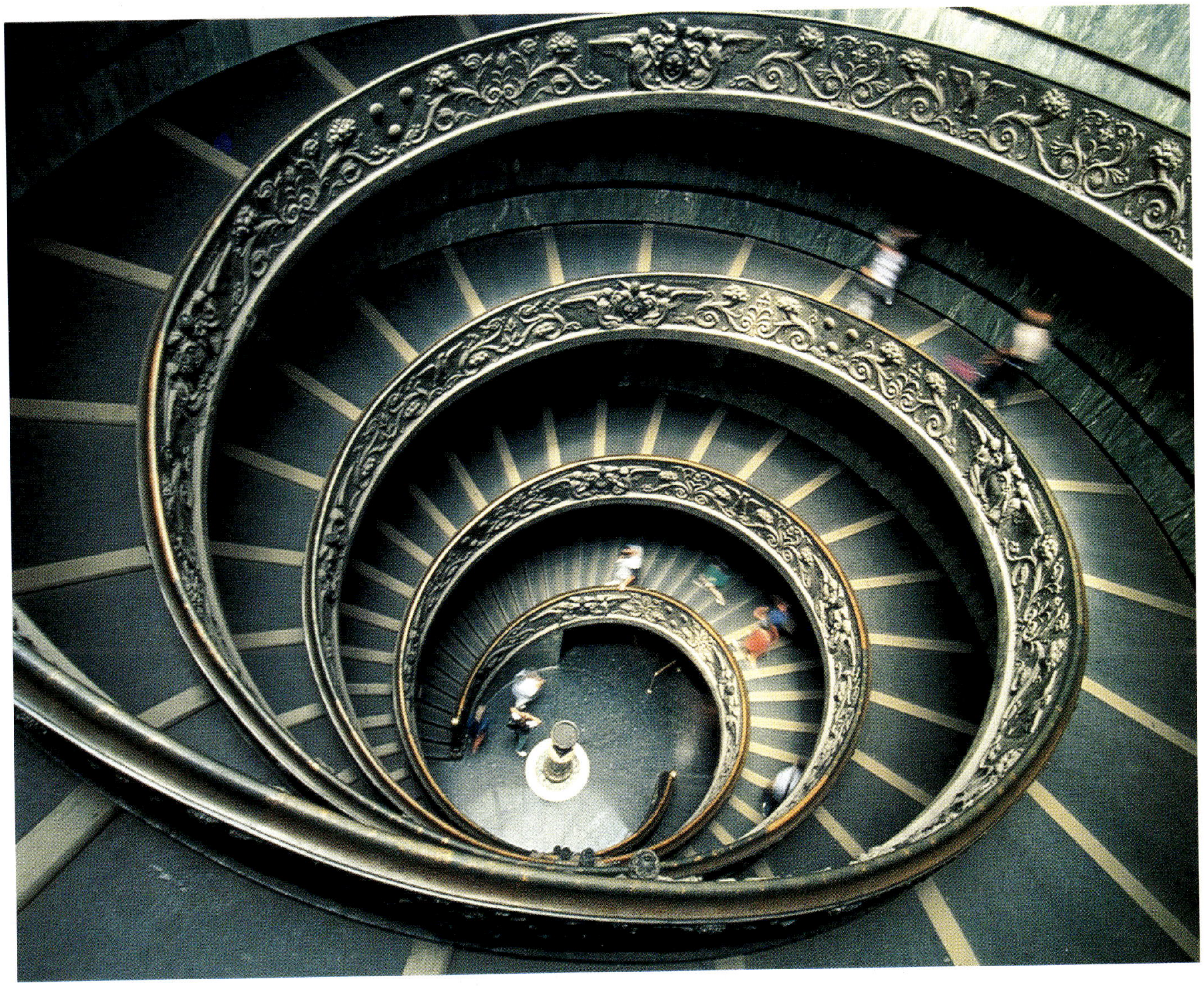

Jianzhang Xu

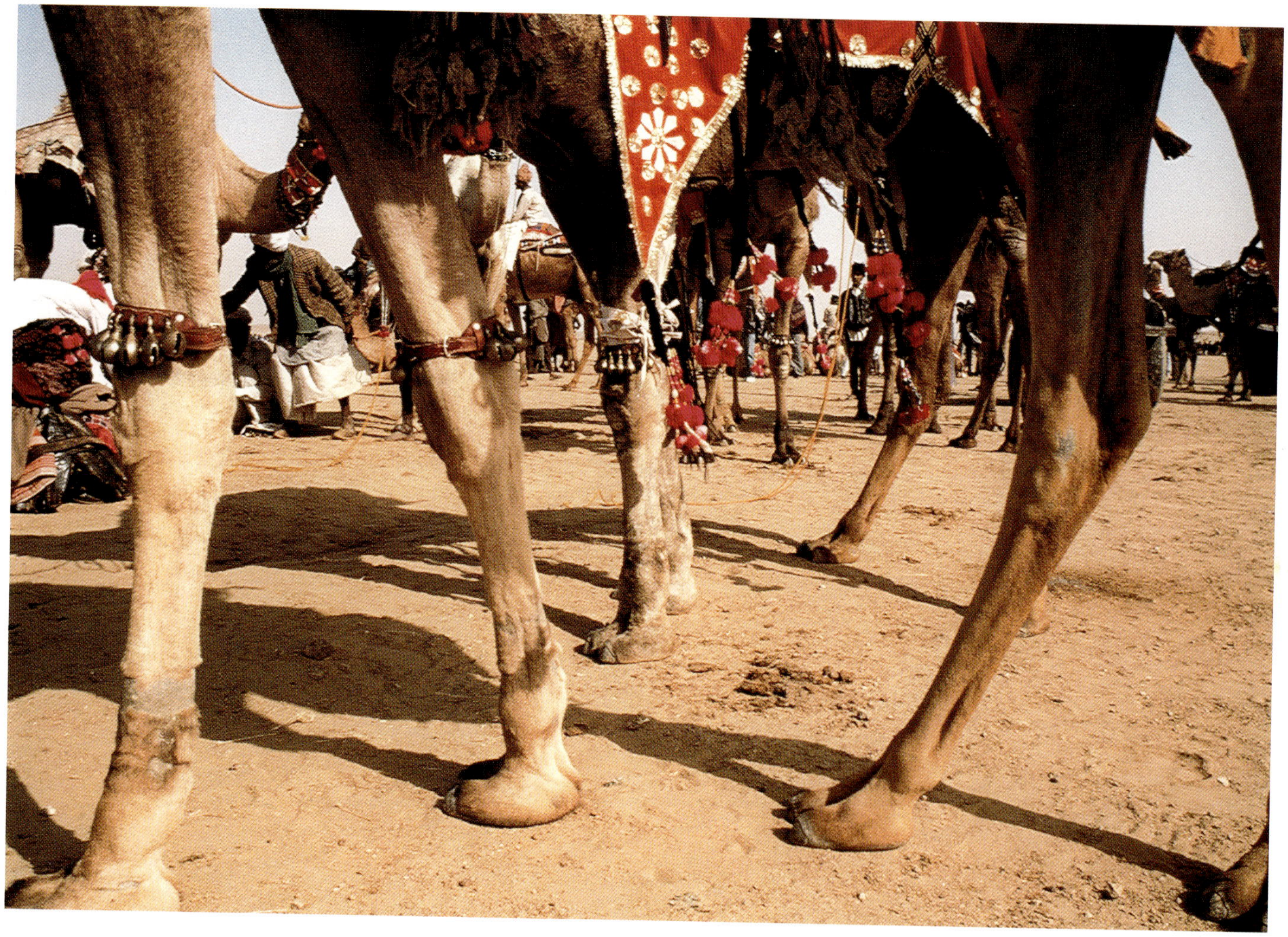

Greg Nielson

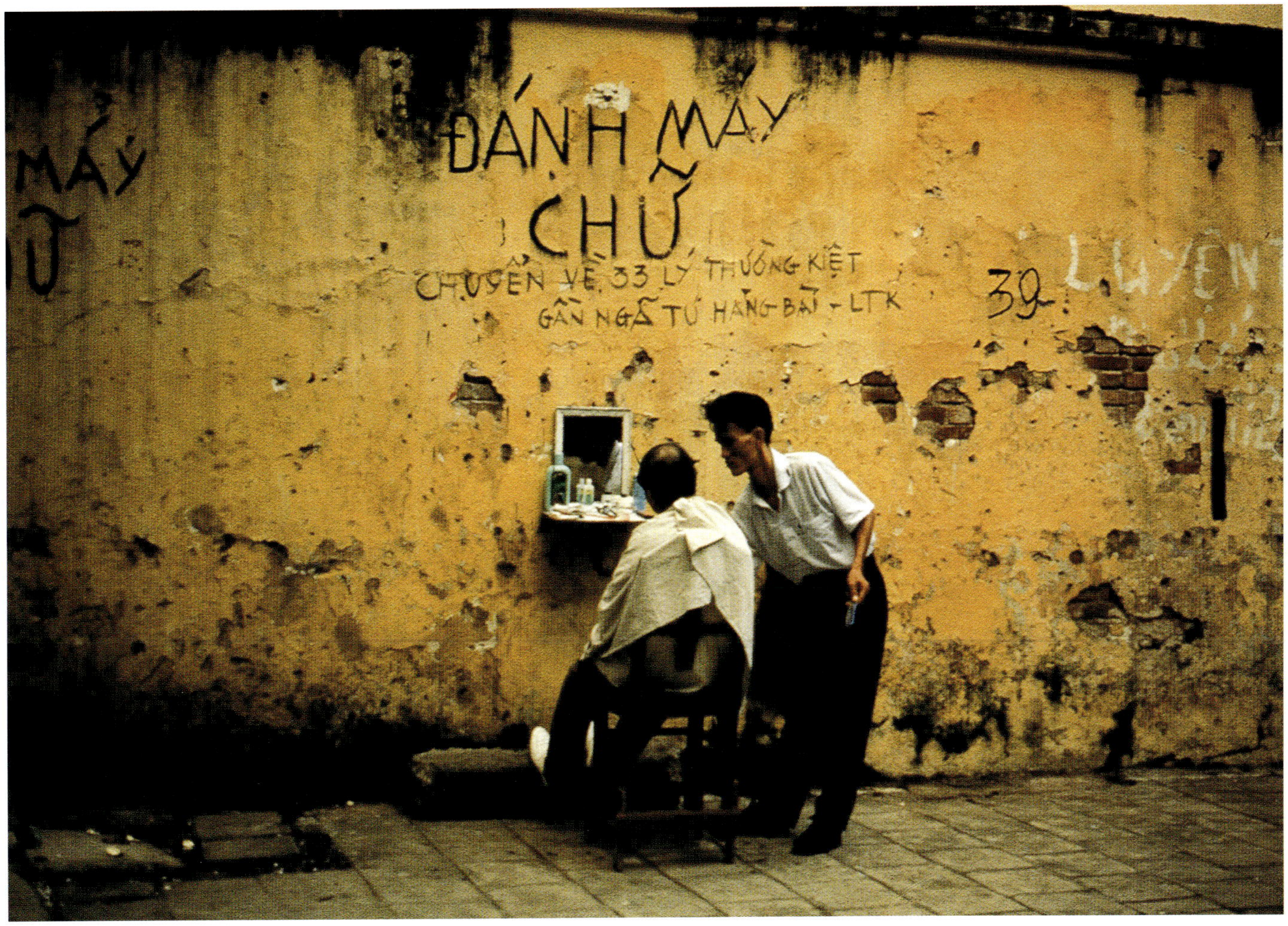

Donald Gurewitz

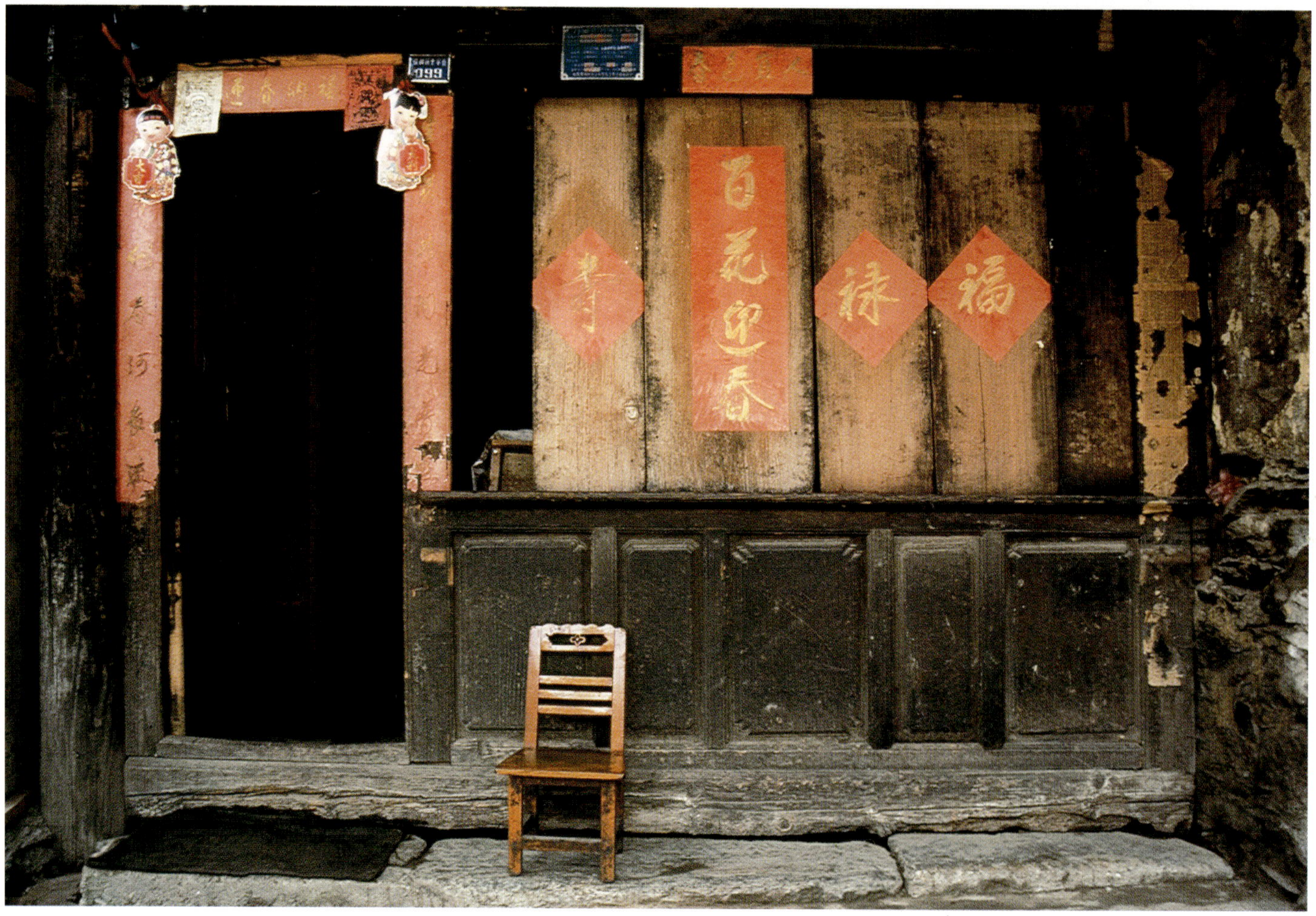

Cindy Ho

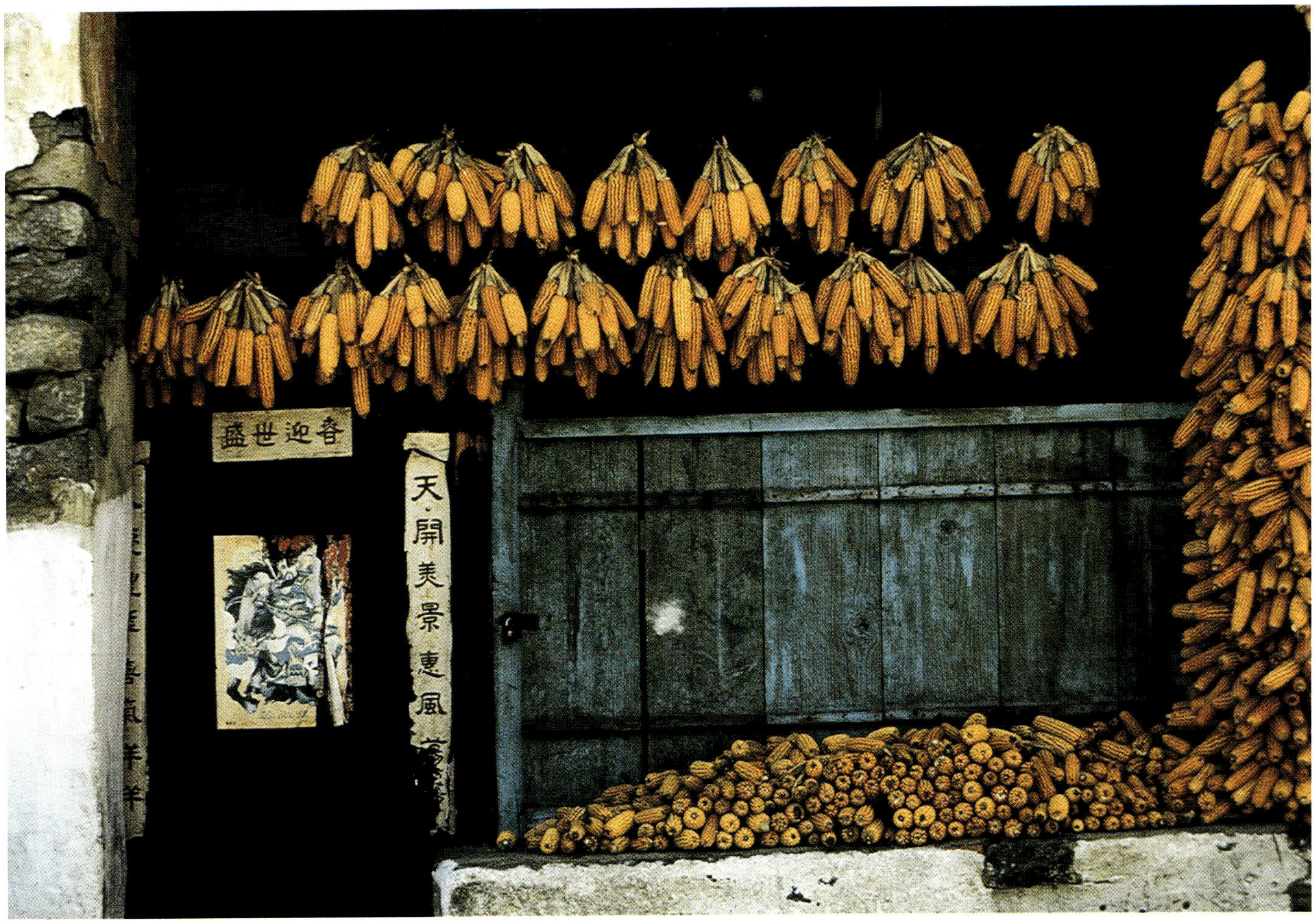

Cindy Ho

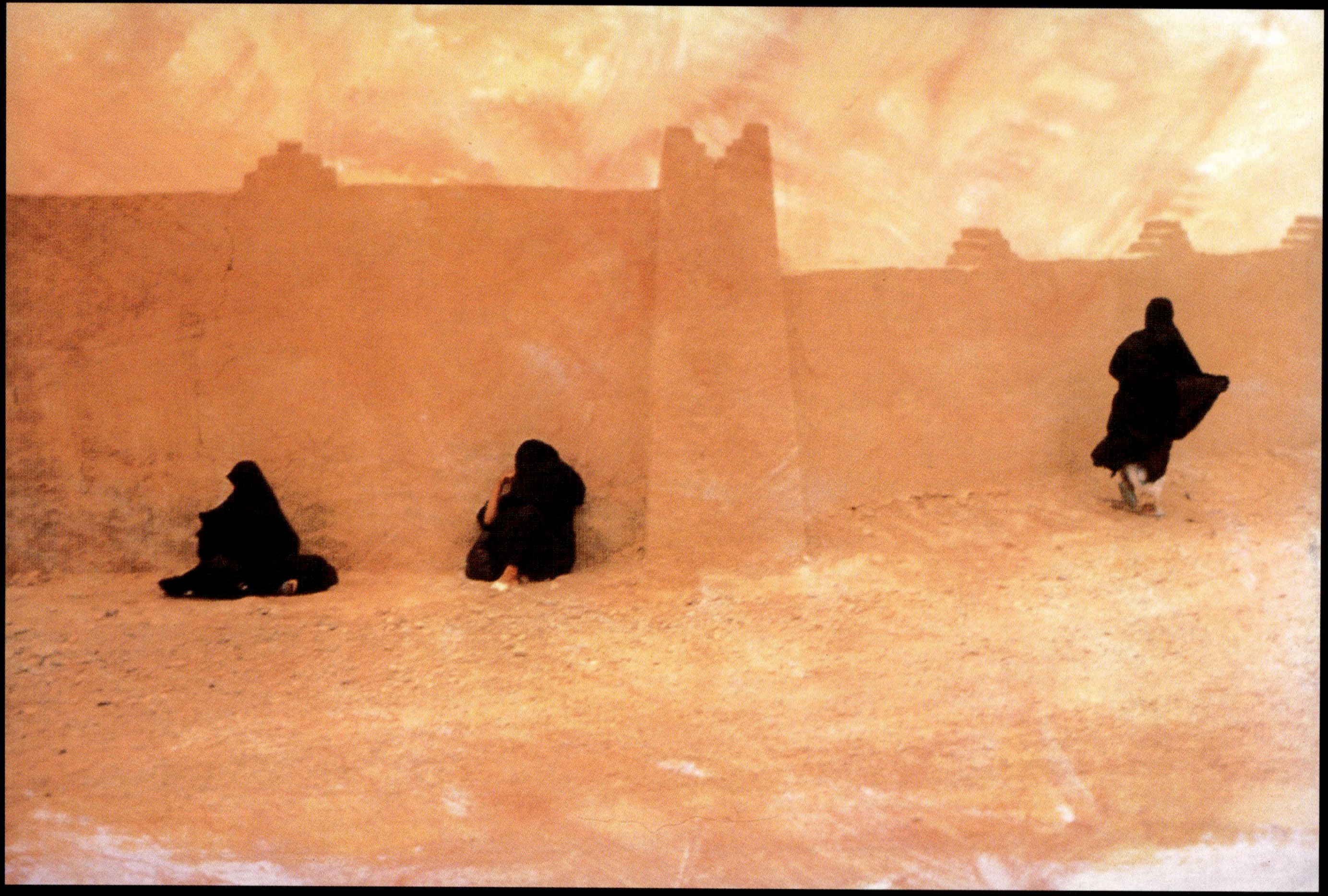

Claudio Gangi

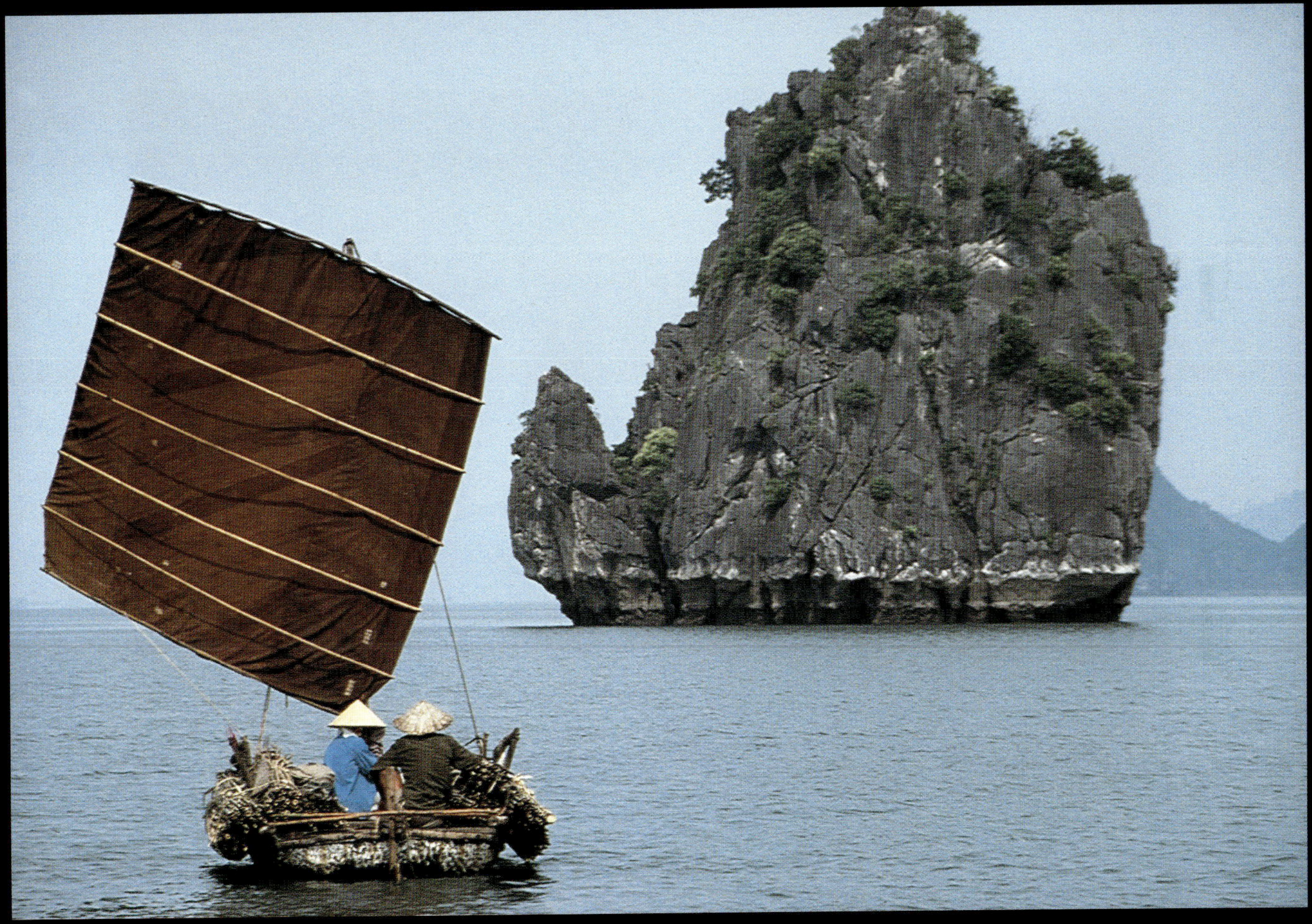

Donald Gurewitz

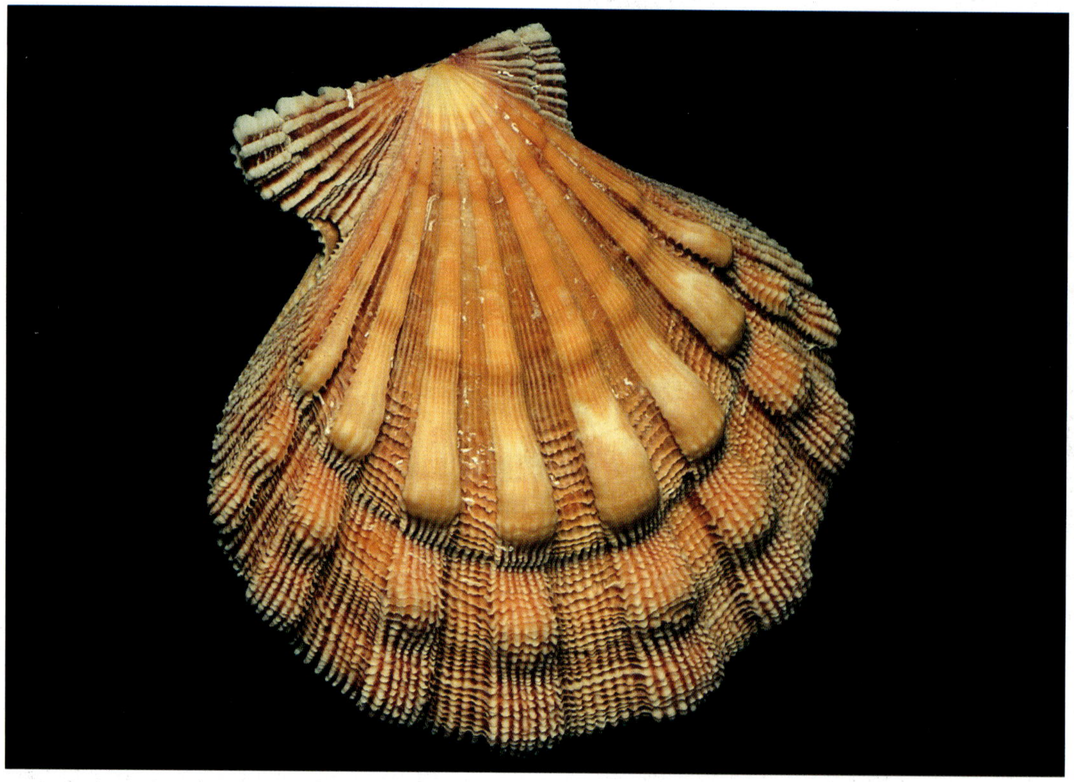

CAPTIONS AND INDICES

LEGENDEN UND KÜNSTLERANGABEN

LÉGENDES ET ARTISTES

COVER *PHOTOGRAPHER: Paul Kozal YEAR: 1996 CAMERA: Canon A2E w/28-105mm FILM: Ilford XP2 PAPER/PROCESS: Forte Polywarm Tone/selenium toned TITLE/DESCRIPTION: E=Mc2 ■ Taken at Marin County, California, civic center designed by Frank Lloyd Wright. ● Aufgenom-men in Marin County, Kalifornien, Civic Center, entworfen von Frank Lloyd Wright. ▲ Photographie prise dans le comté de Marin, Californie. Le centre administratif conçu par Frank Lloyd Wright.*

PAGE 2 *PHOTOGRAPHER: Constantinos Petrinos YEAR: 1996 CAMERA: Nikon F-4 FILM: Fuji Velvia EXPOSURE: f22 @ 1/250 ■ Anemone detail shot from underwater housing with two strobes.*

PAGE 4 *PHOTOGRAPHER: K.C. Armstrong YEAR: 1996 CAMERA: Horseman 4x5 with 150mm lens. PAPER: Agfa semi-matt*

PAGE 6 *PHOTOGRAPHER: Stuart Brown YEAR: 1996 CAMERA: Nikon FM2 FILM: Kodak Ektachrome P1600 EXPOSURE: 1/30 @ f5.6 tungsten PAPER/PROCESS: E6, push to 3200 ASA*

PAGE 14 *PHOTOGRAPHER: Kosuke Yuki CAMERA: Nikon F3*

PAGE 16 *PHOTOGRAPHER: Patrick Sanfacon YEAR: 1996 CAMERA: Nikon F-90 FILM: Kodak Ektapress 400 PAPER/PROCESS: Kodak Supra Ra-4 TITLE/DESCRIPTION: Destruction*

PAGE 17 *PHOTOGRAPHER: Patrick Sanfacon YEAR: 1996 CAMERA: Nikon F-90 FILM: Kodak Ektapress 400 PAPER/PROCESS: Kodak Supra Ra-4 TITLE/DESCRIPTION: Saved ■ This 92-year-old man was saved by a Montreal firefighter. ● Dieser zweiundneunzig Jahre alte Mann wurde von einem Feuerwehrmann der Stadt Montreal gerettet. ▲ Ce vieillard de 82 ans a été sauvé par un pompier de la ville de Montréal.*

PAGE 18 *PHOTOGRAPHER: Jozef Ondko YEAR: 1996 CAMERA: Nikon N70 FILM: Kodak Gold 100, 1200 Royal 200 PAPER/PROCESS: Kodak Ektacolor Supra II N TITLE/DESCRIPTION: Ice Cream Lover*

PAGE 19 *PHOTOGRAPHER: Lorne Resnick ■ Two boys pointing toy (hopefully) pistols in a playground. ● Zwei Jungen, die mit ihren (hoffentlich) Spielzeugpistolen spielen. ▲ Deux garçons jouant avec leur faux pistolet sur une aire de jeu.*

PAGE 20 *PHOTOGRAPHER: Michael Davies YEAR: 1996 CAMERA: 5 x 4 Studio w/150mm lens FILM: Fuji G4t EXPOSURE: 1/30 at f/11 PAPER/PROCESS: normal E6 process TITLE/DESCRIPTION: Coke on the Rocks ■ Can was placed on a bed of ice and illuminated by a blue gelled photoflood from above. ● Die Dose wurde auf eine Eisunterlage gestellt und von oben von einer Photolampe mit Blaufilter beleuchtet. ▲ Le photographe a placé la boîte de conserve sur un lit de glace et l'a éclairée de haut en bas avec un projecteur à filtre bleu.*

PAGE 22 *PHOTOGRAPHER: Andrea Pickens YEAR: 1996 CAMERA: Calomet 4 x 5 view camera FILM: Kodak Tri-X PAPER/PROCESS: Luminos Photo Linen TITLE/DESCRIPTION: Whisper Diptych black-and-white prints*

PAGE 23 *PHOTOGRAPHER: Andrea Pickens YEAR: 1996 CAMERA: Calumet 4 x 5 view camera FILM: Kodak Tri-X PAPER/PROCESS: Luminos Photo Linen TITLE/DESCRIPTION: Whisper Diptych black-and-white prints*

PAGE 24 *PHOTOGRAPHER: James Colony YEAR: 1995 CAMERA: Minolta 370 FILM: Fuji 50d TITLE/DESCRIPTION: Mesembryanthemum I ■ 28-70 zoom lens was reverse mounted. ● Das 28-70 mm Zoomobjektiv war umgekehrt angesetzt. ▲ Le zoom 28-70 mm a été monté à l'envers.*

PAGE 26 *PHOTOGRAPHER: K. Armstrong YEAR: 1996 CAMERA: Horseman 4 x 5 w/210mm lens FILM: Polaroid Pos/Neg PAPER/PROCESS: Agfa semi-matte TITLE/DESCRIPTION: Untitled*

PAGE 27 *PHOTOGRAPHER: K. Armstrong YEAR: 1996 CAMERA: Horseman 4 x 5 w/210mm lens FILM: Fuji Rvp PAPER/PROCESS: Fuji Color TITLE/DESCRIPTION: Untitled*

PAGE 28, 29 *PHOTOGRAPHER: Beth Vagley YEAR: 1996 CAMERA: Canon Rebel FILM: T-Max 400 EXPOSURE: f/8 PAPER/PROCESS: black-and-white silver prints*

PAGE 30 *PHOTOGRAPHER: Marcelino Pagan YEAR: 1996 CAMERA: Canon Ae-1 Program/ 50mm lens FILM: Kodak Ektachrome Rome Elite 200 EXPOSURE: 1/125 at f/11 PAPER/PROCESS: E-6 TITLE/DESCRIPTION: Ladder in Cape May ■ Shot was taken in Cape May, New Jersey. ● Die Aufnahme entstand in Cape May, New Jersey. ▲ Photographie prise à Cape May, New Jersey.*

PAGE 31 *PHOTOGRAPHER: Noel Karzen YEAR: 1996 CAMERA: Nikon 8008 FILM: Provia 100 EXPOSURE: 2 second double exposure at f/5.6*

PAGE 32, 33 *PHOTOGRAPHER: Paul Cutright YEAR: 1996 CAMERA: Polaroid Sx-70 FILM: Sx-70 Time Zero ■ Hand-etched orginals printed on Canon laser color copier or copied onto film to produce large 20 x 20 to 36 x 36 type-r prints or ilfordchrome (cibachrome) prints. ● Handgeritzte Originale, die mit Canon Laserfarbkopierer gedruckt oder auf Film aufgenommen wurden, um davon grössere 20 x 20 bis 36 x 36 Type-r- oder Ilfordchrome-Abzüge (Cibachrome) zu machen. ▲ Originaux gravés à la main, imprimés avec une photocopieuse laser couleur de Canon ou photographiés pour réaliser des tirages positifs ou ilfordchrome (cibachrome) de plus grand format allant de 20 x 20 à 36 x 36.*

PAGE 34-37 *PHOTOGRAPHER: Anthony Lawson YEAR: 1996 CAMERA: 4 x 5 Calumet FILM: T-Max 100 PAPER/PROCESS: Palladium TITLES/DESCRIPTIONS: Breaker, Extinguisher, Raise Blade, Exposed*

PAGE 38 *PHOTOGRAPHER: Karina Serna CAMERA: Sinar F 1 & Sinar P2 FILM: Epp Kodak Ektachrome EXPOSURE: 1/60 at f/22 PAPER/PROCESS: E-6 Process TITLE/DESCRIPTION: Self-promotion*

PAGE 39 *PHOTOGRAPHER: Peter Worth YEAR: 1984 CAMERA: Leica FILM: Agfa-chrome TITLE/DESCRIPTION: Lime and Kiwi Fruit in Porcelain Dish*

PAGE 40 *PHOTOGRAPHER: George Day YEAR: 1996 CAMERA: Canon F-1 FILM: Velvia ISO 50 EXPOSURE: 1/2 at f/22 FILTERS: 8/A TITLE/DESCRIPTION: Multi-Colored Leaves: Still Life ■ Four-foot square still life created on living room floor lit with reflected window light and softbox over Vivitar 285 flash. ● Stilleben, 1,2 x 1,2 m, auf dem Fussboden eines Wohnzimmers mit reflektiertem Fensterlicht und Softbox über Vivitar 285-Blitzlicht aufgenommen. ▲ Nature morte 1,2 x 1,2 m photographiée sur le sol d'un séjour avec la lumière réfléchie d'une fenêtre et un diffuseur de lumière soft équipé d'un flash Vivitar 285.*

PAGE 41 *PHOTOGRAPHER: Roger Pfingston YEAR: 1992 CAMERA: Nikon FM2 FILM: Plus-X EXPOSURE: f/16, flash PAPER/PROCESS: Agfa Portriga-Rapid 2, 111 TITLE/DESCRIPTION: Night Blooming Cereus 1992 ■ Print was selenium toned and slightly bleached.● Der Abzug wurde mit Selen getont und etwas gebleicht. ▲ Le tirage a été viré au sélénium et légèrement blanchi.*

PAGE 42-45 *PHOTOGRAPHER: H. Turk Year: 1992 CAMERA: Pentax K1000 w/50mm f 4 lens FILM: Agfa 100 EXPOSURE: f/16 flash PAPER/PROCESS: C Print*

PAGE 46 *PHOTOGRAPHER: Assaf Haber*

PAGE 47 *PHOTOGRAPHER: Helena Fierlinger YEAR: 1994 CAMERA: Nikon FM 2 FILM: Kodak Epp EXPOSURE: 1 second at f/32 PAPER/PROCESS: E6 TITLE/DESCRIPTION: Tomatoes*

PAGE 48 *PHOTOGRAPHER: Beth Vagley YEAR: 1996 CAMERA: Canon Rebel FILM: T-Max 400 EXPOSURE: f/8 PAPER/PROCESS: black-and-white silver prints TITLE/DESCRIPTION: Untitled*

PAGE 50 *PHOTOGRAPHER: Michael R. Reese YEAR: 1992 CAMERA: Maxxum 9000 FILM: Tri-X EXPOSURE: 1/250 at f/8 PAPER/PROCESS: Ilford Fb/sepia-toned TITLE/DESCRIPTION: Three Plus One ■ Atlanta, during the Rodney King acquittal. ● Atlanta, beim Freispruch für Rodney King. ▲ Lors de l'acquittement de Rodney King, Atlanta.*

PAGE 51 *PHOTOGRAPHER: Miwa Nishio YEAR: 1996 CAMERA: Minolta X700 FILM: Provia 100 EXPOSURE: 1/30 at f/3.5 PAPER/PROCESS: cross process color coupler TITLE/DESCRIPTION: From the "Michelle's Nightmare" series. No 3., "Busy Line."*

PAGE 52 *Photographer:* *Nathan Teutle* *Year:* *1996* *Camera:* *Hasselblad 501c* *Film:* *Kodak Pmc 400* *Exposure:* *1/60 at f/8* *Paper/Process:* *Kodak Supra II* *Title/Description:* *Girl Looking at Clock* ■ *Natural light.* ● *Natürliches Licht.* ▲ *Lumière du jour.*

PAGE 53 *Photographer:* *Norma Zuniga* *Year:* *1996* *Camera:* *Hasselblad* *Film:* *Fuji 400* *Exposure:* *1/25 at f/8* *Paper/Process:* *Kodak* *Title/Description:* *Revine* ■ *An hommage to Avedon's "Dovima and the Elephants" image.* ● *Hommage an Avedons Bild «Dovina und die Elefanten».* ▲ *Hommage à la photographie d'Avedon «Dovina et les Eléphants».*

PAGE 54 *Photographer:* *Charles Brackman* *Camera:* *Mamiya 6* *Film:* *Ilford Hp5* *Exposure:* *15 seconds at f/3.5* *Paper/Process:* *Agfa Classic/Toned* *Title/Description:* *Night Watch*

PAGE 55 *Photographer:* *Charles Brackman* *Camera:* *Mamiya 6* *Film:* *Ilford Hp5* *Exposure:* *5 seconds at f/3.5* *Filters:* *Neutral Density* *Paper/Process:* *Agfa Classic/selenium toned* *Title/Description:* *The Strand*

PAGE 56 *Photographer:* *Charles Brackman* *Year:* *1996* *Camera:* *Mamiya 6* *Film:* *Ilford Hp* *Exposure:* *15 seconds at f/3.5* *Paper/Process:* *Agfa Classic/selenium toned* *Title/Description:* *Morpheus Descending*

PAGE 57 *Photographer:* *Charles Brackman* *Camera:* *Mamiya 6* *Film:* *Ilford Hp* *Exposure:* *5 seconds at f/3.5* *Filters:* *Neutural Density* *Paper/Process:* *Agfa Classic/Toned* *Title/Description:* *Night Sea Journey* ■ *Photo taken in ocean surf with evening sky.* ● *Das Photo wurde in der Ozeanbrandung mit Abendhimmel aufgenommen.* ▲ *Photographie prise le soir, dans les vagues de l'océan.*

PAGE 58 *Photographer:* *Charles Brackman* *Year:* *1996* *Camera:* *Mamiya 6* *Film:* *Ilford Hp* *Exposure:* *100 seconds at f/8* *Paper/Process:* *Agfa Classic/selenium toned* *Title/Description:* *Shadowland*

PAGE 59 *Photographer:* *Melvin Moten Jr* *Year:* *1996* *Camera:* *Crown Graphic w/80 f 3.8 Graphex* *Film:* *Ek Vpl 4 x 5* *Exposure:* *3 seconds at f/ 3.8* *Paper/Process:* *Ek Pro* *Title/Description:* *Ragan with Love Letters*

PAGE 60 *Photographer:* *Catherine Satterwhite* *Year:* *1995* *Camera:* *Minolta 303 Si Super* *Film:* *black-and-white Tri-X Pan* *Paper/Process:* *Multigrade IV Fiber Ilford*

PAGE 61 *Photographer:* *Norma Zuniga* *Year:* *1996* *Camera:* *Mamiya* *Film:* *Kodak 400* *Exposure:* *1/125 at f/11* *Paper/Process:* *Kodak* *Title/ Description:* *The Valentino Suite* ■ *The picture at the left corner is of Valentino.* ● *Das Bild in der linken Ecke ist von Valentino.* ▲ *L'image dans le coin de gauche est de Valentino.*

PAGE 62 *Photographer:* *Martin Cooper* *Year:* *1994* *Camera:* *Fuji Gx680* *Film:* *Tri-X* *Paper/Process:* *Agfa 118* *Title/Description:* *#1 Reclining Horizon, 1994. From the "Emergence" collection.* ■ *All images are toned gelatin silver prints. Original print size: 8 x 10.* ● *Alle Bilder sind getonte Silbergelatine-Abzüge. Originalgrösse: 8 x 10 Inch.* ▲ *Photographies virées aux sels d'argent. Format original: 8 x10".*

PAGE 63 *Photographer:* *Martin Cooper* *Year:* *1994* *Camera:* *Canon Ae-1* *Film:* *Tri-X* *Paper/Process:* *Agfa 118* *Title/Description:* *#2 Twist, 1994. From the "Emergence" collection.* ■ *All images are toned gelatin silver prints. Original print size: 8 x 10.* ● *Alle Bilder sind getonte Silbergelatine-Abzüge. Originalgrösse: 8 x 10 Inch.* ▲ *Photographies virées aux sels d'argent. Format original: 8 x10".*

PAGE 64 *Photographer:* *Michael Wylot* *Year:* *1996* *Camera:* *Hasselblad 500cm-80mm C F* *Film:* *Plus-X Kodak* *Exposure:* *1/250 at f/8* *Filters:* *Soft Focus #2 Net (Black)* *Paper/Process: Kodak Polymax Rc* *Title/Description: The Dream* ■ *The print was split-toned using sepia and selenium.* ● *Der Abzug wurde sowohl mit Sepia als auch Selen getont.* ▲ *Tirage viré au sépia et au sélénium.*

PAGE 65 *Photographer:* *Kevin McWilliams* *Year:* *1996* *Camera:* *Bronica Sq-A* *Film:* *Ilford Delta 100* *Paper/Process:* *Ilford MgIV* *Title/Description:* *Seated Nude* ■ *The picture was taken without a filter, but a diffuser was used during printing. The print was then toned with Berg sepia toner.* ● *Die Aufnahme wurde ohne Filter gemacht, doch beim Vergrössern wurde ein Diffusor verwendet. Danach wurde der Abzug mit Berg-Sepiatoner getont.* ▲ *Photographie prise sans filtre. Un diffuseur a été utilisé pour le tirage, viré au sépia Berg.*

PAGE 66 *Photographer:* *Laura Savidge* *Year:* *1994* *Camera:* *Nikon F3* *Film:* *Ilford Hp5* *Exposure:* *1/60 at f/22* *Filters:* *81a* *Paper/Process:* *Ilford Multigrade IV Deluxe* *Title/Description:* *Kate*

PAGE 67 *Photographer:* *Laura Savidge* *Year:* *1994* *Camera:* *Nikon F3 28-85 lens* *Film:* *Kodak Infrared ASA 200* *Exposure:* *1/60 at f/22* *Filters:* *25 Red* *Paper/Process:* *Ilford Multigrade III Deluxe* *Title/Description:* *Red Shoes*

PAGE 68 *Photographer:* *Christopher Lovenguth* *Year:* *1996* *Title/Description:* *Fallen Angel* ■ *Toned black-and-white print.* ● *Getonter Schwarzweiss-Abzug.* ▲ *Tirage noir et blanc viré.*

PAGE 69 *Photographer:* *R. Michael Walker* *Year:* *1995* *Camera:* *Nikon F3, 24mm lens* *Exposure:* *1/250 at f/8* *Paper/Process:* *C Print/Ep2 Chemistry* *Title/Description:* *Fashion Aftermath*

PAGES 70, 71 *Photographer:* *Scott Gilbertson* *Year:* *1996* *Camera:* *Canon FTB* *Film:* *T-Max 400* *Paper/Process:* *Agfa* *Title/Description:* *Nude Studies* ■ *The print is 8 x 5 1/4* ● *Abzug 8 x 5 1/4 Inch.* ▲ *Tirage 8 x 5 1/4".*

PAGE 72 *Photographer:* *Michael Schreiner* *Year:* *1996* *Camera:* *Nikon F4* *Film:* *Hp-5 +* *Paper/Process:* *Ilford Pearl* *Title/Description:* *Lani*

PAGE 73 *Photographer:* *Joe Rice* *Year:* *1995* *Camera:* *Minolta Xe-7* *Film:* *Kodak Infrared black-and-white* *Exposure:* *1/60 at f/ 5.6* *Filters:* *Red 25* *Paper/Process:* *Oriental Seagull graded papers* *Title/Description:* *Boundless*

PAGE 74 *Photographer:* *Scott Gilbertson* *Camera:* *4 x 5 Orbit* *Film:* *T-Max 400* *Paper/Process:* *Agfa* *Title/Description:* *Series of Five Nude Studies* ■ *Each print is 11 x 14. This series was shot entirely with natural light.* ● *Jeder Abzug im Format 11 x 14 Inch. Diese Serie wurde ausschliesslich bei natürlichem Licht gemacht.* ▲ *Chaque tirage est de format 11 x 14". Série entièrement réalisée à la lumière du jour.*

PAGE 75 *Photographer:* *Scott Gilbertson* *Camera:* *4 x 5 Orbit* *Film:* *T-Max 400* *Paper/Process:* *Agfa* *Title/Description:* *Series Of Five Nude Studies* ■ *Each print is 11x14. This series was shot entirely with natural light.* ● *Jeder Abzug im Format 11 x 14 Inch. Diese Serie wurde ausschliesslich bei natürlichem Licht gemacht.* ▲ *Chaque tirage est de format 11 x 14". Série entièrement réalisée à la lumière du jour.*

PAGE 76 *Photographer:* *Bob Todrick* *Year:* *1994* *Camera:* *Konica Hexar* *Film:* *Tri-X ISO 800* *Exposure:* *1/30 at f/2* *Paper/Process:* *Agfa Multicontrast Classic* *Title/Description:* *My Friend's Breast in Studio Hallway* ■ *Part of a series of nudes.* ● *Aus einer Serie von Aktaufnahmen.* ▲ *Extrait d'une série de nus.*

PAGE 77 *Photographer:* *Jorge Marquardt* *Year: 1995* *Camera:* *Nikon 6006* *Film:* *Kodak Tri-X 3200* *Paper/Process:* *Ilford MgIV Fiber* *Title/Description:* *Kneeling Nude with Shadows*

PAGE 78 *Photographer:* *David Lundberg* *Year:* *1995* *Camera:* *Rollicord Vb* *Film:* *Hp5+* *Exposure:* *Ei 1600* *Paper/Process:* *Ilford MgIV* *Title/Description:* *Nude 9*

PAGE 79 *Photographer:* *Nathan Teutle* *Year:* *1996* *Camera:* *Hasselblad 501c w/80mm* *Film:* *Kodak Pmc 400* *Exposure:* *1/60 at f/8* *Paper/Process:* *Kodak Supra II Normal* *Title/Description:* *Koali* ■ *Natural lighting.* ● *Bleuchtung mit natürlichem Licht.* ▲ *Eclairage à la lumière du jour.*

PAGE 80 *Photographer:* *Wendy Newman* *Year:* *1996* *Camera:* *Yashicamat 24* *Film:* *Agfapan 400* *Exposure:* *1/30 at f/5.6* *Paper/Process:* *Ilford Multigrade IV* *Title/Description:* *Danielle*

PAGE 81 *Photographer:* *Paul Kozal* *Year:* *1996* *Camera:* *Canon A2e w/28-105mm* *Film:* *Ilford Hp5+* *Exposure:* *1/60 at f/5.6* *Paper/Process:* *Forte Polywarm Tone/seleni-*

um toned TITLE/DESCRIPTION: *John and N.C. Wyeth*

PAGE 82 PHOTOGRAPHER: *Paul Kozal* YEAR: *1995* CAMERA: *Nikon N90 w/35-135mm* FILM: *Ilford Hp5+* PAPER/PROCESS: *Agfa Multigrade/selenium toned* TITLE/DESCRIPTION: *John West* ■ *John West is a silversmith in Carrizozo, New Mexico.* ● *John West ist Silberschmied in Carrizozo, New Mexico.* ▲ *John West est orfèvre à Carrizozo, Nouveau-Mexique.*

PAGE 83 PHOTOGRAPHER: *Edie Pereira* YEAR: *1995* CAMERA: *Eos 650* FILM: *Agfa Pan 400* PAPER/PROCESS: *Agfa 118* TITLE/DESCRIPTION: *Man with Cane...Never Looks Up*

PAGE 84 PHOTOGRAPHER: *Paul Kozal* YEAR: *1994* CAMERA: *Kowa 6* FILM: *Ilford Hp5+* EXPOSURE: *1/2 at f/16* PAPER/PROCESS: *Agfa Multigrade/selenium toned* TITLE/DESCRIPTION: *John Meigs*

PAGE 85 PHOTOGRAPHER: *Sergio Leitao* YEAR: *1996* CAMERA: *Hasselblad 500 cm/w 50mm* FILM: *Fuji Super G 100* EXPOSURE: *1 minute at f/22 on tripod* PAPER/PROCESS: *Fujicolor* TITLE/DESCRIPTION: *Hotel Fashion 1* ■ *Imagine asking someone to be still for a one-minute exposure...It is said that one should throw the background out of focus to enhance a model in any scenery, but the opposite suits this hotel.* ● *Stellen Sie sich vor, dass Sie jemanden bitten, sich für eine Belichtungszeit von einer Minute nicht zu bewegen... Es heisst, man solle den Hintergrund unscharf halten, um ein Modell in gleich welcher Umgebung hervorzuheben, doch für dieses Hotel ist das Gegenteil angebracht.* ▲ *Imaginez que vous demandiez à quelqu'un de ne pas bouger pour un temps de pose d'une minute... On vous dit que la toile de fond doit rester floue pour mettre en valeur le modèle dans n'importe quel environnement, mais que le contraire s'applique à cet hôtel...*

PAGE 86 PHOTOGRAPHER: *Norma Zuniga* YEAR: *1996* CAMERA: *Hasselblad* FILM: *Agfa 5d* PAPER/PROCESS: *Kodak* TITLE/DESCRIPTION: *Melissa*

PAGE 87 PHOTOGRAPHER: *Michael Reese* YEAR: *1994* CAMERA: *Rolleiflex Tlr* FILM: *T-Max 100* EXPOSURE: *1/60 at f/16* PAPER/PROCESS: *Ilford Fb/bleached sepia print* TITLE/DESCRIPTION: *Fear or Admiration*

PAGE 88 PHOTOGRAPHER: *Malinda Kilmer* YEAR: *1996* CAMERA: *Nikon N-90* FILM: *Kodak Tri-X* PAPER/PROCESS: *Kodak Ektalure* TITLE/DESCRIPTION: *Austin's Hands*

PAGE 89 PHOTOGRAPHER: *Malinda Kilmer* YEAR: *1996* CAMERA: *Nikon N-90* FILM: *Kodak Tri-X* PAPER/PROCESS: *Kodak Ektalure*

PAGE 90 PHOTOGRAPHER: *Gordon Eckler* YEAR: *1996* CAMERA: *Pentax* FILM: *Kodak Tri-X 400* PAPER/PROCESS: *Agfa fiber matte* ■ *A 60-second shutter speed slightly blurred her hair.* ● *Eine Belichtungszeit von sechzig Sekunden verwischte ganz leicht ihr Haar.* ▲ *Le temps de pose de 60 secondes a légèrement effacé ses cheveux.*

PAGE 91 PHOTOGRAPHER: *Darriel Caston* YEAR: *1994* CAMERA: *Nikon 6006* FILM: *Velvia Fuji* EXPOSURE: *f/8* PAPER/PROCESS: *Fujiflex/R4* TITLE/DESCRIPTION: *A Day with Devon*

PAGE 92 PHOTOGRAPHER: *Robert Parkey III* YEAR: *1987* CAMERA: *Nikon FA* FILM: *Ilford Hp5* PAPER/PROCESS: *Oriental Fiber Baser RC* TITLE/DESCRIPTION: *Father and Son* ■ *Part of an on-going series: "The American Barbershop."* ● *Aus einer laufenden Serie: "The American Barbershop".* ▲ *Extrait d'une série continue: «Le barbier américain».*

PAGE 93 PHOTOGRAPHER: *Robert Parkey III* YEAR: *1987* CAMERA: *Nikon FA* FILM: *Ilford Hp5* PAPER/PROCESS: *Oriental Fiber Baser RC* TITLE/DESCRIPTION: *First Cut* ■ *Part of the series: "The American Barbershop."* ● *Aus der Serie: "The American Barbershop".* ▲ *Extrait d'une série continue: «Le barbier américain».*

PAGE 94 PHOTOGRAPHER: *Sara Jo Matthys* YEAR: *1980* CAMERA: *Minolta Srl 201* FILM: *Tri-X* PAPER/PROCESS: *Brovira* TITLE/DESCRIPTION: *My Best Friend Samuel* ■ *Light source: bare bulb from bedside lamp.* ● *Lichtquelle: Nackte Glühbirne einer Nachttischlampe.* ▲ *Source de lumière: une ampoule nue d'une lampe de chevet.*

PAGE 95 PHOTOGRAPHER: *Liza Betof* YEAR: *1996* CAMERA: *35mm* FILM: *Plus-X 400* EXPOSURE: *8 seconds at f/11* PAPER/PROCESS: *Ilford* TITLE/DESCRIPTION: *Shoemaker (Chinatown, New York City)*

PAGE 96 PHOTOGRAPHER: *Jo Ann Lore* YEAR: *1993* CAMERA: *Canon T90* FILM: *Fuji Chrome 100* EXPOSURE: *1/30 at f/2.8* FILTERS: *Neutral Density* TITLE/DESCRIPTION: *Self Portrait*

PAGE 97 PHOTOGRAPHER: *Michael Dobson* CAMERA: *Nikon Fm-2* FILM: *Kodak Tri-X pushed* PAPER/PROCESS: *Ilford Multi Grade* TITLE/DESCRIPTION: *(Bufp) Kira*

PAGE 98 PHOTOGRAPHER: *Perry Dilbeck* YEAR: *1995* CAMERA: *Pentax 6 x 7* FILM: *T-Max 400* PAPER/PROCESS: *Oriental selenium-toned gelatin silver print* TITLE/DESCRIPTION: *E C Hill*

PAGE 99 PHOTOGRAPHER: *James Rushing* YEAR: *1995* CAMERA: *Minolta SRT 201* FILM: *Tri-X* PAPER/PROCESS: *Kodak F Surface* TITLE/DESCRIPTION: *A Taste of Life*

PAGE 100 PHOTOGRAPHER: *Kevin McWilliams* YEAR: *1988* CAMERA: *Minolta X700* FILM: *Tri-X* PAPER/PROCESS: *Ilford MgIV* TITLE/DESCRIPTION: *Coke Adds Life*

PAGE 101 PHOTOGRAPHER: *Libby Edelman* YEAR: *1996* CAMERA: *Nikon* FILM: *Tri-X 400 ASA* PAPER/PROCESS: *Galleria #3 Ilford* ■ *A school for deaf and mute children.* ● *Eine Schule für taubstumme Kinder.* ▲ *Ecole pour enfants sourds-muets.*

PAGE 102 PHOTOGRAPHER: *Greg Nielson* YEAR: *1991* CAMERA: *Nikon FM2* FILM: *Tri-X 400* FILTERS: *Red filter* TITLE/DESCRIPTION: *Bed of Nails* ■ *The Sadhus of India are renowned for their ability to renounce pain as a means of religious expression. This particular Sadhu stood serenely for hours at a time upon his bed of nails.* ● *Die Sadhus sind berühmt für ihre Fähigkeit, Schmerzen zu überwinden - als Mittel religiösen Ausdrucks. Dieser Sadhu stand während Stunden ganz gelassen auf seinem Nagelbrett.* ▲ *En Inde, les Sadhus sont connus pour leur capacité à vaincre la douleur en signe d'expression religieuse. Ce Sadhu s'est reposé durant des heures et avec la plus grande sérénité sur une planche de clous.*

PAGE 103 PHOTOGRAPHER: *Donald Gurewitz* YEAR: *1993* CAMERA: *Canon 630* FILM: *Fujichrome 100* TITLE/DESCRIPTION: *Ferryboat Captain, Haiphong, Vietnam*

PAGE 104 PHOTOGRAPHER: *Stephen Yu* YEAR: *1994* CAMERA: *Minolta 7xi* FILM: *Kodak Tri-X 400* EXPOSURE: *"P" with flash* PAPER/PROCESS: *Ilford Multigrade IV Rc Deluxe* TITLE/DESCRIPTION: *Machinist*

PAGE 105 PHOTOGRAPHER: *K Armstrong* YEAR: *1996* CAMERA: *Nikon* FILM: *Agfa Apx 100* PAPER/PROCESS: *Agfa semi-matte* TITLE/DESCRIPTION: *Untitled*

PAGE 106 PHOTOGRAPHER: *Stephen Wilde* YEAR: *May 1996* CAMERA: *F90 w/20mm lens* FILM: *Agfa Apx 100* PAPER/PROCESS: *Fuji Fa4-G* TITLE/DESCRIPTION: *Missing You*

PAGE 107 PHOTOGRAPHER: *Davin Ellicson* YEAR: *1995* CAMERA: *Nikon N90* FILM: *Kodak T-Max 400 Professional* PAPER/PROCESS: *geltain silver print* TITLE/DESCRIPTION: *Mt. Greylock, Lansboro, Massachusetts* ■ *Massachusetts's highest peak, standing at 3,491 ft.* ● *Massachusetts höchster Berggipfel (1064 m).* ▲ *Le Mont Greylock, le plus haut sommet du Massachusetts (1064 m).*

PAGE 108 PHOTOGRAPHER: *Christopher Clemente* YEAR: *1996* CAMERA: *Canon Eos-S* FILM: *Kodak* FILTERS: *Quantaray* PAPER/PROCESS: *Kodak* TITLE/DESCRIPTION: *Made in America* ■ *The six-year-old boy was a spectator at the Aspen, Colorado summer rodeo.* ● *Der sechsjährige Junge war Zuschauer am Sommerrodeo von Aspen, Colorado.* ▲ *Ce garçon de six ans faisait partie des spectateurs du rodéo d'Aspen, Colorado.*

PAGE 109 PHOTOGRAPHER: *Richard Langone* YEAR: *1996* CAMERA: *Minolta X-700* FILM: *Tri-X* TITLE/DESCRIPTION: *Part of an on-going series: "Small Town Georgia."*

PAGE 110 PHOTOGRAPHER: *Trevor Nelson* YEAR: *1992* CAMERA: *Canon Ae-1* FILM: *Fujichrome Sensia 100* FILTERS: *none* PAPER/PROCESS: *E-6*

PAGE 111 PHOTOGRAPHER: *Emmanuel Caluag* YEAR: *1991* CAMERA: *Nikon FM2*

Paper/Process: E6 *Title/Description:* Eyes and Snow ■ Taken during the blizzard of 1991, in New York City.The mural belonged to "Club Usa," a disco now demolished. ● Aufgenommen in New York während des Blizzards von 1991. Das Wandgemälde gehörte zum «Club Usa», einer inzwischen abgerissenen Disco. ▲ Photographie prise durant le blizzard de 1991 à New York. La peinture murale appartenait au «Club Usa», une discothèque démolie aujourd'hui.

PAGE 112 *Photographer:* Andre Souroujon *Year:* 1995 *Camera:* Canon A2 w/28-80mm lens *Film:* Kodak Tri-X ■ The photographer's parents in Mexico ● Die Eltern des Photographen in Mexiko. ▲ Les parents du photographe à Mexico.

PAGE 113 *Photographer:* Andre Souroujon *Year:* 1995 *Camera:* Canon A2 w/28-80l lens *Film:* Kodak Tri-X ■ The photographer's parents in Mexico ● Die Eltern des Photographen in Mexiko. ▲ Les parents du photographe à Mexico.

PAGE 113 *Photographer:* Edie Pereira *Year:* 1995 *Camera:* Eos 650 *Film:* Agfa Apx 100 *Paper/Process:* Agfa 118 *Title/Description:* Curiosity ■ Jardin du Luxembourg, Paris. ● Jardin du Luxembourg, Paris. ▲ Jardin du Luxembourg, Paris.

PAGE 114 *Photographer:* William Mercadante *Year:* 1996 *Camera:* Nikonos V *Film:* Fujichrome 100 *Exposure:* f/6 *Paper/Process:* E-6 *Title/Description:* #21 Casino ■ Storm on Santa Catalina Island. ● Sturm über der Insel Santa Catalina. ▲ Tempête sur l'île Santa Catalina.

PAGE 116 *Photographer:* Paul Kozal *Year:* 1995 *Camera:* Nikon N90 with 75-210mm lens *Film:* Ilford Fp4 *Exposure:* 30 seconds at f/22 *Filters:* Red #25 *Paper/Process:* Agfa Multigrade Fb/sepia toned *Title/Description:* Electrical Storm ■ Taken in New Mexico ● Aufgenommen in New Mexico. ▲ Photographie prise au Nouveau-Mexique.

PAGE 117 *Photographer:* Paul Kozal *Year:* 1994 *Camera:* Nikon N90 with 35-135mm lens *Film:* Ilford Hp5+ *Paper/Process:* Agfa Multigrade Fb/sepia toned *Title/Description:* Alta ■ Shot in the ghost town of Alta, Colorado. ● Aufgenommen in der Geisterstadt Alta, Colorado. ▲ Photographie prise dans la ville fantôme d'Alta, Colorado.

PAGE 118 *Photographer:* Ben Salvador *Year:* 1991 *Camera:* Contax Rts11 25mm lens *Film:* Fujichrome Rfp *Exposure:* 1/30 at f/22 *Filters:* Polarizing *Title/Description:* Mono Lake surroundings

PAGE 119 *Photographer:* Susan Shamper *Year:* 1996 *Camera:* Nikon F3 *Film:* Fuji Velvia *Title/Description:* Dalmation Corner

PAGE 120 *Photographer:* Paul Kozal *Year:* 1995 *Camera:* Canon A2e w/28-105mm lens *Film:* Ilford Xp2 *Exposure:* 1/60 at f/11 *Filters:* none *Paper/Process:* Agfa Multigrade Fb/sepia toned *Title/Description:* Road To Mt. Baker

PAGE 121 *Photographer:* Paul Kozal *Year:* 1995 *Camera:* Kanon A2e w/28-105mm lens *Film:* Ilford Hp5+ *Exposure:* 1/60 at f/8 *Paper/Process:* Luminos Antique Ivory/sepia toned Title/Description: Point Reyes, California

PAGE 122 *Photographer:* Paul Kozal *Year:* 1995 *Camera:* Canon A2e with 28-105mm lens *Film:* Ilford Hp5+ *Exposure:* 1/60 at f/8 *Paper/Process:* Luminos Antique Ivory/sepia toned *Title/Description:* Road to Reyes ■ Taken at Point Reyes, California. ● Aufgenommen bei Point Reyes, Kalifornien. ▲ Photographie prise à Point Reyes, Californie.

PAGE 123 *Photographer:* Patricia Jordan *Year:* 1994 *Camera:* Nikon F45 *Film:* Fuji Velvia *Exposure:* f11 *Title/Description:* Zanzibar

PAGES 124, 125 *Photographer:* Paul Kozal *Year:* 1996 *Camera:* Nikon N90 with 35-135mm lens *Film:* Ilford Fp4 *Exposure:* 30 seconds at f/22 *Filters:* Red #25 *Paper/Process:* Luminos Antique Ivory/sepia toned *Title/Description:* Twin Streaks ■ "This is not a double exposure. Sometimes you just get lucky." ● Es handelt sich nicht um eine Doppelbelichtung. Manchmal hat man einfach Glück. ▲ Il ne s'agit pas d'une double exposition. Parfois, on a simplement de la chance.

PAGE 126 *Photographer:* Brian Hite *Year:* 1996 *Camera:* Calumet 4 x 5 with Caltar 90mm lens *Film:* Fuji Nps 160 *Exposure:* 1 second at f/4.5 *Filters:* Cokin Sepia Coef 3 *Paper/Process:* Fuji Fa5 / Ra-4 *Title/Description:* Abandoned House ■ To color correct the washed-out exposure of the house, the photographer added the sepia filter to bring out the sky and give the reddish-yellow tonal change to the landscape. ● Zur Farbkorrektur der überhellen, aufs Haus abgestimmten Belichtung setzte der Photograf ein Sepiafilter an, um den Himmel deutlich sichtbar zu machen und der Landschaft die rötlichgelbe Färbung zu geben. ▲ Pour corriger la couleur de la maison qui a été exposée, le photographe a ajouté un filtre sépia pour rendre le ciel plus soutenu et donner une teinte jaune rouge au paysage.

PAGE 127 *Photographer:* Brian Hite *Year:* 1996 *Camera:* Calumet 4 x 5 with Caltar 90mm lens *Film:* Fuji Nps 160 *Exposure:* 1/2 second at f/4.5 *Filters:* Colin Sepia Coef 3 *Paper/Process:* Fuji Fa-5/Ra-4 *Title/Description:* O'Shaughnessy Dam ■ The white cast at the top right is from a fogging of the negative due to a light leak. ● Der Stich ins Weisse oben rechts ist auf eine Verschleierung des Negativs durch eine lichtdurchlässige Stelle zurückzuführen. ▲ Le blanc à droite est dû au passage de la lumière lors du voilage du négatif.

PAGE 128 *Photographer:* Joshua Even *Year:* 1988 *Camera:* Nikon 801 *Film:* Agfacolor 100 Asa *Exposure:* Auto *Title/Description:* Leisure and Tranquility ■ Taken in Tel Aviv

PAGE 129 *Photographer:* Aaron Landman *Year:* 1996 *Camera:* Canon Ae-1 *Film:* Fuji Neopan 400 *Exposure:* 1/250 at f/8 *Filters:* Red 25 *Paper/Process:* Afga Multicontrast Fiber *Title/Description:* Sunset District, San Francisco, California

PAGE 130 *Photographer:* David Parker *Camera:* Hasselblad 500 C/M *Film:* T-Max 100 *Exposure:* 1/25 at f/16 *Paper/Process:* Poly Max Fine Art *Title/Description:* Boat in Maine

PAGE 131 *Photographer:* Joan Kane *Year:* 1996 *Camera:* Nikon 8008 *Film:* Fuji 100 *Exposure:* 1/60 at f/4 *Paper/Process:* Kodak Ekta Color Supra II *Title/Description:* American Landscape ■ Nature is typically received through a screen in our contemporary culture. ●Die Natur wird in unserer zeitgenössischen Kultur typischerweise über einen Bildschirm wahrgenommen. ▲ Dans notre culture, il n'est pas étonnant que nous découvrions la nature par le biais d'un écran.

PAGE 132 *Photographer:* Paul Kozal *Year:* 1996 *Camera:* Nikon N90 w/35-135mm lens *Film:* Kodak Hie *Exposure:* 1/60 at f/16 *Filters:* Red #25 *Paper/Process:* Forte Poly Warm Tone/selenium toned *Title/Description:* Dune XI ■ Whitesands, New Mexico ● Whitesand, New Mexico. ▲ Whitesand, Nouveau-Mexique.

PAGE 133 *Photographer:* Paul Kozal *Year:* 1996 *Camera:* Kowa 6 *Film:* Ilford Hp5+ *Exposure:* 1/30 at f/16 *Filters:* Red #25 *Paper/Process:* Forte Polywarm Tone Fb/selenium toned *Title/Description:* The Dunes at Stovepipe Wells ■ Death Valley, California ● Death Valley, Kalifornien. ▲ La vallée de la Mort, Californie.

PAGE 134 *Photographer:* Richard Langone *Year:* 1996 *Camera:* Minolta X-700 *Film:* Tri-X *Title/Description:* Part of an on-going series: "Small-Town Georgia"

PAGE 135 *Photographer:* Robert Oliverio *Year:* 1996 *Camera:* Nikon FM with Nikkor 28mm lens *Film:* Fuji Hg200 *Exposure:* 1/60 *Filters:* UV Filter *Paper/Process:* Kodak Professional *Title/Description:* Modern Prairie (John Wayne) ■ John Wayne's Western persona in the context of the modern Western landscape. Taken off the highway between Las Vegas and Los Angeles. ● John Waynes Westernfigur im Kontext der modernen Landschaft des Westens. Aufgenommen abseits der Hauptstrasse zwischen Las Vegas und Los Angeles. ▲ Le personnage western de John Wayne dans un paysage moderne de l'Ouest. Photographie prise à l'écart de la route qui relie Las Vegas et Los Angeles.

PAGE 136 *Photographer:* Jason Costanzo *Year:* 1996 *Camera:* Mamiya *Film:* Tri-X *Paper/Process:* silver pint/Aged Portriga 118

PAGE 137 *Photographer:* Jason Costanzo *Year:* 1996 *Camera:* Mamiya *Film:* Tri-X *Paper/Process:* silver print/Aged Portriga 118 *Title/Description:* Ferris Wheel

PAGE 138 *Photographer:* Jason Costanzo *Year:* 1996 *Camera:* Mamiya *Film:* Tri-X *Paper/Process:* silver print/Aged Portriga 118

PAGE 139 *PHOTOGRAPHER: Jason Costanzo YEAR: 1996 CAMERA: Mamiya FILM: Tri-X PAPER/PROCESS: silver print/Aged Portriga 118 TITLE/DESCRIPTION: Basketball Hoop*

PAGE 140 *PHOTOGRAPHER: Ben Salvador YEAR: 1994 CAMERA: Contax Rts with 25mm lens FILM: Fujichrome Rfp EXPOSURE: unrecorded FILTERS: Polarizing TITLE/DESCRIPTION: Sand Tufa At Mono Lake, California*

PAGE 141 *PHOTOGRAPHER: Voytek Otok YEAR: 1996 CAMERA: Nikon N90s FILM: Fuji Velvia FILTERS: Polarizer TITLE/DESCRIPTION: #04 White Mountains of Sierra Nevada*

PAGES 142, 143 *PHOTOGRAPHER: Malinda Kilmer YEAR: 1996 CAMERA: Hasselblad 501c FILM: Kodak Tri-X PAPER/PROCESS: Sterling Lith TITLE/DESCRIPTION: Cactus and Skull ■ Chemically altered lith developer. Sepia-toned. ● Chemisch veränderter Lithentwickler. Mit Sepia getont. ▲ Révélateur «lith» modifié chimiquement. Virage au sépia.*

PAGE 144 *PHOTOGRAPHER: Darriel Caston YEAR: 1995 CAMERA: 6x6 Konica FILM: Hp5 Ilford EXPOSURE: f/22 PAPER/PROCESS: black-and-white/copper-toned TITLE/DESCRIPTION: Oak and Stone*

PAGE 145 *PHOTOGRAPHER: Ryan Skorecki YEAR: 1995 CAMERA: Mamiya C330 FILM: Velvia PAPER/PROCESS: duplicate slide TITLE/DESCRIPTION: Great Sand Dunes, Colorado*

PAGE 146 *PHOTOGRAPHER: Clara Teufel YEAR: 1994 CAMERA: Canon Eos Rebel FILM: Tri-X PAPER/PROCESS: black-and-white processing on Ilford fiber TITLE/ DESCRIPTION: Chairs ■ The clouds are on a separate negative that has been superimposed upside-down on a photo of chairs. ● Die Wolken stammen von einem anderen Negativ, das verkehrt herum in eine Aufnahme von Stühlen einkopiert worden ist. ▲ Les nuages viennent d'un autre négatif qui a été surimprimé à l'envers sur une photographie de chaises.*

PAGE 147 *PHOTOGRAPHER: Sonia Barrozo YEAR: 1996 CAMERA: Topcon Beseler FILM: Kodak 35mm ISO 200 EXPOSURE: 1/125 at f/5.6 PAPER/PROCESS: Kodak Royal Paper TITLE/DESCRIPTION: Old Pier ■ Brazil ● Brasilien.▲ Brésil.*

PAGE 148 *PHOTOGRAPHER: Robert Fudge YEAR: 1996 CAMERA: Minolta 5000 FILM: Kodak Gold 400 FILTERS: Sky 1 PAPER/PROCESS: Kodak TITLE/DESCRIPTION: Oregon Coast*

PAGE 149 *PHOTOGRAPHER: Paul Kozal Year: 1995 CAMERA: Kowa 6 FILM: Ilford Hp5+ EXPOSURE: 1/2 second at f/16 PAPER/PROCESS: Agfa Multigrade Fb/selenium toned TITLE/DESCRIPTION: Palos Park*

PAGE 150 *PHOTOGRAPHER: Lorne Resnick ■ Sahara Desert, Africa. ● Sahara, Afrika. ▲ Le Sahara, Afrique.*

PAGE 151 *PHOTOGRAPHER: Nathan Teutle YEAR: 1996 Camera: Nikon F90 FILM: Kodak Gold 100 Exposure: 2 seconds at f/22 PAPER/PROCESS: Kodak Supra II TITLE/DESCRIPTION: My Dream*

PAGE 152 *PHOTOGRAPHER: Paul Kozal YEAR: 1996 CAMERA: Canon A2e w/75-300mm lens FILM: Ilford Hp5+ EXPOSURE: 30 seconds at f/22 FILTERS: Red #25 PAPER/PROCESS: Forte Polywarm Tone Fb/selenium toned TITLE/DESCRIPTION: The Artichoke Farm. ■ Carmel, California ● Carmel, Kalifornien ▲ Carmel, Californie.*

PAGE 153 *PHOTOGRAPHER: Edie Pereira YEAR: 1996 CAMERA: Eos 650 FILM: 400 Tri-X EXPOSURE: F8 16 PAPER/PROCESS: Agfa 118 TITLE/DESCRIPTION: Front Row Seating Only ■ Swanson Residence, Irvine, California ●Haus Swanson, Irvine, Kalifornien ▲ La résidence Swanson, Irvine, Californie*

PAGE 154 *PHOTOGRAPHER: Edie Pereira YEAR: 1994 CAMERA: Eos 650 FILM: Kodak 5063 Tri-X EXPOSURE: 17 seconds at f/11 PAPER/PROCESS: Agfa 118 TITLE/DESCRIPTION: Windowpane ■ Huntington Library, Pasadena, California ● Huntington Library, Pasadena, Kalifornien ▲ Bibliothèque Huntington, Pasadena, Californie.*

PAGE 155 *PHOTOGRAPHER: Mathew Courtney YEAR: 1996 CAMERA: Nikon FE2 FILM: T-Max 100 EXPOSURE: 1/125 at f/8 FILTERS: Polarizer and orange PAPER/PROCESS: Ilford Multigrade IV TITLE/DESCRIPTION: Lauderdale Beach ■ Sepia toned ● Mit Sepia getont ▲ Image virée au sépia.*

PAGE 156 *PHOTOGRAPHER: Babs Armour YEAR: 1992 CAMERA: Nikon 6006 FILM: Fuji Velvia PAPER/PROCESS: E6 TITLE/DESCRIPTION: Store Windows with Reflections ■ Single exposures shot hand-held from sidewalk. ● Einzelaufnahmen, vom Bürgersteig aus der Hand aufgenommen. ▲ Scènes urbaines réalisées sans volonté de cadrage, l'appareil à la main.*

PAGE 157 *PHOTOGRAPHER: Babs Armour YEAR: 1992 CAMERA: Nikon 6006 Film: Fuji Velvia Paper/Process: E6 Title/Description: Store Windows with Reflections ■ Single expsoures shot hand-held from sidewalk. ● Einzelaufnahmen, vom Bürgersteig aus der Hand aufgenommen. ▲ Scènes urbaines réalisées sans volonté de cadrage, l'appareil à la main.*

PAGES 158, 159 *PHOTOGRAPHER: Mathew Courtney YEAR: 1996 CAMERA: Nikon FE2 FILM: T-Max 100 EXPOSURE: 1/125 at f/16 FILTERS: Polarizer PAPER/PROCESS: Ilford Multigrade IV TITLE/DESCRIPTION: Lauderdale Sky ■ Print is slightly sepia toned ● Der Abzug ist mit Sepia leicht getont. ▲ Epreuve virée au sépia.*

PAGE 160 *PHOTOGRAPHER: Anthony Lawson YEAR: 1996 CAMERA: 4 x 5 Calumet FILM: T-Max 100 PAPER/PROCESS: Palladium TITLE/DESCRIPTION: The Eternal Garden #7 ■ 4 x 5 negative enlarged to 8 x 10 duplication film, contact-printed on palladium paper. ● 4 x 5-Negativ, vergrössert auf 8 x 10-Duplikatfilm, Kontaktabzug auf Palladiumpapier. ▲ Tirage contact sur papier palladium, réalisé à partir d'un négatif 4 x 5 dupliqué et agrandi sur un film 8 x 10.*

PAGE 161 *PHOTOGRAPHER: Michael Totaro CAMERA: Nikon N2000*

PAGE 162 *PHOTOGRAPHER: Paul Kozal YEAR: 1996 CAMERA: Canon A2e with 28-105mm lens FILM: Ilford Xp2 PAPER/PROCESS: Forte Polywarm Tone/selenium toned TITLE/DESCRIPTION: Frank Lloyd Wright Civic Center, Marin, California*

PAGE 164 *PHOTOGRAPHER: Richard Langone YEAR: 1996 CAMERA: Minolta X-700 FILM: Tri-X TITLE/DESCRIPTION: Part of an on-going series: "Small-Town Georgia."*

PAGE 165 *PHOTOGRAPHER: Timothy Gilbert YEAR: 1996 CAMERA: Pentax Pz-1 with Smc 70-210mm lens FILM: Fuji Velvia FILTERS: Polarizer PAPER/PROCESS: E-6 TITLE/DESCRIPTION: Freeway Columns, Los Angeles*

PAGE 166 *PHOTOGRAPHER: Christopher Lovenguth YEAR: 1996 CAMERA: 4 x 5 TITLE/DESCRIPTION: Broad Street Bridge*

PAGE 167 *PHOTOGRAPHER: Edie Pereira YEAR: 1995 CAMERA: Eos 650 FILM: Agfa Pan 400 EXPOSURE: 10 seconds at f/16 PAPER/PROCESS: Agfa 118 TITLE/DESCRIPTION: Paris in the Springtime ■ As seen from Notre Dame ● Von Notre Dame aus gesehen. ▲ Vue de Notre-Dame.*

PAGE 168 *PHOTOGRAPHER: Jane Evans YEAR: 1996 CAMERA: Hasselblad FILM: Kodak VPL EXPOSURE: 105 seconds at f/22 TITLE/DESCRIPTION: Barbershop*

PAGE 169 *PHOTOGRAPHER: Jane Evans YEAR: 1996 CAMERA: Hasselblad 500 C/M FILM: Kodak VPL EXPOSURE: 80 seconds at f/16 TITLE/DESCRIPTION: Room at the Masonic Temple*

PAGES 170, 171 *PHOTOGRAPHER: Emmanuel Caluag YEAR: 1989 CAMERA: Canon Ae1 Program FILM: Tri-X EXPOSURE: Auto-Program FILTERS: NonePAPER/PROCESS:D76 TITLE/DESCRIPTION: Tale of Two Buildings ■ The photographer used a Vivitar zoom (35-200) to compress & exaggerate space & relationship between the two buildings. ●Verwendung eines Vivitar Zoomobjektivs (35-200 mm), um den Raum und die Beziehung zwischen den beiden Gebäuden zu verdichten und überzubetonen. ▲ Pour mettre en relief et souligner l'espace et la relation entre les deux bâtiments, le photographe a utilisé un objectif Vivitar 35-200 mm.*

PAGE 172 *PHOTOGRAPHER: Fernando Burgleno YEAR: 1996 CAMERA: Minolta X700 FILM:*

Fuji Super HgII 200 EXPOSURE: *1/1000 at f/11* PAPER/PROCESS: *Kodak Utra N Ra* TITLE/DESCRIPTION: *Beach I*

PAGE 173 PHOTOGRAPHER: *Fernando Burgleno* YEAR: *1996* CAMERA: *Minolta X700* FILM: *Fuji Super HgII 200* EXPOSURE: *1/1000 at f/11* PAPER/PROCESS: *Kodak Utra N Ra* TITLE/DESCRIPTION: *Beach I*

PAGE 174 PHOTOGRAPHER: *Gregory Kihlstrom* YEAR: *1996* CAMERA: *Minolta X-700* FILM: *Kodak Tri-X 400* EXPOSURE: *1/250 at f/8* PAPER/PROCESS: *Kodak Ultra II Color Paper* TITLE/DESCRIPTION: *Radio City* ■ *Black-and-white negative printed on color paper.* ● *Schwarzweissnegativ auf Farbpapier abgezogen.* ▲ *Tirage d'un négatif noir et blanc sur papier couleur.*

PAGE 175 PHOTOGRAPHER: *Jan Rosol* YEAR: *1996* CAMERA: *Rolleiflex 6008* FILM: *Kodak T-Max 100* EXPOSURE: *Auto at f/22* PAPER/PROCESS: *Ilford Multigrade/ Universal* TITLE/DESCRIPTION: *From the series: "12 Pictures of Prague"* ■ *Camera on tripod.* ● *Kamera auf Stativ* ▲ *Appareil sur un trépied.*

PAGE 176 PHOTOGRAPHER: *Claudio Gangi* CAMERA: *Nikon F90* ■ *Double exposure during slide duplication.* ● *Doppelbelichtung beim Duplizieren des Dias.* ▲ *Diapositive soumise à une double exposition au moment de la duplication.*

PAGE 177 PHOTOGRAPHER: *Joshua Even* YEAR: *1996* CAMERA: *Nikon 801* FILM: *Fujicolor 400 ASA* TITLE/DESCRIPTION: *A Bar in Amsterdam, 1996*

PAGE 178 PHOTOGRAPHER: *Ron McDonald* YEAR: *1995* CAMERA: *Canon A1* FILM: *Kodak P3200* EXPOSURE: *125 seconds at f/5.6* FILTERS: *Tiffon UV Haze* PAPER/PROCESS: *Agfa Rc Vl* TITLE/DESCRIPTION: *Window and Tree*

PAGE 179 PHOTOGRAPHER: *Paul Kozal* YEAR: *1996* CAMERA: *Kowa 6* FILM: *Konica 750mm* EXPOSURE: *1/4 second at f/22* FILTERS: *Red #25* PAPER/PROCESS: *Agfa Multigrade Fb/sepia toned* TITLE/DESCRIPTION: *Ranchos de Taos, New Mexico*

PAGE 180 PHOTOGRAPHER: *John Cameron* YEAR: *1981* CAMERA: *Nikon FM* FILM: *Kodachrome 64* FILTERS: *Polarizer* TITLE/DESCRIPTION: *Doggie Diner* ■ *An effort to document sites before they disappear forever.* ● *Ein Versuch, etwas festzuhalten, bevor es für immer verschwunden ist.* ▲ *Images documentaires visant à immortaliser des sites avant qu'ils ne disparaissent à jamais.*

PAGE 181 PHOTOGRAPHER: *Russell Kroll* YEAR: *1995* CAMERA: *Olympus Om-1 24mm* FILM: *Kodak Epn-135* TITLE/DESCRIPTION: *Moonrise Over Abandonded Farm House, Minster Ohio* ■ *A long exposure of an old farm house* ● *Lang belichtete Auf-nahme eines alten Bauernhauses.* ▲ *Vieille ferme photographiée avec un long temps de pose.*

PAGES 182, 183 PHOTOGRAPHER: *Terese Mlakar* YEAR: *1993* CAMERA: *Minolta Srt101* FILM: *T-Max 100* EXPOSURE: *1/30 at f/11* PAPER/PROCESS: *black-and-white D76 Ilford* TITLE/DESCRIPTION: *Prague* ■ *Laser copies.* ● *Laserkopien.* ▲ *Copies laser.*

PAGE 184 PHOTOGRAPHER: *Paul Kozal* YEAR: *1996* CAMERA: *Canon A2E w/28-105mm* FILM: *Ilford HP5+* EXPOSURE: *1/30 at f/11* FILTERS: *none* PAPER/PROCESS: *Agfa Multigrade Fb/selenium toned* TITLE/DESCRIPTION: *Arch* ■ *Paris arch* ● *Bogen in Paris.* ▲ *Arc à Paris.*

PAGE 185 PHOTOGRAPHER: *John Crawford* YEAR: *1994* CAMERA: *Nikon FE with 28-210mm lens* FILM: *Fujichrome 50* EXPOSURE: *Auto, about 1/120 at f/5.6* TITLE/DESCRIPTION: *Sonoran-style Row Housing, Florence, Arizona*

PAGE 186 PHOTOGRAPHER: *Amina Baig* YEAR: *1996* CAMERA: *Minolta Maxxum* FILM: *Tri-X 100* EXPOSURE: *1/1000* PAPER/PROCESS: *Ilford Pearl* TITLE/DESCRIPTION: *Entrance to Mysticism*

PAGE 187 PHOTOGRAPHER: *Paul Kozal* YEAR: *1995* CAMERA: *Canon A2E w/75-300mm lens* FILM: *Ilford Hp5+* PAPER/PROCESS: *Agfa Multigrade Fb/sepia toned* TITLE/DESCRIPTION: *The City Sickness* ■ *"Beijing at 11:oo am, from the 17th floor. No, its not fog, and yes, you can stare at the sun without going blind."* ● *Peking, 11 Uhr morgens, vom 17. Stock aus. Nein, es ist kein Nebel, und tatsächlich, man kann in die Sonne blicken, ohne blind zu werden.* ▲ *Pékin à 11 heures du matin, du 17e étage. Non, il n'y a pas de brouillard, et oui, on peut regarder le soleil sans être ébloui.*

PAGE 188 PHOTOGRAPHER: *Michael Guzman* YEAR: *1993* CAMERA: *Nikon FE* FILM: *XP1* FILTERS: *No Red 25* PAPER/PROCESS: *Ilford Mult III RD* TITLE/DESCRIPTION: *Urban Structural Form II*

PAGE 189 PHOTOGRAPHER: *Jason Williams* YEAR: *1994* CAMERA: *Cannon A2 w/75-300 at 100* FILM: *Fuji Sensia 100* PAPER/PROCESS: *Kodak Print From Slide* TITLE/DESCRIPTION: *Harvest Moon*

PAGE 190 PHOTOGRAPHER: *Christopher Lovenguth* YEAR: *1995* TITLE/DESCRIPTION: *Plaster Room*

PAGE 191 PHOTOGRAPHER: *Brian Hite* YEAR: *1995* CAMERA: *Canon Eos I-N with 28mm lens* FILM: *Kodak T-Max 400* EXPOSURE: *1/125 at f/8* FILTERS: *Polarizing* PAPER/PROCESS: *Ilford Multigrade Fb* TITLE/DESCRIPTION: *Franklin Park Conservatory*

PAGE 192 PHOTOGRAPHER: *Brian Hite* YEAR: *1995* CAMERA: *Canon Cos 650 w/28mm lens* FILM: *Kodak T-Max 400* EXPOSURE: *1/250 at f/11* FILTERS: *Polarized* PAPER/PROCESS: *Ilford Multigrade Fb* TITLE/DESCRIPTION: *Wexner Center for the Arts*

PAGE 193 PHOTOGRAPHER: *Stuart Brown* YEAR: *1996* CAMERA: *Nikon Fm 2* FILM: *Kodak Lumiere X100 Asa* EXPOSURE: *8 seconds at f/11* PAPER/PROCESS: *E6* TITLE/DESCRIPTION: *Blue Floodlight Detail of Bridge at Night*

PAGES 194, 195 PHOTOGRAPHER: *Paul Kozal* YEAR: *1996* CAMERA: *Canon A2E w/28-105mm lens* FILM: *Ilford XP2* PAPER/PROCESS: *Forte Polywarm Tone/selenium toned* TITLE/DESCRIPTION: *Inside the Mind of Frank Lloyd Wright* ■ *Taken at the Frank Lloyd Wright civic center in Marin County, California. It's the same negative printed side by side and flipped.* ● *Aufgenommen im Civic Center von Frank Lloyd Wright in Marin County, Kalifornien. Es handelt sich ein Negativ, das einmal richtig und einmal seitenverkehrt vergrössert wurde.* ▲ *Image prise au centre administratif conçu par Frank Lloyd Wright dans le comté de Marin, Californie. C'est le même négatif, inversé.*

PAGE 196 PHOTOGRAPHER: *Paul Kozal* YEAR: *1996* CAMERA: *Canon A2E with 28-105mm lens* FILM: *Ilford HP5+* EXPOSURE: *1/125 at f/8* PAPER/PROCESS: *Forte Polywarm Tone/selenium toned* TITLE/DESCRIPTION: *The Tomb* ■ *Paris in June* ● *Paris im Juni.* ▲ *Paris en juin.*

PAGE 197 PHOTOGRAPHER: *Gregory Morton* YEAR: *1996* CAMERA: *Contax G1 Rangefinder* FILM: *Fuji Super G 400* EXPOSURE: *1/90 at f/2* FILTERS: *Contax 81 B Warming Filter* PAPER/PROCESS: *C41* TITLE/DESCRIPTION: *Woman In Window, Musee D'Orsay*

PAGE 198 PHOTOGRAPHER: *Brian Hite* YEAR: *1995* CAMERA: *Canon Eos 650 with 28mm lens* FILM: *Kodak T-Max 400* EXPOSURE: *1/125 at f/11* PAPER/PROCESS: *Ilford Multigrade Fb* TITLE/DESCRIPTION: *Steel Matrix*

PAGE 199 PHOTOGRAPHER: *Juan Nunez Estevez* YEAR: *1995* CAMERA: *Nikon FM2* FILM: *Negative Infrared black-and-white* EXPOSURE: *1/125 at f/16* FILTERS: *Red #25* PAPER/PROCESS: *Kodak Port IIE D-76* TITLE/DESCRIPTION: *Santo Cerro, Dominican Republic, La Vega*

PAGE 200 PHOTOGRAPHER: *Patricia Jordan* YEAR: *1995* CAMERA: *Nikon F45* FILM: *Fuji Velvia* EXPOSURE: *f/8* TITLE/DESCRIPTION: *Surreal Crinoids*

PAGE 202 PHOTOGRAPHER: *Helena Fierlinger* YEAR: *1994* CAMERA: *Nikon FM2* FILM: *Kodak Epp* EXPOSURE: *2 seconds at f/22* PAPER/PROCESS: *E6* TITLE/DESCRIPTION: *Hibiscus*

PAGE 203 PHOTOGRAPHER: *Jordan Weinstein* YEAR: *1996* CAMERA: *Nikonos V Underwater 35mm* FILM: *Velvia 150.50* EXPOSURE: *1/60 at f/5.6* PAPER/PROCESS: *35mm* TITLE/DESCRIPTION: *Stealth Shark* ■ *Shot at 50-feet off the wreck of the Bahama Mama, Nassau, Bahamas.* ● *Aufnahme des Wracks der Bahama Mama aus einem Abstand von 25 Metern; Nassau, Bahamas.* ▲ *Photographie de l'épave du Bahama Mama, prise à une distance de 25 mètres. Nassau, Bahamas.*

PAGE 204 *Photographer: Mark Scheflen Year: 1996 Title/Description: "Vichwa Na Mikia"*

PAGE 205 *Photographer: Mark Scheflen Year: 1996 Title/Description: "Kiboko"*

PAGE 206 *Photographer: Constantinos Petrinos Year: 1996 Camera: Nikon Rs 50mm lens Film: Fuji Velvia Exposure: "A" at f/16 Title/Description: Octopus ■ Two strobes. Location: Greece. ● 2 Röhrenblitze. Aufnahmeort: Griechenland. ▲ Deux stroboscopes. Grèce.*

PAGE 206 *Photographer: Constantinos Petrinos Year: 1996 Camera: Nikon F4 w/105mm lens Film: Fuji Velvia Exposure: 1/250 at f/22 Title/Description: He's Looking At You, Kid ■ Underwater housing, two strobes ● Unterkunft unter Wasser, zwei Röhrenblitze. ▲ Logement subaquatique, deux stroboscopes.*

PAGE 207 *Photographer: Patricia Jordan Year: 1995 Camera: Nikon F45 Film: Fuji Velvia Exposure: f/16 Title/Description: Jellyfish Ballet*

PAGE 207 *Photographer: Patricia Jordan Year: 1996 Camera: Nikon F45 Film: Fuji Velvia Exposure: f/8 Title/Description: The Hygienist*

PAGE 208 *Photographer: Malinda Kilmer Year: 1996 Camera: Nikon N-90 Film: Infrared Kodak Filters: 25a Red Paper/Process: Forte Title/Description: Zebra in Motion ■ Shot in South Africa ● Aufgenommen in Südafrika. ▲ Image prise en Afrique du Sud.*

PAGE 209 *Photographer: Malinda Kilmer Year: 1996 Camera: Nikon N-90 Film: Infrared Kodak Filters: 25a Red Paper/Process: Forte Title/Description: Impala in Motion*

PAGE 210 *Photographer: William Mercadante Year: 1996 Camera: Nikonos V Film: Fujichrome 100 Exposure: f/22 Filters: None Paper/Process: E-6 Title/Description: #14 Large Star Coral ■ Underwater at Bonaire. ● Unterwasseraufnahme bei Bonaire. ▲ Photographie sous-marine, près de Bonaire.*

PAGE 210 *Photographer: William Mercadante Year: 1996 Camera: Nikonos V Film: Fujichrome 100 Exposure: f/22 Paper/Process: E-6 Title/Description: #6 Giant Kelp Macrocystis Pyrifera ■ Underwater at Santa Catalina Island, California. ● Unterwasseraufnahme bei der Insel Santa Catalina, Kalifornien. ▲ Photographie sous-marine prise dans les eaux de l'île Santa Catalina, Californie.*

PAGE 211 *Photographer: William Mercadante Year: 1996 Camera: Nikonos V Film: Fujichrome 100 Exposure: f/22 Paper/Process: E-6 Title/Description: #3 Giant Anemone (Condylactis Gigantea) ■ Underwater in Bonaire. ● Unterwasseraufnahme bei Bonaire. ▲ Photographie sous-marine, près de Bonaire.*

PAGE 212 *Photographer: Jianzhang Xu Year: 1992 Camera: Nikon N2000 Film: Ektachrome 100 Exposure: 1/125 at f/11*

PAGE 213 *Photographer: Lorne Resnick ■ Elephant in field ● Elefant auf weitem Feld. ▲ Eléphant.*

PAGE 214 *Photographer: Jianzhang Xu Year: 1995 Camera: Nikon N2000 Film: Fuji Chrome Provia 400 Exposure: 1/30 at f/11*

PAGE 216 *Photographer: Donald Gurewitz Year: 1993 Camera: Canon 630 Film: Fujichrome 400 Title/Description: Daybreak at the Ganges, Varanassi, India*

PAGE 217 *Photographer: Jianzhang Xu Year: 1995 Camera: Nikon N2000 Film: Ektachrome 100 Exposure: 1/4 at f/11*

PAGE 218 *Photographer: Greg Nielson Year: 1992 Camera: Nikon F3 Film: Kodachrome 64 Exposure: unrecorded Filters: none Title/Description: Desert Festival ■ Each year the nomadic tribesmen of Rajasthan gather to celebrate in the desert. # Jedes Jahr versammeln sich die Angehörigen von Nomadenstämmen Rajasthans in der Wüste, um ein Fest zu feiern. ▲ Rassemblement de tribus de nomades du Rajasthan à l'occasion d'une fête annuelle célébrée dans le désert.*

PAGE 219 *Photographer: Donald Gurewitz Year: 1993 Camera: Canon 630 Film: Fujichrome 400 Title/Description: Street Scene, Hanoi, Vietnam*

PAGE 220 *Photographer: Cindy Ho Year: 1996 Camera: Canon Eos Elan III Film: Fuji Sensia 100 Filters: Haze 1 Paper/Process: Slide Transparency Title/Description: Happy New Year, Weixi, China ■ The spirit of old China.l ● Der Geist des alten China. ▲ L'esprit de l'ancien empire du Milieu.*

PAGE 221 *Photographer: Cindy Ho Year: 1992 Camera: Minolta Xg2 Film: Uv Fuichrome 100 Filters: Uv Paper/Process: Slide Transparency, Title/Description: The Harvest, Xian China ■ The countryside near the old capital of China.*

PAGE 222 *Photographer: Claudio Gangi Camera: Nikon F90 ■ Double exposure during slide duplication. ● Doppelbelichtung beim Diaduplizieren. ▲ Diapositive soumise à une double exposition au moment de la duplication.*

PAGE 223 *Photographer: Donald Gurewitz Year: 1993 Camera: Canon 630 Film: Fujichrome 100 Title/Description: Fishing in Halong Bay, Vietnam*

PAGE 224 *Photographer: Steven Knyszek Year: 1996 Camera: Minolta 630 Film: Fuji Title/Description: Lyropecten Nodusus—"Lion's paw scallop"*

INDEX

VERZEICHNIS

INDEX